The Service Business Planning Guide

The complete handbook for creating a winning business plan for any service company

Warren G. Purdy

INC. BUSINESS RESOURCES
Boston, Massachusetts

The Service Business Planning Guide
The Complete Handbook for Creating
a Winning Business Plan
for Any Service Company

Published by *Inc.* Business Resources, a division of *Inc.* magazine.

Chief Editor: Bradford W. Ketchum, Jr.
Book and Cover Designer: Cynthia M. Davis
Cover illustration: Annie Bissett

Library of Congress Catalog Card No.: 96-77327

ISBN: 1-880394-27-8

First Edition

Printed in the United States of America.

1 2 3 4 5 6 7 8 9 10

DEDICATION

To Leanne, Blake, and Nathaniel,
Who Light Up My Life

ACKNOWLEDGMENTS

It took the input and support of many people to make this guide a reality, and I extend sincere gratitude to those who gave so generously of their time and expertise. There are several individuals, however, who deserve special mention.

Bradford W. Ketchum, Jr., editorial director of *Inc.* Business Resources, guided this project from its inception. Thanks to Brad's editorial instincts, professionalism, and perseverance, this book progressed from idea stage to start-up and successful conclusion. Special gratitude also goes to Cynthia M. Davis, whose design and layout make this work truly reader friendly; to researchers Tom Misner, Mary Furash, and Jason Wood; and to Ari Soroken, Ken Pereira, Pam and Shoqut Hussien, and Andrew McKee, the entrepreneurs who so graciously allowed us to publish their business plans so that others might learn from their experiences. Thanks, also, to the numerous business owners and managers who allowed portions of their plans to be used and to those who provided the quotations that punctuate the chapters in Section I.

I am also indebted to a panel of experts for reviewing and evaluating dozens of business plans and for helping to select the plans included in Section III. The panel included Ronald Guerriero, director of Emerging Business Consulting, Arthur Andersen; Debra M. Phillips, assistant vice president, Fleet Bank; and Donald J. Rielly, senior management consultant, Massachusetts Small Business Development Center (SBDC) at Boston College. (Don's book, *A Guide to Planning and Financing Your Business in Massachusetts,* served as an important reference.)

Many thanks, too, to Sam Males, director of the Nevada SBDC, and Bradford W. Ketchum III, sales manager of *Inc.* Business Resources, who shared the vision for this joint publication; and to a number of Small Business Development Centers that nominated business plans and provided planning materials. A special nod goes to SBDCs in Georgia, Indiana, Massachusetts, Missouri, New York, and Pennsylvania. In addition, my appreciation goes to Mary Ellen Beck, director of the State University of New York SBDC Research Network, and her staff for their advice and access to the research center and its substantial resources.

I am also grateful to the University of Southern Maine for granting me a sabbatical to undertake this project, and to my colleagues Professors Carter Manny and John Sanders, for their reviews of the legal and financial sections of this guide; and Janice Tisdale, director of business information services at the Maine SBDC, for all her help with secondary resources. I am also grateful to Drew Buckley, of Buckley and Associates, and Scott Small, of Macdonald, Page & Co., for their assistance.

Finally, thanks to my wife, Leanne, who spent hours on her bumpy commutes to Boston, reviewing my dog-eared manuscripts and musings prior to their submission to the sharp-penciled editing staff at *Inc.*

Warren G. Purdy

Rye, New Hampshire

1996

CONTENTS

INTRODUCTION

Why a Business Plan?

Ask successful small-business founders, bankers, and consultants what are the most important factors contributing to the long-run viability of a small business, and they will give you consistent answers. Among the factors cited most often: management skills and business planning.

It is important to understand those observations as you contemplate starting a business. Why? Because most people who start businesses do not succeed. In fact, 80% of businesses fail within the first five years of operation. The good news is that most businesses that fail generally lack a formal, written plan to help guide them through their initial years. You can learn basic planning skills to avoid this pitfall.

Management skills are a crucial topic in any planning guide. Both poor planning and unskilled management are significant causes of business failure and are closely related. Most people go into business based on some specialized skill or interest. You decide to open a restaurant or computer consulting business because you are an accomplished chef or computer programmer. Without a comprehensive business plan, you might have the best food in town or provide a most needed service, but you may fail because you have inadequate working capital, no rational promotion strategy, and a recordkeeping system of the shoebox variety.

The planning process will force you to consider all aspects of your prospective business, helping to reduce the number of mistakes business founders and owners usually make. Is it wise to tie up all your money in inventory? Should you locate downtown, or out in the suburbs? Are you capable of handling your bookkeeping, or do you need an accountant? Your detailed business plan will address these questions before you are caught scrambling for the answers.

A well researched and documented business plan will significantly increase your chances of success. A carefully thought-out plan will force you to take a hard look at your business on paper before you even order your first ream of letterhead. You'll find it easier to staff your business effectively, obtain financing, and attract customers. This planning guide will enable you to approach the task of launching your business with enthusiasm and confidence.

Why the Service Industry?

Of the more than 22 million business in the United States, more than 60% employ fewer than five people. The service sector comprises over 38% of these businesses, and that number is growing. In fact, small business dominates those industries which are projected to grow most rapidly from 1990-2005, and the service industry specifically represents a major portion of those growing businesses.

Although the projections are dramatic, the real question is whether or not they will hold true. Has the growth in the small-business and service sectors simply been a short-term phenomenon or does it reflect fundamental long-term structural changes in our economy? To evaluate these changes, consider two important sets of factors.

Business/economic factors.

During the past few decades, businesses have become increasingly interdependent. Large manufacturers are not only outsourcing more component part production but also much higher levels of work in areas such as design, promotion, distribution, and service. Although much recent outsourcing activity has been the result of downsizing or reengineering, these changes alone will result in very significant long-term increases of demand in the small-business service sector. For example, while companies such as IBM and AT&T have trimmed personnel to increase efficiency and profitability, they still have to perform many of the functions for which they were responsible prior to the layoffs. In many cases, that work is outsourced to small businesses.

Social/demographic factors.

Certain changes are occurring in our society that will affect demand in the service sector.

- ❑ An increase in *two-income families* is driving demand for all types of services (some of which have not been invented yet), ranging from franchised housecleaning to elder day care. Convenience is the common denominator.
- ❑ The *aging of the U.S. population* will have a significant impact. There are more people over 65 years old than teenagers. Baby Boomers, who are now over 50, are traveling for pleasure and enjoying more leisure activities. This fundamental change in the population will have profound effects on the demand for services of all kinds.
- ❑ Nearly two million *people are retiring* each year, and by the year 2000, that number will be three million a year. By 2030, Americans over 65 will outnumber all children under 18. Americans can now expect to spend up to one-third of their lives in retirement.
- ❑ The explosive *growth of credit and credit card use* and *purchase of services via the mail, phone, and online* have created new, direct, and convenient distribution channels to which buyers are flocking.
- ❑ Concern for *health and fitness* has inspired growth in the specialty food, apparel, and educational sectors.

The market potential of the service industry reflects all of these fundamental long-term changes in population and in lifestyles.

Why This Planning Guide?

Whether you plan to start a business from scratch, enter a franchise agreement, or buy an existing business, there is no substitute for personally developing a business plan. Don't just rely on the slick presentation of a potential franchiser, or the bare financial statements and some very convincing jawboning offered by the seller of a business, or a plan that you have paid a consultant to write. The reasons for writing your own plan are simple. This is your business, an enterprise that you will live with day and night for years to come. Your financial security will be dependent on your business's success. It is too important to leave to third parties.

Although information and assistance from others may be essential to the development of your plan, they should not be a substitute for it. You have to be convinced your plan will work because, in the final analysis, you will have to make it work.

This planning guide was created because of a specific need in the marketplace — the need for a resource that combines specific information on how to write a business plan, a directory enabling you to identify and find the resources you will need to complete your plan, and actual business plans that have been used to launch successful enterprises.

This guide is designed to integrate all of the information you need to lead you through the process of designing a plan that will work for you.

To help you research and write your service-business business plan—and to make this guide as user friendly as possible—five simple icons are used:

Sample
p 18

Resource—This icon refers to the page number of the corresponding resource in Section II.

Sample
p 18

Inc.Sheets—This icon refers to the page number of the corresponding *Inc.Sheet* in Section IV.

Sample
p 18

Bibliography—This icon refers to the page number of the corresponding publications in Section V.

Online

Online—This icon refers to the availability of specific information or reference through the Internet (see Section II).

Copy—This icon is an invitation—and reminder—to make copies of the *Inc.Sheets* in Section IV to use in drafting and writing your business plan.

Section I

Developing a Business Plan

WRITING YOUR PLAN

This section illustrates how to develop a business plan for the service industry. It is designed so that you can easily identify the types of information that should be included in each part of your plan. Although individual business plans differ in style and organization, all of the elements covered here are necessary to develop a comprehensive plan for your business.

As you will quickly see when you begin to work on your own plan, you'll want a lot of information that you don't have at your fingertips. This is when the Resource Directory in Section II will be most useful. Every category of information or data identified in this planning section refers you to a specific part of the Resource Directory, where you will find a list of sources to help answer your questions.

As you are writing out your plan, you should refer to Section III, which includes four, real-life business plans developed by inspired entrepreneurs like yourself. Fully tested, these plans will prove useful as you develop your own approach and style in writing your business plan.

And finally, use the *Inc.Sheets* — do-it-yourself worksheets — in Section IV to guide you each step of the way to creating a successful blueprint for your service business.

THE EXECUTIVE SUMMARY

OVERVIEW

The Executive Summary, by definition, should appear at the front of your business plan. Don't assume, however, that because it is a summary, it's supposed to be written after the plan has been completed and then just inserted at the beginning. Although many business owners may have done this, we suggest that you take a slightly different approach.

The Executive Summary represents your vision for your business. If you don't have a clear vision up front, you can't expect anyone else to see it. That's why a great deal of the content in this section should be well thought out beforehand — not after the fact. Write a two- to three-page draft of your Executive Summary first, as best you can. It can always be revised or corrected for accuracy once your entire business plan has been completed.

The Executive Summary could be the most important part of your plan, particularly if you are looking for external sources of debt or equity. If your plan is being evaluated by potential lenders or investors, the Executive Summary is the first and sometimes the last thing they really read. Why? Because most people evaluating your plan probably have a stack of others they are reviewing, and if you don't capture their imagination and enthusiasm at the beginning, your proposal may end up in the reject pile before it has been fully evaluated. Compare this to the process of buying a book. If the author is known to you, you might purchase it without a second look. If, on the other hand, the author is new to you, you will most likely read the reviews on the cover and take a look at the introduction, then make your purchase decision.

THE BASICS

p 268

What, Why, Whom, When, Where

This is the essence of the Executive Summary. The reader needs to know in concise and unambiguous terms:

What are you planning to do? *(describe your business)*	Start a computer-repair and software consulting service focused on the home-based business market.
Why are you planning to do it? *(explain your business)*	The home-based business market is the fastest-growing small business sector, with an estimated 15 million businesses currently in operation. At present there is only one other company providing such service in our proposed market area…
Whom are you planning to do it for? *(identify your customers)*	Primary market will be the estimated 15,000 home-based businesses in our area and 5,000 other small businesses who do not have on-site computer expertise…

When are you planning to do it?
(timetable, schedules)

Our service will be unique to the area in that we will offer both drop off and on-site service. In addition, we will also offer a help line for customers. Our hours of operation will be from 7:30 a.m. to 7:00 p.m. to provide convenience for customers...

Where do you plan to do it?
(specific site selection)

Our fixed-base location will be on Route 101, just four miles from Center City in the Valley Strip Mall. Other stores in the mall include Staples, the office-supply retailer, which will complement our services...

Management Team

The Executive Summary should describe briefly the backgrounds and experience of the owner/managers. In addition, if you plan to have a board of directors or advisers, or if you are using consultants, their backgrounds should also be highlighted. Identify their most relevant experience. Include complete résumés in the Management section or appendices of your business plan.

Objectives

Although you specifically outlined earlier what you intend to do in your business, you need to mention here both your intermediate and your longer-term goals. For example, in your computer service business, you may plan at some point to sell software, develop a user-based newsletter, or offer specific types of training to your customers. If these are significant goals, they should be mentioned.

Investment

If you intend to use your business plan to help you secure financing or equity investors (stockholders), the Executive Summary should include the types of capital and amounts you hope to raise. As with other parts of this section, you don't have to provide every detail here, just enough to enable the reader to get the big picture in terms of your financial needs. In addition, if you already have equity investors or large potential customers interested in or committed to the business, that should also be mentioned, unless you have a compelling reason to keep the information confidential.

PITFALLS

The major problems with most executive summaries is that they are too long, lack focus, and fail to garner the enthusiasm of the reader. This section of your plan should be a few pages long, at most. Even better, try to get it all on one page, with just enough room for a page number at the bottom. Remember, everything in this section will be explained in detail in some other part of the plan, so *focus on the opportunity* that your business presents.

Some Advice —

"Attention to detail is important. I'm a form person as well as a content person. If I see poor wording, bad spelling, and lousy punctuation, it suggests that the writer does things sloppily. If the Executive Summary—something that's pretty important—is sloppy, maybe the business will be run that way, too. I'll read the whole plan, but my expectations will be much lower."

Holly Thomas
Vice President
First Union National Bank of Florida
Tampa, Fla.

AN EXAMPLE

Yruwel Tutoring

Executive Summary

The ideas, plans, goals, and objectives discussed in this plan are those of a full-service tutorial, educational, and computing center to be known as Yruwel Tutoring and Educational Services, located at 436 Broadway, in Kingston, New York. One of the primary purposes of this business is to offer added individualized academic assistance to students who are struggling to develop their conceptual and comprehensive skills, including language and analytical mastery. The second purpose of the business is educational services, which will use computers and educational software as tools to motivate and instruct students. Their sense of motivation will grow as they explore various applications, from experimenting with scientific data and researching new ideas for reports to playing computerized educational games while learning.

Our on-site computers will be strategically used in other ways. First, students at various levels of education can receive computerized instruction in the following courses: literacy programs; PSAT, SAT, and ACT testing; GED preparation and testing; professional standardized testing such as GRE and LSAT instruction; in-school standardized assessments. Second, our word processing services will be available for the creation and completion of résumés, reports, proposals, etc. Third, a personal computing, or Self-Serv, computer service will allow customers the opportunity to create their own forms, reports, bulletins, flyers, financial statements, etc. Fourth, there will be an on-line (Internet) service available for those seeking employment, desiring to surf the World Wide Web, creating and sending electronic mail (E-mail), and researching miscellaneous material. An on-site copying and fax service will also be available to supply the customer with complete one-stop shopping.

Research into Kingston-area businesses reveals that there are no word processing, computer service, and/or copy-printing businesses that provide one-stop shopping to their customers. One-stop computer servicing allows customers the freedom to accomplish the task of creating, copying, and faxing their document without having to rush from store to store. Currently potential customers have to make several service stops to obtain assistance in the handling of their documents. Our business will seek to fulfill the demand for one-stop shopping for all members of today's busy households .

The diversification of our business venture increases the potential target market base. In other words, since our service offers several major divisions, i.e. tutoring, personal computing, and word p[illegible]ng, we are able to cater to a vast segment of the population. Success will result [illegible]shing several different, yet compatible, computerized services to meet the techno- [illegible]and educational needs of the entire community...

Source: Yruwel Tutoring

DESCRIPTION OF BUSINESS

OVERVIEW

Generally speaking, it may not be necessary to include a Description of Business section in your business plan. If you have provided enough information in the Executive Summary so that your reader has a clear sense of the "What, Why, Whom, When, and Where" of your business, a Description of Business section would be redundant.

However, there are some important exceptions to this rule. If you need to elaborate on certain aspects of your business that can not easily be discussed in full detail in the Executive Summary, a Description of Business section is essential. For example, if you are purchasing an existing business, you can include important information about the *background* of the business in this section. If the services you are planning to provide are unique or unusual in the market, or if you will be starting a business that has complex service offerings to multiple target markets, you can use the Description of Business section to give readers of your plan a full understanding of *innovative or complex features* of your business.

To see if you really need to include a Description of Business section, have a couple of friends or colleagues read your Executive Summary. If they have only a few questions when they are finished, you might need to add just a few details or some clarification to the Summary to accommodate them. If, on the other hand, your reviewers have a large number of questions, you probably need to have a Description of Business section as part of your plan.

Description of Business p 305

THE BASICS

A Description of Business expands on the information contained in your Executive Summary and provides further detail regarding your business. Here are some of the situations in which you may find it useful to include a Description of Business section:

Buying an Existing Business

If you are planning to purchase an existing business, this section is a good place to include its business history: when it was founded, how it was financed, how it was organized, how successful it has been, and why the current owners want to sell. In addition, you should explain how you plan to carry out the transition from the current owner's management to yours in a way that maximizes customer goodwill. Often this is accomplished by the current owner providing services (such as working along with you) after you have purchased the business, for a fixed length of time on a contract-for-services basis.

In a separate section of the plan, you will need to provide a business valuation and numerous financial records, such as the last several years' tax returns. Check with your accountant and refer to the appropriate resources for specific business valuation techniques.

A Different Drummer

If your type of service either is new to the marketplace or deviates significantly from the way services are being offered and/or distributed by competitors, it is probably wise to provide additional detail to ensure that those evaluating your plan don't simply discard it as just "one more business doing the same old thing." For an example of a business that may need a substantial explanation in addition to what is provided in the Executive Summary, let's look at Viadal Herrea's business, Autopsy/Post Services. This venture, located in Los Angeles (1-800-AUTOPSY), provides autopsies, drug scans, and other confidential reports on deceased persons. Clients include lawyers, who use this type of information in malpractice suits or to challenge police findings, and families who are seeking information on hereditary diseases, such as Alzheimer's. Herrea is planning to open franchises around the country, which may be a good strategy considering the well-documented national demand for his services and the ubiquitous nature of his clientele. It is clear, however, that he will need to include a Description of Business section to describe this very innovative company.

Complex Service Offerings

If your business has a number of service offerings, a variety of distribution strategies, and multiple target markets, a Description of Business section can be used to describe them in detail. For example, in Nashua, N.H., Matt Mercier recently started a business called WCH Enterprises (We Can Help), which markets a variety of on-line related services ranging from developing and managing a regional cyber-mall to designing Web Pages for businesses that want to market their services over the Internet. Because WCH has such a broad array of services and potential clients, Matt would want to include a Description section in his business plan in order to provide adequate detail on his financial needs and market estimates for a prospective investor or lender.

Another example of a business with complex service offerings is North Atlantic Marketing Inc., a vertically integrated fishing business in Portland, Maine. When its owner, Jerry Kenecth, founded the business, it was the only operation of its type on the Eastern seaboard. Jerry's concept was on-shore management of his fishing boat (later to become vessels). That is, all operations besides the actual dragging for fish were taken care of by an on-shore staff. These operations included: marketing fish while the boat was still several days from port (vessels are equipped with single-side band radios to call in their catch); off-loading; all repairs; provisioning; and refueling. Traditionally these tasks would be performed by the captain and crew, and the work schedule would make it difficult to maintain good crews.

Under Jerry's system, the crew was able to walk off the boat almost immediately upon arrival for a well-deserved break between trips. The captain(s) also became part-owners of the boats, and the crew members were eligible to participate in a profit-sharing program. Jerry was able to market his fish much more profitably through the use of multiple distribution channels, and he was also able to buy services at lower prices because he had a greater ability to shop for the best value, as opposed to the captain/owner doing it when he arrived in port. The Description of Business section of North Atlantic's original business plan was crucial in enabling lenders to fully understand the scope of Jerry's business concept, which led to the financing of his first boat.

PITFALLS

Balance

You need to strike a balance between what the reader of your business plan "needs to know" and unnecessary or incomprehensible detail. In the example of WCH Enterprises, the Description section should not include a technical discussion about how software is actually used to create Web pages but, rather, explain what the Web page is, what customers use it for, and how and why WCH can design good ones.

Expert Knowledge

Don't assume that those evaluating your plan have high levels of expertise about your proposed business. There is nothing worse than a plan that's filled with jargon such as "cyber-malls," "bidboards," "web crawlers," or "shake 'n bake" (the cremation alternative to an autopsy). If the audience for your proposal doesn't have a clear understanding of what you are trying to do because they don't understand the language you are using, there is a high probability that your business plan will not be taken seriously.

Redundancy

Be sure not to let your Description of Business simply repeat the information in your Executive Summary. It needs to be complete but succinct and to the point. If your Description of Business section is redundant, consider eliminating it and adding pertinent details to your Executive Summary.

Some Advice —

"Include a Business Description section if it will help crystallize exactly what your business is. If it's an accounting firm, your plan should include what areas your practice will focus on. This can be covered in the Executive Summary. However, if you're in the computer industry, which is so large and complicated that the reader needs a clearer understanding, a separate Business Description is necessary."

Kevin Burns, Vice President of
Commercial Banking
Park Bank
Milwaukee, Wis.

EXCERPTS

Henry's Lawn and Garden Center

The key to the development and growth of our customer base will be an innovative presentation of premium products/services targeted to the unmet needs of the region's gardeners. The lawn and garden industry in Maine is highly seasonal, peaking in the late spring, summer, and early fall. The late fall, winter and early spring seasons are slow, relying mainly upon winter storm-related products (i.e., snow blowers, shovels, etc.) to carry them through the season. We intend to smooth out the seasonality curve by offering the region's gardeners opportunities to continue their hobbies throughout the year.

The business will offer five major categories of products and services:

Lawn and Garden Products

Educational/Greenhouse Programs

Plant Question Telephone Hot-line

Customer Specific Promotions

Season Specific Promotions

Following is a brief description of the positioning for each.

Lawn and Garden Products: Given the affluent nature of the market, coupled with the large number of home starts, premium garden and garden-related home decorative products will be a major element in our offering. Research on garden centers beyond our region have found that those retailing lawn and garden products targeted to the more selective clients maintained higher customer loyalty. Although low-cost planters will be available, our focus will be on the premium accessory items that the selective new homeowner currently finds in upscale lawn and garden catalogues. New homeowners spend a great deal of money decorating their homes, and understand the value of money; as a result they are looking for quality items that are both attractive and durable.

Garden tools and equipment will also be sold but will be primarily limited to hand-operated equipment. Power equipment such as mowers and tillers can be purchased from a variety of area businesses, many of which have buying power that allows them to sell at sharp discounts that our operation will not be able to match. Therefore, power-equipment sales will be limited to specialized high-end tools for the selective gardener.

Educational/Greenhouse Programs: One of our strategies for attracting new customers and the business seasonality is to offer a series of educational programs and seminars ening related topics. The programs, ranging from one-night seminars to three- classes, will be held in conjunction with local adult education programs. They will promoted...

Source: Marketing Services Associates

THE MARKET

OVERVIEW

The Market section of your business plan is extremely important. In this part of your plan you must convince potential lenders and investors, that is, stakeholders in the outcome, that there is enough potential demand for your service to justify yet another business entering the marketplace. The skepticism that banks and investors often express is based on their knowledge of the very high failure rates of small business. Therefore, your ability to describe your market and its potential is probably the most important tool you have to help relieve their concerns.

What is this thing called *marketing*? Most people would respond with answers like "advertising, sales, and communications." Each of those answers would be correct, but only in part. Marketing is a comprehensive activity that includes determining:

- ❑ what **services to provide** and to whom
- ❑ how to **price** those services
- ❑ how to **promote** those services
- ❑ how to **deliver** them.

Marketing activity per se is critical because it integrates most of the fundamental business activities. Therefore, each of these activities should be explained in detail in your business plan.

The Market section of the plan should address certain activities in particular: overall market size, growth potential, segmentation, and target market strategies. The Executive Summary and Description of Business sections have already presented a good overall view of the services you intend to provide and how you plan to deliver them. Pricing and promotional strategy will be detailed in separate sections of the plan.

As you begin to write the Market section, remember that although this is a significant part of your business plan, it is not a full-blown marketing strategy. What's the important difference? Marketing plans tend to be far more tactical in nature, and their higher levels of specificity are simply not necessary here. In your business plan you want to give enough detail to assure the readers that there is a good, well-documented potential market for your service but not so much information as to overwhelm them. Include a few charts and tables that indicate in general how you plan to market your business, but do not quote specific strategies or dollar amounts. A good Market section can be written in three to four pages.

RESEARCH

Once you are familiar with this book's description of a good business plan, begin gathering the information that you will need to develop your own. The prospect of doing this may be distressing to you for a number of reasons. Perhaps you haven't been inside a library in years and wouldn't know where to start once you got there. Perhaps you think research is really the domain of people with very thick glasses and too much education. Perhaps you think you are beginning to understand the types of information necessary to develop your plan but don't have the skills to go about accessing those information sources yourself. Don't worry! This guide is designed to enable you to find the information you need.

Research is a process of gathering and analyzing data. The gathering part should not be too difficult but will take some time. Much of the "searching" for potential sources of information (e.g. magazine articles) in libraries is now done by computer. In addition, most libraries, particularly those associated with Small Business Development Centers, will have professional reference staffs to assist you.

Small Business Sourcebook p 115

Marketing p 323

Information Needs p 270

Define Information Needs. Figure out what you are looking for before you take your first step into a library or start to do a search from your home computer. Develop a very specific list of questions (information needs that you want answered). Don't make the mistake that most people do, of simply going to the library with the goal of developing a business plan for, say, a car wash, and start looking in reference guides and magazines under "C" for car or "W" for wash. The number of titles available will overwhelm you unless you are prepared to narrow your search to specific topics.

The best way to start the research process is to create a file folder for each topic identified in your Table of Contents. Then, in each file, make a list of the questions you need to answer (information required) to complete that section of your plan. This method will force you to stay focused, keep on schedule, identify areas where you may need help, and keep fishing expeditions where they belong — by a river with a fly rod.

You can start this process right now by generating your questions, chapter by chapter, as you read this guide. Finally, this structured system of gathering information will allow you to maximize use of your time because as you are researching a question for your Market section, for example, and you are reading an article that includes some financial information, you can immediately place it in the appropriate folder to return to at a later time. Remember, the process of writing a business plan is not a linear one. You will constantly be discovering information that you can set aside to use at a later time or that will help you refine data already gathered.

Reader's Guide p 108
NYT Index p 106
Business Periodicals p 90

Data Collection. There are basically two types of data. The lion's share of the information you will be gathering for your business plan will come from *secondary sources*. These are materials that already exist, predominantly in written form — and your job is to find them. (The Reference Section of this guide will direct you to rich sources of secondary information.)

The other type of data comes from *primary sources*. This is information not available in written form, or at least you may be unable to find it. Therefore, you have to create it, using methods such as interviews, questionnaires, observation, and focus groups. Secondary data take much less time and are less expensive to collect, and, for your purposes, are generally more reliable. You will, however, need to gather some information firsthand when you begin to evaluate your competition and start looking for a location.

THE BASICS

The Market section of your business plan should include information on the following topics:

How Big Is the Pie?

The first thing that must be established in terms of your prospective market is just how large it is. Remember that although you may (and hopefully do) know a lot about the market size characteristics for your industry, you can assume that the reader of your business plan knows very little. Start with the big picture, the national or regional market. Then provide information about your local market, if you can find it. In many cases, localized data may not be available, so you'll need to conduct some primary research.

In our example of the computer service business, you know that demand for services will be derived from the growth of small office/home office (SOHO) businesses, small business in general, and the growth in the number of households that own computers. Therefore, the way to start the analysis would be to determine the size of each of these markets. These statistics can be obtained using sources identified in the Resource Section.

Business Periodicals Index p 90
Census p 94
County Business Patterns p 96

Trend Analysis

Related to the size of the market are the industry's growth trends. Often you'll find trend data in the same resources you used to establish market size, but in other cases, you'll have to investigate further. It is very important to collect information that is as credible as possible, because the future market potential for your business is an area that most stakeholders will evaluate very carefully.

It is simply not enough to say that there are a lot of these types of businesses out there already as justification for offering another one. The argument that similar businesses are doing well so there must be room for one more won't hold water. Consider any number of businesses, such as racquetball clubs and diet centers, that at one time were fast-growth industries but now are stagnant, if not in significant decline.

The best way to find trend data for specific service businesses is to search in the periodical indices, trade associations, and franchise literature. Remember, you don't want to overwhelm your readers with factoids, just convince them that your business has a high probability of success.

Trend p 271

WSJ Index p 124
Buying Power p 93
ZIP Code p 116

Segmentation

Now that you have established that there is a large market with positive growth trends for your proposed business on a national/regional basis, you must break down these data to reflect the conditions of the market you plan to serve, i.e. your **target market**. The process by which very large and somewhat homogeneous markets are reduced to smaller target markets is called **market segmentation**.

The purpose of segmenting your market carefully is to ensure that the target market that you have identified is indeed accessible and large enough to sustain your overall operation. How do you do it? There are many ways to break down markets by characteristics: age, sex, ethnic group, education, family size, income, business type, geographic location, and so on. Your job is to find the characteristics that are most important in the definition of **whom** your business is trying to serve, and then measure them. For example, if you are starting a business that will tutor high school students to prepare them for the SAT exams, you might segment your market by age, family income, and geographic location.

Market Segmentation Consumer p 272

Market Segmentation Business p 273

Your Slice

The ultimate aim of the business plan is to convince your reader that the large and growing market you have identified really exists where you intend to do business. Although it would be nice to figure this out now (and perhaps finish your plan in record time), you should first take a look at your competition, then return to this most important issue in a separate section of the plan entitled "Market Share," which deals specifically with this topic. You could also complete your competitive analysis, then return to the Market section of your plan and include the evaluation of your market share here.

PITFALLS

The most significant problems you can encounter while developing a case for your market probably fall into one of these categories.

Unbridled Optimism

Don't overstate your case. Be sure that the market data you are using actually reflect demand for *your services* as closely as possible. For example, if you're planning to open an ethnic restaurant, don't simply use data showing that an average family of four with a certain income level will eat out an average of two times a month and will spend X number of dollars per person. The issue here is ethnic food, and if you researched a little further you could find a breakout of restaurant consumption in your area by type of food.

Stale Data

Be sure that your references are as up-to-date as possible. For example, the US. Census is conducted only once every 10 years, so the farther you are from the first year in each decade, the less reliable the data become. Not to worry, though — not only are portions of the census updated more frequently, there are simple techniques you can use to update it yourself. For example, you might have a figure that is three or four years old regarding the population in your target market area. Although that number alone might be a bit stale, it may become useful when combined with the state or municipal government's estimates of population changes over that period.

Too Little Documentation

Provide very specific references to give the reader confidence that credible sources were used to support your findings. In some cases, you may rely on footnotes. In other cases, you may want to include specific pieces of information, such as trade association studies or articles from business magazines, as appendices.

AN EXAMPLE

Cheap Thrills

B. THE MARKET

The market is diverse in this segment of the travel industry. Impulse trips first became popular in the 1980's for residents of the Northeast Corridor. While a formatted weekend trip may not allow vacationers to forget their cares and escape their 9-to-5 routines, it is a quick fix and, very often, a sanity preserver until a longer vacation can be taken.

Many modern travelers prefer following tour trends:

- ❑ Less time spent in vehicles
- ❑ More leisure / less structure
- ❑ Soft adventure options: hot-air ballooning, biking, hiking, rafting, horseback riding, etc.
- ❑ More opportunities to maintain fitness programs
- ❑ No name tags that peg participants as tour group members
- ❑ Added value, quality of accommodations and meals, tickets to sold-out shows and events
- ❑ Vacation is hassle free — tour operator secures transportation, lodging, restaurants, admissions, permits, etc.
- ❑ Others on trip share similar interests

There is a trend toward what the general public considers to be "fun weekend adventures". Surveys show that romance motivates most weekend getaways. Sightseeing, shopping excursions, and theater/concerts are also popular. Summer remains the favorite season to travel; however, in this region, skiing excursions are also popular. The typical traveler is a married baby-boomer with a combined household income of $40,000 to $65,000. Travelers generally move in [illegible] st prefer to revisit favorite places year after year. The majority of travelers prefer to [illegible] n vacations of less than 830 miles. Although wealthy Americans....

Source: Cheap Thrills Tour Operations Company

Some Advice —

"We decided to focus on two kinds of customers. The first is large multinational corporations that are diversified enough that they aren't dependent on any one industry segment. That way, we can have a corporate contract and not be limited to an industry. The second is customers in remote locations. They pay slightly higher rates to make themselves more appealing, and out there, there's less competition to land contracts."

Joanne Peterson
President and CEO
Abator Information Services
Pittsburgh, Pa.

THE COMPETITION

OVERVIEW

A well thought-out and logically presented competitive analysis is a critical component of your business plan. Although planning experts readily agree on the types of information that should be included in the examination of your competitive environment, often the process of gathering it is more difficult than meets the eye. Keep in mind that every business has competition, and if you think that you've found one without any, you're wrong! For example, let's say you want to start a telephone-answering service and claim that there is no competition in the area because you don't find any listed in the Yellow Pages. Perhaps there are no Yellow Page listings, but identical services only represent a part of the picture. In this situation your potential customer has many alternatives to your service, including answering machines, call forwarding, regional telephone company voice-mail services, sophisticated electronic switchboards, and combinations of these.

The goal of the competitive analysis is to demonstrate that you have a thorough knowledge of *where and who* your competitors are, as well as their relative *strengths and weaknesses.* Once you have accomplished this, you will be able to carve out a market niche for your business and then estimate its size. That there will be competition is a given. How you differentiate your business will be the key to its success.

Competitive Data p 274

THE BASICS

The Competition section of your business plan should include the following:

Where Is Your Competition?

To analyze your competition, it is important to define your service area in unambiguous terms. The best way is literally to take a map and plot the area where you plan to concentrate your business. This process will define your customer base, help identify competition, and be an important factor in the development of your promotional strategy.

For example, consider Ever Green Landscaping Inc., a start-up business that plans to offer premium landscaping services to a clientele located within a one-hour round-trip drive from the owner's base of operation. The first step will be for owner Doug Green to draw a circle with a 20-mile radius (he calculates that his trucks will travel at an average of 40 mph) with his location at the center. The area in the circle defines where his potential customers are located. Next, starting at the same point, he draws another circle with a 40-mile radius. Using the same logic, this new, larger area encompasses most of his competition.

Thomas Reg p 118

For some types of service businesses, defining the market and competition will be a more difficult task than Doug Green's. Consider, for example, a consultant with highly specialized expertise in an area such as aquaculture. She might define her market as national or regional in scope, and may plan to use the Internet as a marketing channel. Her analysis would, by definition, have to focus on competition over a broad geographic area, with particular emphasis on how she would differentiate her services from those of her competitors and how she intends to communicate the advantages she offers to prospective customers.

Who Is Your Competition?

Revisit the basic description of your business as it appears at the beginning of your plan. Make sure you have identified all of the tangible and intangible characteristics that must go into a comprehensive explanation of what customer needs your business expects to satisfy. You may find that you need to add or delete some items. Remember, business plan development is a fluid process. You will end up making many changes to your plan before you have a final version.

Now that you are focused on customer needs, you can begin the process of identifying your competition. Put yourself in the position of a potential customer who is searching to satisfy a need. Let's say you're looking for an efficient, flexible, and cost-effective way to answer the phone when you are out of your home office. Check out the competition as a prospective customer would.

Ulrich's
p 122

General Resources for Identifying Competition

Yellow Pages. The telephone book is an excellent and convenient source for service businesses. Some of your competitors may not be found there, however, because they started their business after the directory was published, are not listed under a category you're looking for, or use a residential number for the business.

Local Papers. Local newspapers have some type of business service directory. This is generally a rich source for identifying competitors. However, you should be aware that many small businesses do not advertise in the paper because they feel it is too expensive.

Trade Associations. Professionals and many other types of service businesses belong to a trade or professional associations. If there is one for your service type, contact the group's offices to see what information is available. This may require contacting a national trade association to access the local chapter.

Business-to-Business Directory
p 92
Encyclopedia of Associations
p 98
Trade Shows
p. 120

CABWA (Competitive Analysis by Walking Around). Many service businesses' sole means of promotion is by word-of-mouth and business cards. Most often, the telephone numbers on these cards are those of the owner's residence and therefore never show up in the Yellow Pages or business-to-business directories. The best way to identify these folks is to go to places where you might find their cards or flyers posted. For example, if you're going into the painting/contracting business, go to all of the local hardware and paint stores. If you don't find a bulletin board with business cards posted on it, ask one of the salespeople to recommend a couple of contractors to you. Any number of businesses, such as grocery and discount department stores, may also have a place where cards are posted, so check them out.

Licensing. If your particular business is required to have a license or permit to operate, chances are that such licenses are a matter of public record. You will be able to get names and addresses from the state or local authority that issues them. For example, if you are planning to start a day-care center, most, if not all, states require some type of registration. All you need to do is contact the state agency responsible and request a listing.

Patents, Copyrights & Trademarks p 323

SWOT Analysis

(Strengths, Weaknesses, Opportunities, Threats)

Once you have discovered who your competitors are and where they are located, develop a detailed and comprehensive profile for each one. The goal here is to identify competitive gaps and weaknesses and then modify your services to exploit them. In the example of Ever Green Landscaping, you may find that as you begin to call your competition to get information about their service area and rates, you always reach an answering machine. Although this may impede your research, think of how their current and prospective customers must feel! A clear weakness of your competitors is the difficulty clients experience trying to contact them. This information should prompt you to offer customers a communications feature, such as a cellular phone or pager, so that you will be able to respond to customer calls immediately or on a very timely basis.

The first step of your SWOT analysis is to make a list of what you consider to be all of the relevant attributes of your business. These would include:

- What specific services will you provide?
- To whom will you provide these services?
- Where will you be located?
- What geographic area will you serve?
- How will you price your services?
- What will be your hours of operation?
- What will be your credit policy?
- How will you promote your service?
- What types of guarantees or assurances will you offer?
- What type of follow-up service will you provide?
- Other (to be added as you evaluate your competition)

At this point, you'll be ready to contact your competitors and compare what they say they do to what you plan to do. In most cases this is easily accomplished over the phone, under the guise of being a prospective customer. During this "conversation," get as many questions answered as possible. Also look for service features and opportunities you hadn't considered. For example, let's say you plan on opening a lube, oil, and filter business. In evaluating your competitors, you discover that one of them is offering mobile services for business clients. This might provide a significant opportunity for your business. It is also important to ask these businesses to send you any promotional material they may have. To facilitate this process, develop a competitive grid. Use the one that follows, created to evaluate competition in the day-care industry, as a model.

Competition Grid

Center & City	Ages Accepted	Number of children in center	Meals provided?	Costs infant/ pre-school	Credentials of teachers	Special services
Bldg Blocks Learning Ctr. 100 Westbrook St. So. Portland 761-3936	12 mo. to 10 yrs.	90	Lunch & 2 snacks	12 mo.—$100/wk. 3/4 yrs.—$90/wk.	B. A. in Early Childhood Ed. M. A. in Early Childhood Ed.	
Children's Circle Ctr. 190 Kelsey St. So. Portland 799-6188	2 1/2 yrs. to 9 yrs.	55	Lunch & 2 snacks	2 1/2 yrs.—$90/wk. 3/4 yrs.—$85/wk.	One degree, rest experience	Nursery school Field trips
Heidi's House Child Care 26 Oak Hill Terrace Scarboro 883-9667	6 wks. to School age		Lunch & 2 snacks	Infant—$127 – $87 After school care Pre-school—$90 – $70	Few with degree, most with experience	Summer swim program
Kountry Kids Nursery Sch. 93 Holmes Rd. Scarboro 883-6017	2 yrs. to 5 yrs	23 total (max. 12 per day)	Lunch & 2 snacks	$90/wk or $23/day	No degrees, 20 yrs. experience in child care	
Lighthouse Day Care 525 Highland Ave. So. Portland 767-2121	18 mo.to Kindergarten age	175 (avg. 100 per day)	Lunch & 2 snacks	18 mo.—$110/wk. 4 yrs.—$98/wk. 25% discount for older sibling	1/2 college degree, 1/2 experienced parents	Newsletters
Lil Folk Farm 192 Black Point Rd. Scarboro 883-4001	2 yrs. to 7 yrs.	55	Lunch & 2 snacks	2 yrs. - $96/wk. 4 yrs. - $93/wk.	Certified with 4 yrs. experience	Separate pre-K and nursery school
	6 wks. to Grade 4	70	Sept.—May hot lunch Other months bring own	Infant - $115/wk. 4 yrs. - $85/wk. 10% discount for second child	Combination, 3 certified, rest experienced	Nursery school

Source: Buckley & Associates

Competitive Grid p 276

Such a grid enables you to look at your competition side by side with your own business, and enhances your ability to identify gaps in service. Once you have gathered this information, you will be in a position to fine-tune your service offerings and begin to evaluate your potential market share. Time spent on this evaluation is well invested, because lack of thoroughness can have a compounding effect as you begin to forecast sales later on in your business plan.

PITFALLS

Initial Service Offering Too Broad

Proposing too many services will leave your business unfocused, with the risk of facing many more specialized competitors in the marketplace.

Underestimating Competition

Failure to identify all relevant competitors will lead to false assumptions in market share and pricing, which could have devastating effects.

Overestimating Your Competitive Strength

Making too-optimistic projections about your new service and customers' reaction to it, compared with that of your competition, can lead to the downfall of an otherwise great idea.

Failure to Modify Your Plan

If you neglect to make adequate changes to your initial plan based on findings in your competitive analysis, your business may be doomed before you begin.

These potential problems can all be avoided by being attentive to detail and flexible as you conduct your analysis. On the one hand, be sure to identify and document your competition as it exists; on the other, look for opportunities and take advantage of them where possible.

Some Advice –

"People aren't stupid. If you're doing something right and it works, then sooner or later they're going to figure it out and come after you. Can your people respond? Can you keep innovating? Can you stay ahead? These are the real questions you should be dealing with."

Ken Hendricks, Founder and CEO
ABC Supply Co.
Beloit, Wis.

AN EXAMPLE

Junior Jamboree

VI. COMPETITION

Competition exists at various locations throughout Long Island. The level of competition is vastly different in what is offered for the individual party. The competitor comparison sheet (attachment 4) describes the offerings of party centers surveyed. This information was gathered through discussions with owners, managers, and employees of the party centers surveyed, and through an analysis of their brochures.

ve that our concept offers a more imaginative, enjoyable experience for children 1 rs old. It should also be noted that there currently are no integrated centers in the cted location at this time.

Competitor Comparison by Price Per Party (abbreviated listing)

Name	Location	Price per party	# Kids min.	Rec. eqpt.	Private party	Pizza/ hotdog	Cake	Cost- umes	Goodie bag	Length of party	Gift for birthday	Com- ments
Perfect Party Place	Woodbury	$425	20	Yes	Yes	Pizza	IC Cake	Yes	Candy/toy	2:00	No	all ages
Perfect Party Place	Woodbury	$375	20	Yes	Yes	Pizza	IC Cake	Yes	Candy/toy	1:30	No	4–12 yrs
Discovery Zone	Huntington	$270	15	Yes	No	P/HD	IC Cake	No	No	!:45	T-shirt	all ages
That's Entertainm	Centereach	$195	15	No	Yes	Pizza	No	Yes	Extra	2:00	Yes	Mon–Thu
	Sayville	$120	12	No	Yes	Pizza	Sund/Cup	No	Extra	2:00	Yes	Crafts
		$225	15	Yes	Yes	Pizza	IC Cake	Yes	Candy/toy	1:45	T-shirt	all ages

Source: Junior Jamboree

DETERMINING MARKET SHARE

OVERVIEW

Market-share analysis gives credibility to your sales projections. It should draw on and be consistent with the information presented in the Market and Competition sections, so that it is clear your entire business plan is based on the same fundamental assumptions.

One of the most serious shortcomings of business plans is a lack of strong connection between the sections on demand, competition and the rationale used to support sales projections. The Market section presents data demonstrating a strong national, regional, and local demand for your service. The Competition section contends that there is a viable niche for your business. But the financial section of the plan, with its cash flow forecasts, makes little or no attempt to quantify the share of the market the business intends to capture, let alone establish a rationale for it. This problem is exacerbated by the use of electronic spreadsheets.

Changing sales forecasts, to make the bottom line look good, can be done so effortlessly that it is easy to lose sight of the fact that strong underlying assumptions are necessary to support them. In addition, the computer printout itself looks so professional that sometimes it obscures the fact that the supporting data are inaccurate or inconsistent. To avoid this problem, support your sales projections with a cogent and thorough market-share analysis.

Determining market share may sound like a complicated task, but it is not. All you are doing is documenting what share of the potential sales in your target market is reasonable for you to capture. This is not a highly scientific process with sophisticated formulas that produces a definitive answer. It is an evaluation in which you look at a combination of factors, many of which you have already discovered in the marketplace, to arrive at logical expectations about sales. Keep in mind, you are not repairing a Swiss watch. Try to see the big picture, and don't expect that the different techniques you learn to use will yield exactly the same answers.

You have several options as to where to put your market-share information. Either you can use a separate section or you can place this information in another area, such as the Market section, or as a long footnote to your cash-flow analysis. The important thing is to have it in your business plan and to present it in a compelling fashion.

THE BASICS

While looking at a display case carrying his chicken dogs in a supermarket, Frank Perdue once commented, "I suppose it would be unreasonable to have the whole area." He was referring to the fact that his competition was also holding shelf space. Market-share information enables you to estimate more accurately the amount of business you can capture.

Although there is no definitive formula to compute market share, there are several factors that should be analyzed. Combined, these factors contribute to a logical basis for your sales projections. Each business situation differs somewhat in terms of characteristics and data availability. Therefore, individual business plans will not all look the same. The important thing to remember is that your general analytical tools can be adapted to meet the needs of your particular situation.

Here are three basic methods that can be used to estimate future sales.

Average Competitor Sales

One way to develop your sales projections is to argue that you have used sales levels reflecting that of your competition. In fact, you'll want to project your sales at lower levels, even though your service may be of a higher quality with more features at a lower price.

Let's say you are proposing to start a hair salon. Here is the formula for establishing the average sales level of your competitors. Generally this calculation is made using statewide data.

$$\frac{\textbf{Retail Sales}}{\textbf{No. of Establishments}} = \textbf{Average Sales Per Business}$$

Marketing
p 323

Sales data: Your state bureau of taxation has information available on sales tax paid, by business category. This is a matter of public record, so you should just have to call the bureau to obtain it. In states which have no sales taxes you can gather this data from a state(s) with similar characteristics (e.g. size) and use it for your projections.

Estimated Competitor Sales/Customer Base
p 278

Number of establishments: There are many potential sources for this information, including *County Business Patterns*, the Yellow Pages, and state-specific service directories.

Other: If your industry has a good trade association, it probably compiles industry or membership studies that contain sales data. The problem is persuading the association to share it with you. For example, there might be an industry report that sells for $100. See if you can get a free copy of the previous study or permission to photocopy the specific information you need from the current one. Remember, you are a potential future member, so if you are polite and patient, you can usually get what you need.

County Business Paterns
p 96

How to use this information: As you begin to project sales, the average sales figure for your type of business is a good place to start. Usually it is wise to make your projections slightly lower than your average competitor's sales figures, because your estimates will look more conservative and attainable.

Total retail sales for hair salons in Tucson, Arizona = $1,570,900

Total number of hairdressing establishments in Tucson = 23

Average sales per establishment ($1,570,900 ÷ 23) = $68,300

Projected sales for your service: $55,300

Average Customer Base

Another important factor that should be considered when developing your market share analysis is the underlying population required to support your business. Generally this calculation is also based upon statewide data. You can approximate this as follows:

$$\frac{\text{Population}}{\text{No. of Establishments}} = \text{Average No. of People Per Business}$$

Estimated Competitor Sales/Customer Base p 278

Number of establishments: Same sources as for competitor's sales.

Population: Bureau of the Census

How to use this information: These data can be used to respond to the question, "Don't we already have enough hairdressing salons in the area?" Perform the same analysis as above, but for your own trading area. That is, divide your target population by the number of competitors you identify in your trading area. If the result in potential customers per salon is significantly higher than the state average, that indicates there is room for another competitor.

Bureau of Census p 94

Buying Power Index p 93

Total number of hair salons in Arizona =	1,349
Total population of Arizona =	3,665,228
State average number of people per salon =	2,717
Total number of hair salons in Tucson =	23
Total population of Tucson =	706,300
Average number of people per salon (706,300 ÷ 23) =	30,709
There is room in the Tucson area for an additional hair salon.	

Source: Sales & Marketing Management, Survey of Buying Power

Sales Projections Using National or Regional Demand Data

Some entrepreneurs will find it difficult to access all of the data necessary to complete the type of analysis described on pages 28–30. Another technique you can use is to gather consumption or spending data on a regional or national basis, then shrink it to fit your target market area.

For example, let's say you are interested in starting a tour agency called Cheap Thrills that would specialize in impulse trips. The business would offer "fun weekend adventures" for people looking for affordable, stress-free weekend getaways. Trips would include concerts, sporting events, and sightseeing tours.

As you begin to search for data on your business, you find a lot of information on the tourism industry but little on your slice of the pie. In that case, start doing key word searches at your local library to dig up volumes of information from sources including:

- ✔ ***Money,*** "How to Beat the Costs to Terrific Destinations"
- ✔ ***American Demographics,*** "Spring Break Grows Up"
- ✔ ***Better Homes and Gardens,*** "A New Generation of Tours"
- ✔ ***Southern Living,*** "Weekends From Our Readers"
- ✔ ***Advertising Age,*** "Sky's the Limit for Tour Operators"

Projections Using National Data p 278 & 279

From the information contained in these articles, among others, you will be able to develop a customer profile.

Lifestyle p 105
Simmons p 112

Cheap Thrills Customer Profile: Married baby-boomer couple with one child. Mean family income: $65,000. One full-time, one part-time worker. Generally looking for one- to three-night excursions.

Armed with this profile, you will be able to measure the potential for your total market by determining how many people who live in your target area fit this profile. Then you can review your competitive data and estimate your market share.

PITFALLS

Unrealistic Market Share Projections

Make your sales and market-share projections conservative. It is usually a good idea to make two projections: one at the level that you think you can reasonably achieve and the other at a level closer to your breakeven point. (For break-even analysis, see page 41.)

Sales Projections Exceed Capacity

Be careful not to show sales levels that cannot be maintained with the resources indicated in your business plan. For example, if you are planning to start a livery service, make sure to plan for enough available cars and drivers to meet your projected demand.

Target Market Too Broad

Do not try to be all things to all people. Segment your market and differentiate your services. You can always expand your business later. For example, if you start a plumbing business focused on homeowner repairs and installation, plan very carefully before taking on any commercial jobs. If you don't plan, you may find yourself spread too thin and unable to service your homeowner market on a timely basis. When the commercial job(s) end, you may have ended up losing some customers and also developing a reputation as a business that can't respond to customer needs.

Profitability

Be sure that your target market is large enough to be profitable. In the landscaping example, the owner might have to expand the area of operations by 5 or 10 miles to reach a large enough customer base to operate profitably.

Some Advice –

"We aimed for the top five name-brand customers in our field. Everything we did was geared toward bringing our product to those companies. Rather than sell to the 27th player in the market, we proactively went after those five. And as a result, within five years, we were leading our industry in market share and pushing the 40%-plus mark."

Ken Marshall, President and CEO
Object Design
Burlington, Mass.

AN EXAMPLE

Henry's Lawn & Garden Center

Projected Market Penetration

Our business will strive to gain customers in both retail and wholesale lawn and garden supply markets. Recent favorable demographic trends, coupled with the opportunity presented by an unfilled premium product's niche, make us confident that we are in a very good position to rapidly acquire a viable and profitable share of the local market.

Following are key variables relevant to our estimation of our potential market:

1994 Maine lawn & garden sales	$122,000,000
Maine population	1,240,000
Number of lawn & garden stores in Maine	79
Local market population	70,000

Using the above information, the characteristics for the lawn & garden market in our target market area can be projected as follows:

Average Maine resident lawn & garden expenditures	$98.00
Average sales per lawn & garden store	$1,544,000
Population served per lawn & garden store	15,755
Projected local market dollar sales	$6,860,000

Given that, on average, there is one lawn & garden store per 15,755 people, we can calculate what the local market can bear:

South Portland, Scarborough, Cape Elizabeth population	70,000
Statewide average population served per store	15,755
Potential number of stores supported by the local population	4.4

Since only three lawn & garden stores are in operation in this area, our calculations suggest that the market is not saturated and should easily be able to support an additional store. This information, coupled with continued increases in population and new housing starts, indicates clearly that there is an opportunity to make inroads into the region.

Another method of evaluating our potential in the market is to calculate a break-even analysis ...ine what percentage of the market's population we would have to capture in order ...cceed. The following break-even projections are based upon the cost assumptions ...nd in the financial section of this business plan and the calculated per capita sales ...timates...

(continued)

(continued)

$Q = fc / (p - vc) = 5{,}700$

Q = number of customers required to break even

FC= fixed operating costs (lease, fixed salaries, utilities, etc.)

P = per capita annual lawn and garden expenditures

VC = variable cost of items sold at the industry average (65% of retail)

FC =	$195,500.00
P =	$98.00
VC =	$63.70

Given these assumptions, Henry's Lawn & Garden Center will have to gain a customer population base of approximately 5,700 people or 8.1% of the region's population. Clearly this is an attainable goal, since the market saturation calculation indicates an underutilization of more than 30%. Under these conditions, we believe that we can capture at least 10% of the underserved region's population as our market base. This conservative estimate would produce the following revenues:

Total market population	70,000
Target percentage of population base	10%
Projected number of customers	7,000
Average sales per person	$98
Total sales	$686,000
Variable costs (@ 65% retail)	$445,900
Fixed costs	$195,500
Pre-tax profits	$44,600

Our unique marketing mix should enable us to easily achieve our 10% goal, exceeding the break-even market share. Additional customers will be gained by our efforts to expand the poten-[illegible] through our educational programs, drawing buyers from beyond the local market [illegible] addition, customer loyalty built over our initial summer season can be reinforced [illegible]ghout the year through our continued specialty programs and promotions.

Source: Marketing Services Associates

LOCATION

OVERVIEW

The location of your business is critical to its eventual success or failure. As you contemplate where to locate your business, analyze such basic factors as proximity to your target market and where your competition is located. In addition, be sure to evaluate your alternatives in the light of changing factors in the economy, such as advances in *telecommunications/computer technologies, co-location* opportunities, and the advent of *virtual business*.

Do not simply look at your competitors and assume that because they have selected a particular type of location, you should make a similar decision. Keep an open mind. Don't just accept how things have already been done. Remember that as times change, so do the ways in which services can be delivered most efficiently. For example, consider the auto glass replacement service. Traditionally, if your windshield got broken, you would have to schedule an appointment and go to a specific place to have your glass replaced, which at best is time-consuming and inconvenient. Today there are companies that will send a mobile van with a technician to replace your window at home, work, or accident site when you call their toll-free number. These companies guarantee that the service will be completed in a certain number of hours, and they file all requisite insurance forms.

Consider the three factors above and their potential effect on a location decision.

1. Telecommunications/computer technologies: Advances in these areas have had a profound impact on every facet of business. Location decisions are no exception. Whether you need cellular telephones, fax modems, or on-line services, each could have an impact on your choice of location, depending on the type of services you intend to provide. For example, there are home decorating businesses that now have their whole showroom set up in a large mobile van which, in effect, brings the location to the customer. These vans carry complete lines of samples and are equipped with cellular phones, computers, and fax machines.

2. Co-location: As the term suggests, co-location refers to two or more businesses sharing the same location. Generally the businesses that enter such arrangements are either complementary, such as an accountant, a secretarial service, and a mailing service, or competitive, such as an ice-cream shop and a cookie store. In the latter situation, which occurs less frequently, both businesses expect to generate sales as a by-product of each other's sale. That is, the customer comes into the store to buy an ice-cream cone and then purchases a dozen cookies to take home.

Co-location arrangements serve two purposes. First, they can significantly reduce overhead. Secondly, they can increase sales potential because the customers for each business are highly probable ones for the other businesses occupying the shared location.

3. Virtual Business: Lionheart Consulting Group (LCG) in Brunswick, Maine, is a company that provides integrated research services from the design stage to data analysis. Among other things, it develops questionnaires, composes and prints them, mails them out, statistically analyzes data, and makes formal recommendations to its clients. It has a fancy brochure, business cards with phone and fax numbers, an E-mail address, and a Yellow Pages listing. On first glance, you might think this is fairly large company. There is a good chance, however, that it is a virtual one. That is, the owner of LCG may be a one-man band who relies on a whole cadre of

Note —

This guide assumes that you intend to rent or lease your location. If you plan to buy the property, you will need to go through a thorough business valuation process. There are numerous references on this subject. Consult your accountant or business advisor for assistance with a valuation analysis.

Location p 323

other small businesses and access to technology to perform many functions.

In this case, the owner probably generates the business, works on the research design (possibly with another consultant), decides on questions for the surveys, and writes the final analyses. Every other aspect of the business may be carried out by subcontractors who perform functions ranging from questionnaire layout and design to computerized data analysis.

In fact, a business like LCG might be operated out of a home office, even though the official address is an office suite (which is nothing more than a mailbox service). The point is that, with the network of services available today, it is possible to develop your business with broad offerings but low overhead, including location expense.

Location Needs p 281

THE BASICS

No matter what you decide concerning location, the following factors should be considered, if applicable. It will be helpful to construct an evaluation grid in order to compare the attributes of the different locations you are contemplating.

Costs

As you compare location alternatives, estimate costs carefully. Remember that your expenses include not only your monthly lease payments but also leasehold improvements, lease and security deposits, utilities, and other possible assessments. One way to determine whether you are paying too much for your location is to compare your costs with those of other, similar businesses. You can look up your business type and compare, on a percentage of sales basis, what similar businesses pay for rent.

Financial Studies p 102
Small Business Profiles p 114

Proximity to Customers

Evaluate the importance of locating close to customers. This factor will vary significantly, depending on your type of business. For example, an industrial cleaning service need not be located just down the street from its customers, as there is no need for the customer to go to the business. On the other hand, photocopying or eldercare services need to be as close to their customers as possible because the convenience of their locations will be an important factor in the minds and lives of their clients. Costs and proximity are directly related. Don't pay the premium for a retail location unless you need it.

Proximity to Competition

This is not an important issue for many service businesses. For others, however, it is. For example, if you are planning to open a shoe-repair business, it does not make sense to open right next door to a well-established competitor with a good reputation. On the other hand, if fast food is your business, you will probably want to locate close to your competition because over time your potential customers will want variety in their food choices. There are no set rules here. Look at the marketplace and see how others in your industry treat the issue of location, then view it as a potential customer would. In fact, it may pay to survey or interview people who fit your customer profile to elicit their opinions on this issue.

Traffic Patterns

If foot or vehicular traffic is important to sustain your business, it is necessary to determine what the volume is, and at what times. Your state Department of Transportation is an excellent source for traffic counts, but, in general, the data will need further analysis. Consider a dry cleaner, for example, that recently went out of business, leaving a considerable amount of debt. As the loan file was being reviewed in a postmortem, the bank examiner noticed that a traffic study had been submitted as part of the original business plan/loan application. Much of the justification for the dry cleaner's original sales projections was based on the high volume of traffic passing in front of the proposed store. In retrospect, the traffic counts were accurate but the problem was that the store was located on a corner where virtually all of the cars commuting to the area's largest manufacturing plant passed each day. The majority of these commuters were blue-collar workers with little demand for dry cleaning.

Potential customer traffic is indeed something that you should evaluate, preferably first hand. Go to the proposed location(s). If it's foot traffic that you are documenting, record information such as volume (number, density, timing) and characteristics of the passersby. Interview some of them. If you are analyzing vehicle traffic patterns, try to determine whether there are special circumstances, such as those in our example, then revise your estimates accordingly.

Equifax
p 100

Site Evaluation
p 282 & 283

Parking

Is the parking adequate? The answer to this question is affected by many variables, such as the length of time your customer is likely to spend at your business, your expected customer flow, and whether you will reasonably be able to restrict a parking area just for your customers. Here, again, there is no substitute for on-site analysis.

Zoning Restrictions

Be sure to check with local government authorities (i.e., town hall) to ensure that the location you are considering is zoned for your particular type of business. Even if you are considering a home office, don't make the assumption that it is allowed until you've checked at the town hall. For example, a young couple started a business in their home that involved a great deal of shipping and receiving. At first the occasional UPS truck went unnoticed. However, as the business quickly grew, more and larger trucks appeared in the neighborhood on a regular basis. Local residents began to complain about the new traffic, and the business was forced to move to a new location that was properly zoned for the amount of trucking that was required.

Permits and Licenses

Make a list of all the permits and licenses that are required for your particular business. Not only are there some that might surprise you, they may also differ from location to location. For example, if you have a storefront location, don't just buy a fancy (and expensive) sign. You may find that there are local regulations restricting its size and how it can be displayed. In addition, certain types of businesses, such as those dealing with food and toxic waste, need both state and federal permits. If you have any doubt, the best place to check is your local Small Business Development Center, Chamber of Commerce, trade association, or appropriate state agency.

Expansion

Will the location accommodate your business two, three, or five years down the road, relative to your growth projections? If not, where could you potentially relocate, and how would such a move affect your customer base?

Home-Based Business

If you operate your business out of your home, you can usually deduct a percentage of your utilities, insurance, and maintenance, and depreciate the portion of your home that you are using *exclusively and regularly* for business purposes. The IRS has very strict rules governing home office expenses, spelled out in publication # 587 (see box below).

Use tests. Whether you are an employee or self-employed, you generally can not deduct expenses for the business use of your home. But you can take a limited deduction for its business use if you use part of your home ***exclusively*** and ***regularly:***

1) as the principal place of business for any trade or business in which you engage;

2) as a place to meet or deal with patients, clients, or customers in the normal course of your trade or business; or

3) in connection with your trade or business, if you are using a separate structure that is not attached to your house or residence.

Employee use. Even if you meet the exclusive and regular use tests, you cannot take any deduction for the business use of your home if you are an employee and either of the following situations apply to you.

1) The business use of your home is not for the convenience of your employer. Whether your home's business use is for your employer's convenience depends on all the facts and circumstances. However, business use is not considered for your employer's convenience merely because it is appropriate and helpful.

2) You rent all or part of your home to your employer and use the rented portion to perform services as an employee.

Trade or business use. You must use your home in connection with a trade or business to take a deduction for its business use. If you use your home for a profit-seeking activity that is not a trade or business, you cannot take a deduction for its use.

Source: Internal Revenue Service Publication #587

Office Suites

If you are looking for an office outside your home, consider a shared office arrangement. These are locations that offer such amenities as shared secretarial services, photocopying, conference rooms, and answering services. Under these arrangements you share the overhead with other tenants, and the cost of additional services is included in your rent. This type of setting looks very professional, at a fraction of the cost of providing the facility and services on your own. For example, if you secure retail space for your eyeglass business, you may pay $25 per square foot for space on the first floor of a downtown office building. If you were to share that space with an optometrist (who doesn't need the frontage, but would like your office space in back), your share of the rent could drop to $5 to $10 per square foot, depending on your negotiations with the optometrist (assuming you hold the lease and sublet to the doctor).

Footprint

Include a floor plan for your business, along with a map that shows the street location; proximity to competitors, suppliers, and complementary businesses; major thoroughfares; and public transportation.

PITFALLS

Underestimated Costs

Identify and project accurately all relevant (often indirect) costs associated with each location. For example, if you need to travel from your location to provide customer services, the costs incurred for you and your crew need to be considered, versus the same costs from other locations.

Location Costs Too High

If your location costs as a percentage of sales are significantly higher than industry averages, evaluate the situation carefully. Local market conditions could justify this, but if not, your higher overhead will have a direct effect on profitability.

Better Locations Available

Don't assume that you have to rent a storefront or any other specific type of location for your business. Evaluate each alternative to ensure that you are getting not only an economical situation that you can afford but also the location that best suits your business in terms of image, efficiency, and cost-effectiveness.

AN EXAMPLE

The Eunice Frye Home

…The population of Portland aged 65+ is 14,000. We feel that a projected market share of 3% is easily attainable. The Eunice Frye Home will attract residents from towns other than Portland, so keeping the home full will present no problems. In other parts of the country, investors are very willing to invest in retirement communities that project a 1% penetration, so a modestly projected 3% market share will be attractive to our investors. "Companies that have to capture 5% of their target audiences find backers a bit reluctant to finance retirement community projects," Breines said. "At 5%, you're on the cusp," he said, adding that a 3% penetration need "is great."

[illegible] is a demonstrated need for assisted living facilities in the Portland area, and our cen- [illegible] ill help fill that need. Our center will be competitively priced, and will offer the full range [illegible] services that are expected and desired in such a facility…

Source: The Eunice Frye Home

Some Advice –

"The first space I leased for my law offices seemed ideal. It was in a building with other professionals, and it was very convenient to the courthouse. Little did I know that the building had poor sound insulation and was quite noisy. In fact, after several months and a lot of wasted time and money, we moved. If I had only spoken to a few tenants before moving in, I could have avoided the problem."

Brian Powers, Esq.
Port Jefferson, N.Y.

PRICING

OVERVIEW

At first glance, setting prices appears to be a simple task. **What is price?** The value the market places on a product or service. **How is it determined?** By calculating the costs of providing the service and then adding a profit margin.

Although establishing prices certainly involves an analysis of costs and profit margins, there are a number of other factors that will ultimately have significant effects on your decision. These include *elasticity of demand*, which measures the relationship between changes in prices and the quantity of demand for your services or for any that are close substitutes. For example, if you are going to provide a service which has no close substitutes, such as the first messenger service in your town, the pricing environment will be relatively inelastic. That is, for a certain level of demand, you can charge relatively high prices. However, if you plan to open the third diet center in town, the demand will be relatively elastic, meaning that you may need to offer your service at a lower price to attract customers from your competitors.

The best way to consider the price of your service is from the consumers' perspective. They don't care about your cost basis or profit margin. What they are looking for is good comparative value within the context of what they can afford to pay and what you and your competition have to offer.

Your company *image* has a significant effect on the prices that you will be able to charge. Consider the distiller who produces Absolut vodka. By definition, vodka is a neutral spirit and therefore all vodkas theoretically taste the same. How, then, is Absolut able to charge four times as much as its lowest-priced competitor? It has created an image that attracts a large number of customers who are willing to pay a premium for something they believe to be of superior value. It's the same way a local livery service, such as Royal Limousine, does it. The company creates an image of sophistication, comfort, and status then charges significantly more than its competition. This theory cuts both ways. What image is Rent-A-Wreck trying to create? The company offers a low-cost alternative, designed to attract a sizable segment of the population that currently does not rent cars because of the high cost.

Market
p 323

Intangibles often have the biggest effect on your customers' perception of value and, accordingly, on their purchase decisions. The quality of your warranty, friendly service, and follow-up add value to your offering, and many people may be willing to pay extra for them. The importance of these factors and their relationship to price cannot be overstated.

Break-even Analysis
p 284
Start-up Cost Estimate
p 289

The first step in determining price is to calculate your costs. Then, establish the return you are looking for in quantitative terms. For start-ups, the return is most often expressed as the amount of salary you will require for yourself over the short term. As your business grows, you can expect earnings to increase as well, but in the formative years, when you are establishing yourself, plan to take a modest amount from the business. If you are more successful than you planned, all the better. This approach will help ensure a viable business and, potentially, more funds for advertising and promotion. As your business grows, you may expand your pricing objectives to include maintaining or improving market share, price stability, or preventing competition.

THE BASICS

These are the fundamental steps and considerations for establishing an introductory pricing strategy.

How Low Can You Go?

The first step is to determine is *your break-even point* (BEP). The BEP is the point at which your total costs are equal to your total revenue. At sales levels below the BEP, you will have a loss, and above the BEP, a profit. You can calculate the BEP in two ways.

The following formula will enable you to determine the *number of transactions* you will need to achieve breakeven. Transactions can consist of hours worked, jobs completed, services provided, or any other single unit of measurement. Then you can estimate the *number of customers* you need, and compare that number to your estimated market-share information. These calculations should indicate how likely you are to achieve the minimum level of sales required in your first year.

BEQ/BEP
p 284

BREAK-EVEN QUANTITY

$$BEQ = \frac{FC}{P\text{-}VC}$$

BEQ = number of transactions necessary to break even (i.e., houses cleaned, meals served, hours billed)

FC = fixed costs for one year

P = price that you will charge for a single service or transaction

VC = direct or variable costs related to each transaction

To complete your break-even analysis, you will have to make a lot of assumptions, any one of which could have a substantial effect on its outcome. That is, however, the nature of this type of analysis. It is advisable to calculate your BEP under a number of different conditions and select the one that seems most reasonable.

AN EXAMPLE

Let's say you are planning to start KleanKare, a residential cleaning service targeting at two-worker families with incomes in excess of $60,000. Follow these steps to calculate your BEP.

1. Establish a prototype.

Design a profile of the *typical job* (transaction). In this case, let's assume your basic service will include vacuuming, dusting, cleaning bathrooms, and mopping floors. The typical client home (established from data you've already collected) will have a total of eight rooms, including three bedrooms and one and a half baths. You estimate (from experience) that it will take two people an hour and a half to complete the task, including time for transportation to the job site.

2. Calculate fixed costs.

Fixed costs, often referred to as *overhead*, are costs that do not change in the short run as the number of your customers increases or decreases. Fixed costs include items such as rent, insurance, utilities, owner's salary, and vehicles. All these costs should be calculated on an annual basis. (For service businesses, most costs are considered fixed because it is difficult to allocate items like advertising or utilities to a specific job.)

For KleanKare:

Owner salary	$18,000
Rent	0[a]
Advertising	3,000
Insurance (liability & bonding)	1,800
Utilities	1,200
Equipment	800
Vehicle	1,800[b]
Total Fixed Costs	**$26,600**

[a] You will establish your office in a spare bedroom in your home.

[b] Reflects loan payment for one year on the purchase of one used van. The family station wagon will also be available for business purposes.

The above calculations show that you will have to generate $26,600 in sales in the first year to cover fixed costs.

3. Estimate variable costs.

Variable costs are costs that change as the volume of your business increases or decreases and that can be readily assigned to each job, such as labor, taxes, supplies, and materials. Your variable costs should be calculated on a per-transaction basis, that is, one house cleaning = one transaction.

For KleanKare:

Labor	$30.00[a]
Supplies	3.00
Fuel	1.00
Total Variable Costs (per transaction)	**$ 34.00**

[a] This figure includes two workers at $8 per hour for 1.5 hours plus worker's compensation and taxes (FICA, social security). Suppose we have two crews consisting of two workers each, working part-time, five days a week. By using two crews on a part-time basis, the owner will be able to draw from a larger employment pool, including mothers of school-age children (who need to start after 8 a.m. and end by 2:30 p.m.).

4. Estimate a price.

At this stage of your analysis you must estimate a price that you can charge. Your best bet is to use the same price as that of the business you think will be your closest competitor. Remember, you are looking for ballpark figures here. You will determine your actual pricing strategy later on.

Estimated price $55 (per cleaning)

5. Compute breakeven.

$$\text{Break-Even Quantity (BEQ)} = \frac{\text{Fixed Costs}}{\text{Price per job} - \text{Variable Costs}}$$

$$\text{Number of cleaning jobs necessary to break even in one year} = \frac{\$\,26{,}600}{\$\,55 - \$34} = 1{,}267$$

On the face of it, this number looks quite large, but consider the situation from some different perspectives:

- ❑ This number represents about 24 cleanings per week, or 12 houses per crew per week, which seems reasonable.
- ❑ Each cleaning job does not represent a new customer, because you assume (based on data gathered during your market research) that the average customer will have you clean at least once a month. This allows you to estimate your total customer base by dividing the total number of cleaning jobs needed by the average frequency of cleaning. Your estimate of total customer base:

$$\text{Total estimated customer base} = \frac{\text{BEQ}}{12 \text{ months}}$$

$$106 = \frac{1{,}266}{12}$$

- ❑ You have assumed that the owner won't be cleaning. However, as the business starts up, the owner will be involved in cleaning. Therefore, your labor costs will drop by $10 per hour for each job the owner participates in completing.
- ❑ You are also assuming that you have two crews out working. Additional crews would add to your capacity, with little, if any, additional overhead, and would increase your revenues accordingly.

6. Evaluate your break-even point relative to your target market and competition.

Let's assume that in the Market Section of your business plan you have identified 10,000 families who fit your customer profile. Furthermore, as a result of other secondary research, you determined a high probability that about one in five of these families would use your type of services. Therefore, you estimate a pool of 2,000 families in your target market. In addition, during your competitive analysis you identified three other businesses with similar services.

7. Make your first year's sales projection.

Based on the foregoing analysis, you estimate on a very conservative basis, that you should be able to capture 10% of the market during the first year. That number (200) would place you at a level significantly above breakeven (106) and would be well within your capacity.

200	customers
x 12	months
2,400	jobs
x $55	per job
$132,000	sales in first year

In other words, your first year's sales projection at $132,000 would be justifiable. Now compare this calculation with the conclusions you've drawn in your Market Share section and modify as appropriate.

In the previous example, you determined the number of transactions you would need to achieve your break-even point. In most cases, you will usually solve for Q (breakeven quantity, or number of transactions), because finding a substitute price (P) is easy to do and is quite accurate. In some situations, however, you may want to solve for price, in which case you must estimate the number of transactions (i.e., demand). That may be hard to do precisely.

Accounting
p 321

For example, consider a plumber who has been working for a large plumbing and heating company for a number of years and who now wants to go out on his own. Based on his experience and contacts in the community, he is confident that he will be able to bill 30 hours per week on a time-plus-materials basis. He also wants three weeks' vacation per year. He has determined his fixed costs to be $51,000 (including his salary) and his variable costs per job (for transportation and consumables) to be $3. In the short run he does not plan to mark up his materials. If Q refers to the number of hours worked, not the number of transactions, break-even price (his hourly charge) would be calculated as follows:

BREAK-EVEN PRICE

$$BEP = \frac{FC}{Q} + VC$$

(Q = 49 weeks x 30 billable hours per week = 1,470)

$$BEP = \frac{\$51,000}{1,470} = \$34.69 + \$3$$

BEP = $37.69

The plumber in this case should charge at least $38 per hour to cover his expenses and generate the income he requires.

WHAT PRICING OPTIONS ARE AVAILABLE?

In the breakeven analysis, you selected a price based on what your closest competitor charges. In the long run, *all pricing,* by definition, has to be *competitive.* In most mature markets, you will find services offered at different price levels (high, moderate, low) reflecting varying degrees of consumer demand, ability and willingness of customers to pay, and the service providers' ability to differentiate their offerings.

In establishing your introductory pricing strategy, you should also consider the following alternatives.

Penetration Pricing

Market p 323

This strategy involves pricing your service at a level below that of your competition. Your goal is twofold: to get customers to switch from your competitors because they perceive that you can give them better value and to attract customers who have never used such services before or have used them infrequently because of the price barrier.

This strategy works most effectively for businesses that can achieve economies with increases in volume. In the KleanKare cleaning service example, a penetration strategy might generate sufficient customer volume to hire more crews, and therefore become more profitable and use management capacity more effectively.

On the downside, you must be very careful when implementing this type of pricing structure, for two reasons.

First, you must be confident that you can achieve your financial goals at these lower price levels. Don't think that if your projected sales levels don't come to fruition, you can always solve the problem by simply increasing the price. At that point, faced with higher prices, your newfound customers may revert to their former service providers, or those new to the market may find they cannot afford to continue the service.

Second, your competitors have the ability to interfere with your plans in the short run, assuming they don't want to decrease their own prices over the long term. For example, they could mail discount coupons to their customers or advertise a special offer to attract new customers. Both of these techniques are inexpensive and can be implemented rapidly.

Premium Pricing

Premium pricing, as the name suggests, is a strategy whereby you price your service at the high end of the market. You are trying to attract customers who are willing to pay more for what they consider to be superior service, who assume that higher price, by definition, means higher quality, or who get some ego gratification from selecting your service. In the case of Royal Limousine, the company may offer tangible advantages such as better scheduling and guaranteed on-time arrival, but there is also the powerful ego benefit of stepping out of a black Cadillac limo, with a uniformed driver, as opposed to riding in a Ford minivan with a driver in a T-shirt.

The upside of this strategy is more profitable sales. The downside is a mirror image of the penetration strategy. That is, if you are forced to lower prices because you misread consumer demand or as new competitors enter the market, you may find that a number of your customers switch back to their former service providers. Some may feel that they were being overcharged in the first place. In addition, at lower pricing levels, it may be impossible for you to maintain your former level of service because of the high costs associated with delivering it.

PITFALLS

A number of factors can have a negative impact on your overall pricing strategy.

Underestimating Costs

The failure to identify and estimate costs accurately can have a devastating effect on your business. In the house-cleaning business, if you omitted fuel costs, that would have a substantial impact on your profit. Forgetting to count fuel as an expense could take $2,400 (200 transactions @ $1 per job for fuel x 12 months) out of your pocket in the first year.

Competition

You need to identify all relevant competitors and their pricing policies. Failure to do so may result in overestimating market share and in pricing errors that could be fatal to your business.

Discounts and Allowances

If you intend to offer discounts, such as 15% off to preferred customers in a dry-cleaning business, or a coupon book at the driving range, be sure to include them in your pricing analysis. A 15% discount to the top 10% of your customers would have a significant effect on your bottom line.

Some Advice —

"When I started out, I didn't realize how tight my margins would be. Although I used industry standards as pricing guidelines, there were many costs—particularly for packaging and shipping— that turned out to be higher than I originally estimated. Also, my labor expenses have continued to rise. Now that I have a better feel for the costs, I've been able to build them into my new pricing structure."

Eileen Sutherland, Owner
Shake, Rattle, and Wrap
(corporate gift service)
New Castle, N.H.

AN EXAMPLE

Frequent Travel Management, Inc.

Pricing/Gross Margin Targets

Price Levels – Business Travelers

Direct FTM AirMax Worldwide Diskette Sales - The list price is $149.95. However, FTM is marketing its product at discounted pricing in order to quickly penetrate the market, gain market share, and rapidly quantify and identify the level of demand. Therefore the selling price for all orders will be $49.95.

On-line/Internet Services - Once development of the on-line and Internet applications is completed, FTM will use the commercial on-line services as its distributor of this service. FTM will be charging a monthly recurring fee of $5.95 per month, which will be charged to the on-line customer's bank card. Annual revenues for this product will be $71.40 per year. FTM benefits from this product application since there is no cost of goods sold (CGS) and marketing costs can be shared with the on-line services.

Price Levels – Travel Agencies

Direct FTM AirMax Diskette Sales (Travel Agencies) - The list price and sale price will be $249.95, which is average pricing for travel agency software. Travel agencies will be charged an annual fee of $120 for monthly updates per location. Because travel agencies need to have accurate and timely information, the monthly program updates are a necessity. The travel agency will need to have the diskette product installed locally in order to execute the point-of-sale features and assure functionality. The CRS companies are improving their systems to make it possible for FTM AirMax data to be downloaded on a daily basis. This will solve many time problems with current data, as well as increase FTM's gross margins.

GROSS MARGIN LEVELS – BUSINESS TRAVELERS

Direct FTM AirMax Diskette Sales

Sale Price	$49.95
Shipping & Handling	8.50
FTM Net Revenue	**$58.45**
Cost of Goods Sold	
Diskettes (4) & Labels (4)	3.52
Package & Assembly	1.90
Registration Card	.10
Quarterly Update Diskettes	6.00
Quarterly Update Disk & Mailing	2.08
CGS Sub total	**13.60**
Credit Card Processing (3.2%)	1.59
UPS Ground Shipping	2.30
Total Product Costs	**$17.49**
Total Retail Sales Margin	**$40.96**
Gross Margin (%)	**70.1%**

Source: Frequent Travel Management, Inc.

PROMOTION

OVERVIEW

Promotion is any form of communication that informs your potential customers that you have a service available to them, convinces them that this service meets their needs, and persuades them to purchase it. You create the message that you want to convey to current and potential customers, select the medium (e.g. TV, radio, newspapers, Internet) to be used to carry your message, and then send it.

The first step in developing a promotional strategy is to create a list of goals you expect to achieve. They should be clearly stated in quantitative terms wherever possible. Each aspect of your promotional campaign should be measured against these objectives. For example, if you decide to use a certain amount of radio advertising, let's say a package that provides 30 spots per week, you can check its effectiveness by determining to what extent it meets your goals in terms of customer reach and frequency.

Evaluating the effectiveness of the various components of your promotional strategy is an important but often difficult task. A comprehensive statement of your **goals** should include the following:

Establish and/or Expand Your Customer Base

How does the proposed strategy ensure that potential customers will become aware of your service? How many new customers will be reached?

Differentiate Your Service

How does the promotional activity make your service look unique, different from that offered by your competitors? Emphasize factors such as price, hours of operation, and personalized customer service to achieve this.

Objectives p 285

Influence People to Become Customers

Does the promotional activity provide an incentive for the prospective customer to purchase? For example, ads reading "Have your house cleaned for the holiday. Call today to make sure your rooms get priority treatment" or "Use this coupon to receive a 20% discount on all spring clean-up services" may help achieve this goal.

Build Goodwill

Does this promotional technique build your reputation as a good citizen and establish a positive image for your business that people will remember? Contributions such as support of community fund-raising activities and buying Little League uniforms for local teams fall into this category.

Goals in hand, your next step is to create a comprehensive promotional plan. Assume that most customers you want to attract to your service will have numerous alternatives or substitutes available to them. That's why the most important factor contributing to your business success will be your ability to inform customers and prospects about your service and differentiate it from that of your competitors.

THE BASICS

This section focuses on promotional mix and several other factors that influence the development of a well-rounded promotional strategy. Before you begin to evaluate your promotional alternatives, consider these three factors.

Reach. This refers to the number of people who will actually see or hear your promotional message. For example, an advertisement in the local newspaper will reach subscribers and their families or roommates, as well as people who buy the paper at the newsstand. Reach is important because you want your promotional material to get to your target market but not too far beyond it. If you have a house-cleaning service operating within a very local area, for example, you might decide not to advertise in the county newspaper because there would be no point in paying to reach a large number of people who are outside your geographic target market.

Frequency. This is the number of times you think your potential customers need to be exposed to your message for it to be effective. For example, if you think that radio would be a good way to promote your day-care services, your customers will probably have to hear your ad several times for it to generate a response. Radio listeners who are concentrating on driving a car may not be paying particular attention to the message, and may not remember your telephone number.

Evaluation Media Reach p 286

CPM. CPM stands for dollar cost per thousand potential customers reached by a particular advertisement. It is a valuable tool to use as part of your analysis of how to allocate your advertising budget. To compute CPM, simply take the cost of the promotional activity and divide it by the number of people reached. For example, if you pay $2,500 to place an ad in a specialty magazine that has a circulation of 375,000, your CPM would be $6.67. You can then compare that figure to the CPMs of your other promotional alternatives.

Cost per thousand is a good analytical tool. However, just because one promotional activity has the lowest CPM, it is not necessarily the best alternative. Other factors to consider are the medium's focus on your target market and overall costs.

The Promotional Mix

The promotional mix includes five basic ways to communicate about your services: advertising, sales promotion, personal selling, publicity, and public relations. The promotional mix is a blend of these options. Which ones you choose depends on factors such as available funds, competition, and stage of your business lifecycle. Your strategy should not be created by happenstance. It should result from an analysis of your alternatives, weighed against your promotional goals.

Advertising

Advertising includes all paid promotional activities that are used to communicate to your target audience about your service. Your alternatives include:

Literature	Print Advertising	Direct Mail
Brochures	Newspapers	Catalogs
Flyers	Buyers' guides	Brochures
Leaflets	Magazines	Coupons
Circulars	Specialty publications	Sales letters
		Cooperative Direct Marketing (e.g. Super-Coups)

Broadcast	Outdoor Advertising	Other
Television	Billboards	Internet postings
Cable TV	Signs	Web pages
Radio	Banners	CD-ROMs

Market p 323

As you evaluate your advertising expenditures in the context of reach, frequency, and CPM, be aware of the general characteristics of each of the options that follow. Specific advertising rates, circulation figures, and readership, viewer, or listener demographics can be obtained by contacting prospective newspapers, magazines, radio stations, or other media directly.

Literature. Brochures and flyers can be easy and inexpensive to produce and change. They can also be used for multiple purposes. For example, you could use the same rafting guide service brochure in a point-of-purchase display at local motels, as a direct mail piece, or for follow-up mailings generated by customer inquiries.

Print Advertising. More small business advertising dollars are spent on *newspapers* than any other medium. Newspapers are timely, widely read, have low CPMs, and are flexible, in that ads generally require short lead time. Their major downside is that their life span is brief. People generally read the paper and throw it away on the same day (with the exception of large-circulation Sunday newspapers such as *The New York Times*, the *Boston Globe*, and the *San Francisco Examiner,* which people tend to keep and read throughout the week).

Specialty magazines, such as *Fly Rod and Reel*, have grown exponentially over the last decade. There are over 10,000 in print on subjects ranging from needlepoint to paint ball. These magazines tend to be highly focused, so there is little wasted circulation. The ads tend to have a long shelf life, as most readers save the magazines for reference. Each time readers consult the magazine or show it to a friend, there is a high probability that they will see your ad again, increasing frequency of exposure. Specialty magazines tend to be far less expensive than their larger-circulation counterparts. However, there is usually a substantial time lag before getting your ad into print. These magazines are good venues for many types of service businesses, from tourism and hospitality to software developers.

Direct mail. Direct mail (DM) has been the fastest growing component of the promotional mix over the past decade. A significant part of this growth can be traced to the fact that many small businesses now have access to DM services that were formerly the domain of larger businesses. Even the smallest firms can afford this form of promotion because the tools needed to use it are readily available, usually at modest cost. You can usually buy mailing lists for between $50 to $60 per thousand names, and there are fulfillment services that do everything from stuffing, labeling, and mailing to taking orders.

Direct mail is successful because it is the most selective advertising technique. With little wasted circulation, DM can be very cost-effective. For example, if you ran a business such as Wilderness Excursions, offering unique group sporting adventures, you could buy a mailing list from *Cross Country Skier*, possibly one with only New England zip codes, and send a brochure promoting your winter skiing adventures to potential customers in your target market area.

The downside of direct mail is that there is so much of it that it is hard to get your prospects to open your envelope rather than simply tossing it away. Don't despair! Start small and keep it personal. Hand-stamped mail, test lists, and follow-up are just a few of the techniques that can have a dramatic effect on your response rates.

Market p 323

There are also companies, such as Val-Pak and Super-Coups, that mail packets of coupons from several different businesses to all residents within a specific zip codes. These types of services may be a cost-effective DM alternative. If direct mail looks like a good alternative for you, because your target audience is clearly identifiable and reachable, there are several good publications and professional help available.

Broadcasting. Radio has a low CPM, is flexible, and can target customer groups. Its disadvantage is that it leaves only an audio impression, and multiple exposures are needed for a radio spot to be effective. In addition, audiences vary a great deal, depending on the time of day your advertisement is aired. "Trip" or "Drive" times are expensive. Packaged plans are often a good idea because they provide a variety of exposures.

Cable TV (CATV) is becoming a popular medium for small-business advertising. Unlike its network cousins, cable's local programming enables you to target specific markets, using color and sound, at costs that will fit most promotional budgets. As CATV expands to systems with hundreds of channels, many programs become akin to specialty magazines. You can promote your services, as in the case of Wilderness Excursions, to a highly targeted group of customers who are watching programs on topics such as hiking, fly fishing, rafting, cross-country skiing, or backpacking.

Outdoor billboards, signage, and banners. These can be important parts of a promotional mix. If you depend on customers coming to your place of business (such as a restaurant), a billboard message not only alerts them to your existence, type of cuisine, and directions, but also stimulates demand by reminding the driver that mealtime is approaching. For those who often travel the same roads, billboards and signs generate frequency of exposure, which can boost patronage.

Signage is important for businesses that depend on customer traffic. The sign makes a statement about your business and is often your customer's first exposure to your service. Banners are effective in drawing attention to your place of business and promoting sales. They are a must for trade shows or other types of special events. Local and/or state regulations often limit the use of billboards and signs, so be sure to check with the appropriate authorities. If you locate your business in a mall, the leasing agent will inform you of any restrictions that apply.

Electronic Commerce. Selling services over the Internet, and particularly the World Wide Web, is becoming a cost-effective way to reach a large number of potential clients. Businesses ranging from consultants to investment publications are using this medium very successfully. Recently, the Schott Letter, a monthly investment newsletter originally targeted to clients in the medical profession, began to use the Internet, and now has information available at the Financial Center (http://www.tfc.com). The Internet has given this young, successful business the ability to reach literally thousands of potential clients worldwide every day, around the clock, at low cost, and with little maintenance.

If you intend to market your business on the Internet, there are many things you should be aware of, including these three rules of thumb on the Net:

> **Only put useful content on your Web site.** Since you are asking your customers to pay for the information they are receiving from you (in terms of download time), they will not be happy if they must spend a great deal of time on the computer to get a cursory overview of your business.
>
> **Limit the graphics used in your home page.** While they look great, graphics can take a long time to download, causing frustration for your customers.
>
> **Include valuable links to other Web sites.** A link (often called a "hyperlink") can direct the customer to other places of interest with the click of a mouse. If your hours vary from week to week, include a link to a listing of your hours. You can update your hours weekly, and your customers will know when you are in. Another link might connect them to your sales department for up-to-the-minute price quotes, or offer a calendar that shows upcoming events.

Internet
p 104

Market
p 323
Buying a Computer
p 322

It is important to keep online time to a minimum, time providing the maximum amount of information. Net customers can be very loyal if you provide them with a service they can utilize for a small investment of time and money, such as complete planning for a trip to Disney World including booking airline tickets, hotel accommodations, and dinner reservations.

Sales Promotion

Sales promotion refers to activities such as displaying at trade shows and giving away premiums that stimulate the trial or purchase of your service by a customer.

Trade shows and expositions. Virtually every industry sponsors events at multiple locations around the country. If you are in the catering business, for example, you might attend a local bridal trade show, which would have photographers, caterers, formalwear stores, limousine businesses, and stationery printers displaying their wares. Trade shows and expos are a cost-effective way to reach highly targeted markets.

Premiums. You can have giveaways, such as pens, hats, key rings, golf tees, or coffee mugs, imprinted with your company name to hand out or mail to customers and prospects. These low-cost items are effective because they repeatedly expose your company name, not only to your customer but to other potential customers as well, as in the case of a hat or T-shirt.

Coupons. Coupons offering price discounts, two-for-one bargains, or free introduction to your services can be a cost-effective way to attract sales. The same coupons can be used simultaneously for many purposes, such as direct mail programs and billing inserts.

Publicity

A form of advertising — generally free — publicity communicates information about your company and your service. It can be effective because it is presented by a third party, and is thus perceived as unbiased. Although you don't usually have to pay for it, you will have to spend some time and money generating it. For example, you would want to send press releases or other materials to local newspapers, most of which run regular articles on new businesses.

Consider the author of a book that was originally a collection of stories about country living, gardening, and recipes, which she had written for her county newspaper over a period of several years. Her local publisher was having little success selling the book to a national distributor. As part of its publicity strategy, the company mailed complimentary copies of the book to editors of 50 magazines that might have an interest in reviewing it. One major magazine reprinted a whole chapter from the book. The publisher no longer had a problem with national distribution.

Public Relations

This is communication designed primarily to influence the opinion of non-customer groups. Public relations can be critical to success. In the recycling business, for example, it pays to invest time supporting politically active environmental groups, the government, and industry to help ensure efficient operational and promotional strategies. However as your business grows, you may rely on outside professionals, who have a rapport with editors and broadcasters and can place your story and target your efforts.

Personal Selling

Customer solicitation face-to-face or over the telephone is the most powerful form of promotion because its flexibility enables you to match the customer's needs to specific attributes of your service. For example, if your business customer is most interested in the on-time reliability of your livery service, you can focus your sales pitch on that feature, offering to refer him or her to other customers for rreferences. You won't have to waste time describing product features that may not be important to that particular customer.

Personal selling is expensive, however. The cost includes the time you, the owner, spend on it, and it takes time away from other responsibilities. In addition, good salespeople are expensive to hire, train, and retain. When you start your business, if you opt for personal selling, be sure to budget plenty of time for it. If you need salespeople, consider providing them with results-based compensation, in the form of commissions or a share of the equity, to offset costs.

OTHER CONSIDERATIONS

Evaluation. One of the most difficult aspects of designing an overall promotional strategy is determining how to measure its effectiveness, particularly if you have more than one activity going on simultaneously, such as a radio promotion and a newspaper ad. There are several methods you can use to determine how each medium is drawing and, therefore, which is most cost-effective. In print advertising, for example, you can include a special offer that must be presented or mentioned when someone calls or comes in for service. If you are using several different print outlets, you can use your address with a different fictitious department number in each ad to see where the responses are coming from.

On radio, a very good strategy is the "mention this ad" ploy, which normally generates results. In addition, as part of every customer contact, whether by phone or in person, you should gather data on how the customer found out about your service.

Even if you use all of these techniques and more, you won't get perfect data. Some customers won't remember, some will inadvertently give the wrong information, and you'll often forget to collect the data. The point here is to collect as much as you can, on a regular basis. At a minimum, this will reduce your uncertainty about how you are spending your advertising dollars.

Guerrilla marketing. Unconventional methods can be used, usually at low cost, to reach potential customers. Techniques such as having people dressed as Sesame Street characters handing out fliers on a beach or parachute into a high-school football championship half-time celebration are examples of guerrilla marketing. Guerrilla marketing has proved to be very successful, and is a strategy that should be seriously considered as you develop your plan of attack.

Budgeting. How much money to spend on promotional activity poses a constant problem. Although there are no hard and fast rules, some guidelines suggest that up to 10% of net sales should be earmarked for promotion during the first year. Comparisons can also be found by looking in *Financial Studies of the Small Business* to determine what other, similar businesses are spending as a percentage of sales. Remember, however, that these figures will reflect average expenditures, and your expenses in the first year will probably be higher. Do remember that you must promote your service, and although promotion is expensive, it is as important (if not more so) than all other expenses. Don't look at it as money that you can afford to spend only after all other bills, including your salary, have been paid. If you do that, eventually all you will have are bills to pay.

Financial Studies p 102

Evaluate your promotional options relative to your competition and your customer base. Let the budget follow the plan. Use financial and trade association data to compare your proposed expenditures with other businesses in your industry, remembering that start-up and location factors will have a substantial effect on the numbers. Consult a local ad agency, a Small Business Development Center counselor, and other marketing professionals for their advice.

Cooperative advertising. One way to reduce advertising expenses is cost-sharing arrangements. These are very common, most often done with suppliers who will share costs up to a certain dollar amount if you mention their products in your ad. In other cases, you can advertise with noncompetitive service providers. If you are a roofing contractor, for example, you might find a carpenter and a stone mason with whom you could pool resources to purchase larger and/or more frequent ads.

PITFALLS

Common mistakes that new businesses make in developing and executing a promotional strategy include:

Underestimating costs

Do not assume that you can leave promotional strategy at the bottom of your list in business planning. Make sure you have provided for an adequate budget allocation at the level required to sustain your sales projections.

Differentiation

Use promotion to adequately differentiate your services from those of your competitors. You do not want to stimulate a general need for this type of service with no compelling reason to purchase from you, thus creating a potential sale for your competitor.

Lack of research

"Gut feel" is an unreliable guide for deciding how to promote your services. Spend adequate time conducting an analysis to find out which promotional techniques most effectively meet your goals, quantifying results as much as possible.

Some Advice —

"Avoid mass promotion. We have some common material that we give each customer, but we also tailor each package to address their specific needs. It's more important to understand the markets you want to serve, and then go out and find the matches. Simply trying to reach as many people as possible is not cost effective."

Paul Stanfield, Operations Manager
ABCO Automation, Inc.
Browns Summit, N.C.

AN EXAMPLE

Sub-Zero Restaurant

E. Promotional Activities

Sub-Zero Restaurant intends to utilize an aggressive promotional campaign to introduce its business to the Latrobe area. We intend to take advantage of several area media sources in announcing our opening and reinforcing awareness of our existence. We intend to utilize the following sources:

The *Latrobe Bulletin*	Publish grand opening information and then follow-up coupons and specials. Weekly advertising will be maintained throughout the prime seasons.
Local Radio Stations	Promote the grand opening and reinforce business presence throughout the year. Thirty-second spots will be read live on the air to give the advertisement a personal touch.
Bell Atlantic Yellow Pages	A small display ad, beginning November, 1996.
Entertainment '96 **Pittsburgh East book**	A coupon ad with a special offer on subs and ice cream.
Queen City Cable	

Source: Sub-Zero Restaurant

FORMS OF OWNERSHIP

OVERVIEW

Analysis of your business's legal form of ownership should be undertaken with a broad perspective. The first question to ask is not "How do I incorporate?" but rather, "What are my organizational options, and which one of them best meets my needs?"

To determine the most appropriate legal structure for your business, consider issues such as capital requirements, business succession, legal liability, taxation, decision-making authority, and control. Many of these issues will be addressed in various sections of your business plan, and therefore no decisions should be made on ownership status until the appropriate sections of the plan have been completed.

Once you have gathered the relevant information, an attorney and an accountant should be consulted for advice on your options in the light of your particular situation. When selecting an attorney, choose one with experience in new ventures. Don't assume that your brother-in-law, the divorce lawyer, is the fellow to call. He is probably not the right choice, nor are other lawyers whose specialties are not business-oriented.

If you do not know a lawyer who fits your needs, ask a successful small-business owner, banker, or accountant for a referral. Each state also supports a Lawyer Referral Service, which can provide you with the name and location of a lawyer with the specialty you seek. In return for a listing with the service, many of these lawyers provide a reduced rate to the client, or a free initial meeting. Contact your state bar association for the phone number of your state's referral service. In addition, if you are considering a franchised service business, select an attorney who has extensive experience with this highly specialized form of business.

Your legal form of ownership does not have to be presented in a separate section in your business plan. The form you selected and your rationale for it should be included in the Introduction or Management section.

THE BASICS

Following are descriptions of the three fundamental forms of ownership and their relative advantages and disadvantages.

Sole Proprietorships

A sole proprietorship is a business that is owned and operated by one person. No legal distinction exists between you as an individual and your business entity. Many proprietorships function on a DBA (doing business as) basis, such as a local dry cleaner owned by Bill Johnson, DBA Sea Coast Cleaners. The DBA status enables your business to use any name you like as long as it has been properly registered and does not infringe on someone else's trademark or trade name. The DBA allows you to create a separate "image" for your business that is appropriate to the services you will provide, but which is not associated with your personal name.

Proprietorships can have employees and, in fact, some are quite large. Over 75% of all businesses operate as sole proprietorships, according to the U.S. Small Business Administration.

Advantages of Proprietorships

- ❑ **Costs.** Start-up costs tend to be low. Once you've registered your name and secured any necessary licenses and permits, you'll be able to solicit your first customers.
- ❑ **Control.** As a proprietor, you have complete control over all business decisions. You are free to hire and fire within the labor laws, and decisions can be made quickly.
- ❑ **Profits.** The owner keeps all profits net of applicable federal, state, and local taxes.
- ❑ **Flexibility.** You can decide to close your business as easily as you started it. There are no forms or costs other than to pay off your suppliers and any debt you may have incurred.

Forms of Ownership p 322

Disadvantages of Proprietorships

- ❑ **Unlimited liability.** As a sole proprietor, you make all of your assets available to satisfy a creditor or a plaintiff in a legal action.
- ❑ **Less available capital.** All financing is based on your personal financial statement, business record, and character. You do not have the ability to raise equity.
- ❑ **Limited scope of management.** As your business grows, it will probably need a professional management staff. It may be difficult to hire and retain this staff if, as a sole proprietor, you are unable to offer equity in lieu of salary.
- ❑ **Business life.** If you become disabled, retire, or die, usually the business will cease to exist unless it is inherited by someone who is ready and able to continue it. This disadvantage has many implications, not the least of which is its effect on your customers. The more they depend on your services, the less comfortable they may become with your status as sole proprietor.

Partnerships

A partnership is a form of organization in which two or more individuals conduct business as co-owners. Partnerships can have anywhere from two to 2,000 partners. For example,Arthur Andersen, the accounting and management consulting firm, has close to 2,000 partners. As with a proprietorship, a partnership does not exist as a legal entity separate from its owners. There are two types: **general partnerships**, by far the most common form of partnership, and **limited partnerships**. Partnerships can be formed by a simple handshake. However, a detailed partnership agreement, signed by all partners, is highly recommended. A sample partnership agreement can be found in Appendix B on page 310.

Legal
p 323

Advantages of a General Partnership

- ❑ **Capital availability.** Partners contribute capital to the business, providing for a potentially larger resource base than proprietorship offers. As the business grows and more partners are added, your capital base will expand.

- ❑ **Continuity.** If one of the partners becomes disabled, retires, or dies, the business can continue, although a new partnership must be created.

- ❑ **Taxation.** Partners can agree to divide profits any way they see fit, typically based on pro rata share of ownership. However, if there is no agreement, they share profits equally. Each partner pays income tax on his or her share of the profits at the individual's tax rate.

- ❑ **Growth potential.** The ability to add new partners to the business provides the opportunity to recruit new expertise and build management infrastructure.

Disadvantages of a General Partnership

- ❑ **Liability.** Generally each partner is responsible for the business debts of the partnership. There is unlimited joint liability, which may mean that if one partner has more substantial personal assets than the others, he or she could end up paying more to satisfy a debt or claim, even though the partnership shares were equal. This would occur, however, only after each partner's assets have been depleted.

- ❑ **Divided authority.** In a partnership, by definition, you have less authority and control than in a proprietorship. As your business grows and partners are added, your authority and control may continue to be diluted.

- ❑ **Capital.** Although capital becomes available as partners are added, you still do not have the ability to sell shares of your business to investors.

Limited Partnership

Designed to attract investors, this type of partnership includes at least one general partner and a number of limited partners. The limited partners are passive investors. They have no say in management issues and no role in running the business. Their legal liability is limited to the amount they have invested in their partnership share. The laws regulating limited partnerships, including the number of limited partners you can have, vary from state to state, so you must check with your state attorney general's or secretary of state's office for the rules and regulations. Limited partners also get tax advantages, so consult both your attorney and your accountant.

Corporations

The corporation is a state-chartered organization owned by shareholders. Shareholders elect a board of directors who are ultimately responsible for the management of the business. The corporation is a separate legal entity and, as such, it can make products and provide services to customers, own and sell property, sue, and be sued. The corporate form of ownership was developed to reduce the number of problems and disadvantages associated with partnerships and proprietorships.

To create a corporation, you must file a Certificate of Incorporation or Corporate Charter with the secretary of state's office. You can obtain information, including forms that may be required, by contacting that office in your state.

There are two forms of for-profit corporation: the C corporation, and the S corporation (so-called because it is defined under subchapter S of the Internal Revenue Code). Although for most start-ups the S corporation, also known as the "Sub S," is the most appropriate, this is an area where professional advice from your lawyer and accountant is imperative. An example of a corporate charter can be found in Appendix A on page 307.

Advantages of the C corporation

- ❑ **Limited Liability.** Stockholders' liability is limited to the amount they have invested in the company. If the company fails, creditors cannot attach the personal assets of stockholders. There are exceptions to this in certain areas of taxation and fraud. If any corporation fails to pay withholding taxes or is involved in some types of fraudulent activity, the "corporate veil" can be pierced and individual stockholders may be held liable. Although this situation doesn't occur frequently, it is something you should be aware of, particularly in the S corporation.

- ❑ **Access to capital.** The corporation can raise money directly through the sale of stock (equity) and bond (debt) offerings. The corporation can also borrow from commercial sources, using corporate assets to secure the loan. However, with a small corporation, most commercial lenders will require the major stockholder(s) to guarantee the loan personally.

- ❑ **Perpetual life.** Because the corporation is a separate legal entity, its existence will not be affected by the retirement, injury, or death of any stockholder. That is not to say that when the president of a closely held company dies suddenly, the business won't have some problems. One of the problems it won't have, however, is losing its legal identity and standing.

- ❑ **Transfer of ownership.** The transfer of ownership in the corporation is simple. Ownership is determined by the number of shares owned, and these shares can be traded or sold, assuming there is a market for them, with little effort.

- ❑ **Ability to attract management.** Often business growth is stymied in a proprietorship or partnership by the inability to attract specialized management expertise and build general management infrastructure, because these organizations cannot pay market salaries or add additional partners. The corporation has the ability to use stock options as a powerful incentive to attract such managerial talent.

Disadvantages of the C Corporation

❑ **Taxation.** Corporate income taxes are paid prior to the distribution of any dividends to stockholders. Once these dividends have been received, they are again taxed as part of the individual stockholder's income. In other words, the profits have been taxed twice.

❑ **Government regulation and paperwork.** Certain government reports, forms, and other paperwork must be filed and/or monitored regularly. This places a particular burden on small enterprises and can create a considerable hidden cost of doing business.

❑ **Costs.** Paperwork and other initial costs, including legal and filing fees, can be significant. They can amount to thousands of dollars, depending on the complexity of the incorporation and the amount of work you are willing to do yourself.

The S corporation

Created in 1958, this has become a very popular form of ownership for small business. The Sub S retains most of the advantages of incorporation, including limited liability, but eliminates the disadvantage of double taxation. All profits, as in the partnership, are distributed on a pro rata basis to the stockholders and are then taxed at the individual's income tax rates.

Disadvantages of the S corporation include taxes on many fringe benefits; limits on retirement benefits, which are treated more favorably in the C corporation; and limitations on the number of stockholders. In addition, the tax benefits of the Sub S will change, for better or worse, with changes in corporate and individual tax rates. Several states do not recognize the S corporation for state tax purposes. All of these issues should be discussed with your lawyer and accountant.

To qualify as an S corporation your business must meet these legal requirements:

❑ It must be an independently owned and managed domestic corporation.

❑ It may have no more than 35 stockholders.

❑ It must have only one class of stock.

❑ It may have no stockholders who are nonresident aliens.

❑ It cannot be a financial institution that takes deposits and makes loans.

❑ It cannot be in the insurance business taxed under Sub-Chapter L of the IRS Code.

❑ It cannot have received tax credits for doing business in the United States.

Limited Liability Company

The limited liability company (LLC) is a state-chartered organization which may offer the best of both worlds in terms of structure for small businesses. An LLC allows for the reduced personal liability of a corporation, but with the tax advantages of a partnership, although not all LLCs qualify for partnership federal income tax treatment. Its partnership approach enables the company to act as a reporting agent and not as a taxable organization, therefore eliminating the "double taxation" of a C corporation (where corporate profits are taxed, and then taxed again as income to the owners/shareholders when the dividends are distributed), yet allows for an unlimited number of partners. There are also no restrictions on member nationality (as there are with an S corporation).

Conversely, the corporate aspect of the LLC lies in its ability to eliminate personal liability for the firm's debts and enjoy perpetual life. As with most small businesses, however, no matter what form of organization you elect to use, bankers are typically not risk takers, and may still require the major partners of a new business to personally guarantee any loans made to their concern. Finally, unlike a Sub S, an LLC can issue several different types of stock (thus allowing for unequal shares of company assets). This gives the company greater access to capital.

Forms of Ownership p 322

First established in Wyoming in 1977, the LLC form of organization took the country by storm. By mid-1996, all states were expected to have their own version of Limited Liability Company laws. Currently, the American Bar Association is reviewing a "Uniform Limited Liability Company Act." However, the legislation is still several years away. Since each state differs somewhat in the regulations used to govern an LLC, resolution of a taxation or liability claim could be difficult and costly if a dispute should arise between businesses in different states. Likewise, the tax and liability benefits associated with an LLC will vary from state to state. Again, it is imperative that you contact a qualified attorney if you are considering this form of organization.

COMPARING ORGANIZATIONAL STRUCTURES

Attribute	S Corp	C Corp	Partnership	Proprietorship	LLC
Liability protection	Yes	Yes	No	No	Yes
Member restrictions	Yes	No	No	Yes	No
Double taxation	No	Yes	No	No	No
Transfer of shares	Yes	Yes	No	No	No
High cost of start-up	Yes	Yes	No	No	Yes/No*
Easy access to capital	Yes	Yes	Yes/No	No	Yes

** Can be high, particularly in states that have only recently adopted LLC regulations.*

Source: Business Week, *July 18, 1994, and* Inc. *magazine*

PITFALLS

Lack of Adequate Analysis

The form of ownership you select is a critical decision. Take time to consider your alternatives carefully, to make sure that your decision will provide the best combination of flexibility, protection, and income at your business's current stage of development.

Lack of Professional Advice

The tax and liability consequences of your choice of ownership structure are potentially enormous. Many of the issues you have to evaluate to make your decision require the advice of a lawyer and an accountant. Although there are costs associated with their services, in many cases they will provide these services on a fixed-fee basis. Good preparation prior to meeting with your advisers can reduce your costs significantly, in both time and money.

Failure to Review Legal Structure

As your business grows, you should evaluate your form of ownership on a periodic basis. You may find that the business you started five years ago as a partnership, which made sense at the time, would now be better off as a limited liability company.

Some Advice —

"The limited liability company (LLC) and the limited liability partnership (LLP) are fast becoming entities of choice for service businesses. Each combines the key advantages of a corporation with those of a partnership. Members of LLCs, like shareholders in traditional corporations, enjoy limited personal liability but gain the greater flexibility of a partnership in areas such as management and income distribution."

Joel I. Cherwin, Senior Partner
Cherwin, Glickman & Theise, LLP
Boston, Mass.

MANAGEMENT AND PERSONNEL

OVERVIEW

How will you staff and manage your business? These are critical issues that require planning and creative thinking. Usually, in a start-up situation, you have limited resources available. Therefore you have to be as creative as possible in order to attract the qualified personnel you need, at the salaries you can afford to pay.

From a management viewpoint, how you organize your business will also be important to your business success and the job satisfaction of your employees. Carefully think through your own contribution to the business, in the short run and longer term, as well as the role that you may want external consultants and others to play.

The Management and Personnel section of your business plan must make those evaluating your plan confident that you have the ability to hire and manage the team needed to make your business a success. The section can be short and concise. The reader should already be well aware of what your business is trying to accomplish. The purpose here is to show how you expect to garner the human resources to do it. You must demonstrate that you will build a team, leveraging all of the appropriate resources available to you, and that you have thought out your staffing needs in detail. Additional information, such as complete resumés of your managers, should be presented in your appendices.

Human Resources p 322

THE BASICS

Although initially you may be relying on some people for pro bono assistance or on others, including yourself, for "sweat equity," you should fully evaluate the staffing needs of your business, as well as the management configuration you will use. The following areas relating to management and personnel should be covered in your plan.

Management

Short one-paragraph profiles (biographies or "bios") should be included for yourself, partners, and any others who will have management responsibility. The profiles should highlight experiences that are directly related to the work at hand. For example, if you are starting a restaurant, you would certainly focus on your work experience as a cook or manager of a fast-food franchise, and on your educational background as a graduate of a hospitality management program. If none of your full-time management team has direct experience, be sure that other individuals closely associated with the business, such as consultants or advisers, do. Include a full resumé for each of these individuals in the appendices.

Management Information p 287

Key Personnel

A short bio should also be included for any key members of your staff who are not in management positions. For example, in the landscaping business, you may have a designer with a significant amount of experience and a well-known reputation in the field. Include a profile of this key person in this section of your plan.

Professional Advisers

Your business should have established a relationship with an attorney, accountant, and insurance adviser as you developed your plan. These individuals are key members of your team; their bios should also be included in this section.

Staff

Although you may have some ideas about particular individuals whom you may want to hire to work in your business, this section should include descriptions of the jobs that need to be performed, salary and benefit levels, and any special requirements or qualifications. For example, if you were staffing a lifeguard position in your health club, you would need an individual who possesses the requisite lifesaving and first aid certificates, is willing to work specific hours at a certain salary and benefit level, and is customer-oriented. The descriptions in this section should resemble well-written want ads, and there should be one for each position.

Consultants

If you plan to use consultants, include their bios. Consultants bring expertise to the business that your management team (in many cases, a team of one) may not possess. Consultants' experience and credentials can make a difference to a potential banker or investor. For example, if you are starting a payroll management service, you might find a retired accountant with a great deal of experience who would be willing to advise you on the tax and/or operational aspects of your business. Any counselors, such as those associated with Small Business Development Centers, should also be mentioned in your plan.

Boards of Directors/Advisers

No matter how small your business, consider establishing a board of directors or advisers. This board can be instrumental in offering advice as you develop and grow your business. Except in the case of a corporation where the bylaws will govern, the structure of your board can be informal and flexible. The board is a low- or no-cost resource that can add significantly to your overall management capabilities, assuming you have selected individuals with substantial backgrounds and experience. Bios of these individuals should also be included in the plan.

Organizational Chart

If your business employs several people, or has a variety of service offerings, include an organizational chart. The chart should show how you plan to organize your human resources to reach your goals. It should indicate areas of responsibility of individuals within the organization and who reports to whom. For example, in a landscaping business, the chart would indicate who is responsible for equipment maintenance, how many work crews there are, whom they report to, who is responsible for new business development, and so on.

Forms p 322 Human Resources p 322

Staffing Plan

Briefly describe your future professional and staffing personnel needs, making sure that the description reflects the business growth projections that appear in other sections of your plan.

Salary and Benefits

Explain your philosophy regarding the work environment and company culture you intend to create, and how you plan to compensate and reward employees. Your long-term goal may be to provide a wide range of fringe benefits, including health insurance, retirement benefits, and incentive saving plans. In the short term, however, you may be able to offer only a life insurance plan or paid vacation time, and build from there as your business grows.

PITFALLS

Estimate of Personnel Needs

Overestimating your human-resources needs will dramatically affect the bottom line — you'll have higher working-capital requirements. On the other hand, underestimating personnel needs will inhibit your ability to provide your services efficiently. Map out your staffing requirements as carefully as possible, and consult your advisers to test your assumptions.

Compensation Package

Your compensation package must be adequate to attract and retain employees. Your employees' satisfaction should come second only to that of your customers. In the long run, your ability to offer a comprehensive and competitive benefit plan will help attract high-quality workers and reduce turnover.

Chain of Command

Employees, particularly in closely held or family-run businesses, need a clear understanding of whom they report to and what they are responsible for. Often employees find themselves answering to more than one boss, which can be very frustrating and lead to confusion and inefficiency.

Management

You want an adequate degree of supervision in your business, but not too much. Your employees should have a clear sense of their superior's duties and responsibilities. They should not feel that there are too many people watching the work being done and not enough doing it.

Some Advice —

"The real key to running a successful business is to hire good people. You cannot make business decisions about competing in today's world without considering the people who have to 'buy' the concept and deliver results."

Steve Burkhart, Chairman of the Board
Advanced Micro-Electronics
(on-site repair service)
Vincennes, Ind.

AN EXAMPLE

Susan's Child Care Center

PERSONNEL

The center will have nine employees; 3 Head Teachers, 3 Assistant Head Teachers, and 3 Assistant Caregivers. The center will also have three work-study positions available.

The Head Teachers will hold a bachelor's degree in early childhood education and have at least two years' previous experience in a head teacher role. The Head Teacher should be experienced in preparing age-related curricula as well as supervising other staff members. He/She will be an enthusiastic teacher excited about the opportunity to work with children. This person will be able to work within a new, undeveloped position. The Head Teacher will be able to inject enthusiasm into his/her staff as well as provide a leadership role for others.

The Assistant Head Teachers will hold an associate's degree in Early Childhood Education and will bring additional experience in the child-care field. This person will be creative as well as enthusiastic about the learning and discoveries that children will achieve in the day-care environ- s person will be excited about developing this role to its fullest capacity.

e Assistant Caregiver will maintain a Maine teaching certificate....

Source: Susan B. Murray

FINANCIAL INFORMATION

OVERVIEW

The Financial Information section of your business plan creates a picture of how you expect your business to perform in quantitative terms, based on market assessments that you make as you develop the plan. This picture will be drawn using financial statements, which are simply standard formats used to present financial information. Most of your statements will be developed on a pro forma basis, which means that you are projecting data, such as future revenues and expenses, using assumptions you have made and can defend.

Complete, accurate, and well-documented financial information is crucial for a number of reasons. For example, if you are using the plan to apply for commercial financing, loan officers usually focus their attention on the numbers. That is, after reading the Executive Summary and the Market overview, they proceed directly to your financial information. This is understandable because loan officers are experts at — and most comfortable with — dealing with financial information, as opposed to marketing data or promotional strategy. Once they have a basic understanding of the type of business you plan to enter, they review your financial information and develop a preliminary assessment as to whether they would be willing to finance you. If the answer is yes, they go back and read through your entire business plan in detail. Accurate financial information is also very important because it establishes the basic framework you will use to monitor and control your business and report information to the government (e.g., for tax purposes), bankers, investors, and other stakeholders.

Although it is wise not to become too dependent on electronic spreadsheets, when used properly they can make your job a lot easier. As you begin to gather and record information for your financial statements, you will want to be able to update them and sometimes change your assumptions. Spreadsheet software enables you to do this with little effort and the highest degree of mathematical accuracy. In addition, a manual "one-write" -type checking system, an electronic checkbook program, or a computerized accounting package are inexpensive and efficient ways to organize your records, both for generating financial statements and for tax purposes.

Finally, be sure to document all of the assumptions you use as a basis for your projections in this section of your plan. Don't simply present statements without explanation. There should be a bright line that links the data presented in the Market, Market Share, and Competitive Analysis sections of your plan to the projections you make in the Financial Information section. When in doubt as to whether you have made it clear enough, restate your assumptions as notes to your cash flow or income statements and/or refer the reader to the appropriate section(s) of your plan for more detail. Of all possible flaws in the presentation of a business plan, lack of clear connection between assumptions and financial projections ranks among the most serious, yet it's one that can be easily fixed.

Note —

If you intend to use your business plan to secure financing, most banks will require:

- ❑ **Three balance sheets (start date, end of Year 1, and end of Year 2)**
- ❑ **One cash flow statement (monthly for the first year)**
- ❑ **Two income statements (annually for Year 1 and Year 2).**

Accounting p 321

THE BASICS

The financial and other related statements described in this chapter should be included in your business plan. We give examples for Hook, Line & Sinker, an imaginary fishing-expedition proprietorship in the mountains of Montana. The business is owned by an experienced fishing guide and subcontracts two additional guides on an "as-needed" basis. The company offers two-, three- and five-day fishing excursions up the Madison, Jefferson, and Gallatin Rivers during the 26-week season from May 1 to October 31. Its services include food, tent, equipment, all licenses and fees, and transportation.

From market research, Hook, Line & Sinker anticipates an average volume of 10 customers per week during the peak season. In the off season (November 1 through April 30) the owner expects to generate sales from guided hunting and ice-fishing trips. The company expects to begin operations on May 1, 1997.

Hook, Line & Sinker is a start-up business, so all its statements will be developed on a *pro-forma* basis, that is, in advance. If you are already in business, you will be generating the same types of statements, but most of the information/data will come from your actual business records. Even if you are working with a consultant while developing your business plan, it is very important for you to understand how your own projections are made and agree with them. They will form the basis of your financing needs and your salary level, which may be with you long after your friendly adviser leaves to sow other seeds.

The best way to complete this section is to use the *Inc.Sheets* in Section IV for each of the following statements. Fill in the information as you locate or develop it. Many of the statements are interdependent, so you will probably be working on them concurrently.

Capital Equipment List

This list should include a description and cost for each item of machinery and equipment you must purchase to start your business. The list should be detailed; however, you can combine similar articles of low unit-value, such as glassware and place settings in a restaurant business. High-ticket items, such as computers or vehicles, should be footnoted to provide a quote from your supplier. The capital equipment list will be used to help determine the amount of fixed-asset financing you will require.

Hook, Line & Sinker

CAPITAL EQUIPMENT LIST APRIL 1997

ITEM	DESCRIPTION	QTY.	UNIT COST	COST
Equipment				
	Telephone system	2.	$150	300
	Photocopier	1	850	850
	4-man dome tent	3	180	540
	St. Croix fly-fishing outfit	10	135	1350
	Miscellaneous equipment	1	500	500
Computer[1]				
	486DX66 w/CD ROM/fax modem	1	1,500	1,500
	Color monitor	1	350	350
	Color ink-jet printer	1	400	400
Software				
	Windows 95	1	95	95
	Lotus SmartSuite	1	370	370
Furniture				
	Office desk	2	350	700
	Chair	2	175	350
	File cabinet	1	200	200
Vehicles[2]				
	Van [2a]	1	8,250	8,250
	Inflatable boat w/35-hp motor [2b]	2	5,500	11,000
	Tomahawk 4-man canoe [2b]	1	400	400
TOTAL				**$27,155**

Cost estimates from:

1. CompuWorld, 155 Edison Drive, Helena, MT
2(a). Caswell RV & Used Truck Center, Route 100, Helena, MT
2(b). Roberts Marina, 673 Riverside Drive, Helena, MT

Capital Equipment List p 288

Start-up Costs

This statement estimates the amount of money you will need to launch and maintain your business until sales receipts can cover operating expenses and debt service. You need to project all monthly expenses such as utilities and salaries; prepaid expenses such as insurance; and one-time expenses like your Grand Opening event. Once these have been calculated, you should "build in a cushion" to provide for some margin of error if sales do not materialize as quickly as you expect. Often this margin will be an amount equal to two or three times your monthly operating expenses, employees' salaries, and your salary (draw). This statement will also be used to estimate working-capital needs.

Start-up Cost Estimate p 289

Almanac p 88

Hook, Line & Sinker

START-UP COST ESTIMATE APRIL 1997

PRE-START-UP

ITEM	Estimate
Capital Equipment	$27,155
Deposits with Public Utilities	200
Legal & Other Professional Services	150
Licenses & Permits	75
Advertising and Promotion	500
Prepaid Insurance	200
Other Expenses	100
SUBTOTAL	**$28,380**

OTHER START-UP COSTS

ITEM	Est. cost per month	# Months coverage	Total estimated cost
Salary of Owner	$1,500	2	$3,000
Other Salaries/Wages/Fees	1,000	2	2,000
Rent	300	3	900
Advertising	300	2	600
Delivery Expense	n/a	n/a	n/a
Supplies	40	3	120
Telephone	50	3	150
Other Utilities	100	3	300
Insurance	600	3	1800
Taxes, Social Security	n/a	n/a	n/a
Interest	200	3	600
Maintenance	50	2	100
Legal and Other Professional Assistance	175	2	350
Miscellaneous	75	2	150
TOTAL FROM OTHER START-UP			10,070
TOTAL FROM PRE-START-UP			28,380
TOTAL ESTIMATED START-UP			**$38,450**

Sources and Uses of Cash Statement

This statement indicates how you plan to secure funds to start your business and how you intend to spend them. Both your sources and uses should be categorized. For example, if you plan to borrow money to purchase a building, a truck, and equipment, these loans should be listed as separate items because the interest rates and repayment terms will be different for each. For the purposes of this analysis, 25% owner equity/investment is assumed. Your sources of cash must always equal your uses. If they don't, you probably haven't calculated your equity properly.

Sources & Uses of Cash p 290

Hook, Line & Sinker

SOURCES AND USES OF CASH – MAY 1997

SOURCES	
Owner's investment	$9,612
Working-capital loan	8,471
Capital-equipment loan	3,593
Computer-equipment loan	2,036
Van loan	6,188
Boat loan	8,550
	$38,450

USES	
Working capital	$11,295
Purchase capital equipment	4,790
Purchase computer equipment	2,715
Purchase van	8,250
Purchase boats	11,400
	$38,450

*Note: The bank will probably combine the equipment loans and the boat and van loans.

Banking p 321

Balance Sheet

The balance sheet answers the question, "What is the financial condition of your company on a particular date?" It lists what your company owns (its assets) and what your business owes (its debts). The balance sheet also reflects net worth, or total owner's equity, which is the amount left over after the total debts are subtracted from the total assets.

The formula for the balance sheet is: **Assets = Liabilities + Equity**

Assets are what your business owns (cash, supplies, accounts receivable, equipment, land, buildings). These are the investments your business has made to earn a profit. *Liabilities* are debts your business owes (accounts payable, loans, mortgages, installment debt, and so on). *Owner's equity* represents the claims against business assets by the owners of that business. This amount includes the owners' investments plus any profits that have been retained by the business (in the case of a corporation these are called "retained earnings"). If your business is incorporated, the *owner's equity* is referred to as *"stockholders' equity."*

Balance Sheet p 291

RMA p 110

Hook, Line & Sinker

BALANCE SHEET JUNE 1, 1997

ASSETS		LIABILITIES	
CURRENT ASSETS		**CURRENT LIABILITIES**	
Cash	$11,295	Notes Payable	$5767
Accounts Receivable	0	Accounts Payable	0
Supplies	0	Accrued Expenses	0
Prepaid Expenses	0		
Other Current Assets	0	TOTAL CURRENT LIABILITIES	$5,767
		LONG-TERM LIABILITIES	
TOTAL CURRENT ASSETS	$11,295	Installment Debt Payable	23,070
PROPERTY, PLANT & EQUIPMENT		TOTAL LONG-TERM LIABILITIES	$23,070
Land	0	TOTAL LIABILITIES	$28,837
Buildings	0		
Equipment	7,505	OWNERS EQUITY	
Vehicles and Boats	19,650	Paid-In Capital	9,613
		Retained Earnings	0
TOTAL NET FIXED ASSETS	$27,155		
		TOTAL OWNER'S EQUITY	$9,613
TOTAL ASSETS	**$38,450**	**TOTAL LIABILITIES & OWNER'S EQUITY**	**$38,450**

If you are in a start-up phase, your balance sheet will be constructed on a *pro forma* basis, meaning that you have to project what your assets and liabilities will look like on the day you start your business. These figures can be derived from your Sources and Uses of Cash statement. For example, if you are transferring ownership of a car to the business, it should be listed as an asset on your company's balance sheet. If your business is already in operation, gather the actual amounts for each category as of the day you plan to generate the statement.

Income Statement

The income statement, also known as the profit and loss statement or simply the P&L, is the record of your business's financial activities over a period of time. The income statement, usually prepared on an annual basis, documents your revenue and expenses and establishes whether a gain or loss has occurred during that period.

As with the balance sheet, a start-up business must project or estimate the numbers to be used on the pro forma income statement. All these figures, with the exception of depreciation, can be obtained from your cash flow projections, which will be covered in the next section of this chapter.

The amount of depreciation (i.e., the part of an asset's the dollar value written off as an expense over its useful life) to include on the income statement will be determined by the number of depreciable assets your business owns and the method you use to depreciate them. The IRS has a depreciation schedule for all property purchased for business use. Most businesses use straight line depreciation, which is simply the total cost of the item divided by the number of years in its useful life. For example, an automobile with a five-year life span and a $10,000 initial price tag will be depreciated by 20% (or $2,000) each year, starting in Year 1, until its value equals zero in Year 5. It is important to remember that depreciation is calculated for tax purposes, and while a vehicle may last more than five years, it is depreciated according to an average lifespan for all vehicles.

Almanac
p 88

Property is generally depreciated over a three-year, five-year, or seven-year period (with greater periods applying to longer-term assets such as real estate). Typically, computer equipment falls in the three-year category, vehicles are a five-year asset, and office furniture is considered a seven-year item. Real estate is generally depreciated over 27.5 to 31.5 years. For specific depreciation guidelines, refer to *How to Depreciate Property* (IRS Publication #946).

In addition, most small businesses are allowed under IRS regulations to expense (write off) $17,500 worth of depreciable assets (not including real estate) purchased in the current tax year. For more information on depreciation, consult IRS publication #946, or ask your accountant.

Accounting
p 321

The formula used for *Income* is: **Revenues - Operating Expenses = Income**

Revenues are the total sales revenue less any sales returns, discounts, or allowances. *Operating expenses* include items such as rent, advertising, salaries, insurance, and other day-to-day operating costs. In the case of restaurants, food and beverage inventory can also be considered as Cost of Goods Sold (See Appendix D, page 316 for a typical income statement from a restaurant business). In the case of a C corporation, income taxes are an additional cost which are listed separately in the Income Statement.

Basic Structure of the Income Statement

It may be helpful to think of the Income Statement as a series of simple calculations:

	Revenues
–	**Operating expenses**
=	**Earnings before interest and taxes**
–	**Interest**
=	**Income Before Taxes**

Income Statement p 292

Hook, Line & Sinker

INCOME STATEMENT FOR 1997

NET SALES (Revenues)		$ 88,000
OPERATING EXPENSES		
Salaries (Owner)	$19,500	
Fees (Subcontractors)	12,750	
Rent	2,400	
Telephone & Utilities	835	
Insurance	800	
Advertising	1,300	
Professional Fees	1,250	
Office Administration	755	
Depreciation	17,500	
Travel & Entertainment	350	
Food Supplies	4,300	
Miscellaneous	475	
Non-Income Taxes	895	
TOTAL OPERATING EXPENSES		$63,110
OTHER REVENUE (EXPENSES)		
Interest Expense		(934)
INCOME BEFORE TAXES		**$23,956**

Cash Flow Statement

The cash flow statement is the most important financial management tool you have. It documents all cash transactions (income and expenses) that occur from month to month. It is like your personal checkbook, where you post your deposits and then draw checks against them. As with your checkbook, if you spend more than you take in, your check bounces. The reason this statement is so useful is that it forces you not only to analyze your sources of income and expenses but to do it on a cash basis. That is, you may sell a service such as office cleaning, but because your customer wants to be billed you may not receive the payment (cash) for 30 to 45 days, or maybe longer. During this same period, you will probably have to pay your workers on a weekly basis. Where does the money come from? Cash received from customers who have been billed for services in previous months? A working capital loan from the bank? Or money you may have to invest in the business?

Cash Flow
p 293

What if your business has seasonal peaks and valleys? Your cash flow statement will reflect them and indicate the amount of cash reserve you must retain from the peak periods to enable you to survive the slow times. In other words, it enables you to project your cash needs and prepare in advance for times when you might need to borrow money, change your billing terms, or pay your suppliers.

Cash flow statements are developed on a 12-month basis, but should be adjusted each month to reflect the actual cash in and cash out during that period. The difference between your cash flow projection and what actually happened is called a variance. As you calculate these variances over time, you will notice trends, which will enable you to adjust your cash flows more accurately into the future.

Layout of the Cash Flow Statement

SOURCES OF CASH	USES OF CASH
Cash flow from operations	Cash drain from operations
+ Cash flow from borrowing	+ Cash drain from debt reduction
= Total cash available in the current period	= Total cash used in the current period

The Difference between **Total Sources** and **Total Uses** is the **Net Cash Flow** in the current period.

Monthly Cash Flow Projections Statement

Hook, Line & Sinker

MONTHLY CASH FLOW PROJECTION

	Pre-Start-Up		Month 1		Month 2		Month 3		Month 4	
YEAR MONTH										
	Estimate	Actual	Estimate	Actual	Estimate	Actual	Estimate	Actual	Estimate	Actual
1. Cash on Hand (beginning of month)	$9,613		$10,070		$13,794		$18,898			
2. Cash Receipts (a) Cash Sales	0		9,500		11,800		12,500			
(b) Collections from credit accounts	0		0		800		900			
(c) Loan or other cash (specify)	28,837		0		0		0			
3. Total Cash Receipts (2a+2b+2c)	$28,837		$9,500		$12,600		$13,400			
4. Total Cash Available (Before Cash Out) (1 + 3)	$38,450		$19,570		$26,394		$32,298			
5. Cash Paid Out (a) Purchases (merchandise)	0		750		750		750			
(b) Gross Wages	0		0		0		0			
(c) Payroll Expenses	0		0		0		0			
(d) Outside Services	0		2,000		2,750		3,500			
(e) Supplies (office/operating)	0		40		40		20			
(f) Repairs and Maintenance	0		50		50		50			
(g) Advertising	500		350		350		150			
(h) Car, Delivery, & Travel	0		0		0		0			
(i) Accounting & Legal	150		125		100		75			
(j) Rent	300		300		300		300			

(Continued)

(Continued)

	Pre-Start-Up		Month 1		Month 2		Month 3		Month 4	
YEAR **MONTH**										
	Estimate	Actual	Estimate	Actual	Estimate	Actual	Estimate	Actual	Estimate	Actual
5. Cash Paid Out ***(cont.)***										
(k) Telephone	0		75		95		95			
(l) Utilities	0		75		75		75			
(m) Insurance	0		67		67		67			
(n) Taxes (real estate, other)	0		0		0		0			
(o) Interest	0		78		78		78			
(p) Other expenses (specify) food for customers	0		900		1,400		1,500			
(q) Miscellaneous	0		40		40		40			
(r) Subtotal (5a thru 5q)	950		3,200		3,945		4,450			
(s) Loan Principal payment	0		976		976		976			
(t) Capital Purchases	27,155		0		0		0			
(u) Other Start-up Costs	275		100		75		40			
(v) Reserve and/or Escrow	0		0		0		0			
(w) Owner's Withdrawal	0		1,500		2,500		2,500			
6. Total Cash Paid Out (Total 5r through 5w)	$28,380		$5,776		$7,496		$7,966			
7. Cash Position (end of month) (line 4 minus line 6)	$10,070		$13,794		$18,898		$24,332			

PITFALLS

Failure to Update Records

It is critical to keep your financial records as up-to-date as possible. For example, as you compare your projected cash sales to actual ones on your cash flow analysis, it doesn't do any good if you don't update the rest of your cash flow based on this information. *Therefore, you must update your income and cash flow statements no less than once a month, and sales receipts should be calculated every day.*

Failure to Document Assumptions

Every financial assumption, from your projected sales levels to your utility bills, needs to be documented. Most expense documentation can be provided as footnotes to your cash flow statement. This will indicate to anyone evaluating your plan that you haven't just pulled numbers from thin air. In the case of your sales projections, detail your methodology in the Market Share or Pricing sections of the plan, and reference the location in the footnote.

Too Much Optimism

Keep your projections and estimates conservative. It is always better to err on the conservative side and possibly borrow a little more money initially, than to run out of working capital because you have failed to achieve unrealistic sales forecasts. If this situation does occur, it will be difficult to borrow additional funds from the bank.

Some Advice —

"Write down supporting data that justifies your projections for revenues and expenses. I worked out 30-, 60-, and 90-day goals for projected revenues and cash flow—with realistic expectations for accounts receivable turnaround. Putting everything down in black and white forces you to ensure that your sales goals are met. A written plan keeps you from sitting back and saying, 'Wow, I'm in business!' "

Shane Jones, CEO
Ace Personnel, Inc.
Overland Park, Kans.

INSURANCE

OVERVIEW

Business insurance protects your business against losses from fire, employee injury, lawsuits, automobile accidents, or other occurrences beyond your control. Although all of these events will probably not happen to you, you can't afford to take the risks.

Insurance has also taken on new dimensions in response to record numbers of lawsuits over issues of liability and alleged malpractice. The cases range from a pet groomer being sued because the owner didn't like his pet's "do" to a multimillion-dollar award to a McDonald's customer because the coffee was too hot! Or take the example of a New Hampshire man who, while on assignment out of town, was having a few drinks with his supervisor. A fight broke out, and the supervisor hit the man with a two-by-four. A court decided the man was entitled to workers' compensation for his injuries.

All businesses need adequate insurance coverage. You must identify the potential risks in your business, then evaluate your insurance options in the context of those risks and how much you can afford to pay. Insurance against some risks, such as workers' compensation, is mandatory. Other risks, such as shoplifting, are uninsurable, and still others, such as fidelity bonding, may be desirable.

Most insurance brokers can be helpful in assessing your needs and alternatives. It is important, however, that you evaluate your needs as thoroughly as possible prior to consulting a broker, so that you will be an educated buyer. This can save you considerable time and money.

It is also important to review your insurance needs on a regular basis. An increase in the value of your assets and the possibility of finding lower premiums in a competitive insurance market are two good reasons to do this annually. Many small-business trade and professional associations offer their members discounted group insurance programs. After you have discussed your needs with an insurance professional, contact a few of these organizations to see what alternative insurance programs they provide.

Note —

Few business plans have a separate section on insurance. Unless your business is unusual and involves high risk, it is probably best to include this information as an appendix, clearly labeled in your Table of Contents.

Insurance p 323

Insurance p 323

Insurance Needs List p 303
Insurance Quotes Grid p 304

Small Business Profiles p 114

THE BASICS

Insurance needs can be broken down into three categories: 1) mandatory, 2) essential, and 3) desirable.

Mandatory Insurance

Workers' compensation insurance. If you plan to hire employees on either a full-time or part-time basis, workers' compensation insurance must be secured before your workers start their jobs. Rates for workers' comp are based on the degree of risk associated with the particular job. A carpenter will have a relatively high rate, while a bookkeeper will have a much lower one. Workers' comp can add significantly to your cost of doing business. The following practices can help reduce costs and potential liability:

- ❑ Review your job classifications to make sure that each one is included in the least costly category.
- ❑ As your business grows, contact your insurance broker when new employees are hired. Failure to do so will require back premium payments when an insurance company audit is performed.
- ❑ If you use subcontractors, obtain a certificate of insurance from them. If they are not insured, you may end up paying the insurance premium on their payrolls.
- ❑ Separate regular pay from overtime pay. Premiums are based on regular pay; overtime pay is excluded.
- ❑ Keep your work environment as safe as possible and maintain records of any claims made by your employees. Your rates will be adjusted on the basis of an "experience modification factor" which is computed each year, based on your loss history over the three preceding years.

Vehicle insurance. You may be legally liable when employees or subcontractors use your vehicle or their own on your behalf. If you are using vehicles to deliver merchandise, make sure that they are covered under your policy. A rider may have to be added to the policy to cover merchandise and personal property. It is imperative to carry adequate coverage for both liability and property damage. Although insurance can be expensive, there are several ways to reduce premiums, such as increasing your deductibles and buying fleet coverage if you use several vehicles.

Essential Insurance

Fire Insurance. Fire insurance is essential, unless you are renting or leasing a property that has coverage. In that case, you should check the policy carefully to make sure that the coverage is adequate. If there is a coinsurance clause in your policy, which may reduce the premium, be sure that you understand the implications. For example, if you insure your property for 75% of its value, in the event of a fire you will be responsible for covering 25% of the cost to rebuild.

You may also want to insure against perils such as vandalism, explosion, wind, and smoke. The need for, and costs of, such insurance should be discussed with your broker.

Liability insurance. Liability insurance protects your business from potential losses caused by accidents suffered by others when using your services or property. This liability usually extends to both your employees and subcontractors. In recent years the number of civil lawsuits has been staggering. According to the U.S. Administrative Office of the Courts, in 1993 there were nearly 20 million civil cases filed in state and federal courts, and that number could range as high as 30 million today, with median awards ranging from $40,000 to $625,000. Therefore, it is very important to assess your potential liability and discuss it in detail with your insurance broker before selecting coverage.

Although premiums have increased dramatically for most businesses, usually you can secure an *umbrella policy*, which provides inclusive coverage for vehicles, liability claims, and personal injury claims, for a single premium. Separate policies must be obtained for workers' compensation, fire, or theft. Even for a small enterprise with low risk factors, liability insurance of $1 million would not be considered high in most cases.

Key-person insurance. If you are in a business that depends on an individual(s) whose skills would be difficult to replace in the short to intermediate term, you should carry life and disability insurance on that person. This policy would be owned by, and payable to, the company and would provide funds needed to operate the business in the short term until the individual is replaced. Key-person coverage is also important as your company grows, to make sure that it has the cash to settle a deceased partner's estate (or a stockholder's estate in a closely held corporation).

Title insurance. If you own real estate, title insurance will protect you against potential claims questioning the validity of your title. Such coverage is generally inexpensive.

Desirable Insurance

Group health insurance. Although it's the subject of great national debate, at this point no employer is required to carry health insurance. However, if you do and you have 20 or more part-time or full-time employees, there are a number of requirements that your plan must satisfy, including provisions for continuing coverage if your employee leaves. Continued coverage is required under the Federal COBRA Act which states that an employee who was covered under a group policy is entitled to health insurance for a period of 18 months after he or she leaves the company (provided such employees apply for the coverage within 60 days of termination). The insurance is normally provided at a higher rate to the former employee, however, and the company is under no obligation to pay any premiums on the employee's behalf. The company is required to maintain the former employee's records throughout the duration of the coverage. Your ability to provide health insurance benefits can offer significant recruiting advantages and help reduce employee turnover. Group policies tend to be significantly less expensive than individual contracts. This possibility should be reviewed in detail with your insurance agent.

Group life insurance. If you offer all employees group life insurance and cover the premiums, up to $5,000 is deductible as a business expense and the value of the insurance is not taxable as income for the employees. Check with your insurance agent to determine the costs and the minimum number of employees required to qualify for the group rate.

Disability insurance. You can purchase low-premium insurance to cover an employee's income for short periods of disability due to a nonwork-related injury.

Business interruption insurance. This insurance provides income when your business is unable to operate owing to certain circumstances, such as a fire. The premiums for this type of insurance tend to be quite high. Sometimes, because of inability to pay bills and payroll, by the time payment is made on a claim an owner may have been forced out of operation.

Fidelity bonding. A fidelity bond protects your business against financial losses caused by a dishonest employee. The fact that employees are bonded can be used as a marketing tool. For example, a house-cleaning service with bonded employees can eliminate potential customer concerns about theft. Obtaining fidelity bond insurance can be difficult for start-up businesses, however, as the underwriter typically looks at a firm's reputation, years in business, and employee-screening methods to determine eligibility.

PITFALLS

Underestimating Insurance Needs

Be sure that you have double-checked your insurance plans and consulted with at least one professional for advice. One adverse liability judgment can easily wipe out your business and personal assets.

The Corporate Veil

Don't get the mistaken impression that just because you are incorporated, you can afford to carry less liability insurance. In some situations, you may find that you can be held personally responsible for claims against your company.

The Fringe Benefit Effect

Insurance can be as powerful a motivator as salary increases, and sometimes more so. Insurance helps satisfy your employees' safety needs and can have a substantial effect on job performance and turnover.

Some Advice —

"We determined what coverage we needed by weighing projected costs and revenue against family obligations and our respective debt. Initially, we left our insurance strategy rather vague in the business plan, but now we make it specific every year to try to pinpoint what percentage of our expenses will be insurance costs. And every year or so, we get two or three quotes on the coverage we need to make sure we're getting the best price."

Nathan Rykse, President
Rykse's
(restaurant & catering)
Kalamazoo, Mich.

Section II

Resource Directory

The following section contains a variety of resources that you will find helpful in researching and writing your business plan. Although the listings in this section do not include all those available in the marketplace, for most plans they will be more than sufficient, and for others, a good start. Resources are grouped into three categories.

Reference materials are listed first. Most are readily available at your local public, college, or university library. Some are also available online, so you may be able to access them from your home computer. These resources are marked with a phone icon and include their Internet or World Wide Web address. References are organized to correspond to the sections of your business plan. Each one gives a specific example of how the particular reference will help you find the information you need.

General resources, or advisers, available to help you find information and/or develop your business plan make up the second category. It is always a good idea to see what type of assistance is available as you start developing your plan. A few phone calls can often identify significant help that is available at low or no cost.

Finally, there is a listing of **financial resources and programs** that are targeted toward small business. Once you have started your plan and have an understanding of what your financing requirements will be, you should review this section. Start by contacting local bankers to apprise them of your situation and to seek their counsel. This will enable them to provide input regarding what they need to see in your plan to consider you a good candidate for financing. It often helps to bring the banker in early on, to make him or her a part of your team.

REFERENCES

Here are some of the most useful materials available to assist you in developing your plan.The names and addresses of the publishers are included so that you may contact them if you are unable to find the resource locally. As indicated, some of these resources are available online, and where applicable, their Internet addresses are listed.

You will find Resource Directory icons throughout Section I to guide you to the appropriate material. As you consult these resources, you are likely to find many additional uses for them beyond creating a business plan.

Index Guide to Resources

Type of Information	Almanac of Business & Industrial Ratios	Business Periodicals Index	Business-to-Business Directory	Buying Power Index	Census of the Service Industries	County Business Patterns	Encyclopedia of Associations	Equifax National Decision Systems	Financial Studies of the Small Business	Internet
MARKET										
Customers		X	X							X
Suppliers		X		X		X				X
Marketing		X								X
FINANCIAL										
Industry Norms										X
Ratios	X								X	
Salaries/Payroll					X	X				
INDUSTRY										
Employment		X								X
Forecasts		X					X			X
Trade Associations		X					X			X
Trade Shows		X					X			X
COUNSELING										
FINANCING										

Index Guide to Resources

Type of Information	Lifestyle Market Analyst	New York Times Index	Reader's Guide to Periodical Literature	RMA Annual Statement Studies	Simmons Media and Market Report	SBA	SBDC's	SBDC Research Network	Small Business Profiles
MARKET							X	X	
Customers	X	X	X		X	X	X	X	
Suppliers							X	X	
Marketing			X		X	X			X
FINANCIAL							X	X	
Industry Norms				X		X	X	X	
Ratios				X			X	X	
Salaries/Payroll									
INDUSTRY							X	X	
Employment		X	X			X	X	X	
Forecasts		X	X				X	X	X
Trade Associations	X		X			X	X	X	
Trade Shows			X			X	X	X	
COUNSELING						X	X		
FINANCING						X			

Type of Information	Small Business Sourcebook	The Sourcebook of Zip Code Demographics	State Economic Development Agencies	Thomas Register	Trade Associations	The 1996 Trade-Shows and Exhibits Schedule	Ulrich's International Periodicals Directory	Wall Street Journal
MARKET								
Customers		X	X		X			X
Suppliers	X		X	X		X		X
Marketing			X		X	X		X
FINANCIAL								
Industry Norms								
Ratios								
Salaries/Payroll								
INDUSTRY								
Employment			X					X
Forecasts					X			X
Trade Associations	X		X			X	X	X
Trade Shows			X			X	X	X
COUNSELING								
FINANCING			X					

Almanac of Business and Industrial Financial Ratios

Publisher:
Prentice Hall Inc.
200 Old Tappan Rd.
Old Tappan, NJ 07675
800-922-0579
http://www.prenhall.com

Type of information available:
Selected Operating and Income Statement figures and financial ratios for various industries.

How to use it:
Find comparable Income Statement figures and financial ratios for your industry.

Situation:

Jim and Patty are developing a business plan for their accounting service, and want to compare their Balance Sheet projections to those in comparable industries. They also want to know roughly how much they should spend on advertising and other expenses based on their projected revenues.

What Jim and Patty can find:

Under the heading "Personal Services," they will find comparable Balance Sheet and expense figures for businesses the same size as theirs (note: personal services all fall under one heading).

How Jim and Patty will use:

They will determine whether their Balance Sheet and Income Statement projections are in line with those for service industries, therefore increasing their likelihood of creating a realistic business plan.

Note —
Excerpt: Next page
Availability: Bookstores, major libraries
Cost to purchase: $89.95

Table I

Corporations with and without Net Income

SERVICES
7200

PERSONAL SERVICES

MONEY AMOUNTS AND SIZE OF ASSETS IN THOUSANDS OF DOLLARS

Item Description for Accounting Period 7/91 Through 6/92		Total	Zero Assets	Under 100	100 to 250	251 to 500	501 to 1,000	1,001 to 5,000	5,001 to 10,000	10,001 to 25,000	25,001 to 50,000	50,001 to 100,000	100,001 to 250,000	250,001 and over
Number of Enterprises	1	78887	4175	53372	11227	5139	3063	1693	104	68	14	12	13	7
Revenues ($ in Thousands)														
Net Sales	2	33398212	337955	7721484	3848120	3175996	2841056	4444590	1417309	1196167	294771	905846	2719952	4694966
Portfolio Income	3	601431	9032	27303	22519	13559	45744	62545	30443	13651	13929	12202	95979	254525
Other Revenues	4	812401	1172	26856	23254	47318	51794	115708	52052	29089	61190	28884	100171	274913
Total Revenues	5	34812044	348159	7775643	3693893	3236873	2938594	4622843	1499804	1238907	369890	946932	2916102	5224404
Average Total Revenues	6	441	83	146	329	630	959	2731	14421	18219	26421	78911	224316	746343
Operating Costs/Operating Income (%)														
Cost of Operations	7	38.1	35.7	35.9	30.2	29.6	35.4	45.7	41.9	50.3	42.5	29.7	30.3	49.5
Rent	8	6.1	16.3	8.9	8.5	6.7	5.2	3.5	4.4	4.1	3.7	11.2	5.2	2.4
Taxes Paid	9	4.4	4.5	4.5	4.6	4.5	4.9	4.3	5.3	4.0	3.9	2.8	4.5	4.2
Interest Paid	10	2.5	0.7	1.0	2.3	2.6	2.0	3.0	0.7	2.0	3.8	3.5	3.6	4.9
Depreciation, Depletion, Amortization	11	4.3	1.6	2.6	5.4	5.1	3.9	3.6	2.1	6.1	4.6	5.0	4.9	6.4
Pensions and Other Benefits	12	1.5	0.3	0.5	0.8	1.5	2.4	2.0	3.1	3.4	3.3	3.1	2.2	0.9
Other	13	38.1	38.8	37.2	39.3	44.0	36.8	33.5	40.6	28.4	53.0	41.3	48.0	34.1
Officers Compensation	14	6.2	4.4	10.0	9.1	7.3	8.8	6.7	2.9	3.0	2.4	1.3	1.3	0.8
Operating Margin	15	•	•	•	•	•	0.6	•	•	•	•	2.2	0.2	•
Oper. Margin Before Officers Compensation	16	5.1	2.2	9.4	8.9	6.1	9.4	4.4	2.0	1.8	•	3.5	1.5	•
Selected Average Balance Sheet ($ in Thousands)														
Net Receivables	17	33	•	1	15	47	101	308	1539	2327	7025	10883	10230	88626
Inventories	18	16	•	1	7	17	34	84	438	950	1688	7829	9690	62100
Net Property, Plant and Equipment	19	97	•	14	82	167	271	713	2263	5210	7938	21211	55762	202690
Total Assets	20	265	•	28	160	344	722	1683	7239	13685	38510	73532	158552	798695

Almanac of Business and Industrial Financial Ratios, 1995 ed., pp. 315 – 316; by Leo Troy.
Used by permission of Prentice Hall/Career & Personal Development

Business Periodicals Index

Publisher:
H.W. Wilson Co.
950 University Ave.
Bronx, NY 10452
718-588-8400

Type of information available:
Index of articles appearing in general business and trade periodicals, organized alphabetically by subject.

How to use it:
Obtain information including general industry trends, news, competitive information, and advances in technology.

Situation:
Evan wants to open a tax-preparation and bookkeeping service. He needs to find articles on proposed changes in tax laws, information on electronic filing, and recent court rulings.

What Evan can find:
Articles on topics ranging from tax auditing and tax consultants to tax return preparation (including electronic filing). Many valuable links to other tax topics can also be found under the heading of "Taxes."

How Evan will use:
This information is crucial to the service he offers to customers. The articles may also lead him to other sources of information.

Note —
Excerpt: Next page
Availability: Most libraries
Cost to purchase: $255 to $2,990

Business Periodicals Index

Excerpts from:
January 1995
Vol. 37, No. 5
pp. 787 – 789
TAX

Business-to-Business Directory

Publisher:

Your local telephone company

Type of information available:

A listing of businesses in your local area that sell goods and services principally to other businesses.

How to use it:

Find potential suppliers or competitors.

Situation:

Hannah is planning to open a hair-care salon, and she needs to find a supplier of equipment and hair care products.

What Hannah can find:

Listings of suppliers of hair-care equipment and supplies who service her area.

How Hannah will use:

She will contact the suppliers to find the best price and credit terms for the equipment and products she wants.

TORRINGTON COMPANY
747 Farmington Av New Britain Ct —203 826-1441

▶ Beauty Salons–Equip. & Supls.

Aries Beauty Supply
74 Main Medway Ma —508 533-4522
Flammia Beauty Supply
363 Highland Av Somerville Ma —617 628-0249
Gregory Beauty Co Inc
Tocco Magico-Connelia-Capelli Inter
934 Branch Av Providence R I —800 556-6446
LMF Nucleic Protein Prod Inc
176 King Hanover Ma —617 878-0168
Masello Bros Inc
Call —800 828-0030
Mid-K Beauty Supply
1134 Blue Hill Av Dorchester Ma —617 287-8813

PAUL MITCHELL SYSTEMS–
AUTHORIZED WHOLESALER & DISTRIBUTOR
HAIR LINES-PAUL MITCHELL SYSTEMS
577 Hartford Trnpk Shrewsbury Ma -800 922-2310

SEBASTIAN PRODUCTS OF RI
16 Stafford Ct Cranston R I —800 666-2580
SHAKOUR R G INC
254 Boston Turnpk Westboro Ma —508 366-8282
Stephan Wm C Inc
368 Park Av Worcester Ma —800 339-1303
Visions Beauty Supply Inc
13½ Pond Newburyport Ma —508 465-9266

▶ Bedding Mfrs.' Supplies

Farnsworth Fibre Corp
185 Old Colony Av South Boston Ma —617

NYNEX Business-to-Business Directory
©1995 NYNEX Information Resources Co.
January 1995 – December 1995
Eastern MA, Southern NH, RI edition
pp. 23
Beauty Salons – Equipment and Supplies

Buying Power Index

Publisher:
Sales & Marketing Management
Bill Communications Inc.
355 Park Ave. South
New York, NY 10010-1789
212-592-6300
800-443-2155

Type of information available:
Annual issue published by *Sales & Marketing Management* magazine. Contains information on population and income for every state by cities and counties, including per capita and per household incomes.

How to use it:
Determine the buying power of a particular city or county, or find cities or counties with certain buying-power characteristics.

Situation:

Marsha and Dick, who live in Sacramento, want to open a catering business that specializes in nostalgia parties (retirement, golden anniversary, "over-the-hill," and the like). They want to know how much of the total amount for eating and drinking is spent by the 50-and-over crowd in the surrounding area.

What Marsha and Dick can find:

The effective buying power of their target market.

How Marsha and Dick will use:

By using population and spending habits data, they can determine whether they should locate in Riverside-San Bernardino, Sacramento, Salinas, or San Diego county. They may choose the city of Hemet in Riverside County, where the 50+ age group comprises more than 54% of the total buying power.

Note —
Excerpt: Not available
Availability: Most major libraries
Cost to purchase: $95 (free with subscription to *Sales & Marketing Management*, $48 per year)

Census of the Service Industries (*Service Annual Survey*)

Publisher:
Bureau of the Census
Washington, DC 20233
301-457-4100
http://www.census.gov

Type of information available:
Numbers of establishments and payroll figures in various industries, organized by town. This resource also provides information on how many businesses are individual proprietorships versus partnerships or corporations.

How to use it:
Determine how many businesses (potential competitors) in a particular industry are located in your market area..

Situation:
Mike is opening a barbershop in Newton, Mass. He wants to get an idea of the number of existing barbershops in Newton, their annual receipts, and the annual payroll for each one.

What Mike can find:
There are four barbershops in Newton, all of which are sole proprietorships, with average annual receipts of $117,000 and an annual payroll of $37,000.

How Mike will use:
This information enables Mike to determine the number of competitors he has, and to project annual receipts and payroll.

Note —
Excerpt: Next page
Availability: Internet World Wide Web; many libraries
Cost to purchase: $6

Table 6. **Summary Statistics for Firms Subject to Federal Income Tax for Places With 350 Establishments or More: 1987**—Con.

[Includes only establishments with payroll. For meaning of abbreviations and symbols, see introductory text. For explanation of terms and comparability of 1982 and 1987 censuses, including revised methodology for presenting establishment counts, see appendix A. For information on geographic areas followed by A, see appendix F]

1987 SIC code	Geographic area and kind of business or operation	Establishments (number)	Receipts ($1,000)	Annual payroll ($1,000)	First quarter payroll ($1,000)	Paid employees for pay period including March 12 (number)	Unincorporated businesses or operations: Individual proprietorships (number)	Unincorporated businesses or operations: Partnerships (number)
	NEW BEDFORD—Con.							
80	**Health services**	139	66 090	34 380	8 292	2 040	71	5
801	Offices and clinics of doctors of medicine	70	33 624	19 555	4 845	714	32	1
802	Offices and clinics of dentists	35	8 587	3 356	743	196	21	2
803	Offices and clinics of doctors of osteopathy	-	-	-	-	-	-	-
804	Offices and clinics of other health practitioners	19	3 043	682	171	62	16	1
8041	Offices and clinics of chiropractors	7	1 342	342	79	27	5	-
8042	Offices and clinics of optometrists	6	(D)	(D)	(D)	(D)	6	-
8043, 9	Offices and clinics of podiatrists and other health practitioners, n.e.c.	6	(D)	(D)	(D)	(D)	5	1
805	Nursing and personal care facilities	10	14 284	6 995	1 588	639	1	1
806	Hospitals	1	(D)	(D)	(D)	(D)	-	-
807, 8, 9	Other health services	4	(D)	(D)	(D)	(D)	1	-
81	**Legal services**	87	22 447	8 111	1 877	362	46	13
823, 4, 9	**Selected educational services**	4	(D)	(D)	(D)	(D)	2	-
83	**Social services**	10	(D)	(D)	(D)	(D)	3	-
87 ex. 8733	**Engineering, accounting, research, management, and related services (except noncommercial research organizations)**	48	18 517	8 955	2 105	449	21	3
871	Engineering, architectural, and surveying services	17	11 773	5 798	1 372	276	4	-
872	Accounting, auditing, and bookkeeping services	22	5 023	2 513	570	135	16	2
873 ex. 8733	Research, development, and testing services (except noncommercial research organizations)	3	(D)	(D)	(D)	(D)	-	1
874	Management and public relations services	6	(D)	(D)	(D)	(D)	1	-
89	**Services, n.e.c.**	8	961	380	78	17	2	-
	NEWTON							
	Total	1 106	558 551	215 107	49 799	10 154	311	67
70 ex. 704	**Hotels, rooming houses, camps, and other lodging places (except membership lodging)**	9	45 583	10 713	2 367	1 287	1	2
7011	Hotels and motels	7	(D)	(D)	(D)	(D)	1	2
7011 pt.	Hotels	3	(D)	(D)	(D)	(D)	-	-
7011 pt.	Motels, motor hotels, and tourist courts	4	(D)	(D)	(D)	(D)	1	2
702, 3	Other lodging places	2	(D)	(D)	(D)	(D)	-	-
72	**Personal services**	115	24 450	9 182	2 111	897	38	5
721	Laundry, cleaning, and garment services	30	9 813	2 753	589	214	10	3
7211	Power laundries, family and commercial*	-	-	-	-	-	-	-
7213	Linen supply*	-	-	-	-	-	-	-
7215	Coin-operated laundries and drycleaning	6	(D)	(D)	(D)	(D)	1	2
7216	Drycleaning plants, except rug cleaning*	16	4 392	1 677	379	142	4	1
7217	Carpet and upholstery cleaning	1	(D)	(D)	(D)	(D)	-	-
7218	Industrial launderers*	1	(D)	(D)	(D)	(D)	-	-
7212, 9	Other laundry, cleaning, and garment services*	6	666	116	17	10	5	-
722	Photographic studios, portrait	1	(D)	(D)	(D)	(D)	-	-
723, 4	Beauty and barber shops	65	11 111	5 532	1 337	417	24	1
723	Beauty shops	61	10 994	5 495	1 329	413	20	1
724	Barber shops	4	117	37	8	4	4	
725	Shoe repair shops and shoeshine parlors	2	(D)	(D)	(D)	(D)		
726	Funeral service and crematories	5	1 006	146	37	7		
729	Miscellaneous personal services	12	2 066	603	115	48		
73	**Business services**	196	171 507	70 872	[illegible]			
731	Advertising	25						
732	Consumer credit reporting agencies, mercantile reporting agencies, and adjustment and collection agencies							
733	Mailing, reproduction, commercial art and photography, and stenographic services							
734	Services to dwellings [illegible]							
735	Miscellaneous [illegible]							
736								
737								

Service Annual Survey

U.S. Census Bureau

Massachusetts, MA-47 — MA-48

Newton, Personal Services, Barbershops

County Business Patterns

Publisher:
U. S. Department of Commerce
Bureau of the Census
Data User Services Div.
Washington, DC 20233
301-457-4100
http://www.lib.virginia.edu/socsci/cbp/cbp.html

Online

Type of information available:
State and county employment, payroll figures, and numbers of establishments of various industries according to size. Updated annually, this resource is similar in content to the *Census of the Service Industries;* however, *County Business Patterns* breaks down the total number of establishments by number of employees, but does not contain information on form of organization.

How to use it:
Find out how many businesses in a particular industry are located in a county.

Situation:

Brad and Joan are thinking about opening an in-home nursing care business. They want to know how many are currently in operation in their area, and how many employees each one has.

What Brad and Joan can find:

How many in-home nursing care businesses are operating in their county, and a breakdown of number of establishments by employee category.

How Brad and Joan will use:

This information contributes to an assessment of whether their county can support another in-home health care business, and how many employees they should anticipate hiring.

Note —
Excerpt: Next page
Availability: CD-ROM, libraries, government bookstores
Cost to purchase: U.S. book, $6.50; state by state, $2.50 to $12.00; CD-ROM (1992-93), $150

Table 2. **Counties—Employees, Payroll, and Establishments, by Industry: 1991**—Con.

[Excludes most government employees, railroad employees, and self-employed persons. Size class 1 to 4 includes establishments having payroll but no employees during mid-March pay period. (D) denotes figures withheld to avoid disclosing data for individual companies. For explanation of terms, statement on reliability, and comparability with other data, see introductory text]

SIC code	Industry	Number of employees for week including March 12	Payroll ($1,000)		Total number of establishments	Number of establishments by employment-size class								
			First quarter	Annual		1 to 4	5 to 9	10 to 19	20 to 49	50 to 99	100 to 249	250 to 499	500 to 999	1,000 or more
	CUMBERLAND—Con.													
	Services—Con.													
73	Business services—Con.													
737	Computer and data processing services	245	1 964	8 424	32	18	7	4	2	1	-	-	-	-
7371	Computer programming services	76	716	2 824	7	3	2	1	1	-	-	-	-	-
7372	Prepackaged software	(B)	(D)	(D)	4	-	1	2	1	-	-	-	-	-
7373	Computer integrated systems design	(B)	(D)	(D)	4	-	2	1	-	1	-	-	-	-
738	Miscellaneous business services	1 362	5 947	22 999	110	61	22	16	6	2	2	1	-	-
7381	Detective and armored car services	535	1 567	6 010	19	5	4	3	3	2	2	-	-	-
7382	Security systems services	(B)	(D)	(D)	3	1	-	1	1	-	-	-	-	-
7384	Photofinishing laboratories	(E)	(D)	(D)	8	2	3	2	-	-	-	1	-	-
7389	Business services, n.e.c.	320	1 255	4 950	78	53	15	8	2	-	-	-	-	-
75	Auto repair, services, and parking	1 215	5 839	23 688	177	108	48	12	6	-	3	-	-	-
751	Automotive rentals, no drivers	480	2 362	9 619	17	7	3	2	2	-	3	-	-	-
7513	Truck rental and leasing, no drivers	(E)	(D)	(D)	7	4	-	1	-	-	2	-	-	-
7514	Passenger car rental	(C)	(D)	(D)	8	2	2	1	2	-	1	-	-	-
753	Automotive repair shops	529	2 682	10 906	125	84	34	4	3	-	-	-	-	-
7532	Top and body repair and paint shops	150	845	3 217	30	19	8	1	2	-	-	-	-	-
7538	General automotive repair shops	244	1 074	4 332	60	42	15	2	1	-	-	-	-	-
7539	Automotive repair shops, n.e.c.	62	351	1 454	18	13	4	1	-	-	-	-	-	-
754	Automotive services, except repair	100	382	1 562	19	11	6	1	1	-	-	-	-	-
7549	Automotive services, n.e.c.	73	267	1 126	9	4	3	1	1	-	-	-	-	-
76	Miscellaneous repair services	522	3 368	13 494	81	59	9	5	6	2	-	-	-	-
762	Electrical repair shops	137	1 092	4 239	14	7	3	2	1	1	-	-	-	-
7629	Electrical repair shops, n.e.c.	82	684	2 586	6	1	2	2	-	1	-	-	-	-
769	Miscellaneous repair shops	340	2 133	8 538	47	34	5	2	5	1	-	-	-	-
7692	Welding repair	(B)	(D)	(D)	6	4	-	1	1	-	-	-	-	-
7699	Repair services, n.e.c.	258	1 542	6 142	40	30	5	1	3	1	-	-	-	-
78	Motion pictures	249	596	2 446	42	23	12	5	2	-	-	-	-	-
783	Motion picture theaters	116	177	793	10	4	1	3	2	-	-	-	-	-
7832	Motion picture theaters, except drive-in	(C)	(D)	(D)	9	3	1	3	2	-	-	-	-	-
784	Video tape rental	(B)	(D)	(D)	19	11	7	1	-	-	-	-	-	-
79	Amusement and recreation services	1 341	2 715	12 507	121	78	17	12	10	1	2	1	-	-
792	Producers, orchestras, entertainers	242	570	2 066	17	12	2	1	1	-	1	-	-	-
7922	Theatrical producers and services	61	230	1 019	8	5	2	-	1	-	-	-	-	-
7929	Entertainers and entertainment groups	180	338	1 024	6	4	-	1	-	-	1	-	-	-
793	Bowling centers	88	175	693	8	3	2	1	2	-	-	-	-	-
794	Commercial sports	166	326	2 077	7	5	1	-	-	-	1	-	-	-
7948	Racing, including track operation	(C)	(D)	(D)	3	2	-	-	-	-	1	-	-	-
799	Misc. amusement, recreation services	796	1 559	7 249	73	45	10	9	7	1	-	1	-	-
7991	Physical fitness facilities	123	211	884	13	4	5	2	2	-	-	-	-	-
7997	Membership sports and recreation clubs	162	463	2 973	16	12	-	-	3	1	-	-	-	-
7999	Amusement and recreation, n.e.c.	453	758	2 692	34	22	3	7	1	-	-	1	-	-
80	Health services	14 283	83 431	369 609	648	372	137	64	36	19	10	6	3	1
801	Offices and clinics of medical doctors	2 038	17 349	92 880	246	153	52	24	14	1	1	1	-	-
802	Offices and clinics of dentists	838	4 386	20 198	133	68	42	18	4	1	-	-	-	-
803	Offices of osteopathic physicians	200	1 527	8 241	52	35	14	3	-	-	-	-	-	-
804	Offices of other health practitioners	495	2 065	9 584	109	82	18	7	1	1	-	-	-	-
8041	Offices and clinics of chiropractors	69	235	974	29	24	5	-	-	-	-	-	-	-
8042	Offices and clinics of optometrists	117	454	2 131	31	23	6	2	-	-	-	-	-	-
8049	Offices of health practitioners, n.e.c.	250	1 065	4 953	31	21	3	5	1	1	-	-	-	-
805	Nursing and personal care facilities	2 293	8 944	37 240	32	5	2	1	8	10	4	2	-	-
806	Hospitals	7 054	43 703	178 308	11	1	-	-	-	1	2	3	3	1
807	Medical and dental laboratories	232	1 047	4 325	24	15	3	3	2	1	-	-	-	-
8071	Medical laboratories	154	697	2 910	16	11	2	2	-	1	-	-	-	-
8072	Dental laboratories	78	350	1 415	8	4	1	1	2	-	-	-	-	-
808	Home health care services	738	1 888	8 465	15	5	-	2	2	3	3	-	-	-
809	Health and allied services, n.e.c.	269	1 936	6 529	18	3	5	5	5	-	-	-	-	-
81	Legal services	1 830	13 711	63 305	187	117	30	17	15	4	4	-	-	-
82	Educational services	2 863	9 693	40 093	68	36	11	5	10	1	3	1	-	1
821	Elementary and secondary schools	476	2 075	8 309	18	3	4	2	7	1	1	-		
822	Colleges and universities	2 259	7 272	30 438	8	-	-	1	3	-	[illegible]			
83	Social services	2 766	9 770	39 941	283	137	63	48						
832	Individual and family services	771	3 227	13 117										
833	Job training and related services		[illegible]											
835	Child day care services													
836														

County Business Patterns

U.S. Department of Commerce, Bureau of the Census

1991, Maine, CBP-91-21

Encyclopedia of Associations

Publisher:
Gale Research, Inc.
835 Penobscot Bldg.
645 Griswold St.
Detroit, MI 48226-4094
800-877-GALE (877-4253)
800-762-4058 fax
http://www.thomson.com

Online

Type of information available:
Lists of trade associations and other groups.

How to use it:
Trade associations are potentially rich sources of information for both start-ups and those already in business. Trade associations may be able to provide you with industry information, consumer demographics, publications, and listings of trade shows, as well as other information.

Situation:

Sally and Jack want to start up a pet-sitting service, and they need to know what types of insurance and bonding are recommended for pet sitters.

What Sally and Jack can find:

Under "Pets," they find a National Association of Pet Sitters.

How Sally and Jack will use:

They will call the association to ask about regulations in the pet-sitting industry, and get publications or information about starting their business.

Note —
Excerpt: Next page
Availability: Internet World Wide Web, most libraries
Cost to purchase: $450 (31st ed., three volumes)

... business. ...
puppies and pet stores ... Conducts correspon...
training program on commercial kennel management. **Formerly:** (198..., Master Kennel Association.
Publications: Newsletter, monthly.

★2711★ NATIONAL ASSOCIATION OF PET SITTERS (NAPS)
1200 G St. NW, Ste. 760
Washington, DC 20005-4709
Patti J. Moran, Exec.Dir.
PH: (202)393-3317 FX: (202)393-0336
Founded: 1989. **Members:** 500. **Membership Dues:** patron, $100 • active/pledge, $120 • corporate, $250 • benefactor, $500. **Staff:** 6. **Budget:** $70,000. **Regional Groups:** 5. Owners or employees of pet-sitting services; professionals or businesses in related fields. Promotes professional and ethical standards in pet sitting and fosters cooperation among members of the pet-care industry. Serves as a network for the exchange of ideas and information on pet sitting and current industry practices. Disseminates information educating the pet-owning public on the advantages of leaving pets in a home environment and how to choose a reliable sitter. Advocates legislation to prevent animal abuse. Provides consulting services. compiles statistics. **Libraries:** Type: reference. **Telecommunication Services:** phone referral service. **Committees:** Education; Ethics; Insurance; Legislation; Product Review; Research and Marketing; Seminar.

★2715★ PET ...
1710 Rhode Is...
Washington, DC ...
Marshall Meyers, ...
PH: (202)452-1...
TF: (800)553-7...
Founded: 1970 ...
retailers, manuf...
industry trade ...
regulations and ...
and industry-rel...
Relations; Rese...
Publications: ...
Alerts members ...
• *Pet Shop Ma...*
on federal and st...
on research an...
Circulation: 2,50...
alerts and public...
Conventions/M...

Encyclopedia of Associations, Section 1, Trade, Business, & Commercial Organizations, p.331;

Equifax National Decision Systems

Publisher:
Decision Systems Inc.
5375 Mira Sorrento Place, Suite 400
San Diego, CA 92121
800-866-6510
619-550-5800
http://www.ends.com

Type of information available:
High-tech information, including detailed databases of demographics, projections, and geographic data; customer segmentation and targeting data; data-analysis services; and consulting services.

Online

How to use it:
Find information related to location factors for your business, such as traffic flow demographics, data by potential trading area, and street maps.

Situation:

Anne and Don want to open a sandwich shop and pub in the Faneuil Hall area of Boston. They are looking for the location with the highest level of foot traffic that consists of white-collar workers with disposable income who eat out for lunch. They would also like a listing of all restaurants within a two-mile radius of their potential site.

What Anne and Don can find:

They will call Equifax and speak with a consultant. For a fee (starting at $70 for a single location report), the consultant will identify locations in Boston that match Anne and Don's criteria.

How Anne and Don will use:

Armed with detailed maps and traffic-flow patterns, Anne and Don will look for restaurant space near upscale, high-traffic locations.

Note —
Excerpt: Next page
Availability: Internet World Wide Web; customized for your location (not in bookstores or libraries)
Cost to purchase: up to five-mile radius, $180

Page 1

RESTAURANT: LOCATION DIRECTORY
(* inc *)
BY EQUIFAX NATIONAL DECISION SYSTEMS 800-866-6510

COORD: 42:21.81 71:03.58

RESTAURANT NAME CATEGORY	ADDRESS CITY	SIC EMP SIZE	DIST/DIR CHAIN
M & M COFFEE SHOP NC RESTAURANT	98 A ST BOSTON, MA	581200 17	1.5 S NO
M COOKE INC NC RESTAURANT	121 LEWIS WHARF BOSTON, MA	581200 60	0.4 E NO
MAK-KWAN RESTAURANT NC RESTAURANT	44 BEACH ST BOSTON, MA	581200 2	0.8 S NO
MALTA ROTISSERIE & GRILL NC RESTAURANT	450 HANOVER ST BOSTON, MA	581200 17	0.4 NE NO
MAMA MARIA'S NC RESTAURANT	118 BUNKER HILL ST CHARLESTOWN, MA	581200 2	1.0 N NO
MAMA'S KITCHEN MIDSCALE FAMILY STYLE	82 BENNINGTON ST BOSTON, MA	581260 2	1.5 NE NO
MAMMA CATINA RESTAURANT NC RESTAURANT	326 HANOVER ST BOSTON, MA	581200 17	0.3 E NO
MAMMA LISA'S PIZZA HOUSE QSR PIZZA	312 BROADWAY BOSTON, MA	581243 2	1.1 S NO
MAMMA MARIA NC RESTAURANT	3 NORTH SQ BOSTON, MA	581200 15	0.3 E NO
MANGIA MANGIA NC RESTAURANT	147 ENDICOTT ST BOSTON, MA	581200 2	0.1 NE NO
MARCELLO'S PIZZERIA QSR PIZZA	272 NEWBURY ST BOSTON, MA	581243 13	1.6 SW NO
MARCO POLO INC NC RESTAURANT	274 SUMMER ST BOSTON, MA	581200 2	1.0 SE NO
MARCO POLO RESTAURANT NC RESTAURANT	17 UNION ST BOSTON, MA	581200 17	0.2 SE NO
MARIA'S SUB SHOP QSR OTHER SANDWICH	43 GORE ST CAMBRIDGE, MA	581244 2	1.2 NW NO

* IN DIRECTION COLUMN MEANS MATCHED TO ZIP CODE CENTROID

Note: Reduced from full page

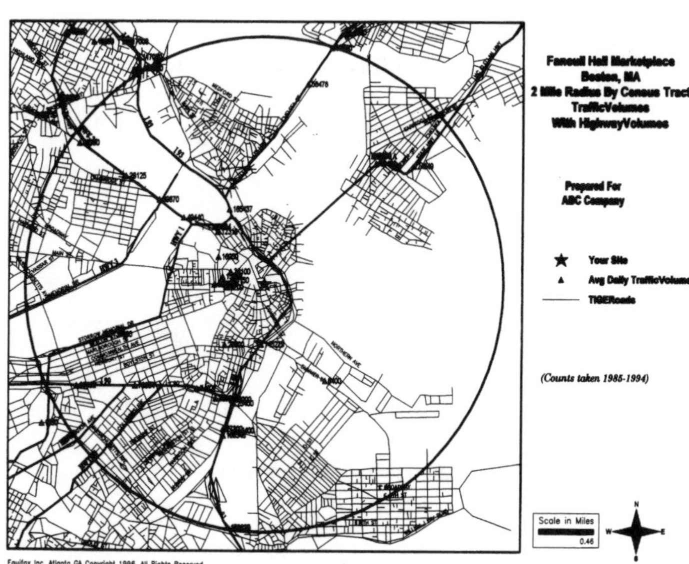

Financial Studies of the Small Business

Publisher:
Financial Research Associates
P. O. Box 7708
510 Ave. J SE
Winter Haven, FL 33880
941-299-3969

Type of information available:
Sales data and ratios for businesses from $10,000 to over $1 million in annual sales. This reference is particularly good for businesses that are anticipating modest sales levels.

How to use it:
Determine whether your business-plan financials and projections are in line with industry norms.

Situation:

Chris and Sid are doing their first-year projections for the upscale restaurant they are opening. They want to know if their advertising budget is in line with that of other businesses with sales levels similar to those they are projecting.

What Chris and Sid can find:

The ratio for advertising expenses as a percent of sales for restaurants with annual sales of $10,000 to $250,000, $250,000 to $500,000, $500,000 to $1 million, and more than $1 million.

How Chris and Sid will use:

Using the figures they find as a guideline, Chris and Sid will develop their advertising budget and allocate the typical percentage of their sales revenues for advertising.

Note —
Excerpt: Next page
Availability: Many libraries and accountants (not in bookstores)
Cost to purchase: $96 hardbound, $125 diskette

SERVICES
RESTAURANT

TOTAL NUMBER OF FIRMS REPORTING	228
NUMBER OF FIRMS INCORPORATED	183
NUMBER OF FIRMS PROPRIETORS	29
NUMBER OF FIRMS PARTNERSHIPS	16

BREAKDOWN BY SALES

TOTAL SALES (IN THOUSANDS)	10-250 AS A PCT OF SALES	250-500 AS A PCT OF SALES	500-1000 AS A PCT OF SALES	1000&OVE AS A PCT OF SALES
NET SALES	100.00	100.00	100.00	100.00
COST OF SALES	42.74	41.22	39.63	37.27
GROSS PROFIT	57.26	58.78	60.37	62.73
GENERAL/ADMINISTRATIVE EXP	50.37	54.43	56.58	58.67
OPERATING PROFIT	6.89	4.35	3.78	4.07
INTEREST EXPENSE	0.29	0.77	0.37	0.27
DEPRECIATION	2.80	1.60	1.50	1.65
PROFIT BEFORE TAXES	3.80	1.97	1.91	2.15
ADDITIONAL OPERATING ITEMS				
LABOR	18.78	25.92	26.60	25.27
ADVERTISING EXPENSE	0.79	1.23	1.37	1.22
TRAVEL EXPENSE	999.99	0.28	0.11	0.14
RENT	8.00	5.28	4.78	5.16
INSURANCE	2.57	2.24	1.99	1.72
OFFICER/EXECUTIVE SALARIES	12.25	6.65	6.61	5.93
RATIOS				
CURRENT	1.2	1.3	1.8	1.0
QUICK	0.6	0.8	1.1	0.6
CURRENT ASSETS/TOTAL ASSETS	19.1	20.4	38.5	36.5
SHORT TERM DEBT/TOTAL DEBT	85.1	31.0	67.4	65.3
SHORT TERM DEBT/NET WORTH	11.5	10.3	20.6	67.8
TOTAL DEBT/NET WORTH	14.3	17.9	37.3	103.2
SHORT TERM DEBT/TOTAL ASSETS	19.0	18.3	24.1	37.1
LONG TERM DEBT/TOTAL ASSETS	2.5	60.0	20.6	25.5
TOTAL DEBT/TOTAL ASSETS	64.9	88.9	60.2	73.6
SALES/RECEIVABLES	0.0	0.0	18.9	132.9
AVERAGE COLLECTION PERIOD	0.	0.	0.	1.
SALES/INVENTORY	45.8	74.9	63.2	65.8
SALES/TOTAL ASSETS	2.8	4.4	4.1	5.2
SALES/NET WORTH	6.5	4.9	5.1	10.0
PROFIT (PRETAX)/TOTAL ASSETS	12.4	7.2	13.1	11.1
PROFIT (PRETAX)/NET WORTH	20.0	10.9	20.0	32.9

SERVICES
RESTAURANT

TOTAL ASSETS $250000-$ 500000

ASSETS

CURRENT ASSETS	AS A PCT OF CURRENT ASSETS	AS A PCT OF TOTAL ASSETS
CASH	56.60	10.52
ACCOUNTS RECEIVABLES	5.37	1.12
INVENTORIES	18.43	4.96
OTHER CURRENT ASSETS	0.79	0.15

FIXED ASSETS	AS A PCT OF FIXED ASSETS	AS A PCT OF TOTAL ASSETS
LAND, BUILDINGS, LEASE-HOLD IMPROVEMENTS	9.27	2.52
EQUIPMENT	63.19	21.50
OTHER FIXED ASSETS	0.00	0.00

LIABILITIES & CAPITAL

CURRENT LIABILITIES	AS A PCT OF CURRENT LIABILITIES	AS A PCT OF TOTAL LIABILITIES
ACCOUNTS PAYABLE/TRADE	20.87	10.59
SHORT TERM BANK LOANS	0.00	0.00
OTHER CURRENT DEBT	54.29	17.09

LONG TERM DEBT	AS A PCT OF LONG TERM DEBT	AS A PCT OF TOTAL LIABILITIES
NOTES PAYABLE	0.00	0.00
MORTGAGES PAYABLE	0.00	0.00
LONG TERM BANK LOANS	0.00	0.00
STOCKHOLDER LOANS (DUE TO OWNERS)	0.00	0.00
OTHER LONG TERM DEBT	0.00	0.00

SERVICES
RESTAURANT

TOTAL ASSETS $250000-$ 500000

INCOME DATA

	AS A PCT OF NET SALES
NET SALES (GROSS INCOME)	100.00
COST OF SALES	40.53
GROSS PROFIT	59.47
GENERAL/ADMINISTRATIVE EXP	55.38
OPERATING PROFIT	4.09
INTEREST EXPENSE	0.70
DEPRECIATION	1.98
PROFIT BEFORE TAXES	1.41

ADDITIONAL OPERATING ITEMS

LABOR	25.41
ADVERTISING EXPENSE	1.35
TRAVEL EXPENSE	0.30
RENT	6.30
INSURANCE	2.00
OFFICER/EXECUTIVE SALARIES	5.31

RATIOS

	MEDIAN	UPPER QUARTILE	LOWER QUARTILE	UNITS
CURRENT	1.1	2.2	0.5	TIMES
QUICK	0.9	1.8	0.3	TIMES
CURRENT ASSETS/TOTAL ASSETS	24.5	51.1	9.1	PCT
SHORT TERM DEBT/TOTAL DEBT	42.4	93.2	20.9	PCT
SHORT TERM DEBT/NET WORTH	28.9	63.6	-32.0	PCT
TOTAL DEBT/NET WORTH	66.4	195.0	-290.7	PCT
SHORT TERM DEBT/TOTAL ASSETS	20.6	31.5	15.0	PCT
LONG TERM DEBT/TOTAL ASSETS	40.5	68.7	1.6	PCT
TOTAL DEBT/TOTAL ASSETS	66.8	106.4	43.1	PCT
SALES/RECEIVABLES	37.2	161.3	0.0	TIMES
AVERAGE COLLECTION PERIOD	1.	5.	0.	DAYS
SALES/INVENTORY	60.9	114.3	30.6	TIMES
SALES/TOTAL ASSETS	2.8	4.0	1.8	TIMES
SALES/NET WORTH	5.9	10.2	-4.6	TIMES
PROFIT (PRETAX)/TOTAL ASSETS	4.1	19.0	-4.5	PCT
PROFIT (PRETAX)/NET WORTH	12.2	57.4	-12.4	PCT

Financial Studies of the Small Business, 1994 Ed., p. 5-22, Copyright ©1994; 1995 Ed., pp.201-202, Copyright ©1995, Financial Research Associates

The Internet

Type of information available:
The Internet is a system that integrates literally millions of computers, from major university mainframes to small PCs. Virtually any information that can be found in a library can be accessed on-line through File Transfer Protocol (FTP) sites. In addition, the government maintains information—from census bureau files, labor statistics, and law documents, to the hours the White House is available for tours—in huge libraries located on the Net. Universities maintain research documents, academic and industrial studies, course descriptions, and library card catalogs. The importance the Internet plays in the research process can not be overstated. For example, a large portion of the research for this book was done on the Net, and practically all of the text traveled on the information superhighway from author to editor and back again.

Marketing on the Internet has grown exponentially over the past year. Large corporations like AT&T, Hewlett Packard, and General Motors, have sites on the Net that not only advertise their products and services but also offer financial data about their company and may have links to other resources for information relating to their industry. Even "mom & pop" stores are joining the Information Age by having a "Web site" to advertise their business. Individuals have FTP sites that contain data for special interest groups, such as environmentalism or military reenactments.

The following example shows how several service businesses provide information to a single customer. It should be noted that this form of advertising can have an extremely low CPM because of its extremely high reach and low price (you can have a Web page that reaches millions of people for as little as $50 per month).

How to use it: The Internet can be accessed through most colleges and universities around the globe (some restrictions for usage may apply if you are not directly affiliated with the institution). In addition, you can log on to the Internet via "Internet Gateways," which are virtual "on-ramps" to the information highway. Most online services such as America Online, CompuServe, and Prodigy have gateways, as do most large corporate E-mail systems. Through such connections you can use the Internet at home with your own PC.

Situation:

Anne and Lilly are planning to go to Cancun for a vacation next January. Adventurous travelers, they want to try scuba diving while they are there. They want information about scuba diving in general, a list of reputable dive schools in their hometown of Chicago, and a guide to scuba tour companies in Cancun. They are also interested in finding the cheapest flight that fits their schedules.

What Anne and Lilly can find:

Using her Internet access through an online service, Lilly calls up the home page of Rodale's *Scuba Diving* magazine (http://www.scubadiving.com/), whose Internet address she got from the magazine. Listed under "Scuba Classes," a local vo-tech school had an advertisement for a six-week open-water scuba course. While Anne looks for good flights through the travel link, Lilly uses a key-word search to check out several dive-tour companies that have sites on the Web.

How Anne and Lilly will use:

They will enroll in the course, and explore the clear waters of Cancun next January. By using a hyperlink to "Equipment" from Rodale's Web site, Anne also found a great deal on a dive suit in a small dive shop in Hawaii. She will have it shipped to her home in Chicago next week.

The Lifestyle Market Analyst

Publisher:
SRDS (Standard Rate and Data Service)
1700 Higgins Rd.
Des Plaines, IL 60018
800-851-SRDS (851-7737)
847-375-5000
847-375-5001 fax
http://srds.com

Type of information available:
Demographic information on popular activities, broken down by geographic market.

How to use it:
Cross-reference specific data to calculate potential market for your service. In addition, you could put together several kinds of information and calculate the total market for a service.

Situation:

Scott and Ken are avid golfers. Ken owns a small chain of summer camps for young golfers. Scott's wife, Jennifer, has the option of relocating her business to either Grand Rapids or Marquette, Mich. Wherever they relocate, Scott and Ken intend to start a franchise of Ken's golf camps.

What Scott and Ken can find:

For each location, Scott and Ken can obtain information on the number of households, the number of children at home (broken down by age), and household income figures specifically for golfers.

How Scott and Ken will use:

They can compare Marquette and Grand Rapids in terms of market potential, based on the market information.

Golf — **Demographics**
Base Index US = 100

Total Households. 19,125,630

Children At Home			
At Least One Child	6,062,825	31.7	105
Child Age Under 2	860,653	4.5	125
Child Age 2-4	1,702,181	8.9	113
Child Age 5-7	1,568,302	8.2	108
Child Age 8-10	1,568,302	8.2	105
Child Age 11-12	1,109,287	5.8	102
Child Age 13-15	1,568,302	8.2	101
Child Age 16-18	1,415,297	7.4	100

Household Income			
Under $20,000	2,256,824	11.8	42
$20,000-$29,999	2,275,950	11.9	77
$30,000-$39,999	2,620,211	13.7	99
$40,000-$49,999	2,562,834	13.4	118
$50,000-$74,999	4,857,910	25.4	143
$75,000-$99,999	2,333,327	12.2	169
$100,000 and over	2,199,447	11.5	185
Median Income	$49,353		

▒ : Denotes DMAs ranked 1 - 10

Designated Market Areas	Lifestyle Rank	Households	%	Index
Glendive, MT	148	735	15.8	80
Grand Junction-Montrose, CO	119	11,079	18.2	92
[illegible]	2	[illegible]	[illegible]	[illegible]
Great Falls, MT	113	12,212	18.6	94
[illegible]	1	[illegible]	[illegible]	[illegible]
Macon, GA	169	27,867	15.0	76
Madison, WI	21	75,641	24.4	123
Mankato, MN	29	14,134	24.0	121
Marquette, MI	88	16,929	19.5	98
Medford-Klamath Falls, OR	128	25,416	17.3	87

770 — **Lifestyle Profiles** — The Lifestyle Market Analyst 1995

Note —
Excerpt: This page
Availability: Only through university and public libraries
Cost to purchase: $295

Reprinted from the 1995 edition of *The Lifestyle Market Analyst,* pp. 770, 772, 773; published by SRDS with data supplied by the Polk Co.

Online

New York Times Index

Publisher:
The New York Times Co.
229 W. 43rd St. (9th Fl.)
New York, NY 10036-3913
212-556-1989
212-556-1629 fax
212-221-5065 (for Index)

Type of information available:
Brief digests of articles related to your business that have appeared in *The New York Times*

How to use it:
Find articles addressing topics relating to your business or industry.

Situation:

Bob and Corinne are hoping to open a new health club in Manhattan. They want to see what kind of coverage the *Times* has given to the industry.

What Bob and Corinne can find:

Recent articles on the health club industry and fitness activities in the New York area.

How Bob and Corinne will use:

They will glean information about industry trends, economics, fashions among users, user demographics, press attitude toward health clubs, and frequency of coverage.

Note —
Excerpt: Next page
Availability: University and major public libraries
Cost to purchase: $735 to $1,120 (monthly, quarterly, annually)

Reader's Guide to Periodical Literature

Publisher:
H. W. Wilson Co.
950 University Ave.
Bronx, NY 10452
718-588-8400

Type of information available:
Listings of recent articles appearing in more than 200 popular periodicals, indexed by subject and author in one alphabetical list. Also available in an abridged format covering more then 50 publications.

How to use it:
Find an index of recent articles about your industry or service.

Situation:

David is interested in starting a backpacking guide service in the Washington mountains. He wants to read the latest news in the popular press about backpacking equipment, safety, and regional points of interest.

What David can find:

Title, author, source, and publication date of several recent magazine articles about various aspects of backpacking.

How David will use:

Reading articles of interest to him, he may find sources of further information by cross-referencing author and publication entries.

Note —
Excerpt: Next page
Availability: Most libraries (not available in bookstores)
Cost to purchase: $200 (subscription; plus $10 handling)

BACKLIST BOOKS *See* Publishers and publishing—Backlist books

BACKPACKERS

Health and hygiene

Truth or consequences. E. A. Weiss. *Backpacker* v23 p16-18 F '95

The whole tooth: how to keep dental problems from ruining your backcountry excursions. B. Tilton. il *Backpacker* v23 p22+ Ap '95

Nutrition

Shrink and shrivel. A. S. Kesselheim. il *Backpacker* v23 p92-4+ Ap '95

Recreation

Tedium relievers [entertainment when stuck in tent] R. B. Jones. il *Backpacker* v23 p30-1 Ap '95

BACKPACKING

Hidden wilderness [small but spectacular wilderness areas] B. Tilton. il *Backpacker* v23 p40-7+ My '95

When backpackers dream [nation's three longest trails; cover story] K. Berger. il maps *Backpacker* v23 p68-71+ My '95

Where wild things gather. L. Rice. il *Backpacker* v23 p34-40+ Ap '95

Accidents and injuries

A kind of deliverance [A. Dunne returns after disappearing while trekking in the Santa Rita Moutains, Ariz.] K. Gray. il pors *People Weekly* v44 p73-4 Ag 28 '95

One step at a time [winter injury] L. B. Goetz. il *Backpacker* v22 p131+ D '94

Paying for another's mistakes [lawsuit following backpackers' deaths may result in limited access to Zion National Park] J. Viehman. il *Backpacker* v23 p7+ F '95

"Things like this happen" [family decides not to sue for lack of warning about landslides in Yosemite National Park] J. C. Gellhorn. il *Backpacker* v23 p143 My '95

Equipment

See also

Backpacks

Camp stoves

Hiking boots

Mountain boots

Sleeping bags

Sleeping pads

Tents

Body-bag bivy sack. il *Backpacker* v22 p28+ D '94

Editors' choice '95 [cover story] il *Backpacker* v23 p60-4+ Ap '95

Gear guide '95 [cover story; special section] il *Backpacker* v23 p18-19+ Mr '95

Tried and true. il *Backpacker* v23 p58-61+ My '95

Maintenance and repair

Miracle workers. D. Getchell. il *Backpacker* v23 p209-14 Mr '95

Psychological aspects

The quest for a vision. B. Tilton. il *Backpacker* v23 p96+ F '95

Safety devices and measures

Face your fears [grizzly bears] J. Rennicke. il *Backpacker* v23 p20-2 F '95

Sanitation

Waste not, want not [how to dispose of trash on the trail] A. Getchell. il *Backpacker* v23 p34+ My '95

Storm hazards

The telescoping effect [husband caught in snowstorm on backpacking trip in Idaho] J. J. Maughan. il *Backpacker* v23 p155+ Ap '95

Alaska

Alaska! Cheap! [backpacking in parks; cover story] L. Rice. il maps *Backpacker* v23 p40-7+ F '95

Arizona

Alone and vulnerable in the Mazatzal Wilderness. T. Kuhn. il map *Arizona Highways* v71 p18-23 My '95

Arizona's Aravaipa Wilderness. C. Maxa. il maps *Backpacker* v23 p104 Ap '95

Bushwhacking to Grand Canyon's hidden Cheyava Falls [cover story] B. Audretsch and G. Ladd. il map *Arizona Highways* v71 p38-44 Mr '95

British Columbia

Green edge [West Coast Trail] D. Bowen. il maps *Backpacker* v23 p130+ Ap '95

California

America's hottest new parks [backpacking in California deserts] G. Wuerthner. il maps *Backpacker* v22 p32-7+ D '94

California's Henry Coe. R. Graybill. il maps *Backpacker* v23 p112 My '95

California's wild Siskiyou. T. Hallstein. il maps *Backpacker* v23 p108 Ap '95

Idaho

The telescoping effect [husband caught in snowstorm on backpacking trip in Idaho] J. J. Maughan. il *Backpacker* v23 p155+ Ap '95

Indiana

Indiana's Hoosier Forest. J. Mahaney. il maps *Backpacker* v23 p81 F '95

Kentucky

Kentucky's gorgeous gorge. T. V. Ress. il maps *Backpacker* v23 p106 Ap '95

Middle Western States

Wild at heart. il maps *Backpacker* v23 p48-54+ Ap '95

Montana

Valley of the Grizzly [backpacking in Glacier National Park with bear manager N. Wedum] D. Petersen. il maps *Backpacker* v23 p54-61 F '95

Nebraska

Nebraska's Indian Cave. D. T. McDermott. il maps *Backpacker* v22 p95 D '94

Utah

The quest for a vision. B. Tilton. il *Backpacker* v23 p96+ F '95

Yukon Territory

"Hell can't be worse than this trail" [Chilkoot Trail] S. Howe. il maps *Backpacker* v23 p30-7+ F '95

BACKPACKS

The mid-size pack test. S. Howe. il *Backpacker* v23 p98-100+ My '95

Packing it in. D. Getchell. il *Backpacker* v23 p21-2+ Mr '95

BACKSPLASHES

A backsplash done with light and mirrors [work Hayden] W. Talarico. il *Home M* '95

BACKUP STORAGE (C

Backing up [FileS Sidecar II an il *Popular*

Backup is *PC C*

Crossr tech *Cc*

Get

H

H

N

P

Th

Su

Tr

BA

BA

B

Readers' Guide to Periodical Literature, ©1995 H.W. Wilson Co., November 1995, p. 78

BACKPACKING

RMA Annual Statement Studies

Publisher:
Robert Morris Associates (RMA)
The Association of Lending and Credit Risk Professionals
One Liberty Place, Suite 2300
Philadelphia, PA 19103-7398
800-677-7621
215-851-9206 fax

Type of information available:
Balance Sheet, Income Statement, and representative financial ratio information for over 400 industries. This resource is also available on disk.

How to use it:
Determine whether the projections and assumptions on your trial Balance Sheet are representative of the industry, or check whether a company's ratios are within industry norms. (RMA cautions that the Studies be regarded as a general guideline and not an absolute industry norm. This is due to limited samples within categories, the categorization of companies by their primary Standard Industrial Classification (SIC) number only, and different methods of operations by companies within the same industry.)

Situation:

Larry has been developing financial projections for his air taxi and freight business. He would like to see whether his assumptions are close to the actual industry averages.

What Larry can find:

Current and historical comparative data that average Balance Sheet and Income Statement figures, sorted by size of the businesses.

How Larry will use:

He will compare the assumptions he has made on his projections to the ratios in the guide to see whether they line up with the norms in the non-scheduled air transportation industry.

Note —
Excerpt: Next page
Availability: University and business libraries, some bookstores
Cost to purchase: $125 (1996 edition); $30 per study

626 SERVICES—AIR TRANSPORTATION, NONSCHEDULED. SIC# 4522

Current Data Sorted By Assets							Comparative Historical Data	
						# Postretirement Benefits		
						Type of Statement		
1	1	1	2	2	4	Unqualified	11	16
1	6	2				Reviewed	6	13
2	3		1			Compiled	11	6
1	1					Tax Returns		1
2	2	4		3	1	Other	12	14
	11 (4/1-9/30/94)			29 (10/1/94-3/31/95)			4/1/90-3/31/91	4/1/91-3/31/92
0-500M	500M-2MM	2-10MM	10-50MM	50-100MM	100-250MM		ALL	ALL
7	13	7	3	5	5	NUMBER OF STATEMENTS	40	50
%	%	%	%	%	%	ASSETS	%	%
	5.2					Cash & Equivalents	7.0	7.0
	28.8					Trade Receivables - (net)	15.5	15.4
	10.2					Inventory	14.8	7.8
	3.8					All Other Current	2.7	1.9
	48.0					Total Current	40.1	32.1
	40.9					Fixed Assets (net)	44.3	51.7
	1.5					Intangibles (net)	6.5	3.9
	9.6					All Other Non-Current	9.1	12.2
	100.0					Total	100.0	100.0
						LIABILITIES		
	4.4					Notes Payable-Short Term	8.3	9.5
	10.1					Cur. Mat. -L/T/D	7.5	6.1
	16.0					Trade Payables	12.4	9.3
	.6					Income Taxes Payable	.5	.5
	10.0					All Other Current	7.9	7.8
	41.1					Total Current	36.6	33.2
	22.1					Long Term Debt	30.8	32.1
	.3					Deferred Taxes	.5	1.3
	6.5					All Other-Non-Current	2.8	2.3
	30.0					Net Worth	29.3	31.0
	100.0					Total Liabilities & Net Worth	100.0	100.0
						INCOME DATA		
	100.0					Net Sales	100.0	100.0
						Gross Profit		
	94.1					Operating Expenses	95.4	92.2
	5.9					Operating Profit	4.6	7.8
	4.9					All Other Expenses (net)	4.1	3.0
	1.0					Profit Before Taxes	.5	4.9
						RATIOS		
	1.9						1.6	1.9
	1.1					Current	1.0	1.1
	.7						.5	.5
	1.2						1.0	1.3
	.8					Quick	.5	.7
	.4						.2	.4
	8 45.0						11 32.8	10 35.8
	37 9.8					Sales/Receivables	20 18.0	31 11.7
	43 8.5						36 9.6	53 6.9

SERVICES—AIR TRANSPORTATION, NONSCHEDULED. SIC# 4522 627

Comparative Historical Data				Current Data Sorted By Sales					
2	3		# Postretirement Benefits						
			Type of Statement						
18	7	11	Unqualified	1		1		1	8
11	11	9	Reviewed	1	5		2	1	
10	11	6	Compiled	2	3			1	
2	2	2	Tax Returns	1	1				
7	17	12	Other		4		1	3	4
4/1/92-3/31/93	4/1/93-3/31/94	4/1/94-3/31/95			11 (4/1-9/30/94)			29 (10/1/94-3/31/95)	
ALL	ALL	ALL		0-1MM	1-3MM	3-5MM	5-10MM	10-25MM	25MM & OVER
46	48	40	NUMBER OF STATEMENTS	5	13	1	3	6	12
%	%	%	ASSETS	%	%	%	%	%	%
7.1	11.2	7.4	Cash & Equivalents		7.0				12.1
18.1	18.6	23.4	Trade Receivables - (net)		23.4				13.7
9.4	7.3	8.0	Inventory		10.6				9.2
1.5	1.1	3.3	All Other Current		4.3				3.0
36.1	38.2	42.1	Total Current		45.3				38.1
51.1	48.9	46.9	Fixed Assets (net)		44.4				53.8
3.1	3.4	3.7	Intangibles (net)		1.2				2.4
9.7	9.5	7.2	All Other Non-Current		9.2				5.8
100.0	100.0	100.0	Total		100.0				100.0
			LIABILITIES						
5.5	5.4	4.7	Notes Payable-Short Term		3.7				2.9
8.7	6.6	6.6	Cur. Mat.-L/T/D		9.5				6.8
9.6	12.7	14.3	Trade Payables		16.2				8.5
.4	.5	.4	Income Taxes Payable		.7				.0
8.2	8.5	10.0	All Other Current		7.4				8.8
32.5	33.6	36.0	Total Current		37.4				27.1
29.5	27.9	25.7	Long Term Debt		26.7				26.0
1.3	1.1	1.3	Deferred Taxes		.3				3.6
2.1	3.0	4.8	All Other-Non-Current		3.5				2.6
34.6	34.5	32.1	Net Worth		32.0				40.7
100.0	100.0	100.0	Total Liabilities & Net Worth		100.0				100.0
			INCOME DATA						
100.0	100.0	100.0	Net Sales		100.0				100.0
			Gross Profit						
93.4	93.5	91.9	Operating Expenses		92.2				92.1
6.6	6.5	8.1	Operating Profit		7.8				7.9
1.9	.0	2.8	All Other Expenses (net)		2.0				2.6
4.8	6.5	5.3	Profit Before Taxes		5.8				5.3
			RATIOS						
1.9	2.2	2.0			2.0				2.5
1.1	1.2	1.1	Current		1.1				1.8
.6	.8	.6			.7				.8
1.0	1.5	1.2			1.5				1.9
.6	.9	.8	Quick		.8				.8
.4	.4	.5			.4				.4
14 26.8	16 23.1	18 19.8			8 43.5				20 18.1
38 9.5	30 12.1	38 9.6	Sales/Receivables		37 9.8				48 7.6
48 7.6	47 7.8	49 7.4			40 9.1				58 6.3

RMA Annual Statement Studies, 1994 ed., p618; Copyright © 1994, Robert Morris Associates, Reprinted with permission.

Simmons Media and Market Report

Publisher:
Simmons Market Research Bureau, Inc.
309 W. 49th St., 14th Fl.
New York, NY 10019-7316
800-999-SMRB
212-373-8900
212-373-8918 fax

Type of information available:
Extensive information about the consumers of various products. For example, for the product consumed, one can determine the age, income, educational level, race, television viewing habits, etc. of the typical consumer.

How to use it:
A rich source of information about the consumers of approximately 800 products. You can develop a demographic profile of your customer, determine market share and size, and position advertising according to your findings.

Situation:

Leanne plans to open a travel service that specializes in cruise ship vacations. She needs to develop a demographic profile of her potential customer so that she can position her advertising appropriately.

What Leanne can find:

The bureau can provide a breakdown, by percentage of the total U.S. population, of how many adults have taken a cruise within the last three years, and many other demographic characteristics of such passengers including their television and reading habits.

How Leanne will use:

This information will enable Leanne to develop her promotional and direct marketing strategies and to penetrate markets that fit her customer profile.

Note —
Excerpt: Next page
Availability: By subscription; also university and business libraries
Cost to purchase: Custom reports, price varies

CRUISE SHIP VACATION WITHIN THE LAST 3 YEARS
(ADULTS)

	TOTAL U.S. '000	ADULTS A '000	ADULTS B % DOWN	ADULTS C % ACROSS	ADULTS D INDX	MALES A '000	MALES B % DOWN	MALES C % ACROSS	MALES D INDX	FEMALES A '000	FEMALES B % DOWN	FEMALES C % ACROSS	FEMALES D INDX	A '000	B % DOWN	C % ACROSS	D INDX
TOTAL ADULTS	185822	9976	100.0	5.4	100	4655	100.0	2.5	100	5322	100.0	2.9	100				
MALES	88958	4655	46.7	5.2	97	4655	100.0	5.2	209	**0	0.0	0.0	0				
FEMALES	96866	5322	53.3	5.5	102	**0	0.0	0.0	0	5322	100.0	5.5	192				
PRINCIPAL SHOPPERS	112016	5917	59.3	5.3	98	1696	36.4	1.5	60	4222	79.3	3.8	132				
18-24	23965	802	8.0	3.3	62	*327	7.0	1.4	54	*475	8.9	2.0	69				
25-34	42832	1892	19.0	4.4	82	769	16.5	1.8	72	1124	21.1	2.6	92				
35-44	39908	2106	21.1	5.3	98	1323	28.4	3.3	132	782	14.7	2.0	68				
45-54	27327	1842	18.5	6.7	126	815	17.5	3.0	119	1027	19.3	3.8	131				
55-64	21238	1539	15.4	7.2	135	655	14.1	3.1	123	884	16.6	4.2	145				
65 OR OLDER	30552	1798	18.0	5.9	109	787	16.5	2.5	100	1029	19.3	3.4	118				
18-34	66798	2694	27.0	4.0	75	1095	23.5	1.6	65	1599	30.0	2.4	84				
18-49	121918	5797	58.1	4.8	89	2844	61.1	2.3	93	2952	55.5	2.4	85				
25-54	110067	5840	58.5	5.3	99	2907	62.4	2.6	105	2933	55.1	2.7	93				
35-49	55120	3103	31.1	5.6	105	1749	37.8	3.2	127	1353	25.4	2.5	88				
50 OR OLDER	63905	4180	41.9	6.5	122	1810	38.9	2.8	113	2369	44.5	3.7	129				
READ ANY MAGAZINE(MEASURED)	150758	8457	84.8	5.6	104	3838	82.4	2.5	102	4621	86.8	3.1	107				
YELLOW PAGES:USED LST 7 DAYS	83395	5070	50.8	6.1	113	2186	47.0	2.6	105	2884	54.2	3.5	121				
OUTDOOR																	
100 SHWG - 30 DAY AV FREQ	29.05	30.02				33.81				26.94							
30 DAY REACH	164854	9251	92.7	5.6	105	4271	91.8	2.6	103	4980	93.6	3.0	105				
50 SHWG - 30 DAY AV FREQ	15.22	15.80				17.92				14.02							
30 DAY REACH	156465	8876	89.0	5.7	106	4060	87.2	2.6	104	4816	90.5	3.1	107				
25 SHWG - 30 DAY AV FREQ	8.23	8.31				9.52				7.27							
30 DAY REACH	143986	8344	83.6	5.8	108	3849	82.7	2.7	107	4495	84.5	3.1	109				
TELEVISION AVG. DAILY CUME (SUN.-SAT.,6:00AM-2:00AM)	145308	7813	78.3	5.4	100	3515	75.5	2.4	97	4298	80.8	3.0	103				
TELEVISION AVG. HALF HOUR																	
WKDAY 7:00 AM - 9:00 AM	20273	1062	10.6	5.2	98	409	8.8	2.0	80	654	12.3	3.2	113				
WKDAY 9:00 AM - 1:00 PM	22421	1087	10.9	4.8	90	337	7.2	1.5	60	750	14.1	3.3	117				
WKDAY 1:00 PM - 4:30 PM	25918	1365	13.7	5.3	98	373	8.0	1.4	57	992	18.6	3.8	134				
WKDAY 4:30 PM - 7:30 PM	46027	2580	25.9	5.6	104	892	21.9	2.2	86	1588	29.8	3.4	120				
WKDAY 7:30 PM - 8:00 PM	62766	3291	33.0	5.2	98	1326	28.5	2.1	84	1965	36.9	3.1	109				
WKDAY 11:00 PM - 11:30 PM	55220	2817	28.2	5.1	95	1331	28.6	2.4	98	1486	27.9	2.7	94				
WKDAY 11:30 PM - 1:00 AM	18628	884	8.7	4.7	87	439	9.9	2.3	93	431	8.1	2.3	81				
M-SAT 8-11 PM+SUN 7-11 PM	69001	3808	38.2	5.5	103	1693	36.4	2.5	98	2115	39.7	3.1	107				
TELEVISION																	
TV NTWK SHOW TYPES																	
WEEKDAY DAYTIME: DRAMA	6397	314	3.1	4.9	91	66	1.4	1.0	41	248	4.7	3.9	135				
NEWS	4014	217	2.2	5.4	101	85	1.8	2.1	85	132	2.5	3.3	115				
QUIZ/AUD. PARTICIPATION	3644	182	1.8	5.0	93	46	1.0	1.3	50	136	2.6	3.7	131				
WKEND DAY: INFORMATIONAL	2467	153	1.5	6.2	116	68	1.5	2.8	110	85	1.6	3.4	120				
REG. SCHEDULED SPORTS	2784	169	1.7	6.1	113	98	2.1	3.6	142	70	1.3	2.5	88				
SPECIAL SPORTS	4453	238	2.4	5.3	99	167	3.6	3.8	150	70	1.3	1.6	55				
EARLY EVENING: WKDAY NEWS	12164	696	7.0	5.7	107	300	6.4	2.5	99	396	7.4	3.3	114				
WEEKEND NEWS	5187	293	2.9	5.7	105	143	3.1	2.8	110	151	2.8	2.9	101				
PRIMETIME:																	
COMEDY/VARIETY	7533	336	3.4	4.5	83	151	3.2	2.0	80	185	3.5	2.5	88				
DOCUMENTARY/NEWS	13312	787	7.9	5.9	110	320	6.9	2.4	96	467	8.8	3.5	123				
FEATURE FILM	15342	822	8.2	5.4	100	326	7.0	2.1	85	496	9.3	3.2	113				
GENERAL DRAMA	11726	646	6.5	5.5	103	240	5.1	2.0	82	406	7.6	3.5	121				
SITUATION COMEDY	12331	696	7.0	5.6	105	266	5.7	2.2	86	430	8.1	3.5	122				
SUSPENSE & MYSTERY DRAMA	12213	682	6.8	5.6	104	257	5.5	2.1	84	425	8.0	3.5	122				
SPECIALS:																	
COMEDY/VARIETY	10900	577	5.8	5.3	99	253	5.4	2.3	93	323	6.1	3.0	103				
DOCUMENTARY/NEWS	7160	358	3.6	5.0	93	149	3.2	2.1	83	*208	3.9	2.9	102				
FEATURE FILM	8948	491	4.9	5.5	102	198	4.3	2.2	88	293	5.5	3.3	114				
GENERAL DRAMA	10730	546	5.5	5.1	95	240	5.2	2.2	89	306	5.7	2.8	99				
SITUATION COMEDY	11796	619	6.2	5.2	98	276	5.9	2.3	93	343	6.4	2.9	102				
SUSPENSE & MYSTERY DRAMA	9782	586	5.9	6.0	112	268	5.8	2.8	110	*318	6.0	3.3	114				
CABLE TV: HOME WIRED/SATLT	106901	5910	59.2	5.5	103	2833	60.9	2.6	106	3077	57.8	2.9	101				
HOME NOT WIRED/NOT SATLT	78921	4067	40.8	5.2	96	1822	39.1	2.3	92	2245	42.2	2.8	99				
RADIO AVG. DAILY (M-F) CUME																	
6:00 AM - 10:00 AM	99956	5465	54.7	5.5	102	2734	58.7	2.7	109	2721	51.1	2.7	95				
10:00 AM - 3:00 PM	72687	4045	40.5	5.6	104	1925	41.4	2.6	106	2120	39.8	2.9	102				
3:00 PM - 7:00 PM	80444	4296	43.1	5.3	99	2138	45.9	2.7	106	2158	40.5	2.7	94				
7:00 PM - MIDNIGHT	32865	1553	15.6	4.7	88	752	16.2	2.3	91	801	15.1	2.4	85				
MIDNIGHT - 6:00 AM	19915	791	7.9	4.0	74	377	8.1	1.9	75	415	7.8	2.1	73				
6:00 AM - MIDNIGHT	136421	7526	75.4	5.5	103	3575	76.8	2.6	105	3951	74.2	2.9	101				
ENTIRE DAY	137621	7601	76.2	5.5	103	3588	77.1	2.6	104	4013	75.4	2.9	102				

SIMMONS MARKET RESEARCH BUREAU, INC. 1993

*PROJECTION RELATIVELY UNSTABLE BECAUSE OF SAMPLE BASE-USE WITH CAUTION
**NUMBER OF CASES TOO SMALL FOR RELIABILITY-SHOWN FOR CONSISTENCY ONLY

Simmons Media and Market Report, 1993 ed., Travel, Excerpts from pp. 0007 – 0018, CRUISE SHIP VACATION. Copyright © 1993 Simmons Market Research Bureau Inc.

Small Business Profiles

Publisher:
Gale Research, Inc.
835 Penobscot Bldg.
Detroit, MI 48226-4094
313-961-2242
800-877-4253
http://www.thomson.com

Type of information available:
This source contains information for 60 different business types on various aspects of starting a business. Information given includes estimates of start-up costs and profit potential, choosing a location, franchise opportunities, and obtaining licenses and insurance.

How to use it:
Gain targeted, industry-specific information relating to starting your small business.

Situation:

Eleanor is planning to start a packing and shipping service. She needs information on location analysis, as well as on what start-up costs she should plan for.

What Eleanor can find:

A five-page article called "Packing/Shipping and Mail Service."

How Eleanor will use:

She will glean many ideas for analyzing data, writing her business plan, providing services, and launching her business, as well as references to helpful publications.

Note —
Excerpt: Not available
Availability: Major business libraries
Cost to purchase: $95 per volume

Small Business Sourcebook

Publisher:
Gale Research, Inc.
835 Penobscot Bldg.
Detroit, MI 48226-4094
313-961-2242
800-877-4253
http://www.thomson.com

Type of information available:
This resource gives an overview of information resources, arranged by business type, for start-ups or established businesses, including start-up information, primary trade associations, educational programs, reference works, sources of supply, statistical sources, and trade periodicals. Volume II of the set contains information on topics of general interest such as venture capital, funding, and compensation. Volume II also contains listings of governmental, academic, and commercial organizations helpful to small business.

How to use it:
Look up a wide range of sources of start-up information for over 100 types of businesses.

Situation:

Jim and Ellen wish to translate their love of movies from an avocation to a vocation by opening a movie theater downtown.

What Jim and Ellen can find:

Listings of movie theater trade associations, statistical information sources, and a franchise opportunity (Cinema & Drafthouse).

How Jim and Ellen will use:

They will call the trade associations to obtain information about trends in the industry and about starting a movie theater. They will also investigate the franchise opportunity. Then they will consult reference works for sources of financing, insurance, and film distributors.

Movie Theatre Operation

Primary Associations

11495 • **National Association of Theatre Owners (NATO)**
4605 Lankershim Blvd., Ste. 340
North Hollywood, CA 91602
(818)506-1778 • Fax: (818)506-0269

Membership: Owners, operators, and executives of motion picture theaters. **Purpose:** Maintains a speakers' bureau; compiles statistics. **Publications:** *Encyclopedia of Exhibition* (annual) • *National Association of Theatre Owners—News and Views* (monthly) • Also publishes handbook and brochures.

Other Organizations of Interest

11496 • **American Film Marketing Association (AFMA)**
12424 Wilshire Blvd., Ste. 600
Los Angeles, CA 90025-1040
(310)447-1555 • Fax: (310)447-1666

Membership: Independent producers and distributors of feature length theatrical films; private and governmental organizations involved in selling film rights to domestic and foreign territories. **Purpose:** Contributes to negotiations with foreign producer associations; has developed standardized theatrical and video contracts in English, French, Italian, and Spanish. Established and maintains the International Arbitration Tribunal, a system through which prominent entertainment attorneys throughout the world assist members and consenting clients in reaching equitable and binding agreements. Facilitates the formulation of policies, standardized private and governmental contracts, and the exchange of information and experience among members. Deals with predominantly English language products, but handles a limited number of foreign films. Sponsors fundraising events. Future plans include establishment of a reference library, employment referral service, insurance and travel assistance programs, and a liaison among international markets and producers organizations. **Publications:** *Newsletter* (quarterly).

11497 • **Motion Picture Association of America (MPAA)**
1600 Eye St. NW
Washington, DC 20006
(202)293-1966 • Fax: (202)452-9823

Membership: Principal producers and distributors of motion pictures in the U.S. **Purpose:** To establish and maintain high moral and artistic standards in motion picture production by developing the educational as well as the entertainment value and general usefulness of the motion picture. Maintains Motion Picture Association Political Action Committee.

11498 • **Theatre Equipment Association (TEA)**
244 W. 49th St., Ste. 200
New York, NY 10019
(212)246-6460 • Fax: (212)265-6428

Membership: Firms (49) who sell theatrical equipment and supplies to motion picture theatres; manufacturers (61) of theatrical equipment and supplies. **Publications:** *Teaspout* (quarterly).

Franchises and Business Opportunities

11525 • **Cinema 'n' Drafthouse, Inc.**
PO Box 28467
Atlanta, GA 30358
(404)250-9536 • Fax: (404)250-9536

Operates art deco styled motion picture theatres designed to provide a lounge atmosphere. Theatres offer food and beverages, in addition to being multimedia facilities for seminars and teleconferencing. Franchisor provides technical and management training.

Note —
Excerpt: This page
Availability: Business libraries
Cost to purchase: $280 (two volumes)

Small Business Sourcebook, 8th ed., pp. 1261 – 1264, Movie Theater Operation.

The Sourcebook of Zip Code Demographics

Publisher:
CACI Marketing Systems
1100 N. Glebe Rd.
Arlington, VA 22201
800-292-CACI (2224)
703-841-2916
703-522-6376 fax

Type of information available:
Provides demographic information such as population, income, race, age, and purchase potential, from the national to the local level, arranged by zip code.

How to use it:
Determine the demographic characteristics of inhabitants of a certain geographic area.

Situation:

Larry and Charlene plan to start a landscaping business in the Bangor, Maine, area. They want to be sure that there are enough people in their trading area who fit the demographic profile they have established for their target customers.

What Larry and Charlene can find:

Income data on the suburbs near their planned location (Brewer, Hampden, Kenduskeag, Orrington).

How Larry and Charlene will use:

They will determine the disposable income of residents of the areas near their business, as well as the number of housing units versus owner-occupied homes.

Note —
Excerpt: Next page
Availability: Most major libraries
Cost to purchase: $395 (county), $495 (zip), $995 (CD-ROM)

MAINE — **SOCIAL PROFILE**

A 04438-04628

ZIP CODE #	POST OFFICE NAME	COUNTY FIPS CODE	POPULATION: Total	% Urban	% Rural	Place of Birth: % Native	Foreign Born: % Foreign Born	Foreign Born: % Immigrated 1980–1990	POPULATION 5+ YEARS: Total	Residence in 1985: % Same House	Different House: % Movers: Same County	Different House: % Migrants: Different County	Language Spoken at Home: % English Only	Speak Other Language: % Other Language	Speak Other Language: % Do Not Speak English Well	EDUCATIONAL ATTAINMENT: POPULATION 25+ YEARS: Total	% High School Graduate	% Bachelor's Degree	% Graduate/ Professional Degree
04438	FRANKFORT	027	1141	0.0	100.0	98.6	1.4	6.3	1058	59.6	22.2	17.9	97.5	2.5	11.5	743	78.9	13.1	4.2
04441	GREENVILLE	021	1911	0.0	100.0	95.4	4.6	8.0	1767	58.6	22.5	18.3	89.8	10.2	1.7	1322	75.2	14.1	4.5
04442	GREENVILLE JUNCTION	021	85	0.0	100.0	95.2	4.8	0.0	78	59.0	23.1	17.9	89.7	10.3	0.0	59	76.3	15.3	5.1
04443	GUILFORD	021	2832	0.0	100.0	98.7	1.3	21.6	2660	61.8	22.6	15.2	94.3	5.7	23.2	1858	70.5	7.9	2.0
04444	HAMPDEN	019	6752	58.8	41.2	97.6	2.4	14.5	6153	57.4	21.4	21.1	97.5	2.5	11.2	4244	86.1	25.6	9.3
04446	HAYNESVILLE	003	243	0.0	100.0	97.9	2.1	0.0	223	71.7	13.9	14.3	95.1	4.9	27.3	158	66.5	4.4	2.5
04448	HOWLAND	019	1628	0.0	100.0	96.5	3.5	3.5	1496	68.0	21.1	10.7	92.6	7.4	13.6	1077	68.1	5.4	1.3
04449	HUDSON	019	1048	0.0	100.0	98.2	1.8	0.0	962	62.9	25.4	11.6	95.7	4.3	24.4	651	70.4	12.4	3.4
04450	KENDUSKEAG	019	1234	0.0	100.0	98.7	1.3	0.0	1159	56.3	31.6	12.2	97.7	2.3	11.1	767	79.4	6.8	2.2
04451	KINGMAN	019	364	0.0	100.0	98.9	1.1	0.0	341	65.1	16.7	18.2	97.4	2.6	11.1	233	61.8	6.9	2.6
04453	LAGRANGE	019	707	0.0	100.0	98.2	1.8	7.7	650	61.8	21.7	16.3	97.1	2.9	5.3	437	78.7	12.8	4.1
04455	LEE	019	832	0.0	100.0	98.5	1.5	7.7	790	68.9	18.4	12.4	96.2	3.8	13.3				
04456	LEVANT	019	1627	0.0	100.0	99.0	1.0	31.3	1477	65.4	22.7								
04457	LINCOLN	019	4715	62.9	37.1	97.6	2.4	10.6											
04458	LINCOLN CENTER	019	1528																
04459	MATTAWAMKEAG																		

EMPLOYMENT PROFILE — **MAINE**

04438-04628 **B**

ZIP CODE #	POST OFFICE NAME	LABOR FORCE: Population 16+ Years: Total	% in Labor Force	Civilian Labor Force: Employed	Civilian Labor Force: % Unemployed	Females 16+ Years: Total	% in Labor Force	With Children <18: Total	With Children <18: % in Labor Force	EMPLOYMENT CHARACTERISTICS: By Select Industry (%): Manufacturing	Trade	Services	Public Admin.	By Select Occupation (%): Manager/ Professional	Technical/ Sales/ Admin.	Service	Operator/ Laborer	JOURNEY TO WORK: Means of Transportation (%): Drive Alone	Car-pool	Public	Average Travel Time
04438	FRANKFORT	864	62.4	477	11.3	448	52.5	159	61.0	23.8	21.9	30.3	3.8	19.6	22.3	15.8	23.8	80.7	15.1	0.4	24.3
04441	GREENVILLE	1478	63.4	790	15.7	781	56.7	223	83.4	13.5	23.3	36.2	3.5	24.4	21.9	19.0	14.3	78.6	11.3	0.0	13.2
04442	GREENVILLE JUNCTION	66	63.6	35	16.7	35	57.1	11	81.8	13.2	21.1	36.8	2.6	25.7	20.0	17.1	14.3	78.8	12.1	0.0	12.9
04443	GUILFORD	2180	61.0	1230	7.3	1117	54.2	360	70.0	45.0	15.8	19.6	2.0	13.9	20.4	11.2	35.3	70.7	17.7	0.4	15.4
04444	HAMPDEN	4981	67.7	3188	5.0	2695	63.0	1000	73.5	6.2	26.5	39.4	4.7	31.9	32.7	13.0	9.8	85.7	10.5	0.3	18.2
04446	HAYNESVILLE	184	45.1	69	16.9	90	30.0	35	34.3	36.2	11.6	24.6	1.4	5.9	11.8	11.8	51.5	70.1	25.4	0.0	29.8
04448	HOWLAND	1287	56.0	640	11.0	676	43.9	205	50.2	24.7	21.8	26.1	4.1	11.7	21.6	18.2	29.6	74.3	18.7	0.8	24.3
04449	HUDSON	768	63.5	443	7.9	383	52.5	152	62.5	19.9	16.7	31.6	3.6	22.1	20.5	11.3	17.8	75.5	19.6	0.7	31.0
04450	KENDUSKEAG	917	66.5	549	9.3	464	54.5	187	54.5	14.2	26.6	28.2	4.9	17.1	28.4	12.0	15.3	85.0	13.4	0.0	25.1
04451	KINGMAN	279	48.4	111	17.2	137	34.3	50	42.0	26.4	13.6	23.6	1.8	9.9	17.1	13.5	35.1	73.3	21.9	0.0	31.1
04453	LAGRANGE	520	66.0	315	8.2	261	54.4	101	56.4	22.9	17.1	29.2	3.5	15.2	21.5	13.0	30.1	79.5	18.4	0.0	25.6
04455	LEE	639	56.3	313	13.1	318	47.2	115	49.6	29.9	14.0	33.8	1.3	20.8	18.8	12.5	23.6	78.8	17.1	0.7	22.7
04456	LEVANT	1193	66.6	713	9.7	607	54.7	264	73.1	15.3	25.2	32.5	2.5	16.5	22.9	17.5	17.8	86.0	11.8	0.0	23.7
04457	LINCOLN	3584	52.5	1752	6.9	1887	37.4	651	51.0	31.2	19.5	28.6	3.6	20.4	22.5	14.3	23.9	81.0	13.4	0.0	14.5
		1134	57.3	586	9.7	579	41.6	229	51.1	32.0	21.9	24.6	4.3	15.4	21.5	16.9	29.0	81.8	11.8	0.2	15.4
			51.5	306	10.3	335	35.5	104	51.9	44.1	16.3	20.6	3.9	10.1	16.7	15.0	37.3	74.4	16.2	1.7	20.8
						686	45.3	300	52.0	38.2	26.4	17.0	1.2	8.6	18.4	17.9	37.3	84.8	11.0	0.3	17.3
										28.2	19.8	35.3	2.3	14.0	29.6	14.3	21.6	89.1	8.6	0.4	17.5
													3.0	18.7	21.4	15.7	25.1	74.9	13.8	0.2	11.4
																7.5	30.9	82.5	11.5	0.0	21.1
																					22.8

MAINE — **DETAILED HOUSING PROFILE**

C 04438-04628

ZIP CODE #	POST OFFICE NAME	HOUSING UNITS: Total	Condominium: % of Total	Condominium: % Occupied	Year Structure Built (%): 1985–March 1990	1980–1984	1970–1979	1960–1969	1959 or Earlier	% Lacking Plumbing Facilities	OCCUPIED HOUSING UNITS: Total	% Without Telephone	Vehicles Available (%): None	1	2	3+	MORTGAGE STATUS: SPECIFIED OWNER-OCCUPIED UNITS: With Mortgage: Total	Average Value	Average Monthly Owner Cost	No Mortgage: Total	Average Value	Average Monthly Owner Cost
04438	FRANKFORT	436	0.2	100.0	14.2	7.1	20.9	10.3	47.5	8.3	354	4.8	6.5	30.0	43.1	20.4	75	80455	576	77	66973	206
04441	GREENVILLE	1577	4.4	13.0	16.3	6.2	22.1	9.2	46.2	8.5	795	3.7	10.0	40.4	39.0	10.6	189	75307	556	211	55964	188
04442	GREENVILLE JUNCTION	68	4.3	0.0	16.2	5.9	22.1	8.8	47.1	5.8	36	2.9	11.4	40.0	40.0	8.6	8	126164	591	9	114937	198
04443	GUILFORD	1402	0.2	100.0	11.8	7.9	24.2	10.1	46.0	11.7	940	5.9	8.0	38.4	39.3	14.3	184	57809	487	218	48824	167
04444	HAMPDEN	2633	0.0	0.0	15.3	10.3	17.8	13.7	42.9	0.8	2472	2.5	3.9	28.5	46.5	21.1	990	106302	807	470	84149	252
04446	HAYNESVILLE	138	0.0	0.0	12.3	10.9	31.2	9.4	36.2	11.6	61	9.7	6.5	33.9	33.9	25.8	7	3247	493	16	6246	163
04448	HOWLAND	669	0.0	0.0	9.8	7.3	26.2	12.2	44.5	3.3	560	3.5	8.0	30.8	44.1	17.1	128	61860	533	164	50832	192
04449	HUDSON	594	0.0	0.0	16.3	14.3	32.8	11.1	25.4	4.4	420	7.8	5.5	25.5	48.1	21.0	79	68339	520	55	44520	
04450	KENDUSKEAG	453	0.0	0.0	18.5	6.6	33.3	14.1	27.5	2.9	436	8.3	3.9	28.8	48.5	18.8	122	66208	564			
04451	KINGMAN	176	0.0	0.0	15.3	6.8	27.7	13.6	36.7	24.4	109	8.2	5.5	36.4	39.1	19.1	13	82300				
04453	LAGRANGE	313	0.0	0.0	19.4	10.2	21.7	11.5	37.3	6.1	275	8.4	3.6	29.5	51.3							
04455	LEE	365	0.0	0.0	14.4	11.1	20.6	14.9	39.0	16.8	294	5.7										
04456	LEVANT	570	0.0	0.0	18.0	15.4	34.0	7.0	25.6	2.1	551											
04457	LINCOLN	2141	0.0	0.0	12.2	10.6	21.8	13.9	41.6													
04458	LINCOLN CENTER	660	0.0	0.0	11.0	11.5	27.2															
04459	MATTAWAMKEAG	345	0.0	0.0																		
04460	MEDWAY	674	0.0																			
04461	MILFORD																					
04462	MILLINOCKET																					
04463	MILO																					

MAINE

DETAILED INCOME PROFILE — 04438-04628 **D**

ZIP CODE #	POST OFFICE NAME	HOUSEHOLD INCOME: Household Income Base	Distribution (%): Less than $15,000	$15,000 to $24,999	$25,000 to $49,999	$50,000 to $99,999	$100,000 to $149,999	$150,000 or More	By Quartile: Q1 (25%)	Median Q2 (50%)	Q3 (75%)	AVERAGE FAMILY INCOME: All Families: Family Income Base	Average	By Number of Workers in Family: 1	2	3+	Per Capita Income	POVERTY STATUS: Persons: Poverty Status Determined: Total	% Below Poverty	Households: % Below Poverty: Total HHs	Family HHs	Non-family HHs
04438	FRANKFORT	351	29.9	20.2	36.5	12.8	0.6	0.0	12730	24922	38813	272	30147	28213	31438	34748	10586	1134	15.8	15.8	12.5	27.2
04441	GREENVILLE	800	38.1	19.3	34.4	7.1	1.1	0.0	10593	20988	35303	521	29287	22484	34141	42881	10533	1859	12.5	13.9	10.0	21.1
04442	GREENVILLE JUNCTION	34	41.2	17.6	35.3	5.9	0.0	0.0	10417	20000	34375	24	42052	684	1022	17578	12427	82	12.2	11.8	8.7	18.2
04443	GUILFORD	949	34.0	23.0	34.6	7.8	0.3	0.3	11100	21505	33797	700	28370	24669	32297	49325	9672	2827	17.2	17.6	13.2	30.1
04444	HAMPDEN	2413	16.0	18.1	41.7	20.8	2.2	1.1	21044	32303	49367	1836	43955	40532	46770	52712	14050	6584	6.6	8.0	3.9	21.3
04446	HAYNESVILLE	61	34.4	23.0	36.1	6.6	0.0	0.0	9583	22250	33438	49	21713	3142	8992	14455	8649	241	17.0	22.6	16.0	50.0
04448	HOWLAND	566	35.2	17.8	32.5	13.3	0.9	0.4	10625	23910	37277	430	31661	24703	36969	53640	10447	1584	15.7	14.3	13.3	17.4
04449	HUDSON	424	29.7	18.9	40.6	9.2	0.9	0.7	12500	25577	38235	335	32427	20026	38012	41015	9875	1036	14.1	17.2	11.6	38.6
04450	KENDUSKEAG	429	26.8	21.0	38.5	12.6	1.2	0.0	14031	25880	40344	333	31814	22132	36266	47484	10250	1208	14.2	15.9	12.7	27.1
04451	KINGMAN	109	40.4	25.7	24.8	8.3	0.9	0.0	9236	18036	29875	90	23699	32977	35407	27730	8826	362	24.9	25.5	20.2	47.6
04453	LAGRANGE	270	24.1	20.0	43.7	10.0	0.7	1.5	15694	26667	40268	214	29622	19999	43739	53623	11389	699	12.2	11.4	9.3	19.6
04455	LEE	305	26.6	21.0	37.4	14.1	0.0	1.0	14340	26103	37991	251	34004	27490	43937	55142	10939	846	11.8	9.8	8.7	14.8
04456	LEVANT	549	20.9	23.3	40.1	15.7	0.0	0.0	16545	27461	40099	449	31605	24650	34617	48480	10260	1627	8.5	8.6	6.7	17.0
	LINCOLN	1784	34.9	18.9	33.4	12.8	0.0	0.0	12229	22982	39368	1342	29290	26060	38516	43322	10478	4619	17.4	16.9	13.6	27.2
		584	32.0	17.1	36.1	14.0	0.5	0.2	12344	25568	41042	463	31372	26143	41417	56794	10739	1511	16.7	17.6	13.4	33.1
		226	35.0	19.0	34.4	11.7	0.0	0.0	11116	23088	40074	250	30849	31983	36016	47367	10442	825	12.2	11.1	6.8	25.0
					42.2	18.3	0.8	0.2	15862	32039	46316	533	35572	28620	40378	54289	10932	1908	13.0	14.3	10.7	34.7
							0.0	0.0	15750	26968	41042	457	33010	23986	36772	41617	10829	1730	9.4	8.7	6.3	14.8
									16087	32344	48271	1957	40323	42811	46077	51256	14321	6875	9.5	11.1	7.9	19.6
											36143	835	29231	23034	32417	41921	9365	3042	16.6	17.1	10.9	35.9
														7035	62712	13116	11869	267	19.1	14.8	13.2	18.8
																53956	9709	419	19.8	21.5	19.0	
																		9159	16.1	17.0	10.1	
																				20.8	17.9	

The Sourcebook of ZIP Code Demographics, Census Edition, 1992, pp. 131–A–131–D, Maine: Social, Employment, Housing, and Income Profiles. Copyright © 1992, CACI Marketing Systems

Thomas Register of American Manufacturers

Publisher:
Thomas Publishing Co.
Five Penn Plaza
New York, NY 10001
212-695-0500
212-290-7206 fax
http://thomasregister.com

Type of information available:
Lists companies and the products that they produce. Published annually in February, information is organized by both product type and company name.

How to use it:
Identify potential customers, competitors, or suppliers.

Situation:

Blake and Nathaniel are owner/operators of a mall amusement center/video arcade. They are adding a small snack bar to the business and need to find a supplier of popcorn poppers and soda fountains.

What Blake and Nathaniel can find:

Potential suppliers of popcorn machines and soda fountains, listed by state and city.

How Blake and Nathaniel will use:

They will call potential suppliers in their area to determine the best prices and credit terms they can get when purchasing or leasing their equipment.

Note —
Excerpt: Next page
Availability: Most libraries
Cost to purchase: $240 (plus $15.80 shipping)

★POPCORN MACHINES **THOMAS REGISTER.1995**

★POPCORN MACHINES

(see also Poppers: Corn)

OH: CINCINNATI
GOLD MEDAL PRODUCTS CO. 2001 Dalton Ave., Dept. TR, Ste. 5 (ZIP 45214) (513-381-1313).... 10M+

POPPERS: CORN

IL: CHICAGO
Cretors, C., & Co. 3243-T N. California Ave. (Production Automatic Commercial Poppers & Caramel Corn Equipment)....5M+
Krispy Kist Korn Machine Co. 120-T S. Halsted St..... 1M+
MO: BISMARCK
Echols, S.T. Div., DCR Ltd. 1001-T Echols St.....1M+
MO: ST. LOUIS
Star Mfg. Co. P.O. Box 8492 (Commercial)..... NR
NY: BROOKLYN
Carts Mobile Food Equipment Corp. 113 8th St.....NR
OH: CINCINNATI
GOLD MEDAL PRODUCTS CO. 2001 Dalton Ave., Dept. TR, Ste. 5 (ZIP 45214) (Electric & Gas Popcorn Machines) (513-381-1313).....10M+
TX: FORT WORTH
CANTRELL INTERNATIONAL 3245 May St., Dept. T (ZIP 76110-0216) (Snack Food, Vegetable Oil & Peanut Processing Equipment) (817-923-7382).....NR

CORNPOPPERS
Complete popping and coating systems
CANTRELL INTERNATIONAL 1-800-363-6862

Cantrell International, Manley Div. P.O. Box 11216 Dept. T..... 1M+
VA: GLEN ALLEN
Proctor-Silex, Inc. 4421-T Waterfront Dr. (Air)..... 1M+
WI: EAU CLAIRE
National Presto Industries, Inc. 3925-T Hastings Way (Hot Air).....25M+
WI: KEWAUNEE
Leyse Aluminum Co. Norman St., Dept. TR..... 1M+
WI: TWO RIVERS
Metal Ware Corp. 1700-T Monroe St.....5M+
WI: WEST BEND
West Bend Co., The 400 W. Washington (Hot Air, Hot Oil).....50M+
CANADA: PQ, POINTE CLAIRE
Toastess Inc. 815-T Tecumseh St..... NR

GA: MARIETTA
SOUTHERN PORCELAIN, INC. 1000 E
PT (ZIP 30060) (Infrared Burner T
Ceramic Pour Cups. Long Run St
Extrusions For Resistor Cores &
Housings) (404-428-8646).....
GA: NORCROSS
Alliancewall Corp. P.O. Box 920
IL: BELLEVILLE
Peerless-Premier Appli
ROESCH, INC. P.O. D
Burners, Barbecue
Call Toll Free 800
(See Our Full-Pag
vices)
IL: CHICAGO
WILKENS-AN
60651) (M
Supplies &
315-459
(See Ou
Suppli
IN: NAPP
VITCO

Thomas Register of American Manufacturers, 1995 ed., POP/24806, Popcorn Machines.

The 1996 TradeShows & Exhibits Schedule

Publisher:
Bill Communications
P.O. Box 888
Vineland, NJ 08360
800-266-4712
609-691-5800
609-691-3371 fax

Type of information available:
Information about trade shows and exhibitions throughout the country. Listings are indexed by industrial/professional classification as well as geographically, chronologically, and alphabetically by event name. They include such information as contact person, phone and fax numbers, number and type of exhibits, dates, and number and type of attendees.

How to use it:
Locate trade shows or exhibitions with participants from your market area or specialty, enabling you to meet potential suppliers, customers, and others in similar businesses.

Situation:

Renae is an interior decorator in suburban New Jersey who needs to know dates and locations of home furnishing and interior design trade shows in New York and around the country.

What Renae can find:

Under the heading "House Furnishings and Design," there is a list of trade shows directly related to interior design throughout the world, with several in New York and other cities she can get to easily.

How Renae will use:

She will make time in her schedule to attend several of the local trade shows, as well as some in other states, gathering ideas and products to use in her decorating business. Eventually, she may even add the cost of a booth to her budget and exhibit her services at a local show that draws clients from her market area.

Note —
Excerpt: Next page
Availability: Many libraries
Cost to purchase: $125 prepaid, $195 invoiced (plus $12.50 shipping)

HOUSE FURNISHINGS & DESIGN

ACCENT ON DESIGN

CARLA EDSON, EXH MGR
GEORGE LITTLE MGMT
10 BANK ST, STE 1200
WHITE PLAINS, NY 10606-1954
PHONE: (914) 421-3223 **FAX:** (914) 948-6180
SCOPE: INTERNATIONAL **FREQ:** SEMI-ANNUAL
EXHIBITS: 370 BOOTHS **PRE/POST MTG:** NO
EXHIBIT NOTES: A JURIED DIVISION OF THE NY INTL GIFT FAIR HIGHLIGHTING THE LATEST & MOST INNOVATIVE GIFT LINES SUCH AS DECORATIVE ACCESSORIES, HOUSEWARES, HOME FURNISHINGS, STATIONERY, TABLETOP, GOURMET ITEMS AND GENERAL GIFT MERCHANDISE, SELECTED ON THE BASIS OF CREATIVITY, ORIGINALITY & GOOD CONTEMPORARY DESIGN.
SHOW DATES, LOCATIONS & ATTENDANCE:
96 JAN 21 - 25 NEW YORK NY
JACOB JAVITS CONV CENTER 45,000
96 AUG 11 - 15 NEW YORK NY
JACOB JAVITS CONV CENTER 45,000

ACCENT ON DESIGN WEST

LESLIE NATHAN-STREET, DIV MGR
GEORGE LITTLE MGMT
10 BANK ST, STE 1200
WHITE PLAINS, NY 10606-1954
PHONE: (914) 421-3223 **FAX:** (914) 948-6180
SCOPE: REGIONAL **FREQ:** SEMI-ANNUAL
EXHIBITS: 150 BOOTHS
EXHIBIT NOTES: A JURIED EVENT HIGHLIGHTING CONTEMPORARY, INNOVATIVE ITEMS--A WIDE ARRAY OF DECORATIVE ACCESSORIES, LIGHTING & HOME FURNISHINGS, HOUSEWARES, STATIONERY, TABLETOP, GOURMET AND GENERAL GIFT MERCHANDISE--ALL SELECTED ON THE BASIS OF CREATIVITY, ORIGINALITY AND GOOD DESIGN. DIVISION OF SAN FRANCISCO INTL GIFT FAIR.
SHOW DATES, LOCATIONS & ATTENDANCE:
96 FEB 3 - 7 SAN FRANCISCO CA
MOSCONE CONV CENTER 30,000
96 JUL 27 - 31 SAN FRANCISCO CA
MOSCONE CONV CENTER 30,000

AMER SOC INTERIOR DESIGNERS NATL CONF & INTL EXPO OF DESIGN SOURCES

JAYNE L KATZ, DIR SPEC PROJ
608 MASSACHUSSETTS AVE,NE
WASHINGTON, DC 20002
PHONE: (202) 675-2365 **FAX:** (202) 546-3240
SCOPE: NATIONAL **FREQ:** ANNUAL
EXHIBITS: 250 BOOTHS **PRE/POST MTG:** NO
EXHIBIT NOTES: EXHIBITS CONSIST OF INTERIOR DESIGN MERCHANDISE INCLUDING WALL COVERINGS, LAMINATES, LIGHTING FIXTURES, PLUMBING FIXTURES, CARPETS, FURNITURE, OFFICE SYSTEMS, FABRICS, AND COMPUTER SOFTWARE.
ATTENDEES: COMMERCIAL & RESIDENTIAL DESIGNERS, SPECIFIERS, AND INTERIOR DESIGN STUDENTS.
SHOW DATES, LOCATIONS & ATTENDANCE:
96 JUL 29 - AUG 4 BALTIMORE MD
HYATT REGENCY BALTIMORE 3,000

FALL DECOR

TERI FLOTRON, SHOW PUBLCTY
1050 N LINDBERGH BLVD
ST LOUIS, MO 63132-2994
PHONE: (314) 991-3470 **FAX:** (314) 991-5039
SCOPE: INTERNATIONAL **FREQ:** ANNUAL
EXHIBITS: 609 BOOTHS **PRE/POST MTG:** NO
EXHIBIT NOTES: MAJOR DISPLAYS OF PAINTS, WALLCOVERINGS, WINDOW TREATMENTS AND FLOORING (CARPETING) ALONG WITH TOOLS, LADDERS, BRUSHES & ROLLERS, SUNDRIES AND MANY SERVICES CONNECTED WITH THE RETAIL DECORATING PRODUCTS OUTLETS, COMPUTER SOFTWARE, TRUCK LEASING, OTHER BUSINESS SERVICES.
ATTENDEES: INDEPENDENT RETAILERS, MASS MERCHANDISERS, CHAIN STORES, INTERIOR DESIGNERS, ARCHITECTS, SPECIALTY STORES & IMPORTERS, AS WELL AS DISTRIBUTORS & MANUFACTURER REPS.
SHOW DATES, LOCATIONS & ATTENDANCE:
96 NOV 1 - 3 MINNEAPOLIS MN CONV CENTER 7,500
97 OCT 24 - 26 ST LOUIS MO
CERVANTES CONV EXH CENTER 7,500

INTERIORS DECOR SHOWCASE

TERI FLOTRON, SHOW PUBLCTY
1050 N LINDBERGH BLVD
ST LOUIS, MO 63132-2994
PHONE: (314) 991-3470 **FAX:** (314) 991-5039
SCOPE: NATIONAL **FREQ:** ANNUAL
EXHIBITS: 200 BOOTHS **PRE/POST MTG:** NO
EXHIBIT NOTES: EXHIBITS CONSIST OF PAINTS, WALLCOVERINGS, WINDOW TREATMENT & FLOORING (CARPETING) ALONG WITH TOOLS, LADDERS, BRUSHES & ROLLERS, SUNDRIES, AND MANY SERVICES RELATED TO THE RETAIL DECORATING PRODUCTS OUTLETS, COMPUTER SOFTWARE, LABELING SERVICES, COLOR COMPUTERS, INSURANCE, ETC.
ATTENDEES: INDEPENDENT RETAILERS, DISTRIBUTORS, INTERIOR DESIGNERS, HOME CENTERS, DEPT. STORES, DISCOUNT STORES, WHOLESALERS, OWNERS, BUYERS AND SALES PEOPLE.
SHOW DATES, LOCATIONS & ATTENDANCE:
96 FEB 24 - 26 TORONTO ON CONGRESS CENTRE 6,000

MILAN INTL FURNISHING ACCESSORIES EXPO

MANLIO ARMELLINI, EXH MGR
COSMIT EXHIBITIONS
CORSO MAGENTA 96
MILAN, ITALY 20123
PHONE: 39-2-485921 **FAX:** 39-2-4813580
SCOPE: FOREIGN **FREQ:** ANNUAL
EXHIBITS: 20,000 SQ METERS
SHOW DATES, LOCATIONS & ATTENDANCE:
96 APR 18 - 22 MILAN FAIRGROUNDS 147,500

MILAN INTL FURNITURE EXH (SALONE DEL MOBILE)

MANLIO ARMELLINI, EXH MGR
COSMIT EXHIBITIONS
CORSO MAGENTA 96
MILAN, ITALY 20123
PHONE: 39-2-485921 **FAX:** 39-2-4813580
SCOPE: FOREIGN **FREQ:** ANNUAL
EXHIBITS: 170,000 SQ METERS
EXHIBIT NOTES: INTL EXHIBITION OF FURNITURE FOR THE BEDROOM, DINING ROOM, LIVING ROOM & BATH-ROOM, HALL, GARDEN & OCCASIONAL FURNITURE, AND ACCESSORIES.
SHOW DATES, LOCATIONS & ATTENDANCE:
96 APR 18 - 22 MILAN FAIRGROUNDS 147,000

NATL AREA RUG MARKET ATLANTA

JOSEPH BOWERS, SHOW MGR
AMC TRADE SHOWS
240 PEACHTREE ST NW,STE 2200
ATLANTA, GA 30303
PHONE: (404) 220-2209 **FAX:** (404) 220-2442
SCOPE: NATIONAL **FREQ:** ANNUAL
EXHIBITS: 300 BOOTHS
EXHIBIT NOTES: THE LARGEST AREA RUG SHOW IN THE U.S., FEATURING EVERY IMPORTANT MANUFACTURER AND IMPORTER OF AREA RUGS IN THE U.S. DISPLAY INCLUDES MACHINE MADE AND HAND MADE RUGS FROM AROUND THE WORLD.
SHOW DATES, LOCATIONS & ATTENDANCE:
96 JUN 27 - 30 ATLANTA GA MARKET CENTER 8,000

VALENCIA INTL TEXTILES HOME DECORATION EXH (TEXTILHOGAR)

EXHIBIT MANAGER
FERIA MUESTRARIO INTL VALENCIA
PO BOX 476
VALENCIA, SPAIN 46080
PHONE: 34-96-3861100 **FAX:** 34-96-3636111
SCOPE: FOREIGN **FREQ:** ANNUAL
EXHIBITS: 25,227 SQ METERS
EXHIBIT NOTES: EXHIBITION OF RUGS, CARPETS, MATS, UPHOLSTERY, DECORATIVE TEXTILES, CURTAINS, BLANKETS, TABLES, BEDS, BATH LINEN, FIBERS, YARNS, DYES, PRINTING, ACCESSORIES AND OTHER ITEMS FROM ALLIED INDUSTRIES.
SHOW DATES, LOCATIONS & ATTENDANCE:
96 JAN 16 - 19 VALENCIA PALACIO FERIAL 14,000

The 1996 TradeShows & Exhibits Schedule, ©1996 Bill Communications, pp. 247 – 252
House Furnishings & Design

Ulrich's International Periodicals Directory

Publisher:
R. R. Bowker
121 Chanlon Rd.
New Providence, NJ 07974
800-521-8110
908-771-7725
http:www.reedref.com

Type of information available:
Magazines and journals listed alphabetically within subject category. The data include items such as subscription rates, publisher address, description of the periodical, and the ISSN (International Standard Serial Number). This directory is updated annually in November.

How to use it:
Find periodicals (domestic and international) that cover the area of your business.

Situation:

Ken and Caroline have developed a specialty software application. They are looking for trade magazines in which to advertise the software and/or offer their consulting services.

What Ken and Caroline can find:

Listings of publications whose subject matter involves computer software.

How Ken and Caroline will use:

They will go to the library and look over a wide variety of publications, to determine which ones might be appropriate ones in which to advertise. This may also yield marketing ideas, such as names of companies that could use the software application they have developed.

Note —
Excerpt: Next page
Availability: Many libraries
Cost to purchase: $425; CD-ROM, $525

001.642 US ISSN 0895-2108
C A S E OUTLOOK; the journal of software design automation. 1987. 6/yr. $395 (foreign $495). C A S E Consulting Group, Inc., 11830 Kerr Pkwy., Ste. 315, Lake Oswego, OR 97035.
TEL 503-245-6880; 800-775-6880.
FAX 503-245-6935. Ed. Gene Forte. bk.rev.; cum.index. circ. 1,000. (back issues avail.)
—BLDSC (3058.137500). CCC.
Description: Covers developments in the field of computer-aided software engineering (CASE). Provides current source of information on technology, products, events, and trends essential to those responsible for the acquisition and application of CASE within their organizations.

001.642 US ISSN 0730-3157
QA76.6
C O M P S A C/I E E E COMPUTER SOCIETY'S INTERNATIONAL COMPUTER SOFTWARE & APPLICATIONS CONFERENCE. PROCEEDINGS. 1977. a. price varies. (Institute of Electrical and Electronics Engineers, Inc.) I E E E Computer Society Press, 10662 Los Vaqueros Circle, Los Alamitos, CA 90720-1264. TEL 714-821-8380.
FAX 714-821-4641. **Indexed:** Comput.Lit.Ind.
Document type: proceedings.
—BLDSC (3368.300000); UMI. CCC.
Description: Provides papers primarily dealing with software engineering and developmental themes, along with major applications areas.

001.642 US ISSN 1050-3048
C PLUS PLUS JOURNAL. 1990. q. $32 (foreign $52). 2 Haven Ave., Port Washington, NY 11050.
TEL 516-767-7107. FAX 516-944-3050. Ed. Livleen Singh. adv.; bk.rev.

001.642 340 US
COMPUTER SOFTWARE PROTECTION LAW. (In 2 vols.) a. $550 includes Supplement. B N A Books (Subsidiary of: The Bureau of National Affairs, Inc.), 1250 23rd St., N.W., Washington, DC 20037.
TEL 202-833-7470; 800-372-1033.
FAX 202-833-7490. (Subscr. to: BNA Books Distribution Center, 30 Raritan Center Pkwy., Box 7816, Edison, NJ 08818-7816. TEL 908-225-1900. FAX 908-417-0482) (looseleaf format)
Description: Provides analysis of law of copyright, trade secret, and patent protection as it applies to computer programs and databases.

005.3 US ISSN 0893-0570
ADA STRATEGIES; the monthly source of Ada competitive strategies and trends and issues. 1987. m. $337 to institutions (overseas $407); academic institutions $100 (overseas $170). (Software Strategies & Tactics, Inc.) S S T, Inc., Box 713, Harpers Ferry, WV 25425. TEL 304-725-6542.
FAX 304-725-6543. Ed. Ralph Crafts. **Indexed:** Comput.Lit.Ind. **Document type:** trade publication.
Description: Information on Ada training programs, strategies, and related software and hardware, for government contractors, government procurement offices and agencies, insurance and financial institutions, vendors, and manufacturers worldwide.

001.642 US
ADVANCES IN SOFTWARE ENGINEERING. 1985. a. $68.50 to institutions. J A I Press Inc., 55 Old Post Rd., No. 2, Box 1678, Greenwich, CT 06836-1678. TEL 203-661-7602. Ed. Stephen S. Yau.
Refereed Serial

001.642 US ISSN 1044-7997
QA76.75
ADVANCES IN SOFTWARE SCIENCE AND TECHNOLOGY. 1989. irreg., vol.4, 1993. (Japanese Society for Software Science and Technology, JA) Academic Press, Inc., 525 B St., Ste. 1900, San Diego, CA 92101-4495. TEL 619-231-6616.
FAX 619-699-6715. (Subscr. to: Order Dept., 6277 Sea Harbor Dr., 4th Fl., Orlando, FL 32887. TEL 800-321-5068) (back issues avail.)
—BLDSC (0711.407000); Faxon.
Refereed Serial

001.642 US
APPLICATIONS SOFTWARE REPORTS. 1971. base vol. (plus m. updates). $670. Faulkner Information Services, Inc., 114 Cooper Center, 7905 Browning Rd., Pennsauken, NJ 08109-4319.
TEL 609-662-2070. FAX 609-662-3380. Ed. Betsy Yokum. (looseleaf format)
Formerly: Auerbach Applications Software Reports; Supersedes in part: Auerbach Software Reports (ISSN 0004-7775)
Description: Accounting, human resource management, project management, word processing, decision support - EIS, and manufacturing software for mainframe, mini, and micro computers.

ULRICH'S INTERNATIONAL PERIODICALS DIRECTORY 1994-95

Ulrich's International Periodicals Directory, 1994–1995 ed., Vol. 1, pp. 1827 – 28.

Wall Street Journal Index

Publisher:
UMI Co.
P.O. Box 1346
Ann Arbor, MI 48106
800-521-0600
800-864-0019 fax

Online

Type of information available:
Monthly digests of articles appearing in the *Wall Street Journal.* For a more definitive listing, this resource is also available online through many colleges and universities. We have used the on-line format for this example.

How to use it:
Find *Wall Street Journal* articles relating to your industry.

Situation:

Peter and Julie are starting a microbrewing business and want to know what the *Wall Street Journal* recently published about microbrewing.

What Peter and Julie can find:

Searching for "Beer" and "Breweries," they may find recent articles on the topic. They can also check the index for customer trends in pubs, entrepreneur biographies, potential competitors, and other related topics by searching key words.

How Peter and Julie will use:

They will learn more about the brewery industry and monitor trends on a national level.

Note —
Excerpt: Next page
Availability: University and business libraries
Cost to purchase: Transactional account, $25 per month (minimum), Internet or local dial-in; full-text CD-ROM, $2,730; entire subscription, $5,800 per year

Access No: 03758195 ProQuest - Newspaper Abstracts
Title: Pete's Brewing files for offer
Source: The Wall Street Journal [WSJ] ISSN: 0099-9660
Date: Oct 31, 1995 Sec: B p: 10 col: 5
Type: News Length: Short
Companies: Petes Brewing Co
Subjects: Going public; Stock offerings; Breweries; Beer

Abstract: Pete's Brewing Co, the brewer of Pete's Wicked beers, said it filed a registration statement with the SEC for a public offering of 3 million shares of its common stock at an estimated price of $14 to $16 a share.

Access No: 03655480 ProQuest - Newspaper Abstracts
Title: Beverages: When these drinkers crack open a cold one, it can cost $75
Authors: Ortega, Bob
Source: The Wall Street Journal [WSJ] ISSN: 0099-9660
Date: Aug 18, 1995 Sec: B p: 1 col: 3
Type: News Length: Long Illus: Illustration
Subjects: Beer; Beverage industry; Consumer behavior

Abstract: Some drinkers who several years ago abandoned Coors and Budweiser for microbrewery lagers and ales are increasingly willing to spring for something even rarer-luxury beers. A Belgian import called Duvel sells for $75 for a three liter bottle-a price which amazes even the brewers.

Access No: 03429664 ProQuest - Newspaper Abstracts
Title: Microbrewery toasts new library with tale of beer-drinking dogs
Authors: Charlier, Marj
Source: The Wall Street Journal [WSJ] ISSN: 0099-9660
Date: Mar 20, 1995 Sec: B p: 1 col: 1
Type: Feature Length: Medium
Companies: Wynkoop Brewing Co
Names: Thompson, Hunter S; Ginsberg, Allen
Subjects: Breweries; Labeling; Beer

Abstract: To commemorate the opening of Denver's new $64 million public library, Wynkoop Brewing Co will put out a special brew with special labels that feature short stories and essays by such writers as Hunters S. Thompson and Allen Ginsburg. Thompson's narrative tells of his two dogs, who occasionally sip beer and poke each other laughing while reading a copy of 'Lassie' he bought for them.

GENERAL RESOURCES

Here are organizations that can assist you with the development of your business plan. Many of their services are free and can provide invaluable advice and information on recruiting and hiring, staffing, organization, motivation, compensation, training, finance, and other factors related to business planning.

- ❑ Small Business Development Centers (SBDC)
- ❑ State Development Agencies
- ❑ Service Corps. of Retired Executives (SCORE)
- ❑ National SBDC Research Network
- ❑ Chambers of Commerce

Small Business Development Centers (SBDC)

A Small Business Development Center counsels, conducts research, and trains business people in a wide variety of business topics and provides comprehensive information services and access to experts in many fields. SBDCs develop and maintain partnerships among community organizations and local, state, and federal agencies, providing a focal point for broad networks of public and private resources at the community level. SBDC partnership programs and activities serving small businesses have contributed significantly to economic growth in each state.

Following is a list of SBDCs for each state plus the District of Columbia, Puerto Rico, and the Virgin Islands.

State	Headquarters	Phone
Alabama	Alabama SBDC Consortium Medical Towers Building 1717 11th Ave., Suite 419 Birmingham, AL 35297-4410	205- 934-7260
Alaska	Alaska SBDC University of Alaska, Anchorage 430 W. 7th Ave., Suite 110 Anchorage, AK 99501	907- 274-7232
Arizona	Arizona SBDC Network 2411 W. 14th St., Suite 132 Tempe, AZ 85281	602- 731-8720
Arkansas	Arkansas SBDC University of Arkansas at Little Rock 100 South Main, Suite 401 Little Rock, AR 72201	501- 324-9043
California	California SBDC Program Department of Commerce 801 K St., Suite 1700 Sacramento, CA 95814	916- 324-5068
Colorado	Colorado SBDC Colorado Office of Business Development 1625 Broadway, Suite 1710 Denver, CO 80202	303- 892-3809
Connecticut	Connecticut SBDC University of Connecticut 2 Bourn Place, U-94 Storrs, CT 06269-5094	203- 486-4135
Delaware	Delaware SBDC University of Delaware Purnell Hall, Suite 005 Newark, DE 19716-2711	302- 831-2747
District of Columbia	District of Columbia SBDC Howard University 6th and Fairmont St., NW, Room 128 Washington, DC 20059	202- 806-1550

State	State Center Address	Phone
Florida	Florida SBDC Network University of West Florida 19 West Garden St,, Suite 300 Pensacola, FL 32501	904- 444-2060
Georgia	Georgia SBDC University of Georgia Chicopee Complex, 1180 East Broad St. Athens, GA 30602-5412	706- 542-5760
Hawaii	Hawaii SBDC Network University of Hawaii at Hilo 200 West Kiwili Hilo, HI 96720	808- 933-3515
Idaho	Idaho SBDC Boise State University 1910 University Dr. Boise, ID 83725	208- 385-1640
Illinois	Illinois SBDC Department of Commerce and Community Affairs 620 East Adams St., 6th Floor Springfield, IL 62701	217- 524-5856
Indiana	Indiana SBDC Economic Development Council One North Capitol, Suite 420 Indianapolis, IN 46204	317- 264-6871
Iowa	Iowa SBDC Iowa State University 137 Lynn Ave. Ames, IA 50014	515- 292-6351
Kansas	Kansas SBDC Wichita State University 1845 Fairmount Wichita, KS 67260-0148	316- 689-3193
Kentucky	Kentucky SBDC University of Kentucky Center for Business Development 225 Business & Economics Building Lexington, KY 40506-0034	606- 257-7668
Louisiana	Louisiana SBDC Northeast Louisiana University, CBA 700 University Ave. Monroe, LA 71209-6435	318- 342-5506
Maine	Maine SBDC University of Southern Maine 96 Falmouth St. Portland, ME 04103	207- 780-4420
Maryland	Maryland SBDC Department of Economic and Employment Development 217 East Redwood St., 10th Floor Baltimore, MD 21202	410- 333-6995

State	State Center Address	Phone
Massachusetts	Massachusetts SBDC University of Massachusetts - Amherst Room 205, School of Management Amherst, MA 01003	413-545-6301
Michigan	Michigan SBDC 2727 Second Ave. Detroit, MI 48201	313-964-1798
Mississippi	Mississippi SBDC University of Mississippi Old Chemistry Building, Suite 216 University, MS 38677	601-232-5001
Missouri	Missouri SBDC University of Missouri 300 University Place Columbia, MO 65211	314-882-0344
Montana	Montana SBDC Montana Department of Commerce 1424 9th Ave. Helena, MT 59620	406-444-4780
Nebraska	Nebraska SBDC University of Nebraska at Omaha 60th & Dodge St., CBA Room 407 Omaha, NE 68182	402-554-2521
Nevada	Nevada SBDC University of Nevada, Reno College of Business Administration - 032, Room 411 Reno, NV 89557—0100	702-784-1717
New Hampshire	New Hampshire SBDC University of New Hampshire 108 McConnell Hall Durham, NH 03824	603-862-2200
New Jersey	New Jersey SBDC Rutgers University Graduate School of Management 180 University Ave. Newark, NJ 07102	201-648-5950
New Mexico	New Mexico SBDC Santa Fe Community College P.O. Box 4187 Santa Fe, NM 87502-4187	505-438-1362
New York	New York State SBDC State University of New York SUNY Central Plaza, S-523 Albany, NY 12246	518-443-5398
North Carolina	North Carolina SBDC University of North Carolina 4509 Creedmoor Rd., Suite 201 Raleigh, NC 27612	919-571-4154

State	State Center Address	Phone
North Dakota	North Dakota SBDC University of North Dakota 118 Gamble Hall, UND Box 7308 Grand Fork, ND 58202	701-777-3700
Ohio	Ohio SBDC 77 South High St. P.O. Box 1001 Columbus, OH 43266-0101	614-466-2711
Oklahoma	Oklahoma SBDC Southeastern Oklahoma State University P.O. Box 2584, Station A Durant, OK 74701	405-924-0277
Oregon	Oregon SBDC Lane Community College 44W. Broadway, Suite 501 Eugene, OR 97401-3021	503-726-2250
Pennsylvania	Pennsylvania SBDC The Wharton School, University of Pennsylvania 444 Vance Hall, 3733 Spruce St. Philadelphia, PA 19104-6374	215-898-1219
Puerto Rico	Puerto Rico SBDC University of Puerto Rico P.O. Box 5253 College Station Mayaguez, PR 00681	809-833-5822
Rhode Island	Rhode Island SBDC Bryant College 1150 Douglas Pike Smithfield, RI 02917	401-232-6111
South Carolina	The Frank L. Roddey SBDC University of South Carolina College of Business Administration Columbia, SC 29201-9980	803-777-4907
South Dakota	South Dakota SBDC University of South Dakota 414 E. Clark Vermillion, SD 57069	605-677-5279
Tennessee	Tennessee SBDC Memphis State University Building 1, South Campus Memphis, TN 38152	901-678-2500
Texas (Dallas)	North Texas-Dallas SBDC Bill J. Priest Institute for Economic Development 1402 Corinth St. Dallas, TX 75215	214-565-5831
(Houston)	University of Houston SBDC University of Houston 1100 Louisiana, Suite 500 Houston, TX 77002	713-752-8444

State	State Center Address	Phone
(Lubbock)	Northwest Texas SBDC Texas Tech University 2579 S. Loop 289, Suite 114 Lubbock, TX 79423	806-745-3973
(San Antonio)	UTSA South Texas Border SBDC UTSA Downtown Center 1222 North Main St., Suite 450 San Antonio, TX 78212	210-558-2450
Utah	Utah SBDC University of Utah 102 W. 500 South, Suite 315 Salt Lake City, UT 84101	801-581-7905
Vermont	Vermont SBDC Vermont Technical College P.O. Box 422 Randolph, VT. 05060	802-728-9101
Virgin Islands	UVI SBDC Sunshine Mall, Suite 104 Frederiksted, St. Croix USVI 00840	809-776-3206
Virginia	Virginia SBDC 901 East Byrd St., Suite 1800 Richmond, VA 23219	804-371-8253
Washington	Washington SBDC Washington State University Kruegel Hall, Suite 135 Pullman, WA 99164-4727	509-335-1576
West Virginia	West Virginia SBDC 950 Kanawha Boulevard East Charleston, WV 25301	304-558-2960
Wisconsin	Wisconsin SBDC University of Wisconsin 432 North Lake S., Room 423 Madison, WI 53706	608-263-7794
Wyoming	WSBDC/State Network Office P.O. Box 3275 Laramie, WY 82071-3275	307-766-3505

State Economic Development Agencies

Every state has some kind of economic development agency that provides services ranging from management assistance to financing. The types of services provided vary from state to state. As you develop your business plan, it is important to contact your state economic development agency to find out what types of help may be available. Following is a list of contact information for each state.

State	State Center Address	Phone
Alabama	Department of Community and Economic Affairs P.O. Box 5690 Montgomery, AL 36103	334-242-8672
Alaska	Economic Development Department of Commerce & Economic Development P.O. Box 110804 Juneau, AK 99811	907-465-2017
Arizona	Department of Commerce 3800 N. Central Ave., Suite 1500 Phoenix, AZ 85012	602-280-1306
Arkansas	Industrial Development Commission 1 Capitol Mall, Room 4C-300 Little Rock, AR 72201	501-682-2052
California	Trade and Commerce Agency 801 K St., Suite 1700 Sacramento, CA 95814	916-322-3962
Colorado	Office of Business Development Governor's Office 1625 Broadway, Suite 1710 Denver, CO 80202	303-892-3840
Connecticut	Department of Economic Development 865 Brook St. Rocky Hill, CT 06067	203-258-4302
Delaware	Delaware Economic Development Office 99 Kings Highway P.O. Box 1401 Dover, DE 19903	302-739-5749
Florida	Division of Economic Development Department of Commerce 536 Collins Building Tallahassee, FL 32399-2000	904-488-6300
Georgia	Department of Industry, Trade & Tourism 258 Peachtree Center Ave., NE, Suite 1000 Atlanta, GA 30303	404-656-3556

State	State Center Address	Phone
Hawaii	Department of Business, Economic Development & Tourism 220 S. King St., #1100 Honolulu, HI 96813	808-586-2359
Idaho	Division of Economic Development Department of Commerce P.O. Box 83720 Boise, ID 83720-0093	208-334-2470
Illinois	Department of Commerce & Community Affairs 620 E. Adams St., 3rd Floor Springfield, IL 62701	217-782-3233
Indiana	Business Development and Marketing Group Department of Commerce 1 N. Capitol, Suite 700 Indianapolis, IN 46204	317-232-0159
Iowa	Department of Economic Development 200 E. Grand Des Moines, IA 50309	515-242-4814
Kansas	Department of Commerce & Housing 700 SW Harrison, Suite 1300 Topeka, KS 66603-3712	913-296-3480
Kentucky	Economic Development Cabinet Capital Plaza Tower, 23rd Floor 500 Mero St. Frankfort, KY 40601	502-564-7670
Louisiana	Department of Economic Development P.O. Box 94185 Baton Rouge, LA 70804-9185	504-342-5388
Maine	Department of Economic & Community Development #59 State House Station Augusta, ME 04333	207-287-2656
Maryland	Department of Business & Economic Development 217 E. Redwood St. Baltimore, MD 21202	410-333-6901
Massachusetts	Executive Office of Economic Affairs 1 Ashburton Place, Room 2101 Boston, MA 02108	617-727-8380
Michigan	Industry and Investment Relations Michigan Jobs Commission 201 N. Washington Sq. Lansing, MI 48913	517-373-8500
Minnesota	Economic Development Division Department of Business Development 500 Metro Square, 121 9th Place East St. Paul, MN 55101-2146	612-296-5005

State	State Center Address	Phone
Mississippi	Department of Economic and Community Development P.O. Box 849 Jackson, MS 39205-0849	601-359-3449
Missouri	Department of Economic Development 301 W. High St. P.O. Box 1157 Jefferson City, MO 65102	314-751-3946
Montana	Business Development Division Department of Commerce 1424 Ninth Ave. Helena, MT 59620	406-444-3923
Nebraska	Department of Economic Development 301 Centennial Mall South P.O. Box 94666 Lincoln, NE 68509-4666	402-471-3747
Nevada	Commission on Economic Development 5151 S. Carson St. Carson City, NV 89710	702-687-4325
New Hampshire	Office of Business and Industrial Development Division of Economic Development P.O. Box 856 Concord, NH 03301	603-271-2341
New Jersey	Division of Economic Development Department of Commerce and Economic Development 20 W. State St., CN823 Trenton, NJ 08625	609-292-7757
New Mexico	Department of Economic Development 1100 St. Francis Dr. Santa Fe, NM 87503	505-827-0380
New York	Department of Commerce 1 Commerce Plaza Albany, NY 12245	518-474-4100
North Carolina	Business/Industry Development Department of Commerce 430 N. Salisbury St. Raleigh, NC 27603-5900	919-733-4151
North Dakota	Department of Economic Development & Finance 1833 E. Bismarck Expressway Bismarck, ND 58504	701-328-5300
Ohio	Department of Development 77 S. High St., 29th Floor Columbus, OH 43266-0101	614-644-9389
Oklahoma	Department of Commerce 6601 Broadway Extension Oklahoma City, OK 73116	405-843-9770

State	State Center Address	Phone
Oregon	Department of Economic Development 775 Summer St., NE Salem, OR 97310	503-986-0110
Pennsylvania	Department of Commerce 433 Forum Building Harrisburg, PA 17120	717-787-3003
Rhode Island	Department of Economic Development 7 Jackson Walkway Providence, RI 02903	401-277-2601
South Carolina	Department of Commerce P.O. Box 927 Columbia, SC 29202	803-734-0400
South Dakota	Governor's Office of Economic Development Capitol Lake Plaza Pierre, SD 57501	605-773-5032
Tennessee	Department of Economic and Community Development 320 Sixth Ave. North, 8th Floor Nashville, TN 37243	615-741-1888
Texas	Department of Commerce P.O. Box 12728, Capitol Station Austin, TX 78711	512-472-5059
Utah	Division of Business and Economic Development Department of Community and Economic Development 324 S. State St., 5th Floor Salt Lake City, UT 84111	801-538-8820
Vermont	Department of Economic Development 109 State St. Montpelier, VT 05602	802-828-3221
Virginia	Department of Economic Development 901 E. Byrd St. Richmond, VA 23219	804-371-8106
Washington	Department of Trade and Economic Development P.O. Box 48300 Olympia, WA 98504	360-753-2200
West Virginia	Development Office Building 6, Room B504 1900 Kanawha Blvd. East Charleston, WV 25305	304-558-2234
Wisconsin	Bureau of Business Exp. & Recruitment Department of Development 123 W. Washington P.O. Box 7970 Madison, WI 53703	608-255-9467

State	State Center Address	Phone
Wyoming	Division of Economic and Community Development Department of Commerce 2301 Central Ave., 4N Cheyenne, WY 82002	307-777-6435
Plus—		
American Samoa	Office of Economic Development Planning Utulei Pago Pago, AS 96799	684-633-5155
Guam	Economic Development Authority 590 S. Marine Dr., Suite 911 Tamuning, GU 96911	671-646-4141
Northern Mariana Islands	Economic Development Department of Commerce P.O. Box 10007 Saipan, MP 96950	670-322-8711
Puerto Rico	Industrial Development Co. P.O. Box 362350 San Juan, PR 00936-2350	670-322-8711
U. S. Virgin Islands	Department of Economic Development & Agriculture P.O. Box 6400 St. Thomas, VI 00804	809-774-8784
Washington, DC	Economic Development Office of the Mayor 441 4th St., NW, 11th Floor Washington, DC 20001	202-727-6365

Source: State Leadership Directory, 1995 edition

Service Corps of Retired Executives (SCORE)

SCORE, an organization sponsored by the U.S. Small Business Administration, is a nonprofit association with over 13,000 retired (and active) business executives who provide free counseling on a wide variety of small-business topics. They assist in the analysis and definitions of your problems, and help you find solutions based on their experiences with similar situations. There is no limit on the length of time you may utilize SCORE resources. All information about your business is kept strictly confidential, and is not released to anyone outside SCORE. In addition, SCORE conducts seminars and workshops focused on small-business needs.

SCORE has 400 chapters with counselors in all 50 states, Puerto Rico, Guam, the Virgin Islands, and the District of Columbia. Contact the SBA at 800-827-5722 or the National SCORE Office at 202-653-6279 to locate the SCORE office nearest you.

National SBDC Research Network

The National SBDC Research Network provides research support to the more than 900 Small Business Development Centers throughout the United States. The Research Network is funded by the U. S. Small Business Administration and administered by the State University of New York.

A rich source of information and materials for entrepreneurs, the Network and its research may be accessed only through your local SBDC and its counselors. The counselor may determine that the research services of the Network would be useful to a client and request that the Network provide such services.

The Network has a home page on the World Wide Web (http://www.smallbiz.suny.edu/), which provides computer links to numerous other sources of information for entrepreneurs.

Chambers of Commerce

The U.S. Chambers of Commerce
1615 H St. NW
Washington, DC 20062
202-659-6000
800-638-6582 (membership services)

Almost every city and state has a chamber of commerce, a non-profit association that caters to the business community. Many of these have small-business sections that help their members and the community by conducting seminars, publishing educational and informational books and tapes, acting as advocates to governmental agencies, and providing advice and information on entrepreneurship.

Often membership has other benefits for small business. It often enables members to obtain group rates on medical, dental, and life insurance, and other programs. The main headquarters can give you a list of chambers in your area and a catalog of books and tapes offered. Your local chamber should also be listed in your phone book and with Directory Assistance. Find out what services your local chamber offers.

Many chambers have sections that deal with minorities, women, and ethnic groups. Contact the national chamber or your local chamber and ask for the person who deals with your special interest group, or ask for a referral to chambers that deal with these groups.

American chambers located in foreign countries can provide information about other countries, help make business contacts, and assist in a variety of other ways. Contact the national headquarters listed above to get lists of overseas chambers. Also, many foreign countries and cities have branches of their chambers of commerce in the United States. Foreign chambers are located in Washington, D.C., and in major U. S. cities (look in phone books or call the U.S. State Department or the U.S. Chamber of Commerce above to find them). Chambers from other countries can be invaluable sources of information on those countries and their markets, and their representatives can help arrange introductions to their businesspeople.

FINANCIAL RESOURCES

Several potential sources of financing for your business are described here. The best place to start your search is your local bank(s). Explain your business plan and financing requirements, and obtain loan information. Find out what subsidies or other assistance may be available to small businesses.

- ❑ The U.S. Small Business Administration
- ❑ Export-Import Bank (EXIMBANK)
- ❑ Venture Capital

U.S. SMALL BUSINESS ADMINISTRATION

Main Office
1441 L St. NW
Washington, DC 20416
800-827-5722 Small Business Answer Desk
202-205-7717 General questions and answers
800-697-4636 Computer access (9600 baud)

The U.S. Small Business Administration (or SBA) has a variety of loan programs (see table on the following pages). A description of these programs follows along with eligibility requirements and terms. Most of these programs are administered at the local level. Therefore the best place to start is at your SBA district office. The SBA also maintains a "Small Business Answer Desk" (800-827-5722) which can provide you with information relative to its various programs as well as the telephone numbers and addresses of the district SBA offices.

What you should know about SBA loans

- ❑ All SBA lending takes the form of loan guarantees, except for direct SBA loans to handicapped business owners.
- ❑ SBA-guaranteed loans are generally administered through commercial lending organizations (i.e., banks). While most banks and other lending institutions can make SBA-guaranteed loans, certain ones, called certified and preferred lenders, have special relationships with the SBA, which enable the institutions to expedite loans to creditworthy small businesses. Contact your local SBA office for a list of certified and preferred lenders.
- ❑ To obtain an SBA-guaranteed loan, you must demonstrate your ability to repay the loan from the cash flow and profits from your business.
- ❑ SBA-guaranteed loans can be used only to finance the start-up, operation, or expansion of a business. The proceeds may not be used to repay other debts, be reinvested in financial instruments, or be used for speculative purposes.

How to obtain an SBA-guaranteed loan

1. Attempt to obtain a loan from at least one commercial lender. If you are turned down for reasons other than your ability to repay the loan, ask if the lender would be willing to make the loan if it were guaranteed by the SBA. Reasons for rejection may include the amount of the loan, the period of repayment, or the length of time the business has been in operation.

2. The bank will contact the SBA to determine if the loan can be guaranteed by the SBA. If the loan meets SBA criteria, the decision on whether to make the loan rests solely with the bank. The bank will make all necessary arrangements with the SBA to secure the guarantee. If a bank refuses to make a guaranteed loan, the borrower may try another bank.

3. Borrowers must be prepared to pay closing costs on SBA-guaranteed loans. While closing costs depend on many factors, total closing costs between 3% and 5% of the loan amount are common.

Small Business Investment Companies

Small Business Investment Companies (SBICs) are privately capitalized, owned, and managed investment firms licensed by the SBA that provide equity capital, long-term financing, and management assistance to small businesses. For more information on SBICs, contact the nearest SBA office. A directory of SBICs is available by sending $10 to:

National Association of Small Business Investment Companies
NASBIC Directory
P.O. Box 4039
Merrifield, VA 22116

Export-Import Bank (EXIMBANK)

811 Vermont Ave. NW
Washington, DC 20571
800-565-3946

EXIMBANK is an independent government agency that provides export financing to large and small businesses and to potential exporters who have had difficulty obtaining working-capital loans from commercial lenders. For more information about specific EXIMBANK programs, call the EXIMBANK Financing Hotline at 800-565-3946.

Venture Capital

Venture capital companies are different from other sources of financing in that the venture capitalist takes part ownership in the company in return for the funding. Sources of venture capital include individual investors, partnerships, and investment companies seeking to invest in fast-growing small businesses and start-ups with excellent growth potential. The following associations and organizations can help growing businesses find potential sources of venture capital:

The Capital Network	512-794-9398
National Association of Small Business Investment Companies	703-683-1601
National Venture Capital Association	703-351-5269
Seed Capital Network	615-573-4655

The National Venture Capital Association sells a directory listing over 150 venture capital firms. The price: $25. Order by calling 703-351-5269.

Note —

Terms and conditions of SBA loan programs are subject to change periodically. Contact your nearest SBA district office for the latest information on these and other SBA loan programs.

SBA's Economic Development Loan Programs

Type of Loan	Lender	Amount	Maturity
BASIC 7(A)	Banks	Up to $750,000 guaranteed portion	Working Capital - 7 yrs Equipment - 10 yrs. Real Estate - 25 yrs.
CAPLINE PROGRAMS	Banks	Up to $750,000 guaranteed portion	
STANDARD-ASSET BASED	Banks with an asset-based department	Guaranty up to $750,000	Up to 5 yrs.
SMALL-ASSET BASED	Banks	Up to $200,000	Up to 5 yrs.
SEASONAL LINE OF CREDIT	Banks	Up to $750,000 guaranteed portion	12 months to 5 yrs., renewed annually
CONTRACT LOAN	Banks	Up to $750,000 guaranteed portion	Generally 12 months; larger contracts 18 months. Up to 5 yrs.
BUILDERS	Banks (guaranteed portion)	Up to $750,000	Up to 5 yrs.
EXPORT WORKING CAPITAL (pilot program)	Banks	Up to $750,000 guaranteed portion	12 months with 2 options to renew, each for another 12 months
SMALL LOAN PROGRAM	Banks	Up to $50,000 total loan amount	Working capital – 7 yrs. Machinery and equipment - 10 yrs. Real estate – 25 yrs.
FA$TRAK (pilot program)	Banks (selected)	Up to $100,000 total loan amount	
MICROLOAN	Designated microlenders	Up to $25,000 total loan amount	Up to 6 yrs.
504 PROGRAM	Banks and Certified Development Companies (CDC)	Up to $750,000 SBA priced out debenture amount	Debenture of 10 of 20 yrs.
WOMEN'S PREQUALIFICATION (pilot program)	Banks do lending, SBA does prequalifying	Up to $250,000 total loan amount	Working Capital –7 yrs. Equipment – 10 yrs. Real Estate – 25 yrs.
LOWDOC	Banks	$100,000 or less total loan amount	Working Capital – 7 yrs. Equipment – 10 yrs. Real Estate – 25 yrs.

Interest Rate	Collateral Guarantees	SBA % Guaranty	Comments
Maturity less than 7 yrs., max. is 2.25% over Wall Street prime. Maturity greater than or equal to 7 yrs., max. is 2.75% over prime.	Personal guarantees Pledge of assets	$100,000 or less 80% Over $100,000 75%	Owners must have sufficient equity injection, meet SBA size standards and eligibility requirements. Must be for-profit business. Former Veterans program now folded in here.
2.25% over Wall Street prime	Accounts receivable Inventory	75%	
2.25% over Wall Street prime	Accounts receivable Inventory	75%	Must cash flow over 7–yr. term.
Maximum 2.25% over Wall Street prime	Personal guarantees Pledge of assets	$100,000 or less 80% Over $100,000 75%	Must be in business one year. Structured to be repaid from seasonal cash flow. 30-day payout. Only one per season.
Not to exceed 2.25% over Wall Street prime	Personal guarantees Pledge of contract proceeds Assignment of contract	$100,000 or less 80% Over $100,000 75%	Applicants must be contractors or subcontractors.
Not to exceed 2.25% over Wall Street prime	Personal guarantees Pledge of real estate being developed	$100,000 or less 80% Over $100,000 75%	Must be in business at least one year
May be fixed or variable with no minimum	Personal guarantees Pledge of export inventory, foreign receivables, contract and L/C proceeds	Up to 75%	Covers both pre- and post-shipment financing. Can be transaction-driven; single or multiple
Maturity less than 7 yrs., max. is 4.25% over Wall Street prime for loans less than $25,000. Maturity greater than or equal to 7 yrs., max. is 4.75% over Wall Street prime for loans upto $25,000 and 3.75% over prime for loans $25,000 to $50,000	Personal guarantees Pledge of assets	Up to 80%	This program is particularly valuable for service firms
		Up to 50%	Lenders approve loans without SBA review. Reviewed every 2 yrs.
Up to 4% over Wall Street prime	Personal guarantees Pledge of assets	None	Funding for this program provided by the SBA
Fixed	No less than 2nd lien on assets being financed	Lender funds up to 50% of the cost of the assets.	Private lender puts up 50%, CDC 40%, equity 10%. Long-term fixed rate financing for fixed assets
Maturity less than 7 yrs., max. is 2.25% over Wall St. prime. Maturity 7 yrs. or more, max. is 2.75% over prime	Pledge of personal and business assets Personal guarantees	$100,000 or less 80% Over $100,000 75%	Businesses must be at least 51% owned and operated by women. SBA does prequalifying, intermediaries assist applicants in preparing a business plan.
Same as in 7(a) above except loans under $50,000 may be higher (see SBA for more detail)	Personal guarantees Pledge of assets	Up to 80%	Focuses on character, credit, and experience. One-page application. Lenders use normal credit analysis. SBA responds quickly (2 to 3 days).

Source: U.S. Small Business Administration (revised 1/25/96)

❧ *Picaro's Management Company* ❧ 1

Picaro's
Management Company
1995 Business Plan

Picaro's Management Company (PMC) is soliciting proposals from sources that may be interested in participating in the development, design, and funding of the project described herein. This business plan has been prepared solely for informational purposes from data developed by PMC and is not to be reproduced or used for any other purpose.

The information contained herein has been developed to assist interested parties in making an assessment or evaluation of the business and does not purport to be complete. In all instances, interested parties should make their own investigation, analysis, and conclusions of the business entity described. PMC does not make representation or warranty as to the accuracy or completeness of the information or data contained herein beyond the assertion of a "good faith" presentation of the information as of the day it was written.

Any individual or entity that has obtained the business plan with the intent to rely on the information provided to further an interest in an investment in PMC should seek alternative sources to properly assess conclusions with regard to concept utility, worthiness, marketability, etc. In this regard, potential investors may be required to represent in writing that such investor has sufficient knowledge and experience in financial and business matters as to be capable of evaluating the merits and risks of any investment in PMC. Given the development and start-up nature of the project, individuals or entities not in a position to lose an entire investment should not invest.

This document is not an offer to sell or a solicitation of an offer to buy any securities in, or related to, Picaro's as described herein in any jurisdiction in which, or to any person to whom, it is unlawful to make such an offer or sale.

Picaro's Management Company
business plan p 144

Healthcare Automation, Inc.

HEALTHCARE
AUTOMATION, INC.
BUSINESS PLAN

OCTOBER 14, 1991

18352 Dallas Parkway • Suite 136 • Dallas, TX 75287
Tel: (214) 931-7097 • Fax: (214) 931-7098

Healthcare Automation
business plan p 190

ASAPS Xpress–Car Wash and Lube PAGE 2

MARCH 1995

This document contains
confidential and proprietary information
belonging exclusively to:

ASAPS *Xpress* — Car Wash and Lube
Highway 92 & Londonderry Road
Woodstock, Georgia 30188

Shoqut Hussien
President

Pamela Hussien
Vice President

4650 Waters Road
Woodstock, Georgia 30188
404-928-9216

ASAPS Xpress—Car Wash and Lube
business plan p 218

Adventure Media, Inc. PAGE 1

Preliminary Business Plan for

Adventure Media, Inc.

This document contains proprietary and confidential information related to the business plan of Adventure Media, Inc. and has been provided for analysis by the person to whom it has been transmitted by the Company. This document may not be reproduced, distributed, nor its contents divulged or otherwise used, in whole or in part, without the prior written consent of Adventure Media, Inc.

This is not an offer to sell, nor the solicitation of an offer to buy, any securities. Such an offer, if made, will be made only through a prospectus or private placement memorandum issued in accordance with the United States Securities Act and other applicable laws, rules, and regulations.

Prepared By:

Andrew McKee, Chief Executive Officer
Adventure Media, Inc.

Adventure Media, Inc.
business plan p 251

Section III

Sample Business Plans

In this section you'll find three fully documented business plans and one preliminary or *venture* plan. The venture plan is the type of document you would send to potential investors or venture capitalists. It thoroughly explains your business concept and highlights certain parts of your strategy without going into the comprehensive detail that one would expect to find in a complete business plan.

Because we have yet to see a perfect business plan, we asked a panel of experts to comment on the strengths of the individual plans and on areas which could be improved. We have also included some brief biographical information about the founder(s) of these businesses.

Each plan was developed for a real business by individuals who have generously allowed us to publish them in the hope that their hard work might benefit you as you create your business plan.Please note that in the case of Picaro's Management Co. the identity of the owner(s), the business location, and certain proprietary information have been disguised. Because of these changes, some of the demographic data may not match the actual business profile. No changes have been made to any of the financial data, but, due to space, the number of appendices had to be limited.

These examples will provide you with a great deal of insight into how business data and information can be used and communicated effectively. They will be an invaluable tool as you develop and write your own business plan.

Picaro's*

Location:	Minneapolis, Minn.
Business Description:	Mexican Restaurant
Founder:	Simeon Robbins
Education:	B.A., Carleton College, St. Paul, Minn. Economics and Spanish M.B.A., Kellogg School of Management Entrepreneurial Management and Finance
Year Founded:	Start-Up
Starting Capital:	Seeking $800,000 for initial location
Sales 1995:	n/a
Owner's Equity:	n/a
Employees:	40 – 50 employees at start-up

Simeon Robbins was raised in an entrepreneurial environment. His family owned and operated a chain of floral and nursery supply stores. He grew up believing that one day he would work in the family business. But that wasn't to be: The family business failed shortly before he graduated from college. After working in the corporate world for several years and receiving his M.B.A. from Kellogg School of Management, Robbins began to look for entrepreneurial ventures for himself.

Immediately following business school, Robbins worked on a restaurant start-up that never got off the ground. He took his knowledge from the venture to begin working in his own start-up, a chain of Mexican restaurants. He saw that there was a clear void in that category, and had lots of ideas for the concept from recent visits to Texas, New Mexico, and Arizona.

The idea really began to take off when Robbins brought on a partner — a 13-year veteran of the restaurant business. Next they found a location for their first store, and were then able to write the plan based on the location. It took four months to research and write the plan, during which time Robbins relied on credit-card debt, retirement funds, and occasional consulting fees to support himself. When writing the plan, Robbins used a wide variety of resources, including online data, restaurant magazines, and demographic publications based on zip codes. He also contacted trade associations (National Restaurant Association) and the Cornell Hotel Management School. Robbins spent countless hours in the library doing research for his plan.

The plan is designed for raising capital, and has succeeded in opening several doors to investors. Although the concept has not been funded yet, Robbins is hopeful that it will be in the coming months. He believes that his business plan has been invaluable, saying, "The plan is indispensable in getting funding. No one will take you seriously without it. There is no way that we would have gotten entrées in the investment community if we hadn't had this business plan."

** Names and locations have been disguised for competitive reasons.*

***Note:** References to tabular material appear in the text to demonstrate the extent of detail in the original business plan. With the exception of Table 1-1 (page157), however, tables, schematic drawings, architectural sketches, photos, and area maps have been deleted from this guide due to confidentiality and space limitations.*

EXPERT EVALUATION
Picaro's

SECTION

Executive Summary: Good overall description of business. Financing needs and projected sales and profits are useful information for the reader to have as he/she goes on to evaluate the plan. Also includes a good summary of competition, target market, location, and experience of principals.

Description of Business: (Background Section) An interesting way to introduce concept of the restaurant and give the reader a good comprehensive view of the plan, theme, background of people running it, and its ambiance. The downside is its length. It tends to give too much detail, some of which might be more appropriate in other sections of the plan.

Market: Excellent detail of demographic profiles of potential customer in his trading area. However there is quite a lot of unnecessary information, including much of the psychographic data. Market information is also included in several sections of the plan.

Market Share: The issue of market share is almost completely ignored except in the statement that the "area is underserved by Mexican restaurants." This section should be expanded to provide greater detail.

Competition: The competitive analysis section is excellent. The detailed analysis of competitive strengths and weakness validates the promotional strategy proposed by management.

Location: Excellent detail and support documentation. Also addressed issues such as future road construction and its potential impact on the restaurant.

Pricing: Includes menu prices but does not discuss pricing strategy.

Promotional Strategy: Buried in the Marketing Section, which tends to get a bit bogged down in psychographic/demographic data. The promotional strategy is clear but would be strengthened if it included more narrative and were tied more directly to the budget.

Insurance: Identified in the financials as a substantial expense; more information should be provided to document and explain coverage.

Forms of Ownership: Form of ownership is not discussed. This should be spelled out for the reader, along with an organizational chart.

Management/Personnel: Lacks job descriptions, responsibilities, line management, and outside advisers. It does thoroughly describe senior management qualifications but there are no job descriptions, staffing plans, or most important, identification of outside professional advisers.

Financial Information: Very good. Should have endnotes from the text to help connect this section to the projections made.

Overall Comments: A very strong plan. The organization and ordering of information creates problems for the reader. In total the plan is a bit too long. Areas such as "Getting to Know the Customer" could be pared back. Notes to Financial Statements would be helpful.

Picaro's Management Company

1995 Business Plan

Picaro's Management Company (PMC) is soliciting proposals from sources that may be interested in participating in the development, design, and funding of the project described herein. This business plan has been prepared solely for informational purposes from data developed by PMC and is not to be reproduced or used for any other purpose.

The information contained herein has been developed to assist interested parties in making an assessment or evaluation of the business and does not purport to be complete. In all instances, interested parties should make their own investigation, analysis, and conclusions of the business entity described. PMC does not make representation or warranty as to the accuracy or completeness of the information or data contained herein beyond the assertion of a "good faith" presentation of the information as of the day it was written.

Any individual or entity that has obtained the business plan with the intent to rely on the information provided to further an interest in an investment in PMC should seek alternative sources to properly assess conclusions with regard to concept utility, worthiness, marketability, etc. In this regard, potential investors may be required to represent in writing that such investor has sufficient knowledge and experience in financial and business matters as to be capable of evaluating the merits and risks of any investment in PMC. Given the development and start-up nature of the project, individuals or entities not in a position to lose an entire investment should not invest.

This document is not an offer to sell or a solicitation of an offer to buy any securities in, or related to, Picaro's as described herein in any jurisdiction in which, or to any person to whom, it is unlawful to make such an offer or sale.

Table of Contents

Executive Summary

Picaro's restaurant combines the fun and excitement of a tropical resort with the wholesome freshness of an outdoor Mexican vegetable stand. There is no value-based, casual-dining restaurant like it in the Midwest. The design, atmosphere and menu borrow from the most successful concepts around the country. Created with national expansion in mind, the food has a broad appeal, combining Mexican standbys like fajitas and burritos with American favorites like hamburgers, brick oven pizza, ribs, and rotisserie chicken.

Picaro's management seeks $700,000 to develop the first site. Projected gross sales are approximately $1,900,000 during Year One with a net profit before taxes of $200,000. Management's confidence in these projections comes from experience in the restaurant industry and from a thorough analysis of the local market.

First, Minneapolis-St. Paul is underserved by Mexican restaurants. There are only 15 full-service independent operators and one national chain in the surrounding Twin Cities area. When high-end Spanish restaurants and low-end taco houses are eliminated, the playing field becomes even smaller. If consistency and quality are used as a benchmark, few of the remaining operators make the cut, leaving Chi Chi's as the primary competition. Picaro's concept and product are different from Chi Chi's, positioning it to avoid direct competition and to gain market share.

Second, the target market around the proposed site is populated by heavy restaurant users. Baby Boomers, the largest group of potential customers, are likely to have children under thirteen years of age, head dual-income households, and have a relatively high level of education and income. Due to the demands of work and parenting, Baby Boomers eat often at restaurants that offer convenience, value, fun, and relaxation.

Third, Picaro's has the opportunity to lease a Class A commercial property in a prime location. The Marriott Corporation has made a strategic decision to exit the restaurant industry, making one of its former Hamburger Hut sites available. The 6,000-square-foot structure has good visibility, access, and parking, and is in a high traffic area that is a haven for retailers, shoppers, employers, and hotels.

Finally, the founders bring prior restaurant experience and management and start-up skills to the project. James Munoz, General Manager for Picaro's, currently oversees nine stores for the Beefhaus restaurant chain. He has worked for the parent company, Euro-Eateries, for 13 years in every operations capacity. Simeon Robbins, Assistant Manager, is currently devoted to the project full-time. For the past three years, he has worked on his own as a restaurant consultant, and for the Minnesota Small Business Development Center as a small business consultant specializing in finance and marketing.

Management

Name	Position
James Munoz	Chief Operating Officer
Simeon K. Robbins	Chief Financial Officer

James Munoz, age 36, will be the Chief Operating Officer. He will be responsible for the daily operations of the restaurant. Mr. Munoz's responsibilities include: on-site start-up, staffing, training, equipment & service procurement, budgeting, menu development, and quality control and customer service.

Currently, Mr. Munoz is Vice President of Operations and Regional Manager with Euro-Eateries. His responsibilities included nine full-service restaurants with 30 General Managers and 400 hourly employees. Mr. Munoz was also responsible for the start-up of Euro-Eateries' most recent acquisition, Papa Doc's. Under his guidance, the new concept has grossed over $65,000 per week since its opening. Mr. Munoz has worked in the full-service restaurant industry for 13 years and has served in every operations capacity including planning, forecasting, training, marketing, design, and development.

Simeon K. Robbins, age 34, will be the Chief Financial Officer. He will oversee the concept development, financing, and strategic planning of the restaurant. Mr. Robbins' responsibilities include financial oversight, marketing, and legal and regulatory issues, as well as daily management.

Formerly, Mr. Robbins was Partner and Chief Operating Officer of Pub Ventures Inc., an Illinois-based corporation formed to develop a chain of brewpubs in cities along the Mississippi River. His responsibilities included all aspects of the pre-opening and start-up process including concept development, site selection, financing, capital structure, and legal and regulatory matters. In addition, Mr. Robbins served as a restaurant and retail consultant for the Minnesota Small Business Development Center. Previously, he was Vice President of The Illinois Continental Bank, where he spent six years in marketing and small business banking. Mr. Robbins graduated from Carleton College in 1983 and received a Master of Business Administration degree from the Kellogg School of Management in 1994.

Concept Development

Theme Development

Value and convenience reign supreme in the 1990s, according to Standard & Poor's Industry Surveys. Baby Boomers fill the ranks of adults aged 45 to 54, typically the peak earning years. Also, the years when financial and personal priorities focus on college tuition and retirement planning. Standard & Poor's concludes that saving—not spending—takes precedence. Consumer attitudes towards spending, perceived value, and convenience have been impacted by slowing growth in incomes and jobs. Many consumers no longer shop from store to store, but turn to retailers that give them good value every day.

To meet this demand, Picaro's seduces the customer with its physical appearance and strives for an entertainment experience similar to what one would find at Disney World. Baby Boomers no longer define 'dining value' simply by food & service quality. With children in tow, higher living expenses, and stressful lives, relaxation and entertainment have become important. In today's environment, consumers perceive a restaurant as an oasis, a place where they can have fun with family and friends in a safe setting, as well as connect with their community, according to the National Restaurant Association.

The Target Market

With an eye toward national expansion, Picaro's was designed to attract all ages. The shopping habits of today's maturing Baby Boomers reflect the priorities of parents. Because children tend to be loyal customers and often influence the decision to eat out, the environment is 'kid-friendly'. Young people enjoy Picaro's stimulating visual appeal and informal approach to a meal while dining out. Menu offerings such as sandwiches, tacos, and chips can be eaten easily with small hands. Families enjoy the relaxed pace and comfortable approach evidenced by spacious isles, casual cement floors, and a menu that has value-oriented American and Mexican food with a wide range of choices and prices. Older people are attracted to the restaurant as a destination because the theme makes it identifiable and familiar, while providing a comfortable level of distraction. Heart-healthy items on the menu are an added attraction. For single people, the bar area is an unforgettable experience. Unlike bars that are smoky, dark, and stale, Picaro's is bright, fun, and comfortable. Multicolored margaritas swirl around in frozen drink machines that are lined up next to crates of fresh oranges, lemons, limes, and coconuts.

Why National?

There is room in the Mexican casual-dining segment for a well managed, start-up concept with mass appeal. Casual dining is a growing niche, according to Ron McDougall, CEO of Brinker International. Chains comprise 70% of the restaurants in the fast-food segment, compared with only 26% of the casual dining segment. Only 4,000 of the 68,000 casual dining units in existence belong to one of the top 20 chains. The remainder are independents. The independents are not growing significantly and the chains grew only 1% over the last year.

Small, regional chains have the flexibility and energy to grow exponentially. As they emerge, they combine the entrepreneurship of the hands-on operator with the development of sophisticated systems. Because of their size, they can react to trends quickly. And, when the product is unique, either nationally or in its market, the company has a distinct advantage. The Picaro's concept is unique in the Midwest, and therefore has that advantage.

Finally, efficiencies gained through expansion will help Picaro's to grow beyond its small independent competitors and become a national player. Expansion fosters economies of scale and learning curve effects which add to the bottom line.

Why Mexican?

First, Mexican food is hot. Experts predict that sales of Mexican food will grow by more than 10% a year through the middle of the decade and will reach nearly $4 billion in 1997. As many as 79% of all restaurants already have at least one Mexican item on the menu. In fact, salsa has replaced ketchup as the top-selling condiment. H.J. Heinz hopes to take advantage of this trend with its new Salsa Style Ketchup, and H.J. Heinz is not the only one hoping to cash in.

Second, consumers are more willing to experiment with different forms of Mexican food, including authentic fare which is more nutritious. In the past, Mexican food had been marketed primarily as a fast food and customers perceived that it was low in quality and fat-laden. Now, it has been determined that carbohydrates are the preferred source of nutrition and Mexican is well accepted. The widespread acceptance of Mexican food mirrors the concurrent rise in popularity of pasta.

Third, the growing diversity of the nation's population represents a tremendous opportunity to market ethnic foods. From 1981 to 1991, the Hispanic-origin population grew by 40%. From 1992 to 2000 the Hispanic population is expected to contribute 33% of the nation's population. As Americans are exposed to a wider variety of cuisines through different types of "fusion"cooking, it is expected that their acceptance of and demand for different menu items and ingredients will rise.

Fourth, in the Midwest, Mexican restaurants are the exception, whereas in markets west of the Rockies, Mexican restaurants are quite common. As a matter of fact, many operators are heading East, fearing that western markets are saturated. For example, Taco Bell targeted the Northeast region because it felt that it has density, a strong economic picture, and an underpenetration of restaurants.

Finally, there is something on Picaro's menu for every taste, not only Mexican food. To attract a broad customer base and grow beyond a niche player in the restaurant industry, a full menu offering is needed. For this reason, Picaro's offers a blend of Mexican and American cuisine. The menu has a full selection of classic Mexican best-sellers like burritos, enchiladas, and fajitas, and American favorites like brick-oven pizza, ribs, and rotisserie chicken.

Why Not Italian?

There is little room in the Italian segment for an independent operator that wishes to become a national player. Competition is increasing as the segment is divided up, but only one or two regional concepts will have the resources to go up against Olive Garden. Those concepts that do not have the management team, financial resources, or ability to travel will consolidate.

The sign of maturation in the Italian segment, analysts and many operators agree, is the division of markets along food and price lines. Instead of one broad category which Olive Garden defined for so long, the casual dining business appears headed toward different tiers. Romano's and a couple of other chains go after customers willing to pay $13 or more per check. Lower-end casual concepts such as Spageddies, a Brinker entry Mozzarella Cafe, a Morrison concept, and East Side Mario's from PepsiCo look for customers willing to pay under $13 per check. Even Chili's and Ruby Tuesday's offer Italian-inspired dishes.

Food Quality

Fresh, home-made, and simple is Picaro's message. The current popularity of fresh-roasted coffee, home-brewed beer, and bread specialty stores is evidence of the consumers' desire for natural, healthful, and wholesome foods. Picaro's sauces, soups, breads, and dressings are made fresh on the premises, and each entrée is cooked to order. The pizza is baked in 900-degree wood-burning ovens which are the latest rage. Ingredients are displayed before they are served, so the customer's anticipation and appreciation for the food is heightened. Produce is packed in wooden farm crates which reinforce the perception that the food is healthful and natural. To add an element of authenticity to the displays, the staff picks fruit and vegetables from the crates whenever possible. Behind the bar, piles of oranges, lemons, limes, and coconuts add to the perception that the frozen drinks are fruity and fresh. Bottled beer packed in galvanized tubs of ice invokes an image of purity and old-fashioned value.

Service Quality

The Picaro's experience will leave the customer overwhelmed by value, hospitality, and a sense that the norms of dining out have been broken. To reinforce the customer's perception of value, Picaro's will strive for consistency. Consistency provides patrons with a sense of assurance in the anxiety-provoking 1990s, according to the National Restaurant Association. To ensure quality and consistency some dishes will be presented by a team of servers.

The Picaro's customer will feel as if he is getting special attention and receiving better treatment than he normally receives at restaurants. Hot chips and salsa or oven fresh tortillas will be delivered to the table as soon as the customer is seated and not after the order is entered into the point-of-sale system. To create the feeling of being at home, seconds will always be offered on items such as chips and tortillas. Instead of asking the customer "May I get you more," the server will say, "Let me refill that for you."

THE CONCEPT

The Story of Picaro's

In a secluded bay, a boat ride away from the beaches of Treasure Key sits a *bodega* (small grocery store/market) shaded by palm trees. This market is known more for its fresh-cooked food than for its groceries. Neighbors argue as to how long Pablo Picaro has stood behind the counter—-some say 50 years, some say 100. But one thing is for sure, every full moon, revelers come by foot from the surrounding towns to eat the food that he prepares for the celebration of the tides. No one will admit that it's the secret to his long life, but why argue with the gods. We didn't!

The Design Theme

Kitchen & Bar Walls

Unlike most Mexican restaurants, the walls are not covered with ponchos, sombreros and wagon wheels. To convey the feeling of being in a market, Picaro's walls are lined with the groceries that one would find in a Mexican corner market. Real cans and boxes of food are stacked on shelves above the bar and near the kitchen. The institutional-size cans are easy to read and are generally ethnic brands. Whether it is a can of beans or a box of rice, the visual effect is colorful and eye-catching. From a dining perspective, the customer feels as if the food is homemade and fresh.

Dining Room Walls

Portions of the walls are formed by old, colorful, mismatched pieces of wood such as doors that may have been pulled from a junk pile or boards that may have washed up from the ocean. The feeling is that of a shack in a rural, happy-go-lucky village. The surroundings, much like the food, are simple and honest, not pretentious.

Bar Area

Attractive and upbeat enough for the dinnerhouse crowd, yet casual enough for families — the main attraction of the bar area is a row of frozen-drink machines swirling brightly colored margaritas with names like Banana Split and Tropical Breeze. The machines bring the art of the margarita to new heights and support the Latin theme. In addition, they provide a visual stimulus and add an element of fun.

Because the machines occupy the back bar space where bottles of liquor are normally displayed, the bottles are kept out of sight, below the bar. This supports the family theme, as does a selection of non-alcoholic frozen drinks. The soft-sell approach to liquor is also reflected in the limited bar seating capacity and gives way to a bar designed to serve food and liquor at the same time, with the appropriate seat height and leg room.

Floors

Keeping in line with the comfortable, unpretentious theme, the floors are made from bare cement and show evidence of wear. To achieve this effect, the borders of the aisles and thruways are painted with multiple layers of paint in various colors, while the center portions of the aisles are left bare. Additionally, cases of beer are stacked warehouse style in various locations. Mexican brands such as Tecate, Corona, and Carta Blanca play off of the current popularity of beer, while supporting the neighborhood market theme. Picaro's approach to merchandising is unique.

Windows
The bright colors and eye-catching displays of Picaro's interior will serve as the best form of advertisement. For this reason, the front of the restaurant will have large windows that people can easily see into as they pass by. Ambient light will bring the tropical colors to life and add to the open and airy feeling of the market.

Bathrooms
Faithful to the Picaro's theme, the bathrooms are strictly business. Counter tops and stall dividers are fashioned from 1 1/2-inch galvanized pipe and unfinished sheet steel. To add a touch of humor, speakers in the ceiling broadcast Spanish lessons. A Berlitz-style instructor offers Spanish translations of offbeat phrases such as "Will you marry me?" or "Can I pet your dog?" The bathroom walls, designed much like a travel brochure, offer a brief geography lesson on Treasure Kay and the Bahamas. Even a trip to the bathroom at Picaro's is an adventure, offering the chance to discover something new.

Gas-Fired Tortilla Maker
There is nothing like the sight, sound, and smell of freshly baked bread to stimulate the appetite. To meet the demand for tortillas, a five-foot-high mechanical tortilla maker will be installed in a highly visible location. When the operator feeds chunks of fresh dough onto the machine's conveyor belt, it flattens them out and cooks them over a gas-fired flame, automatically flipping them over to be cooked on both sides. To increase the sense of drama, the machine is mounted in a window or on a viewing platform surrounded by a rail. There is never a dull moment at Picaro's.

Adobe Style Wood-Burning Oven
Pizza is a popular menu choice and a key ingredient in Picaro's blend of American and Mexican cuisine. Brick-oven cooking compliments the wholesome, fresh approach and provides an interesting visual display. The sight, sound, and smell of burning wood adds to the allure and drama of the dining experience and offers the customer menu choices normally available only at pizza specialty houses, thereby broadening the Picaro's appeal. Also, the National Restaurant Association reports an increase in the demand for premium baked goods.

Table Settings
The customer will have direct contact with the table settings. For this reason, it is important to pay particular attention to what is put on the table. Mismatched crockery and brown unbleached paper napkins convey a sense of informality and simplicity focusing the customer's attention on the food. Salt and pepper left in their original cardboard and tin containers, as opposed to salt and pepper shakers, reinforce the market theme. Wooden toothpicks suggest a relaxed pace and imply that the food is worth savoring. The Picaro's approach is full service yet relaxed.

Over-Sized Booths
Customers generally expect to have more fun at a Mexican restaurant. In anticipation of large "party" groups on weekends and after work, Picaro's will offer free-standing, eight-person booth seating. Accessible from both sides, the booths will facilitate the movement of large groups in and out, and make families and children more comfortable by not boxing in those who cannot sit still.

Uniforms
Servers wear polo shirts with the Picaro's logo. The short sleeves are appropriate for the tropical setting and brisk work environment, while the collar adds formality. The uniform is completed by khaki shorts in the summer and khaki pants in the winter. The kitchen staff wears starched whites to convey a sense of expertise, knowledge, and value to the customer. Uniforms make teamwork and consistency part of the Picaro's message.

Colors
The psychology of colors plays an important role in the design of Picaro's. To appeal to the broadest range of tastes, the colors are simple. There is an air of accessibility, not richness. While the palette evokes a tropical feeling, the tones have different messages, dependent on their placement. Certain colors are used for their ability to attract attention, while others are used for their ability to stimulate the appetite. Overall, the message is fun.

Restricted Smoking
In keeping with its family-oriented and wholesome theme, Picaro's will join a growing number of restaurants in becoming a restricted-smoking establishment. Smoking will be allowed in the bar area only.

Lighting
With an increased emphasis on visual appeal, bright lighting will be used strategically. Focused spotlights will highlight food preparation areas and various props or design elements. Wherever possible, ambient light will add to the tropical, outdoor-market feeling.

Noise
A comfortable level of noise adds excitement to the atmosphere and in some applications, fast-paced music increases table turnover by discouraging customers from lingering at a casual pace. Although noise from the display kitchen will create a distraction, music will be used strategically to enhance the dining experience. Picaro's will use a prerecorded mix of American pop songs and Spanish remakes of American pop songs. Familiarity with the music will give customers a sense of fun & comfort while providing Mexican authenticity.

Menu Design
The menu design will be simple in response to customers' refined tastes, the decline in liquor sales, and research indicating that consumers prefer a simple listing. A shorter menu is cleaner, easier to read, and communicates a high price-to-value relationship. The silly headlines, humorous headings, and other lighthearted touches of the 70s and 80s are not in line with the customers' new focus on quality and value.

Kid-Friendly
Since family dining decisions are often based on how well restaurants cater to kids, and how well they satisfy parents' nutritional objectives, smart operators will tailor the atmosphere and menu to the needs of children. For Picaro's, this means fresher and lighter kids menus that are nutritionally up-to-date and are presented through hand-held Viewmaster toys. Balloons, activity books, and crayons are also part of the child-friendly atmosphere.

Property & Equipment

Picaro's plans to lease the Hamburger Hut restaurant, located at the intersection of 10th Street and Marquette Avenue in Minneapolis, from the Marriott Corporation. The 6,000-square-foot building is a stand-alone, single-story structure situated along the boundary line of a shopping mall which faces a heavily traveled twelve-lane road. The building is well maintained and the current operation is in compliance with local licensing and permit requirements.

Property

The structure is relatively new, having been built in 1987. It is constructed of red brick with the exception of a glass greenhouse which faces east along 10th Street. While the entranceway also faces east, it will be moved to the north side of the building, which abuts a larger parking area. The back side of the building has a loading area with double doors to facilitate loading, and the entire perimeter of the structure is well lit and secured by an alarm system.

Architect for the project, Peter Laney, AIA, will completely renovate the building's exterior, raising the roof line by five feet, repositioning the entranceway, changing the color, and increasing signage, all of which will result in improved highway visibility (see architect's sketch at end of section). By imparting a distinct architectural style to the building, the structure will become an icon that customers can easily recognize and remember. The cost of leasehold improvements is estimated at $140,000.

Lease Terms

The Marriott Corporation has tentatively agreed to lease the property for a three-year term with two five-year options. Annual rent for the initial term is $85,000, increasing to $98,000 during the first option and $109,000 during the second option. In addition, 1½% of sales over $1,500,000 will be passed through to the landlord.

Equipment

The site is fully equipped and currently operating as a table-service hamburger restaurant with a salad bar (see Table 1-1 for a list of current equipment). The following equipment is needed to prepare the set-up for a Mexican food operation: brick oven, grills, hoods, steam tables, and a tortilla maker. Since Hamburger Hut does not serve liquor, a complete bar set-up which includes frozen drink machines is also needed. Management has allocated $100,000 of the start-up cost to the purchase of kitchen equipment, and $20,000 to smallwares.

Liquor License

Management will apply for and expects to obtain a liquor license without difficulty. The State of Minnesota allocates liquor licenses based on population density, and license prices are dictated by supply and demand. The cost of acquiring a liquor license can be a large portion of start-up expenses depending on the township in which the site is located. Due to the high population density of Minneapolis-St. Paul, licenses are plentiful and consequently prices are low. While licenses in the surrounding suburbs, if available at all, can cost between $150,000 and $200,000, a license in Minneapolis will cost approximately $30,000.

Count	Hamburger Hut Equipment Description	Dimensions in Inches
3	NCR Terminals — 2126	
2	Printers	
1	Cecilware Coffee Urn — FE 100	
5	Stainless Steel Glass Racks	24W x 21D x 35H 32W x 21D x 26H
1	Stainless Steel Counter — Ice, Coffee	113W x 32D
1	Cecilware Coffee Maker — 5 Burner	
1	Juice Dispenser — Two Flavors	
1	Silver King Milk Dispenser	
1	Iced Tea Dispenser	
1	Three Compartment Reach—In	66W x 33D
1	Stainless Steel Shelves — Two Door	35W x 33D
1	Kelvinator Ice Cream Freezer	43W x 30D
1	Hamilton Beach Blender	
1	One Door Stainless Steel Shelves	145W x 18D
1	Toastmaster Warmer — Two Drawers	25W
5	Stainless Steel Shelves	66W x 32D
4	Vulcan Grill	36W x 30D
1	Velfield/Alco Freezer — Two Door	26W x 32½D x 80H
1	Traulsen Freezer — One Door	24W x 34D x 82H
1	Alto Sham Halo Heat — One Door	17½W x 25D x 27H
1	Menu Master Microwave — F516EVP	
1	Stainless Steel Table/Shelves	54W x 32½D x 22H
1	Bainmarie — Three-Door w/Inserts	60W x 32D
1	Pass-Through Window	14-ft. W x 22D x 23H
1	Heat Lamps	102W
1	Stainless Steel Table/Shelves	54W x 32½D
1	Call System	
1	Microwave Panasonic — 1700 w/Table	
1	Traulsen Stand-Up Cooler	24W x 34D x 78H
1	Traulsen Stand-Up Freezer	24W x 34D x 78H
2	Pitco Fryolaters	
1	Vulcan Oven	40W x 34D x 38H
1	Cleveland Trunion Soup Kettle — Double	
1	Safe	
1	Stainless Steel Table	78W x 30 1/2D
1	Hobart Slicer	
4	Stainless Steel Tables	7-ft. W x 30½D
2	Alto Shams	22W x 30D x 60H
1	Traulsen Reach-In	24W x 34D x 78H
1	Ice Machine w/Bin	56W x 33D
1	Hobart Dishwasher	
1	Universe Mixer — Table Top	
3	Comp Sink — 20 x 24 Sinks	10 ft. W x 29½D
1	Comp Sink w/Table — 18 x 20 Sinks	40W x 27½D
1	Time Clock	
1	Stainless Steel Ventilation Hood	7-ft. W x 49D
1	Stainless Steel Ventilation Hood	48W x 30D
1	Stainless Steel Ventilation Hood	78W x 30D

Location

In choosing the site for Picaro's, management sought an existing stand-alone restaurant property in a high-traffic area. The objective was to minimize up-front financial risk, maximize visibility, access a clearly defined customer base, and establish a prototype for expansion. The Hamburger Hut restaurant at the 10th Street Plaza Shopping Center in Minneapolis provides such an opportunity (see map at end of section).

The opportunity is unique for two reasons. First, the Marriott Corporation, which owns Hamburger Hut, has made a strategic decision to leave the restaurant industry and concentrate on the hotel industry. If it were not for Marriott's new strategy, this choice property would not be available. Second, because of Marriott's belief in the strength of Picaro's management team and the concept, they are willing to negotiate with a start-up. Normally, a small business would not have the credibility or creditworthiness to lease a Class A commercial property.

Just as favorable as the events which led to the property are the factors which make it a prime location. The site has good access, visibility, and parking. It is located in a thriving retail shopping district which supports 15 national anchor stores and hundreds of smaller ones. There are also several hotels, office complexes, and employers that will be a good source of lunch customers. Expectations for strong dinner sales are supported by the demographics which show densely populated residential communities nearby with above-average household incomes (See Trade Area Demographics). Additionally, traffic volume in front of the site is high and crime around the site is low, making it safe during the day and night. The Buying Power Index for the trade area is also high (a relative measure used to determine the level of potential retail sales volume). Finally, future changes to the area, which include $14 million in roadway improvements and a multiscreen cinema, are a sign of continuing growth and investment in the local economy.

Description of the Site

The site is located in the heart of northeast Minneapolis's prime retail shopping district at the intersection of 10th Street and Marquette Avenue. It is in one of the Twin Cities' largest and most conveniently located one-stop shopping centers, drawing from over 350,000 people within a five-mile radius. The open-air strip center has 375,000 square feet of retail space spread out over 28 acres. Kmart and Kroger's are the anchor tenants, along with a wide variety of retail and service tenants serving the comparison and convenience goods needs of the surrounding community (see lease plan at end of section).

The 6,000-square-foot building is a stand-alone, single-story structure located along the boundary line of the mall property facing a heavily traveled twelve lane road (see aerial view at end of section). While the restaurant has the advantage of being near a mall, it is not totally dependent on mall traffic. As a stand-alone structure with separate access and high visibility, it can function as an independent destination.

The success of the adjacent Bennigan's and Applebee's restaurants confirms the existence of a clearly defined, tractable, and accessible customer base. The nearby operations are viewed as healthy competition because they are not segment competitors, and because they help to attract a larger and more varied pool of customers. Bennigan's and Applebee's will attest to the ability of the Picaro's prototype to differentiate itself from the national chains.

Ingress/Egress

Tenth Street is one of the primary arteries in the Twin Cities metropolitan area and is a freely moving 10-lane highway. Tenth Street Plaza is the only shopping center which has its own left-turn signal and left-turn lane on 10th Street for northbound traffic. This makes it convenient for shoppers to enter the Center safely and without congestion or delay. Consequently, there is no problem attracting cars driving by on the opposite side of the roadway. Southbound traffic is able to make a right turn directly into the shopping center without passing through a median or waiting for a signal.

There is an additional side entrance to the site from Marquette Avenue, which is a major residential road that intersects with 10th Street on one end and Broadway on the other end. It serves the densely populated residential communities to the west of the property.

Visibility

Management's architect for the project, Peter Laney, AIA, will completely renovate the building's exterior, raising the roof line by five feet, repositioning the entranceway, changing the color, and increasing signage, all of which will result in improved highway visibility (see Property and Equipment). Presently, the building is covered with red brick in the style of an industrial complex rather than a restaurant. The color does not stand out and the shape is unfamiliar. By imparting a distinct architectural style to the building, the structure will become an icon that customers can easily recognize and remember.

Parking

There are 75 parking spaces directly adjacent to the restaurant, and the shopping center has space for an additional 1,500 cars. Given the broad range of operating hours for the stores in the plaza, parking utilization will be even throughout the day and availability should not be an issue (see land development plan at end of section).

Major Daytime and Evening Traffic Generators Within 2½ Miles

"Cluster marketing" has become a buzzword of the 90s. General Mills, at one time the largest restaurant operator in the industry, practiced it by locating all of its restaurant concepts at a site (Red Lobster, China Coast, and Olive Garden), instead of just one of them. General Mills's objective was to offer customers a broader range of complementary choices and thereby attract a larger pool of customers. Retailers achieve the same outcome by bundling complementary services together such as a video store and a laundromat. Ultimately, the result is an increase in sales.

The heavy concentration of stores and restaurants around the Hamburger Hut location creates the same cluster marketing effect. There are two national chain restaurants nearby and five more within 2½ miles. Consequently, customers come to the area knowing that they will find a restaurant that matches their taste. Other lunch-time traffic generators include shopping centers, office complexes, and hotels (see Table 6-1 on previous page). The majority are on 10th Street, within a five-minute drive of the site.

For its dinner business, the restaurant expects to attract diners from the surrounding residential communities (see Trade Area Demographics, p.25). Because customers have more time for dinner and are willing to travel further, Picaro's expects to draw from within a five mile-radius of the site.

Total Number of Retail Establishments

Northeast Minneapolis is a haven for national retail chains as well as smaller businesses. The total number of retail establishments in the area is significant for two reasons. First, a heavy concentration of stores in one area can create the critical mass necessary to make the region a shopping destination. There are 327 retailers in the region adjacent to the site. One hundred and nineteen of them have between 5 and 19 employees and 15 have more than 50 employees (see Table 6-2).

Second, a successful retail sector is a sign of a healthy economy. The region can support numerous merchants because it is populated by a desirable customer base. In demographic terms, the trade area has many residents and an above-average household income. The retail sector also thrives because local government has created a favorable business climate. Northeast Minneapolis will continue to be a prime location for retailers of all sizes and types.

Average Daily Traffic Counts — 56,400 Cars Pass the Site Daily

The traffic volume and the traffic speed at the site are ideal. The average daily traffic count is 56,400. According to *American Demographics* magazine, the average daily traffic count for some major-chain hamburger restaurants is 35,000, with no less than 14,000 in any location. While traffic at the sight far exceeds 35,000, the concept is not as dependent on passing traffic as is a fast food concept. Picaro's is a destination restaurant, not an impulse or convenience concept. It is expected that the uniqueness of the restaurant will draw people to the location, lessening its reliance on passing traffic.

Average Daily Traffic Count In Front of Site

The speed of traffic in front of the site is also favorable. According to *Restaurant Management* magazine, fast-moving traffic is less likely to stop. The ideal speed is between 35 and 40 miles per hour. Given the modest congestion and traffic signals on 10th Street, traffic travels at approximately that pace. The traffic patterns are heaviest and the speeds slowest in the morning hours and during rush hour. The morning traffic should have no impact on business since Picaro's will not serve breakfast, while slow-moving evening traffic could increase sales.

Sales figures for a nearby competitor were examined in an effort to tie local traffic volume to sales. A Rib-It restaurant is located down the street from the site at the intersection of 10th Street and University Avenue. In comparison, 65,000 cars per day pass through that intersection. The full-service, 200-seat concept with an average check of $13.50 grosses $45,000 per week. The comparison is encouraging, even though traffic volume is only one factor in the site selection process.

As Picaro's expands to multiple locations, traffic volume will become a more critical issue. Popular concepts like TGI Friday's were unique to the marketplace upon their inception and were considered destination restaurants at one time. With Friday's growth in popularity came familiarity with the concept and a change in the customerís perception. Eventually, TGI Friday's became less destination oriented and more impulse oriented. Consequently, the volume of traffic became a crucial issue in the site selection process.

Buying Power Index

Residents of the neighborhoods surrounding the site have substantial disposable income and spend it frequently. This is evidenced by the Buying Power Index (BPI). The BPI represents a region's share of total buying power out of all U. S. households. It can be used to gauge the overall retail sales potential of an area and serves as a relative measurement. The figure is expressed as a percentage and is based on a weighted average of a ZIP code's total population, retail sales and income. The BPI for the region was obtained from the 1993 *Lifestyle ZIP Code Analyst* and was derived by Market Statistics.

The graph in Figure 6-1 shows that with the exception of one ZIP Code, the region is a good one for retailers. The area surrounding the site also compares favorably with downtown Minneapolis, an area generally considered to be economically healthy. The eastern portion of northeast Minneapolis is the only aberration. It falls short of expectations due to a combination of low income levels and low population density.

The ZIP codes in Table 6-4 represent the contiguous geographic area surrounding the site. The area covers roughly a five-mile radius. Downtown Minneapolis was added in the last row for comparison purposes. Restaurant sales are included in the column containing Retail Sales (000s) for all goods in the area. The indirect correlation between the BPI and the level of retail sales is a result of the weighting given to other variables in the BPI equation, such as total population and income.

Crime Trends — Crime Around the Site Dropped by 12%

The area around the site became safer between 1992 and 1993 while crime in Minneapolis increased on the whole. The level of crime in the area is a good indicator of the desirability of the location. No matter how well run the operation may be, it is unlikely that patrons will risk their safety to frequent it, especially at night.

Figure 6-3 shows that despite a citywide increase in crime, the area around the site trended favorably. The 6th District experienced a 7% decrease in crime. More specifically, crime in Sector G of the 6th District fell by 6% and crime in Sector H (where the site is located) dropped by 12%. At the same time, it is clear from Figure 6-2 that crime in the entire city increased over the period in question. There were approximately 300 more crimes committed in Minneapolis in 1993 than in 1992.

The number of major offenses in the trade area was examined over a two-year period to determine what, if any, trends were present. Major crime offenses in the area surrounding the site, Sectors G & H of the 6th District, were also compared to the city as a whole. The offenses that were examined include: murder, rape, robbery, aggravated assault, burglary, theft, and auto theft. A map showing the police districts in question appears at the end of this section.

Note: Supporting the text of the original plan is full-page material not included here: an aerial photograph of the downtown area; a map of the greater metropolitan area; a downtown street map showing the restaurant's location; a plaza lease plan; a land development layout plan; and a district map.

Trade Area Demographics

The demographics of this site make it a winner — just ask the nearby Olive Garden, Applebee's, and Rib-It restaurants which rack up over $2 million apiece in annual sales. The average income, age, occupation, density, and ethnic composition of the surrounding neighborhoods are all favorable. The result is a target market with an above-average tendency to dine out.

A concept that meets the consumer's needs in terms of price, convenience, and uniqueness could capture a sizable share of the disposable income spent in local restaurants. Picaro's fills a void in the marketplace for value-based Mexican food, positioning it to attract market share and achieve a high volume of sales.

A closer look at the demographics reveals why the market is so attractive. First, the age distribution is favorable. Baby Boomers aged 35 to 54 have the strongest representation as a group and are expected to grow the most. Considered to be close to the ideal customer, Baby Boomers lead hectic lives, they have children, they have higher than average incomes and are considered to be heavy restaurant users.

Second, there will be a dramatic increase in the number of households with incomes above $50,000 by 1998. This translates into increased buying power and is consistent with the assertion that Baby Boomers typically have higher than average incomes. It is also a sign of the existence of dual-income households. For the restaurateur this means more customers with less time, again indicating the presence of potentially heavy restaurant users.

Third, anecdotal evidence suggests that the location is surrounded by a closely knit community that has a penchant for ethnic foods and that relies on word of mouth. From a marketer's perspective, a good product will sell itself in this environment.

In conclusion, a Picaro's restaurant at this location could achieve equal or better sales volumes than the national chains that sell a product of competing quality. This is so because there is a positive correlation between household income and spending habits. And, the average household income in the trade area is on par with the average household income in the larger Minneapolis Designated Market Area (DMA), which supports several national chains.

The following section looks at the prospective customer in the trade area, the ideal customer, and trends in the trade area.

Customer Demographic Profile — The Baby Boomer

While there are other convenient labels for demographic segments, none fits the trade area (the area within a five-mile radius of the site) quite as well as "Baby Boomer." The largest group of residents in the trade area exhibits a similar age distribution, average household income, and occupation profile as the Baby Boomer.

History
According to the Simmons Research Bureau, in the decade immediately following the Second World War, over three and a half million babies were born in the United States each year. In comparison, the total number of births each year before the war averaged 2.5 million. The first wave of Baby Boomers was born between 1946 and 1955 and numbers approximately 36 million adults. The second wave was born between 1955 and 1960. Since then, this generation's priorities have been studied and chronicled by marketers across the nation. From this information, their needs, desires, and lifestyles were profiled. The impact this has had on the housing industry, baby care products, home furnishings, and education has been dramatic.

In 1986, the first of 76 million Boomers (first and second wave) turned 40. As the first wave made the transition through middle age, their tastes and preferences dominated the priorities of marketers and impacted younger Boomers as they approached middle age. Today, their presence is still felt.

Education, Occupation, Income, Age

Baby Boomers are likely to have children under thirteen years of age, be short on time due to both parents working, and have a relatively high level of education and income. A hassle-free, value-oriented, child-friendly restaurant that features healthful food will meet their lifestyle needs and could gain substantial market share and a loyal following.

Boomers are different from the previous generation in that they achieved a higher level of education. High-school graduation was the norm for them, whereas the majority of their predecessors did not complete high school. Moreover, the college experience, once the province of a select few, was more widespread. Forty-seven percent had some exposure to college, while 10% went on to receive graduate degrees.

The presence of a better-educated consumer has impacted the development and marketing of the Picaro's concept (Figure 7-1). The growing sophistication of the Baby Boomer has been taken into account in concept development, food ingredients, and marketing claims. The restaurant is positioned as fresh, healthful, and value-oriented.

According to Simmons, the Baby Boomers' desire for a formal education paid off. Boomers are 55% more likely than the average adult to be in professional and managerial occupations, and 24% above average in representation among white-collar workers. Figure 7-2 on the following page shows that 24% of the trade area works in Professional and Executive functions, and 39% is in Sales, Support, and Technical functions.

The dual-income household is the norm for Baby Boomers. This group is among America's most affluent, with about 50% earning $40,000 or more per year. Their households are 36% more likely to have two wage earners than the average home. Time and convenience are important to parents who spend most of their day at work. A comfortable, stress-free atmosphere is Picaro's solution to the harried lifestyle of a working household.

Statistics citing a mini-baby boom among the Baby Boomers indicate a need for restaurants that are child-tolerant. Baby Boomers are getting married and having children later in life. As seen from Figure 7-3, the 0- to 5-year-old and 6- to 13-year-old categories are well represented in the trade area and provide an opportunity for astute marketers. The informal atmosphere of Picaro's accommodates children.

Ideal Customer Profile

The customer profile in the trade area compares favorably with the generally accepted ideal customer profile. The age distribution and housing characteristics are similar, and while the income and education levels are slightly below the ideal, they are above average for Minneapolis. More importantly, Picaro's was designed with future expansion in mind and meets the needs of the ideal customer everywhere.

Micro-Vision Restaurant, a site-selection service, and *Restaurants & Institutions* magazine defined ideal customers as affluent families and suburban homeowners that are long on income but short on time. As one would expect, these lifestyle segments have the highest away-from-home consumption rate of any group of diners, and are much like residents in the trade area.

Ideal customers dine out frequently at restaurants from all segments. In fact, they have below-average eating-out tendencies only for quick-serve fish/seafood restaurants and midscale steakhouses. On the whole they prefer upscale restaurants for lunch and dinner. They also show a very strong preference for quick service. They are 1.3 times more likely to frequent midscale, family-style concepts, and they like casual dining and full-service Mexican and Oriental concepts.

As described by *Restaurants & Institutions*, these customers are largely dual-income families, predominantly white (94%), with school-age children. Fourteen percent are in their 40s; 11% are in their 50s; 9% are between 30 and 34; and 8% are 35 to 39. They are well educated — 2.5 times more likely than average to be college graduates. Nationwide they represent about 6% of households. Their average income is $61,000. Sixty-three percent of these households have two incomes, 1.2 times the national average.

Upscale families live on the fringe of the metropolitan area. Seventy-eight percent are home-owners, and 84% live in single-family homes. They are most likely to have three- to four-person households (40%) or even five (15%).

Affluent families and suburban homeowners travel often. Because of their propensity for travel, they have a high tendency to use rental cars and to spend more than $60 a month on long-distance phone calls. Almost two-thirds of upscale families own two or more cars. Thirty-eight percent commute 15 to 29 minutes to work. Thirty-five percent have a longer drive. Typically their radios are tuned to all-news or easy listening stations. Their hobbies are upscale and health oriented and include tennis, skiing, golf, and racquetball. They tend to read airline, business, computer, dining, and travel magazines.

Trade Area Trends

The proposed site has the population density and income level appropriate for a value-based restaurant. Picaro's can maintain a sales volume and average ticket price equal to its casual dining competitors because the projected Average Income for the trade area is similar to that for the 14-county DMA which supports many successful value-based restaurant chains. A lower average income would have signaled a price-sensitive market and would have indicated the need for a concept that is competitively priced and volume-oriented. An higher Average Income would have indicated the need for an upscale, premium-priced concept.

A close examination of the demographic data yields additional clues to the future needs of customers. The data in Table 7-1 on the following page cover the area within a five-mile radius of the site for the years 1993 and 1998. Age and income characteristics are broken out in the first column of the table. The last column, Percent Change, highlights 1998 projected age and income trends.

Age

The most significant population growth in the trade area is projected to occur in the 35- to 54-year-old range. This suggests the presence of Baby Boomers and reflects the aging of the group. The 35 to 44 category is expected to grow by 1.3 % and the 45 to 54 group is expected to increase by 5.3%. The expected increase in Median Age from 39 to 40 is a result of this growth pocket. Due to their busy lives and higher incomes, Baby Boomers dine out frequently.

A large number of young professional couples, aged 25 to 34, also live in the area. As the popularity of the nearby town of Golden Valley grows, the demand for affordable housing in the St. Louis Park section of Minneapolis is outstripping the supply. Young professionals who have a desire to be near downtown are moving to the northeast as an alternative. Affordable housing and good public schools are the reason. This migration will help to fuel the retail sector.

Income

There is a projected increase in upper Household Income ranges as a result of the presence of Baby Boomers and young professionals. While a decrease is expected in the ranges below $49,999, a dramatic expansion will take place in the upper ranges. The number of households in the $75,000 to $99,999 income range is expected to grow by 25.8% and the number in the $100,000 to $149,999 range will jump by 64.3%. There will be a 48.8% climb in Household Incomes over $150,000.

The projected rise in Household Income levels is also caused in part by an increasing number of dual-income households. In a two income household there is more time spent at work and less time for cooking. Studies by GDR/CREST Enterprises show that of the first $10,000 of the second income, as much as 60% is spent on dining away from home. This is good news for restaurants that cater to families.

As Household Incomes in the trade area rise, 1998 Per Capita Income is expected to grow by 17.1% to $21,575. In 1993, Per Capita Income for the trade area was higher than the Minneapolis Designated Market Area (DMA). It is expected that the 1998 Per Capita Income will also be higher. Like rising Household Incomes, a rising Per Capita Income is a good sign.

A favorable pattern also emerges for 1998 Median and Average Household Incomes. The Median Income is expected to increase 14.9% to $45,104 and the Average Income is projected to increase 16% to $54,736. Projected incomes for the trade area are well above the level for all of Hennepin County and are close to the average for the larger DMA which includes 14 counties. Because of the positive correlation between income levels and retail spending, this is a good sign. As stated earlier, residents with similar income levels are able to sustain several national restaurant chains located throughout the DMA.

Demographic Maps

The thematic maps at the end of this section were designed to graphically depict the future demographic composition of the target market with respect to Household Income, Per Capita Income, Median Age, and Workforce Composition. The visual images were created using 1998 projected demographic data from the U.S. Census Bureau at the block group level. There are approximately 4,200 block groups in the Minneapolis MSA (Metropolitan Statistical Area).

The scale used to measure a given demographic characteristic is shown in the legend to the right of each map. In most cases, the scale was broken into ranges containing an equal number of block groups. For example, on a quartile scale 25% of the block groups in the entire MSA (or 1,125 block groups) fall into each range. Naturally, the map shows only those within the radius of the target site. This allows the viewer to look for favorable pockets within the site, and to determine if a demographic characteristic is proportionately or disproportionately represented in comparison to the 25% present in the entire MSA.

Household Income

The red area in the Household Income map depicts households with incomes ranging from $103,847 to $564,999. Surrounding the red is a heavy concentration of yellow, representing incomes in the $63,586 to $103,847 range. The presence of high incomes in the trade area is promising, given that only 3% of the block groups in the entire Minneapolis MSA belong in the red range and only 12% belong in the yellow range. In other words, the target market has a disproportionately large share of these households. This is one reason why the area has a strong Buying Power Index, as noted in the section titled Location.

Per Capita Income

Interestingly, the red concentration on the map, which represents the highest Per Capita Income range, runs parallel with the border of Meeker County. This pattern may be a result of the city wage tax forcing those in the upper income brackets to move out of the city. The blue area closest to the site is a local airport, thereby registering no Per Capita Income.

Median Age

The 35- to 47-year-old age group is strongly represented in the trade area east of the site, as seen from the red shading. This group could be characterized as "Second Wave" Baby Boomers and represents approximately 14% of the Minneapolis MSA. Given boomers' predisposition to dine out frequently, it is fortunate that the site has a disproportionately large share of them.

Work-force Composition

The red area, representing blue-collar workers, is almost nonexistent in Meeker County. Higher property values outside of Minneapolis and fewer craft/trade jobs could account for this division. As a matter of fact, most of the blue-collar workers in the trade area reside east of Tenth Street, closer to I-35.

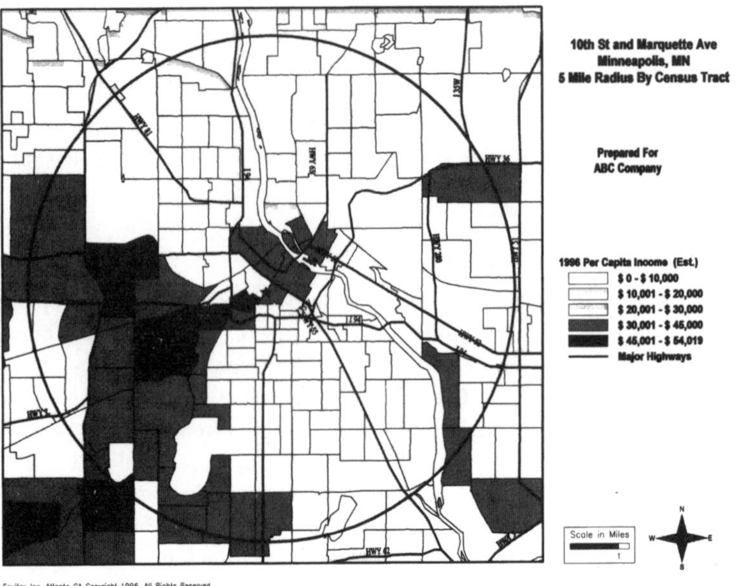

Note: Supporting the text of the original plan is full-page material not included here: four demographic maps documenting — within a five-mile radius — household and per capita income, workforce composition, and median age data *(see sample above).*

Competition

The metropolitan Twin Cities area is underserved by Mexican restaurants. Within a five-mile radius of Minneapolis, there are approximately 12 full-service independent operators and one national chain. Penetration of the market for Mexican food is negligible when compared to other ethnic segments such as Italian and Chinese. When the market is segmented by average check price, the playing field becomes even smaller, with Southwestern and Spanish gourmet restaurants dropping out at the high end, and taco houses dropping out at the low end. If quality and consistency are used as the next benchmark, few of the independent operators survive the cut. A sampling of restaurant reviews is offered as evidence under Segment Competitors. When it comes to national chains, this leaves Chi Chi's as the closest competitor. With two stores in the Minneapolis area, Chi Chi's has not pursued an expansion strategy. Flagging sales and the recent acquisition of the company have left Chi Chi's in a holding pattern. Picaro's management sees opportunity in the marketplace for a fresh, new provider of Mexican food.

The competitors discussed below fall into the major categories of direct and indirect competitors, but for purposes of this analysis a conservative approach was taken and all restaurants, even those not in the Mexican or casual theme segments, were examined. Some were examined because of their geographic proximity to the site, while others were studied because they are segment leaders. Still, some were reviewed simply because significant competitive information on the concept was available. For example, International House of Pancakes was analyzed because there is an IHOP location adjacent to the site. Olive Garden was examined because it is a segment leader.

This information was compiled from on-line services, 10-K's, 10-Q's, business & general periodicals, research bureaus, and in some cases directly from competitors. Wherever possible, current information including actual financials was used, although in some cases, facts, figures, and estimates have changed. This section is broken down into two subsections titled Neighboring Competitors and Segment Competitors. Competitors appear alphabetically in the subsections.

Neighboring Competitors

Chi Chi's

During the late 70s and early 80s, Louisville, Kentucky-based Chi Chi's made its bid to be the country's premiere Mexican dinner-house chain. Started in 1976 by Mexican restaurant magnate Marno McDermott and investor Max McGee in Minneapolis, Chi Chi's galloped into the American heartland with its brand of Sonoran-style Mexican food. It seized an opportunity to develop the Midwest, practically virgin territory for Mexican food. On the West Coast, El Torito was entrenching. On the eastern horizon was the appealing prospect of developing the urban centers of the East Coast.

During the nine-year tenure of Chi Chi's chairman and CEO Shelly Frank, who retired in April 1986, rapid expansion was the byword. In fiscal years 1981–1983, company-owned restaurants increased in number from 11 to 46. In fiscal 1985 alone, 42 new Chi-Chi's opened, 27 company-owned and 15 franchised, increasing total units by more than a third and company units by more than 50%. By the time Frank departed, the company had grown to a 200-unit chain.

Chi Chi's blazed new territory into markets it later regretted. During the rapid expansion period, Chi Chi's, like most of the industry, was building large-scale 10,000 to 12,000-sq.-ft. units. As the optimistic growth projections faded, it became difficult to run these stores profitably. The company was also criticized for clustering restaurants for competitive advantage and market share when the result was a decline in the average unit volumes of established units. In a profitability move, Chi Chi's began the disposal of 21 marginal stores by 1987.

As company performance indicated, there were fundamental problems that needed attention. The next three years were characterized by declining store sales and net income. Arguably, the rapid pace of expansion during Frank's tenure heightened company weaknesses in operations and personnel management. Symptomatic of the problems was a manager turnover rate as high as 80%. And, overall franchisee confidence was low in the wake of the Chapter 11 bankruptcy of Chi Chi's Food Services Inc., a large Oklahoma City-based franchise. The company was increasingly closed to communications, both external and internal. It was said that Chi-Chi's seemed to have forgotten how to treat staff, store management, employees, franchisees, and the customer. The result was inconsistent food and service and an alienated customer base.

Suffering from flattened customer traffic and a sharp decline in liquor sales, the company was vulnerable to a takeover attempt. Consequently, the Washington D.C. Carlyle Group made an $185-million offer to take the company private. Carlyle proposed to merge Chi Chi's into a new company. The move would have allowed it to concentrate on development rather than satisfying shareholder needs. Chi Chi's was not interested and responded with a stock repurchase program.

As part of its turnaround attempt in 1988, Chi Chi's launched G.W. Sharkey's Oyster Bar & Grill, Papanda's Border Cafe, and Chajita's Mexican quickserve restaurant. The new weapons were designed to bolster the company's presence in current markets, provide a more appealing and cost effective means for penetrating new ones, and serve as the means for entering areas where the Chi Chi's concept had failed. The medium-priced Sharkey's concept was designed to catch new business in saturated markets, while Papanda's and Chajita's were positioned to lead a charge back into the South and Southwest.

G.W. Sharkey's was an oyster bar and grill in a 6,500-sq.-ft. bright red building with green and white awnings. Informality, price/value, and display mesquite grilling were featured. Sharkey's had a projected $6 lunch and $11 dinner check average, and occupied a price point midway between Red Lobster and Bay Street. Papanda's was a Mexican dinner house with some American menu items designed for the Southeast and South Central U.S. Chajita's was Chi Chi's first fling with fast food. The concept incorporated touches more common with dinner houses than fast food, but it had a limited menu, quick service, relatively low prices, and a drive-through window. Customers ordered by number and dispensed their own soft drinks. The average start-up cost for a Sharkey's or Papanda's was about 1.2 million. Papanda's measured about 6,000 square feet, and Chajita's 4,500 square feet.

The company also brought in Hal Smith, formerly of Chili's, as president. His work involved changing policies, and freshening up stores with new decor, new uniforms, and a new plate presentation. Smith's move to improve profitability also included writing off marginal units, cutting administrative staffing and overhead, and developing a downsized unit prototype. He traced unit sales declines to inconsistent customer satisfaction, made worse by the company's high management turnover. To reduce turnover, he improved compensation, reduced excessive work hours, and established a new training program. Smith's revised 10-week training program included basic business skills such as following a P&L, personal time management, interweaving, and specific job-area training in the kitchen, bar, and dining room. His new bonus plan rewarded a store's top-line and bottom-line performance. Previously, managers who ran high-profit restaurants were taken care of but, managers of lower-volume stores often weren't making bonuses even thought they may have worked as hard. Paperwork reduction resulted in greater management attention to service. Improved recruiting and hiring policies brought in more qualified candidates.

At the store level, the Chi Chi's structure is led by a general manager who supervises a kitchen manager, service manager, and bar manager, each of whom may have an assistant, depending on the store volume. An hourly office manager lightens the paperwork load on the GM.

In close competition with Chi Chi's is Irvine, California-based El Torito Restaurants, Inc., a division of Restaurant Enterprises Inc. with 195 units and $400 million in annual sales. El Torito Restaurants is the parent for several concepts, including 24 Casa Gallardos, 10 Casa Marias, 160 El Toritos, and one El Torito Grill. Restaurant Enterprises acquired El Torito Restaurants from W.R. Grace & Co. in New York.

Olive Garden

In December 1994, General Mills spun off its $3.2-billion restaurant business to concentrate on breakfast cereals and other foods. Its nearly 1,200 restaurants included Red Lobster and Olive Garden. At the time, it had halted expansion of China Coast and was experiencing stubborn sales with Olive Garden. The Olive Garden had been on a winning streak since expanding from a single restaurant in 1982 to 458 when fiscal 1994 ended. However, last year for the first time, the chain experienced a decline in same-store sales of 4%. The trend continued into fiscal 1995's first quarter, when same store-sales fell 6%. One explanation for General Mills's decision is that it was experiencing what happened at PepsiCo, which had problems after installing corporate headquarters executives atop its restaurant business.

When Olive Garden trailblazed its way across the nation during the late 80s, accomplishing what many critics said couldn't be done, the chain's competition came almost entirely from local restaurants. Some believe that, competitively speaking, Olive Garden is a victim of its own success. It pioneered a niche and showed the world how successful it could be. Before long, everyone wanted to be in it. In meeting the challenge of finding sites and then building, staffing, and training to open 50 restaurants per year, the chain may not have paid enough attention to keeping the concept current. In today's marketplace, customers have too many choices, and a concept that stands still will not prosper.

Aside from the numerous regional operators that battle Olive Garden for customers, such deep-pocketed firms as Brinker International have sandwiched the chain from a check-average standpoint, with its Romano's Macaroni Grill and Spageddies concepts. PepsiCo also jumped into the fray with its East Side Mario's concept, and corporate competition is heating up from the likes of Morrison Restaurants, Outback Steaks, TGI Friday's and Golden Corral, all of which have Italian concepts that they are looking to expand. There are also the likes of Chili's and Ruby Tuesday, which offer Italian- inspired dishes.

Along with the sheer number of competitors, the sign of maturation in the Italian segment, analysts and operators say, is the division of markets along food and price lines. Instead of one broad category which Olive Garden defined for so long, the casual dining business appears headed toward different tiers. Romano's and one or two other chains go after customers willing to pay $13 or more per check. Then there are lower-end casuals such as Spageddies and Mozzarella Cafe, a Morrison concept. In the meantime, Olive Garden is trying to span all segments. Nevertheless, competition will continue to increase as the Italian segment is divided up by a number of competitors who are trying to go national. It is thought that only one or two can achieve the necessary size, but the competition will adversely affect Olive Garden no matter what happens.

By late 1994, Olive Garden knew that some strategic changes had to be made. It is hoping to recharge both traffic and consumer appeal through an evolutionary push that includes new unit prototypes, an expanded advertising budget, and quarterly menu promotions. One of the problems that Olive Garden faces against leaner, smaller restaurants is overhead. With its new prototype, a cafe, it is hoping to add capacity and extend its name without taking on heavy labor or management costs. Each cafe acts as a satellite for a nearby full-service Olive Garden, usually within three to five miles, and serves light pasta and breakfast items. The units are about 800 square feet in size, with approximately 40% of the menu offerings of a full size store. They will serve as outposts in malls and other locations where Olive Garden hasn't gone before and where there is the promise of tremendous exposure. In another attempt to polish its image, all general managers and kitchen managers are being trained at the Culinary Institute of America to sharpen their skills in food preparation and presentation.

Up to now, Olive Garden has made its name as a suburban concept. The average customer is a white-collar customer who dines out several times a week. The menu is changed four times per year with seasonal items. The main selling point is the soup, salad, and breadsticks. Lasagna Classico is the top seller, along with Seafood Linguine. Olive Garden units average $2.6 million per year. Highlights:

* All stores are company owned.
* Television local spot buys are the company's primary medium.
* The chain stresses regional and store-level marketing.
* There are more than 100 different menus in circulation.
* It does not relocate managers, they are all local.
* Managers' incentives are based on gross sales and operating profits. They can earn bonuses for high quality assurance.
* Servers receive raises when they pass $25,000 in sales and again at $50,000, $100,000 and each $100,000 thereafter.
* Olive Garden often staffs higher than its competitors, adding extra people to each shift to ensure that service won't suffer if there is a sudden surge.

Applebee's Neighborhood Grill & Bar

Applebee's International, headquartered in Overland Park, Kans., develops franchises and operates a rapidly expanding chain of 535 Applebee's Neighborhood Grill and Bar restaurants. Applebee's Neighborhood Grill and Bar, which recently purchased five franchise restaurants in the Minneapolis area for approximately $9.5 million, is considered by some analysts to be the low-cost producer in the industry. Some believe that the low average check at Applebee's should allow it to steal a portion of the market for inside fast-food dining and make it the fast-food chain of the '90s. And, according to a poll by *Restaurant Business* magazine, it was recently ranked No. 1 in employee training.

Applebee's International has been on a roll for some time. At year-end 1993, there were 361 restaurants open in 40 states. Systemwide comparable sales were up 3.2% for fiscal 1994. Comparable sales for company-owned restaurants were up 3.7%, while comparable sales for franchised restaurants were up 3.1%. By 1995 same-store sales had increased or were better for two years in a row. For the year ended in December 1994, sales totaled $888.9 million, compared with $608.5 million in fiscal 1993. The company added 145 restaurants during the same period for a total of approximately 535 Applebee's Neighborhood Grill and Bar restaurants in 43 states, one Canadian province, and the island of Curaçao.

The company has often stated that it aimed to acquire an additional casual dining concept which could be expanded as a franchising vehicle complementary to Applebee's Neighborhood Grill and Bar. In March 1995, it completed its acquisition of Rio Bravo Restaurant Concepts Inc., which owns and operates 13 Rio Bravo Cantina restaurants, for about $66 million in stock and debt. Rio Bravo Cantinas are Tex-Mex restaurants similar to Chi-Chi's Mexican restaurants. The acquisition represents Applebee's entry into the fast-growing ethnic segment of the casual dining market.

The Atlanta-based Rio Bravo also operates three other specialty restaurants. They are Green Hills Grille, Ray's on the River, and an upscale Rio Bravo concept called Rio Bravo Grill. Rio Bravo's restaurants are in Georgia, Florida, and Tennessee. Rio Bravo reported sales of $54 million in fiscal 1994, including $38.5 million from the 12 Rio Bravo restaurants that were opened at the end of 1994.

Bay Street Restaurants Inc.

S & A Restaurant Corporation launched the Bay Street concept in 1984 to diversify its dinner-house holdings. It is known primarily for fresh seafood and "library-style" bars with high ceilings. The restaurants offer a daily array of fresh fish that can be cooked to order, which represents about 40% to 50% of sales. Among Bay Street's signature items are deep-fried crawfish tail, blackened fish, shrimp, chicken breasts, and garlic shrimp served on linguine. Each restaurant emphasizes its bar, accounting for 15% to 30% of sales, which shows all labels on shelves that reach to the ceiling. The beverage list contains not only wines and Champagnes but also specialty drinks, beers, liqueurs, and kids' nonalcoholic drinks. Suburban locations have a broader family appeal.

In 1988 Pillsbury, S & A's parent company, kicked off its long-publicized restaurant divestiture program by selling the 16-unit Bay Street chain to a management group backed in part by Restaurant Associates, a New York dinner-house operator. Pillsbury sold Key West, 30 Steak and Ales, and at least 130 Burger Kings in an effort to focus on its core businesses and boost the stagnant Steak and Ale chain.

After acquiring it from Pillsbury, S & A Restaurant Corp. Senior Vice President Alan Palmieri, who became president of the Bay Street chain, planned to sell 12 of the original 16 restaurants. The new president's philosophy was to tailor the remainder of the stores to their regions through menu, uniform, decor, and servic,e and erase the chain mentality. At one time, five different menus existed for nine units. The Northeast units offered more fresh fish selections, and servers were a bit more formal, with shirts and ties.

By 1991, Palmieri discovered that customers were perceiving Bay Street as too upscale, so three units were shuttered and one was opened in Washington Township, N.J. After selling off five more Texas-based units in 1994, Bay Street relocated its headquarters from Plano, Tex., to Red Bank, N.J., and made some minor concept changes. The words "Seafood Restaurant" were placed adjacent to the restaurant name on all buildings, while neon signs advertising seafood offerings were placed in the windows. The three remaining Bay Street units generated aggregate sales of $7.3 million during 1993. The per-person check averaged $20 with liquor, which represented about 20% of the mix.

In September 1994, Uno Restaurant Corp., operator and franchisor of the Pizzeria Uno chain, acquired the remaining three units of Bay Street Restaurants Inc. with plans to expand the seafood dinner-house concept throughout the Northeast. Bay Street operates as a separate division under the umbrella of Uno Corp., which operates about 120 Pizzeria Uno restaurants. Presently, the three Bay Street units are located in Philadelphia, Woodbridge, N.J., and Schaumburg, Ill.

Pizzeria Uno expects to spend the next year familiarizing itself with the concept. Mr. William Bouffard, President of Bay Street Restaurants Inc. and Mr. James Vinz, Vice President of Operations, will be joining the Uno management team and heading up the Bay Street operation. They are targeting the aging Baby Boomer market. Primary customers are 30- to 55-year-olds who have comfortable incomes, want to eat right, and appreciate freshness and lighter fare.

Bennigan's

Launched in 1976 by Steak and Ale founder Norman Brinker, Bennigan's quickly became one of the rapid growth chains in the casual segment through the remainder of the 1970s and into the 1980s. The restaurant was founded as a "fern bar" concept, but it was not all smooth sailing. In 1983 and 1984, liquor represented 43% of sales. By 1986, it had dropped to 37%. AUV had declined from $2.4 million in 1983, to $2.3 million in 1984, and $2.2 million in 1985. This caused a shift in emphasis away from the original concept of the happy-hour gathering place. By 1986, sales had increased for the first time in four years, back to $2.3 million.

At the time, Bennigan's generated 70% of the profits of S & A Restaurant Corp., but its parent had two other concepts, Bay Street and Steak and Ale. However, Steak and Ale was also struggling, reporting stagnant sales while losing market share to more contemporary and vibrant casual themers like Outback Steakhouse, Chili's, and Applebee's Neighborhood Grill and Bar. By March 1989, Grand Metropolitan P.L.C. (the latest corporate parent) decided to sell Pillsbury's Steak and Ale and Bennigan's restaurant chains for $431 million.

Over the years, the outlook for the concepts has not improved. In 1993 the chain's problems were compounded by top management firings at S&A. In 1994 Bennigan's aimed to revitalize the once-powerful brand equity of its 223-unit concept, and to position it for market share battles against casual theme competitors through new marketing efforts.

Chili's Grill & Bar

In 1983, Norman Brinker joined Chili's, a small, but fast growing company gaining a lot of attention. He brought in a whole new management team and steered a course away from the company's gourmet burger concept. Brinker added char-broilers, used fajitas to get away from the hamburger niche, and made the concept more upscale. This necessitated a major adjustment in service from baskets to tray and platter, but paid off. The restaurant moved toward the broader, trendy menu of a casual themer while maintaining its reputation for being fun and casual.

Since the initial public offering in 1984, Chili's has continued to thrive. It grew with the Baby Boomer generation while keeping the warmth and personality of owner-operated stores. The restaurant has a cocoon-like atmosphere that offers privacy, as opposed to the see-and--be-seen fern bars of yesteryear. Calming green and gray tones, modest plants, and booth seating provide a pleasant, nonthreatening atmosphere. Service personnel are dressed in jeans or slacks, knit shirts, and aprons to reinforce the casual, informal environment.

Emphasis is placed on serving substantial portions of fresh, quality food at modest prices. Regulars return to Chili's for the signature fajitas, baby back ribs, half-pound burgers, sandwiches, salads, and margaritas, not to mention quick service and affordable prices. Entrée selections range in menu price from $4.75 to $9.95, with the average revenue per meal, including alcoholic beverages, approximating $8.55 per person. Chili's lower average check is one reason why the company feels it has higher customer frequency than TGI Friday's and Bennigan's. The 45-minute table turn is another reason, and new items are only added to the menu begrudgingly. A full-service bar is available at each Chili's, with frozen margaritas offered as the concept's specialty drink. During the year ended June 1994, food and nonalcoholic beverage sales constituted approximately 86% of revenues, and beverage sales accounted for the remaining 14%. With 200 seats, Chili's AUV is around $2 million.

Chili's markets to a 25- to 55-year-old target population with increasing family business. As of June 1994, there were 277 company-operated stores and 83 franchises. It is growing at a rate of 30 to 34 company units and 25 to 30 franchises per year. During the past two years, the company entered into several international franchise agreements, which will bring Chili's to Australia, France, Puerto Rico, and the United Kingdom. In fiscal 1994, the first Chili's outside North America opened in Singapore and Malaysia. In October 1993, the company acquired the assets of a franchisee, which operated four Chili's restaurants in Pennsylvania and Ohio for approximately $8,165,000 in cash.

Brinker International, Inc., is the parent company of Chili's. The corporation owns over 458 restaurants in 43 states and overseas. In addition to Chili's there is Grady's American Grill, Romano's Macaroni Grill and Spageddies Italian Kitchen. Grady's is an upscale dinner house with an average check of $10.95. Macaroni Grill is an upscale theme restaurant with an average check of $13.50. Spageddies is a casual, family-oriented, moderately priced Italian restaurant with an average check of $9.25.

Most recently, Brinker acquired ownership of On The Border restaurants which included 14 company-owned and 7 franchised stores. On The Border are full-service, casual Tex-Mex theme restaurants featuring Southwest mesquite-grilled specialties and traditional Tex-Mex entrées and appetizers served in generous portions at modest prices. On The Border serves "Texas-sized" nonalcoholic beverages in addition to offering a full-service bar. On The Border restaurants feature an outdoor patio, booth and table seating, and brick and wood walls with a Southwest decor. On The Border restaurants also offer enthusiastic table service intended to minimize customer waiting time and facilitate table turnover, while simultaneously providing customers with a satisfying, casual dining experience.

Entrée selections range in price from $5.45 to $12.95, with the average revenue per meal, including alcoholic beverages, approximating $10 per person. During the year ended June 1994, food sales constituted approximately 74% of sales, with alcoholic beverages accounting for the remaining 26%. Brinker recently teamed up with the new Mexican fast-food chain Taco Cabana as an expansion vehicle.

International House of Pancakes

International House of Pancakes, franchiser of pancake and sausage houses, is noted for its treats. In 1987, it was on the brink of financial failure and was taken private by Kelso & Co. In an attempt to become a player in the three-meal market it was brought public in 1991. By 1992, operating standards were inconsistent, the chairman sold 12,000 shares of his stock, and the buyout firm that brought the company public sold a huge 80% stake of its holdings. Nevertheless, some believe that the IHOP Corporation has been rejuvenated into a financially strong and briskly growing national restaurant with a unique franchising strategy. For 120 months prior to 1992, it consistently improved average store sales.

What some find so attractive about IHOP is that quarterly earnings are only loosely tied to the amount of food that it sells. Its franchising strategy provides a consistent cash stream which has been likened to a "restaurant annuity." As a franchiser, IHOP develops everything from the design of each restaurant to the land it stands on before it turns over operations to a franchisee. IHOP gets paid $200,000 to $350,000 for developing the sites, with 20% of that paid up front in cash. At that point, the restaurant is essentially a turnkey operation, giving IHOP unusual control over its performance. Franchisees pay the company rent and royalties, buy pancake mix from IHOP, and contribute to their own advertising. There are multiple, high-margin revenue streams including rent, leasing of equipment, and pancake batter.

IHOP earned $4.7 million in 1991 on revenues of $105 million. But less than half of those revenues came directly from selling food. About $52 million was from rent, service fees, and other renewable charges from the franchise system. Naturally, with royalties tied to the franchise system, IHOP stands to make more profit when business is brisk.

IHOP has also gained fans on Wall Street because of its skill in remodeling old stores and turning them into powerful producers. On average, remodeling increases store sales by 15%. At the same time, it is bringing in new franchisees who are not only investors but are taking an interest in running operations.

Segment Competitors

The number of Mexican restaurants in Metropolitan Minneapolis-St. Paul is small, given the total number of restaurants of all types in the region and its sizable population. If the market for Mexican is segmented by price, location, and quality, the playing field becomes even smaller, with only a handful of competitors existing within a five mile radius of the site. The table on the following pages alphabetically lists the independent Mexican restaurants in the area. Because they are not public companies, competitive information is limited to restaurant reviews and anecdotal evidence.

Marketing

The Picaro's marketing strategy can be described in three steps:

1) Get to know the customer.
2) Orchestrate the opening.
3) Reach the customer with guerrilla marketing (flyers, take-one's, advertising specialties, etc.).

This strategy is short-term, cost-effective, and most appropriate for the size and nature of the business.

There is no need for a costly advertising program, given limited financial resources. Instead, hiring and training will be emphasized. Ultimately, it is the quality of the product and the operational skill and experience of the staff that will attract customers. During the start-up phase, word-of-mouth from satisfied customers will play a large part in increasing awareness and gaining exposure for the restaurant. Nevertheless, the importance of marketing cannot be overlooked.

A business must differentiate itself from the local competition and understand the marketplace to succeed in a competitive environment. There was a time when QSC (Quality, Service, Cleanliness) was all that a restaurant needed to stay ahead of the competition. In today's market, this program is no longer a primary marketing advantage but a necessity. Quality food, competent service and cleanliness will facilitate market entry, but will not insure success or longevity—understanding the customer will.

Customer focus has become the gospel of leading businesses. Like most industries that mature, the restaurant industry is moving from a product-driven focus to a customer-driven focus. This is evidenced by the introduction of heart-healthy menus and child-friendly environments. These concepts were born from an identification of the consumer's needs. By gathering information about the customer and using it to position the concept, the customer is less of a mystery and product acceptance is less of a gamble.

Getting to Know the Customer

Marketers should be anxious to pinpoint customers who dine out frequently, according to George Rice, president of GDR/CREST Enterprises, a restaurant consulting firm. There is a customer segment that dines out on a regular basis. These individuals are considered heavy buyers and dominate the restaurant industry. This is not to be confused with the operations perspective that says that everybody who walks through the door is a customer. From an operational perspective it's true, but from a marketing perspective, efforts must be structured to have the greatest impact.

It is also necessary to define the pool of customers as precisely as possible. Different locations and concepts have different factors that drive sales. For example, there are differences between dinner business on weekends and weekdays. The variables that should be considered are: product mix, price, timing, party composition, prior activity, subsequent activity, time available, and the entire rationale for eating out.

Picaro's will collect customer information and feedback on an ongoing basis. Accepting the premise that identification of the consumer and consumer needs is crucial to success, it is also important to understand that niche marketing is at best an imprecise and neverending science. It is necessary to continually determine what customers are seeking and to adjust the concept to their changing tastes.

Before the Store is Open

Management used psychographics to identify consumer needs and preferences in the trade area. Psychographics are based on lifestyle data and can give clues to an individual's hobbies and interests. While it is difficult to fully identify and understand the prospective Picaro's customer prior to having an established customer base, data extracted from the *Lifestyle ZIP Code Analyst* offers some insight (see Table 9-1).

For example, management knows that the blue- collar community living in northeast Minneapolis prefers to spend instead of save. It is not surprising that the area is a haven for retailers. While moneymaking opportunities are a priority for residents, they are not interested in the traditional approaches to earning income such as career and investing. They prefer sweepstakes and gambling.

Residents of the trade area also have simple tastes. Dieting, health foods, and fashion are high priorities for them — they support 94 apparel stores. Yet, they are not interested in high fashion or culture. Fine art, antiques, wines, and foreign travel are eschewed for more common pleasures. Free time is likely to be spent on bowling, crossword puzzles, video games, science fiction, self-improvement, and veterans' affairs, but not on high-tech computers.

As a result of their urban lifestyles, outdoor activities do not interest residents of the trade area. Camping, hiking, hunting, recreational vehicles, pets, and the environment are low priorities. There is also a healthy disdain for upscale sports and leisure activities, e.g., running, tennis, skiing, golfing, and boating.

While several conclusions can be drawn from this psychographic profile, it is clear that dieting and games of chance are popular with residents. Therefore, it can be assumed that low-fat menu items will be popular, and that contests will be one of the most effective ways to grab the customer's attention. These are only two examples of how knowing the customer is helpful, yet customer needs and preferences will be reflected in every aspect of the Picaro's concept.

The primary interests of customers in the trade area are summarized below. Descriptions were prepared by Mediamark Research.

> Fashion: Single-female households account for more than one third of fashion-clothing enthusiasts. Fashion-conscious householders are heavy credit users (four out of every ten are frequent users of department store credit cards). Compared to a typical U.S. household, male fashion enthusiasts are at least 2.8 times more likely to spend $250 or more per item for business suits and sports jackets. Female fashion enthusiasts are at least 1.5 times more likely to spend $75 or more per item for swim suits, sweaters, skirts, blouses, dresses, and designer jeans. Over 5% of fashion-conscious householders purchased a fur coat in the last 12 months.
>
> Moneymaking Opportunities: Nearly 20% of people with an interest in moneymaking opportunities are heavy lottery players (played six or more times during the past 30 days). They are 1.5 times more likely to participate in casino gambling than the general U.S. population.
>
> Bowling: Over 33% of the people with an interest in bowling bowl at least once a week. Over 50% own a bowling ball. They are several times more likely than the general adult population to watch bowling on TV and attend bowling matches. They are also more inclined to watch sports programs on TV.

Home Video Games: Households with an interest in home video games are two times more likely to own a personal computer and 1.8 times more likely to play electronic games than the general adult population. Nearly 60% of households that contain home video-game enthusiasts also contain children under age 18 years living at home. Over 10% of these households have purchased at least one children's video game in the past 12 months.

Science Fiction: More than 60% of science fiction enthusiasts are between 25 and 44 years of age. They are well informed on issues concerning science, nature, the environment, and new technology. They surround themselves with high tech toys, including personal computers (35%), photographic equipment (36%), stereo equipment (65%), video recorders (63%), and video games (24%).

Bible/Devotional Reading: Bible/devotional reading enthusiasts are regular church attendees. Over 10% are active church board members. They are 1.4 times more likely to work as volunteers and take part in civic issues than the general U.S. population. Other prominent interests of Bible/devotional readers include walking for health (52%), sewing (31%), entertaining and visiting grandchildren (30%), and health foods (24%).

Casino Gambling: Casino gamblers are generally older, married, and have a household income greater than $40,000. Over one-third are between the ages of 55 and 74. They enjoy the "good life", and when compared to the U.S. population are 2.5 times more likely to participate in moneymaking opportunities and real estate investments. They also have a high interest in traveling across the USA (62%) and watching sports on TV (58%).

Crossword Puzzles: Nearly 50% of crossword puzzle enthusiasts are 55 years of age or older. They are heavy book-readers. Other prominent interests of crossword puzzle enthusiasts are needlework and knitting (35%), working on craft projects (41%), and home decorating (30%).

Dieting/Weight Control: People interested in dieting/weight control are three times more likely to be active in controlling and monitoring their diets compared to the general U.S. population. Over 46% of these dieters consider weight loss to be the primary reason for dieting. Other reasons cited by dieters include monitoring cholesterol levels (29%), maintaining current weight (26%), and being physically fit (21%). Over 44% of dieters buy low-cholesterol prepared foods. The majority of methods used by dieters to control weight are based on either doctor-approved and recommended diet plans or personal exercise programs.

Entering Sweepstakes: People who enjoy entering sweepstakes are in search of convenient moneymaking opportunities. Over one-third of sweepstakes entrants are aged 45 and over with total household income under $30,000. Other activities of sweepstakes enthusiasts include catalog shopping (40%), solving crossword puzzles (34%), and collecting coins and stamps (16%).

Health Foods/Vitamins: People interested in health foods are twice as likely to take vitamins (particularly vitamin C, vitamin E, and calcium) than the general adult population. They enjoy fashion (26%), self-improvement programs (36%), gourmet cooking (31%), and attending cultural and arts events (28%). They are also very much inclined to read health magazines.

Self-Improvement: People with an interest in self-improvement seek to improve the physical, mental, and financial aspects of their lives. Compared to the U.S. adult population, they are 2.4 times more likely to be involved in career-oriented activities such as attending seminars and night classes, 2.2 times more likely to eat health foods, 1.8 times more likely to attend cultural arts events, and 1.9 times more likely to invest in real estate. Other prominent interests of self-improvement enthusiasts include home decorating (44%) and fashion (28%).

Veterans' Benefits/Programs: Households with an interest in veterans' benefits/programs are primarily headed by military veterans age 55 years or older. They enjoy spending their time visiting with grandchildren (45%), entering sweepstakes (34%), participating in community and civic activities (23%), and collecting coins and stamps (17%).

The interests summarized above were identified from Table 9-1. If three or more out of nine ZIP codes in the trade area exhibited an extremely strong interest in a hobby or activity, it is highlighted in the table. The first column of the table is grouped into convenient categories to facilitate understanding. The last column on the right side of the table shows downtown data for comparison purposes.

Numbers in the center columns reflect the degree of interest in an activity for a particular ZIP code. While an index of 100 is average, an index of 120 reflects an interest 20% above average and an index of 80 reflects an interest 20% below average. The average is based on the Minneapolis ADI (Area of Dominant Influence). The ADI is a market defined by measurable TV viewing patterns of individuals making up the area. Each county in the U.S. is allocated exclusively to one ADI. ADI's are defined by the Arbitron Ratings Company.

After the Store Is Open

Once the store is open, survey cards will be used to gather current customer information and feedback on quality, service and cleanliness. ZIP codes collected from the cards will be supplied to a marketing research firm which will use the corresponding demographic and psychographic data to develop a more accurate profile of the Picaro's customer. The information will be used to fine-tune the concept, but, more importantly, it will allow management to pinpoint its marketing efforts through market segmentation.

Segmentation will be employed through positioning, media, and creative strategies. Marketing efforts will be aimed at the target population segment that is most interested in and can best be served by Picaro's. Since it is impossible to satisfy the whole market and since resources for advertising and promotion are limited, this approach is economical.

A positioning strategy dictates how the product is positioned in relation to the competition. In other words, Picaro's will be aimed at customers who want a fun, family-oriented restaurant that serves fresh Mexican and American food in large portions at reasonable prices. Employing a media strategy means selecting the appropriate medium to reach the population segment identified as being most interested in Picaro's. For example, if families with children are the target market, then it would make sense to sponsor a children's event or charity. The creative strategy relates to the design of marketing materials. The graphics, pictures and writing of everything from menus to mailers, will reflect the tastes and preferences of the target audience.

In summary, a key part of the Picaro's marketing strategy will be to get to know the customer. This information will flow through to the positioning, media, and creative strategies. Management now has a partial understanding of tastes and preferences in the trade area. To form a complete picture and segment the market, additional data will be gathered with customer survey cards. By leveraging this information, Picaro's management expects to attract and fulfill the needs of its heaviest users.

Orchestrating the Opening

<u>Public Relations</u>
Public relations will be used prior to the opening, to help establish the restaurant's identity as a value-oriented provider of fun and fresh Mexican food, and to lend credibility to the operation. Public relations is one of the most effective marketing tools because it is free, believable, widely read, and lends credibility to the business, but it goes beyond free press. Public relations encompasses community relations and the joining of clubs and organizations. Community service can be helpful in making powerful contacts, and if the work truly benefits the community and is not self-serving, the positive impact on the business can be enormous. Joining clubs and organizations is also a great way to network and to introduce the organization to other local businesses.

<u>Training</u>
Picaro's management recognizes the importance of training as a marketing tool. Two weeks prior to opening the restaurant, the staff will be schooled in product, service, and selling techniques unique to the Picaro's style of operating. Training for servers will cover topics from team serving to the differences between a burrito and an enchilada. Special arrangements have been made for the cooks to train in the kitchen of a Mexican restaurant that serves a style of food similar to Picaro's. While the customer will already have made the decision to patronize Picaro's before coming into contact with its staff, it is ultimately the staff that is responsible for repeat business.

<u>Opening</u>
A professional public relations firm will coordinate the Grand Opening of Picaro's. There will be a soft opening and a formal opening prior to the Grand Opening. The soft opening, which will occur first, will be attended by family and friends of the staff, as well as suppliers and contractors. The formal opening will be attended by local politicians and community and business leaders. To maximize publicity surrounding the formal opening, the event will be linked to a popular local charity. The restaurant will charge a flat fee for admission and donate the proceeds to the charity. While increasing customer awareness, the openings will serve as a dry run for the staff and allow for fine-tuning of the concept.

Guerrilla Marketing

Like guerrilla warfare, guerrilla marketing takes advantage of the small size of a business by exploiting marketing opportunities through the speed and flexibility with which decisions can be made and acted on. In their article in the *Harvard Business Review*, John Welsh and Jerry White remind business owners that "a small business is not a little big business." So, while Picaro's may apply positioning, media, and creative strategies like Fortune 500 firms, its pool of financial resources will be smaller and its outlook narrower.

<u>Tactics</u>
The primary marketing objective of Picaro's is to create an economical marketing program. One way to do this is through barter. Advertising space in local publications will be exchanged for banquet or party facilities, and house charge accounts will be traded for other services and products. Coop advertising is another way to meet the objective. By including brand names and logos on the menu and on point-of-sale merchandise, production costs for these materials will be subsidized. Picaro's will also establish its own in-house advertising agency. This will allow the company to capture the 15% discount or commission normally received by advertising agencies when placing advertising. Finally, to save money when getting its message out, Picaro's will choose media that cost less, are narrowly focused and have a longer shelf life. Some examples are listed below.

> * Take-One's/Flyers: Picaro's will produce a brochure that provides customers with information on different Mexican spices and chili peppers, styles of cooking, and types of food. The restaurant will assume the role of educator and establish itself as an expert on Mexican food.

* Word-of-Mouth: To speed the word-of-mouth process along, take-out menus that tell the Picaro's story will be used to remind customers of why they patronized the restaurant in the first place. Also, two-for-one coupons will be presented to customers to motivate them to return with new patrons.

* In-Store Sampling: Offering samples of a top-quality product is one of the most effective methods of marketing, according to Jay Conrad Levinson, author of *Guerrilla Marketing*. It is the essence of honesty, since a poor product cannot be hidden. Because this marketing method does not require repetition like print advertising, and because small portions can be served, the cost of sampling can be insignificant in comparison to other media.

* Contests: Research shows that customers in the trade area have an affinity for contests and sweepstakes (see "Getting to Know the Customer"). Foot traffic at the restaurant can be increased by requiring participants to come to the location to enter contests and to return to determine if they have won a prize. While they may be initially attracted by the promotion, they will eventually become involved with the restaurant.

* Point-of-Purchase: Point-of-purchase signs on tables can create impulse sales. Since the customer is already in a buying mood, it is a good time to influence his/her decision. The signs make it easier for customers to make decisions by helping them to select products. They also create extra selling or cross-merchandising opportunities. Ultimately, signs serve as silent salespeople by offering product information and reinforcing the concept's message and positioning.

* Advertising Specialties: While matchbooks and refrigerator magnets will not do the whole selling job, they can increase take-out business by facilitating customer recall. They may also remind customers of Picaro's expertise in Mexican food.

* Shirts/Sweatshirts: Clothing with a unique design can attract attention and become a novelty item. Customers will associate top-quality materials with a top-quality operation. Like advertising specialties, these items will not do the whole selling job, but they can convey a positive message.

* Signage: Picaro's will take two approaches to signage. The traditional approach includes mounting a sign outside the building on pylons. Unfortunately, an increasing number of townships have limited the height and size of commercial signs in the name of aesthetics. So, the second approach involves using the interior and exterior surfaces of the building to gain additional attention. The building itself will have a distinct shape, color, and texture that makes it recognizable and easy to remember. From outside the building, customers will see neon lights and brightly lit displays through Picaro's large windows.

* Local Print Media: Magazine advertising provides the opportunity to match the mood of a specific publication. It also provides the opportunity to present a longer message, since readers normally become more involved with magazines and spend more time reading them. Newspaper advertising will lend Picaro's message the same importance as the news.

* Direct Mail: Once the Picaro's customer profile is established, direct mail will allow management to pinpoint the target audience and deliver its desired message, whether it is an announcement or a coupon.

Ultimately, a superior operation will be the best form of marketing for Picaro's. Since a good portion of sales will come from repeat business, it is the staff's responsibility to ensure that customers have a positive experience and pass the word along. Yet, the simplicity and low cost of Picaro's marketing program will not undermine its effectiveness. Segmentation, guerrilla marketing, and knowledge of the customer will enable Picaro's to maximize the impact of its message without investing large sums of money in advertising.

Appendix A: Financials

YEARLY PROJECTED INCOME STATEMENT
FOR THE FISCAL YEAR ENDING DECEMBER 31

	Pro Forma	1996	1997	1998	1999	2000	2001
SALES							
Sales - Food (Table #1)		$1,528,800	$1,559,376	$1,590,564	$1,622,375	$1,654,822	$1,687,919
Sales - Beverage		382,200	389,844	397,641	405,594	413,706	421,980
NET SALES		$1,911,000	$1,949,220	$1,988,204	$2,027,968	$2,068,528	$2,109,898
COST OF SALES							
Food Costs		$504,504	$506,797	$512,957	$519,160	$529,543	$540,134
Beverage Costs		85,995	87,715	89,469	91,259	93,084	94,945
TOTAL COST OF SALES		$590,499	$594,512	$602,426	$610,419	$622,627	$635,079
GROSS PROFIT		$1,320,501	$1,354,708	$1,385,778	$1,417,560	$1,445,901	$1,474,819
PAYROLL & RELATED EXPENSES							
Salaries & Wages (Table #2)		$517,881	$516,543	$521,904	$527,272	$537,817	$548,574
Employee Bonuses	0.50%	9,555	9,746	9,941	10,140	10,343	10,549
Taxes & Benefits		72,503	72,316	73,067	73,818	75,294	76,800
TOTAL PAYROLL & RELATED EXPENSE		$599,939	$598,605	$604,911	$611,230	$623,454	$635,923
OCCUPANCY EXPENSES							
Rent (Table #3)		85,500	85,500	85,500	98,325	98,325	98,325
CAM Charges (Table #3)		14,250	14,250	14,250	16,530	16,530	16,530
Telephone		4,500	4,500	4,500	4,500	4,500	4,500
Water		5,200	5,200	5,200	5,200	5,200	5,200
Sewer		3,000	3,000	3,000	3,000	3,000	3,000
Gas		13,000	13,000	13,000	13,000	13,000	13,000
Electric		40,000	40,000	40,000	40,000	40,000	40,000
Property Taxes (Table #3)		9,975	10,274	10,582	10,900	11,227	11,564
Insurance		35,000	35,000	35,000	35,000	35,000	35,000
TOTAL OCCUPANCY COSTS		$210,425	$210,724	$211,032	$226,455	$226,782	$227,119
MAINTENANCE & SUPPLY EXPENSES							
Cleaning Supplies		$12,000	$12,000	$12,000	$12,000	$12,000	$12,000
Kitchen & D.R. Supplies		30,000	30,000	30,000	30,000	30,000	30,000
Office Supplies		6,000	6,000	6,000	6,000	6,000	6,000
SUBTOTAL SUPPLIES		$48,000	$48,000	$48,000	$48,000	$48,000	$48,000
Cleaning & Extermination		$6,000	$6,000	$6,000	$6,000	$6,000	$6,000
Protection Services		2,000	2,000	2,000	2,000	2,000	2,000
Repairs & Maintenance - Building		5,000	5,848	7,953	7,953	7,953	7,953
Repairs & Maintenance - Equipment		15,000	15,789	18,093	18,093	18,093	18,093
Trash Removal		12,000	12,000	12,000	12,000	12,000	12,000
Uniforms		4,000	4,093	4,175	4,259	4,344	4,431
SUBTOTAL MAINTENANCE		$44,000	$45,730	$50,221	$50,304	$50,389	$50,476
TOTAL MAINTENANCE & SUPPLY EXPENSES		$92,000	$93,730	$98,221	$98,304	$98,389	$98,476
OPERATING EXPENSES							
Advertising		$19,110	$38,984	$39,764	$40,559	$41,371	$42,198
Bank Service Charges		1,000	1,000	1,000	1,000	1,000	1,000
Cash Over/Short		500	500	500	500	500	500
Comp. Dinners		3,822	3,898	3,976	4,056	4,137	4,220
Employee Meals		4,778	4,873	4,971	5,070	5,171	5,275
Equipment Rental		20,000	20,000	20,000	20,000	20,000	20,000
Management Fee	3.50%	66,885	68,223	69,587	70,979	72,398	73,846
Merchant Fees	2.00%	19,110	19,492	19,882	20,280	20,685	21,099
Misc. Operating Expenses		5,924	6,043	6,163	6,287	6,412	6,541
Music		2,000	2,000	2,000	2,000	2,000	2,000
Taxes & Licenses		5,000	5,000	5,000	5,000	5,000	5,000
TOTAL OPERATING EXPENSES		148,129	170,013	172,844	175,731	178,675	181,679
OPERATING INCOME (LOSS)		$270,008	$281,635	$298,770	$305,831	$318,600	$331,622
OTHER INCOME (EXPENSE)							
Depreciation (Table #4)		(11,319)	(14,176)	(17,033)	(19,890)	(22,747)	(25,604)
Amortization (Table #4)		(60,800)	(60,800)	(60,800)	(60,800)	(60,800)	0
Interest Earned		4,800	4,800	4,800	4,800	4,800	4,800
Interest Expense		0	0	0	0	0	0
Legal & Accounting		(15,000)	(15,000)	(15,000)	(15,000)	(15,000)	(15,000)
TOTAL OTHER INCOME (EXPENSE)		($82,319)	($85,176)	($88,033)	($90,890)	($93,747)	($35,804)
NET INCOME BEFORE TAXES		$187,689	$196,459	$210,737	$214,940	$224,853	$295,818

YEARLY PROJECTED INCOME STATEMENT - COMMON
FOR THE FISCAL YEAR ENDING DECEMBER 31

	Pro Forma	1996	1997	1998	1999	2000	2001
SALES							
Sales - Food (Table #1)		80.00%	80.00%	80.00%	80.00%	80.00%	80.00%
Sales - Beverage		20.00%	20.00%	20.00%	20.00%	20.00%	20.00%
TOTAL SALES		100.00%	100.00%	100.00%	100.00%	100.00%	100.00%
COST OF SALES							
Food Costs		33.00%	32.50%	32.25%	32.00%	32.00%	32.00%
Beverage Costs		22.50%	22.50%	22.50%	22.50%	22.50%	22.50%
TOTAL COST OF SALES		30.90%	30.50%	30.30%	30.10%	30.10%	30.10%
GROSS PROFIT		69.10%	69.50%	69.70%	69.90%	69.90%	69.90%
PAYROLL & RELATED EXPENSES							
Salaries & Wages (Table #2)		27.10%	26.50%	26.25%	26.00%	26.00%	26.00%
Employee Bonuses		0.50%	0.50%	0.50%	0.50%	0.50%	0.50%
Taxes & Benefits		3.79%	3.71%	3.68%	3.64%	3.64%	3.64%
TOTAL PAYROLL & RELATED EXPENSE		31.39%	30.71%	30.43%	30.14%	30.14%	30.14%
OCCUPANCY EXPENSES							
Rent (Table #3)		4.47%	4.39%	4.30%	4.85%	4.75%	4.66%
CAM Charges (Table #3)		0.75%	0.73%	0.72%	0.82%	0.80%	0.78%
Telephone		0.24%	0.23%	0.23%	0.22%	0.22%	0.21%
Water		0.27%	0.27%	0.26%	0.26%	0.25%	0.25%
Sewer		0.16%	0.15%	0.15%	0.15%	0.15%	0.14%
Gas		0.68%	0.67%	0.65%	0.64%	0.63%	0.62%
Electric		2.09%	2.05%	2.01%	1.97%	1.93%	1.90%
Property Taxes (Table #3)		0.52%	0.53%	0.53%	0.54%	0.54%	0.55%
Insurance		1.83%	1.80%	1.76%	1.73%	1.69%	1.66%
TOTAL OCCUPANCY COSTS		11.01%	10.81%	10.61%	11.17%	10.96%	10.76%
MAINTENANCE & SUPPLY EXPENSES							
Cleaning Supplies		0.63%	0.62%	0.60%	0.59%	0.58%	0.57%
Kitchen & D.R. Supplies		1.57%	1.54%	1.51%	1.48%	1.45%	1.42%
Office Supplies		0.31%	0.31%	0.30%	0.30%	0.29%	0.28%
SUBTOTAL SUPPLIES		2.51%	2.46%	2.41%	2.37%	2.32%	2.27%
Cleaning & Extermination		0.31%	0.31%	0.30%	0.30%	0.29%	0.28%
Protection Services		0.10%	0.10%	0.10%	0.10%	0.10%	0.09%
Repairs & Maintenance - Building		0.26%	0.30%	0.40%	0.39%	0.38%	0.38%
Repairs & Maintenance - Equipment		0.78%	0.81%	0.91%	0.89%	0.87%	0.86%
Trash Removal		0.63%	0.62%	0.60%	0.59%	0.58%	0.57%
Uniforms		0.21%	0.21%	0.21%	0.21%	0.21%	0.21%
SUBTOTAL MAINTENANCE		2.30%	2.35%	2.53%	2.48%	2.44%	2.39%
TOTAL MAINTENANCE & SUPPLY EXPENSES		4.81%	4.81%	4.94%	4.85%	4.76%	4.67%
OPERATING EXPENSES							
Advertising		1.00%	2.00%	2.00%	2.00%	2.00%	2.00%
Bank Service Charges		0.05%	0.05%	0.05%	0.05%	0.05%	0.05%
Cash Over/Short		0.03%	0.03%	0.03%	0.02%	0.02%	0.02%
Comp. Dinners		0.20%	0.20%	0.20%	0.20%	0.20%	0.20%
Employee Meals		0.25%	0.25%	0.25%	0.25%	0.25%	0.25%
Equipment Rental		1.05%	1.03%	1.01%	0.99%	0.97%	0.95%
Management Fee		3.50%	3.50%	3.50%	3.50%	3.50%	3.50%
Merchant Fees		1.00%	1.00%	1.00%	1.00%	1.00%	1.00%
Misc. Operating Expenses		0.31%	0.31%	0.31%	0.31%	0.31%	0.31%
Music		0.10%	0.10%	0.10%	0.10%	0.10%	0.09%
Taxes & Licenses		0.26%	0.26%	0.25%	0.25%	0.24%	0.24%
TOTAL OPERATING EXPENSES		7.75%	8.72%	8.69%	8.67%	8.64%	8.61%
OPERATING INCOME (LOSS)		14.13%	14.45%	15.03%	15.08%	15.40%	15.72%

THE COMPANY LIMITED PARTNERSHIP

MONTHLY PROJECTED INCOME STATEMENT
FOR THE FISCAL YEAR ENDING DECEMBER 31

	Pro Forma	Jan	Feb	Mar	Apr	May	Jun	Jul	Aug	Sep	Oct	Nov	Dec	TOTAL
SALES														
Sales - Food		$125,600	$132,000	$133,600	$130,400	$123,200	$94,400	$133,600	$123,200	$138,400	$130,400	$132,000	$132,000	$1,528,800
Sales - Beverage		31,400	33,000	33,400	32,600	30,800	23,600	33,400	30,800	34,600	32,600	33,000	33,000	382,200
NET SALES		$157,000	$165,000	$167,000	$163,000	$154,000	$118,000	$167,000	$154,000	$173,000	$163,000	$165,000	$165,000	$1,911,000
COST OF SALES														
Food Costs		$41,448	$43,560	$44,088	$43,032	$40,656	$31,152	$44,088	$40,656	$45,672	$43,032	$43,560	$43,560	$504,504
Beverage Costs		7,065	7,425	7,515	7,335	6,930	5,310	7,515	6,930	7,785	7,335	7,425	7,425	85,995
TOTAL COST OF SALES		$48,513	$50,985	$51,603	$50,367	$47,586	$36,462	$51,603	$47,586	$53,457	$50,367	$50,985	$50,985	$590,499
GROSS PROFIT		$108,487	$114,015	$115,397	$112,633	$106,414	$81,538	$115,397	$106,414	$119,543	$112,633	$114,015	$114,015	$1,320,501
PAYROLL & RELATED EXPENSES														
Salaries & Wages		$42,547	$44,715	$45,257	$44,173	$41,734	$31,978	$45,257	$41,734	$46,883	$44,173	$44,715	$44,715	$517,881
Employee Bonuses	0.50%	785	825	835	815	770	590	835	770	865	815	825	825	9,555
Taxes & Benefits		5,957	6,260	6,336	6,184	5,843	4,477	6,336	5,843	6,564	6,184	6,260	6,260	72,503
TOTAL PAYROLL & RELATED EXPENSE		$49,289	$51,800	$52,428	$51,172	$48,347	$37,045	$52,428	$48,347	$54,312	$51,172	$51,800	$51,800	$599,939
OCCUPANCY EXPENSES														
Rent (Table #3)		$7,125	$7,125	$7,125	$7,125	$7,125	$7,125	$7,125	$7,125	$7,125	$7,125	$7,125	$7,125	$85,500
CAM Charges (Table #3)		1,188	1,188	1,188	1,188	1,188	1,188	1,188	1,188	1,188	1,188	1,188	1,188	14,250
Telephone		375	375	375	375	375	375	375	375	375	375	375	375	4,500
Water		433	433	433	433	433	433	433	433	433	433	433	433	5,200
Sewer		250	250	250	250	250	250	250	250	250	250	250	250	3,000
Gas		1,083	1,083	1,083	1,083	1,083	1,083	1,083	1,083	1,083	1,083	1,083	1,083	13,000
Electric		3,333	3,333	3,333	3,333	3,333	3,333	3,333	3,333	3,333	3,333	3,333	3,333	40,000
Property Taxes (Table #3)		831	831	831	831	831	831	831	831	831	831	831	831	9,975
Insurance		2,917	2,917	2,917	2,917	2,917	2,917	2,917	2,917	2,917	2,917	2,917	2,917	35,000
TOTAL OCCUPANCY COSTS		$17,535	$17,535	$17,535	$17,535	$17,535	$17,535	$17,535	$17,535	$17,535	$17,535	$17,535	$17,535	$210,425
MAINTENANCE & SUPPLY EXPENSES														
Cleaning Supplies		$1,000	$1,000	$1,000	$1,000	$1,000	$1,000	$1,000	$1,000	$1,000	$1,000	$1,000	$1,000	$12,000
Kitchen & D.R. Supplies		2,500	2,500	2,500	2,500	2,500	2,500	2,500	2,500	2,500	2,500	2,500	2,500	30,000
Office Supplies		500	500	500	500	500	500	500	500	500	500	500	500	$6,000
SUBTOTAL SUPPLIES		$4,000	$4,000	$4,000	$4,000	$4,000	$4,000	$4,000	$4,000	$4,000	$4,000	$4,000	$4,000	$48,000
Cleaning & Extermination		$500	$500	$500	$500	$500	$500	$500	$500	$500	$500	$500	$500	$6,000
Protection Services		167	167	167	167	167	167	167	167	167	167	167	167	2,000
Repairs & Maintenance - Building		417	417	417	417	417	417	417	417	417	417	417	417	5,000
Repairs & Maintenance - Equipment		1,250	1,250	1,250	1,250	1,250	1,250	1,250	1,250	1,250	1,250	1,250	1,250	15,000
Trash Removal		1,000	1,000	1,000	1,000	1,000	1,000	1,000	1,000	1,000	1,000	1,000	1,000	12,000
Uniforms		333	333	333	333	333	333	333	333	333	333	333	333	4,000
SUBTOTAL MAINTENANCE		$3,667	$3,667	$3,667	$3,667	$3,667	$3,667	$3,667	$3,667	$3,667	$3,667	$3,667	$3,667	$44,000
TOTAL MAINTENANCE & SUPPLY EXPENSES		$7,667	$7,667	$7,667	$7,667	$7,667	$7,667	$7,667	$7,667	$7,667	$7,667	$7,667	$7,667	$92,000
OPERATING EXPENSES														
Advertising		$1,593	$1,593	$1,593	$1,593	$1,593	$1,593	$1,593	$1,593	$1,593	$1,593	$1,593	$1,593	$19,110
Bank Service Charges		83	83	83	83	83	83	83	83	83	83	83	83	1,000
Cash Over/Short		42	42	42	42	42	42	42	42	42	42	42	42	500
Comp. Dinners		319	319	319	319	319	319	319	319	319	319	319	319	3,822
Employee Meals		398	398	398	398	398	398	398	398	398	398	398	398	4,778
Equipment Rental		1,667	1,667	1,667	1,667	1,667	1,667	1,667	1,667	1,667	1,667	1,667	1,667	20,000
Management Fee	3.50%	5,495	5,775	5,845	5,705	5,390	4,130	5,845	5,390	6,055	5,705	5,775	5,775	66,885
Merchant Fees	2.00%	1,570	1,650	1,670	1,630	1,540	1,180	1,670	1,540	1,730	1,630	1,650	1,650	19,110
Misc. Operating Expenses		494	494	494	494	494	494	494	494	494	494	494	494	5,924
Music		167	167	167	167	167	167	167	167	167	167	167	167	2,000
Taxes & Licenses		417	417	417	417	417	417	417	417	417	417	417	417	5,000
TOTAL OPERATING EXPENSES		$12,243	$12,603	$12,693	$12,513	$12,108	$10,488	$12,693	$12,108	$12,963	$12,513	$12,603	$12,603	$148,129
OPERATING INCOME (LOSS)		$21,754	$24,410	$25,074	$23,746	$20,757	$8,803	$25,074	$20,757	$27,066	$23,746	$24,410	$24,410	$270,008

THE COMPANY LIMITED PARTNERSHIP

MONTHLY PROJECTED INCOME STATEMENT - COMMON
FOR THE FISCAL YEAR ENDING DECEMBER 31

	Pro Forma	Jan	Feb	Mar	Apr	May	Jun
SALES							
Sales - Food		80.00%	80.00%	80.00%	80.00%	80.00%	80.00%
Sales - Beverage		20.00%	20.00%	20.00%	20.00%	20.00%	20.00%
NET SALES		100.00%	100.00%	100.00%	100.00%	100.00%	100.00%
COST OF SALES							
Food Costs		33.00%	33.00%	33.00%	33.00%	33.00%	33.00%
Beverage Costs		22.50%	22.50%	22.50%	22.50%	22.50%	22.50%
TOTAL COST OF SALES		30.90%	30.90%	30.90%	30.90%	30.90%	30.90%
GROSS PROFIT		69.10%	69.10%	69.10%	69.10%	69.10%	69.10%
PAYROLL & RELATED EXPENSES							
Salaries & Wages		27.10%	27.10%	27.10%	27.10%	27.10%	27.10%
Employee Bonuses		0.50%	0.50%	0.50%	0.50%	0.50%	0.50%
Taxes & Benefits		3.79%	3.79%	3.79%	3.79%	3.79%	3.79%
TOTAL PAYROLL & RELATED EXPENSE		31.39%	31.39%	31.39%	31.39%	31.39%	31.39%
OCCUPANCY EXPENSES							
Rent (Table #3)		4.54%	4.32%	4.27%	4.37%	4.63%	6.04%
CAM Charges (Table #3)		0.76%	0.72%	0.71%	0.73%	0.77%	1.01%
Telephone		0.24%	0.23%	0.22%	0.23%	0.24%	0.32%
Water		0.28%	0.26%	0.26%	0.27%	0.28%	0.37%
Sewer		0.16%	0.15%	0.15%	0.15%	0.16%	0.21%
Gas		0.69%	0.66%	0.65%	0.66%	0.70%	0.92%
Electric		2.12%	2.02%	2.00%	2.04%	2.16%	2.82%
Property Taxes (Table #3)		0.53%	0.50%	0.50%	0.51%	0.54%	0.70%
Insurance		1.86%	1.77%	1.75%	1.79%	1.89%	2.47%
TOTAL OCCUPANCY COSTS		11.17%	10.63%	10.50%	10.76%	11.39%	14.86%
MAINTENANCE & SUPPLY EXPENSES							
Cleaning Supplies		0.64%	0.61%	0.60%	0.61%	0.65%	0.85%
Kitchen & D.R. Supplies		1.59%	1.52%	1.50%	1.53%	1.62%	2.12%
Office Supplies		0.32%	0.30%	0.30%	0.31%	0.32%	0.42%
SUBTOTAL SUPPLIES		2.55%	2.42%	2.40%	2.45%	2.60%	3.39%
Cleaning & Extermination		0.32%	0.30%	0.30%	0.31%	0.32%	0.42%
Protection Services		0.11%	0.10%	0.10%	0.10%	0.11%	0.14%
Repairs & Maintenance - Building		0.27%	0.25%	0.25%	0.26%	0.27%	0.35%
Repairs & Maintenance - Equipment		0.80%	0.76%	0.75%	0.77%	0.81%	1.06%
Trash Removal		0.64%	0.61%	0.60%	0.61%	0.65%	0.85%
Uniforms		0.21%	0.20%	0.20%	0.20%	0.22%	0.28%
SUBTOTAL MAINTENANCE		2.34%	2.22%	2.20%	2.25%	2.38%	3.11%
TOTAL MAINTENANCE & SUPPLY EXPENSES		4.88%	4.65%	4.59%	4.70%	4.98%	6.50%
OPERATING EXPENSES							
Advertising		1.01%	0.97%	0.95%	0.98%	1.03%	1.35%
Bank Service Charges		0.05%	0.05%	0.05%	0.05%	0.05%	0.07%
Cash Over/Short		0.03%	0.03%	0.02%	0.03%	0.03%	0.04%
Comp. Dinners		0.20%	0.19%	0.19%	0.20%	0.21%	0.27%
Employee Meals		0.25%	0.24%	0.24%	0.24%	0.26%	0.34%
Equipment Rental		1.06%	1.01%	1.00%	1.02%	1.08%	1.41%
Management Fee		3.50%	3.50%	3.50%	3.50%	3.50%	3.50%
Merchant Fees		1.00%	1.00%	1.00%	1.00%	1.00%	1.00%
Misc. Operating Expenses		0.31%	0.30%	0.30%	0.30%	0.32%	0.42%
Music		0.11%	0.10%	0.10%	0.10%	0.11%	0.14%
Taxes & Licenses		0.27%	0.25%	0.25%	0.26%	0.27%	0.35%
TOTAL OPERATING EXPENSES		7.80%	7.64%	7.60%	7.68%	7.86%	8.89%
OPERATING INCOME (LOSS)		13.86%	14.79%	15.01%	14.57%	13.48%	7.46%

	Jul	Aug	Sep	Oct	Nov	Dec	TOTAL
SALES							
Sales - Food	80.00%	80.00%	80.00%	80.00%	80.00%	80.00%	80.00%
Sales - Beverage	20.00%	20.00%	20.00%	20.00%	20.00%	20.00%	20.00%
NET SALES	100.00%	100.00%	100.00%	100.00%	100.00%	100.00%	100.00%
COST OF SALES							
Food Costs	33.00%	33.00%	33.00%	33.00%	33.00%	33.00%	33.00%
Beverage Costs	22.50%	22.50%	22.50%	22.50%	22.50%	22.50%	22.50%
TOTAL COST OF SALES	30.90%	30.90%	30.90%	30.90%	30.90%	30.90%	30.90%
GROSS PROFIT	69.10%	69.10%	69.10%	69.10%	69.10%	69.10%	69.10%
PAYROLL & RELATED EXPENSES							
Salaries & Wages	27.10%	27.10%	27.10%	27.10%	27.10%	27.10%	27.10%
Employee Bonuses	0.50%	0.50%	0.50%	0.50%	0.50%	0.50%	0.50%
Taxes & Benefits	3.79%	3.79%	3.79%	3.79%	3.79%	3.79%	3.79%
TOTAL PAYROLL & RELATED EXPENSE	31.39%	31.39%	31.39%	31.39%	31.39%	31.39%	31.39%
OCCUPANCY EXPENSES							
Rent (Table #3)	4.27%	4.63%	4.12%	4.37%	4.32%	4.32%	4.47%
CAM Charges (Table #3)	0.71%	0.77%	0.69%	0.73%	0.72%	0.72%	0.75%
Telephone	0.22%	0.24%	0.22%	0.23%	0.23%	0.23%	0.24%
Water	0.26%	0.28%	0.25%	0.27%	0.26%	0.26%	0.27%
Sewer	0.15%	0.16%	0.14%	0.15%	0.15%	0.15%	0.16%
Gas	0.65%	0.70%	0.63%	0.66%	0.66%	0.66%	0.68%
Electric	2.00%	2.16%	1.93%	2.04%	2.02%	2.02%	2.09%
Property Taxes (Table #3)	0.50%	0.54%	0.48%	0.51%	0.50%	0.50%	0.52%
Insurance	1.75%	1.89%	1.69%	1.79%	1.77%	1.77%	1.83%
TOTAL OCCUPANCY COSTS	10.50%	11.39%	10.14%	10.76%	10.63%	10.63%	11.01%
MAINTENANCE & SUPPLY EXPENSES							
Cleaning Supplies	0.60%	0.65%	0.58%	0.61%	0.61%	0.61%	0.63%
Kitchen & D.R. Supplies	1.50%	1.62%	1.45%	1.53%	1.52%	1.52%	1.57%
Office Supplies	0.30%	0.32%	0.29%	0.31%	0.30%	0.30%	0.31%
SUBTOTAL SUPPLIES	2.40%	2.60%	2.31%	2.45%	2.42%	2.42%	2.51%
Cleaning & Extermination	0.30%	0.32%	0.29%	0.31%	0.30%	0.30%	0.31%
Protection Services	0.10%	0.11%	0.10%	0.10%	0.10%	0.10%	0.10%
Repairs & Maintenance - Building	0.25%	0.27%	0.24%	0.26%	0.25%	0.25%	0.26%
Repairs & Maintenance - Equipment	0.75%	0.81%	0.72%	0.77%	0.76%	0.76%	0.78%
Trash Removal	0.60%	0.65%	0.58%	0.61%	0.61%	0.61%	0.63%
Uniforms	0.20%	0.22%	0.19%	0.20%	0.20%	0.20%	0.21%
SUBTOTAL MAINTENANCE	2.20%	2.38%	2.12%	2.25%	2.22%	2.22%	2.30%
TOTAL MAINTENANCE & SUPPLY EXPENSES	4.59%	4.98%	4.43%	4.70%	4.65%	4.65%	4.81%
OPERATING EXPENSES							
Advertising	0.95%	1.03%	0.92%	0.98%	0.97%	0.97%	1.00%
Bank Service Charges	0.05%	0.05%	0.05%	0.05%	0.05%	0.05%	0.05%
Cash Over/Short	0.02%	0.03%	0.02%	0.03%	0.03%	0.03%	0.03%
Comp. Dinners	0.19%	0.21%	0.18%	0.20%	0.19%	0.19%	0.20%
Employee Meals	0.24%	0.26%	0.23%	0.24%	0.24%	0.24%	0.25%
Equipment Rental	1.00%	1.08%	0.96%	1.02%	1.01%	1.01%	1.05%
Management Fee	3.50%	3.50%	3.50%	3.50%	3.50%	3.50%	3.50%
Merchant Fees	1.00%	1.00%	1.00%	1.00%	1.00%	1.00%	1.00%
Misc. Operating Expenses	0.30%	0.32%	0.29%	0.30%	0.30%	0.30%	0.31%
Music	0.10%	0.11%	0.10%	0.10%	0.10%	0.10%	0.10%
Taxes & Licenses	0.25%	0.27%	0.24%	0.26%	0.25%	0.25%	0.26%
TOTAL OPERATING EXPENSES	7.60%	7.86%	7.49%	7.68%	7.64%	7.64%	7.75%
OPERATING INCOME (LOSS)	15.01%	13.48%	15.65%	14.57%	14.79%	14.79%	14.13%

SUMMARY OF INCOME & CASH FLOW
FOR THE FISCAL YEAR ENDING DECEMBER 31

Pro Forma	1996		1997		1998		1999		2000		2001	
SALES	$1,911,000	100.00%	$1,949,220	100.00%	$1,988,204	100.00%	$2,027,968	100.00%	$2,068,528	100.00%	$2,109,898	100.00%
COST OF GOODS SOLD	590,499	30.90%	594,512	30.50%	602,426	30.30%	610,419	30.10%	622,627	30.10%	635,079	30.10%
GROSS PROFIT	$1,320,501	69.10%	$1,354,708	69.50%	$1,385,778	69.70%	$1,417,550	69.90%	$1,445,901	69.90%	$1,474,819	69.90%
TOTAL PAYROLL & RELATED EXPENSES	$599,939	31.39%	$598,605	30.71%	$604,911	30.43%	$611,230	30.14%	$623,454	30.14%	$635,923	30.14%
TOTAL OCCUPANCY COSTS	210,425	11.01%	210,724	10.81%	211,032	10.61%	226,455	11.17%	226,782	10.96%	227,119	10.76%
TOTAL MAINTENANCE & EXPENSES	92,000	4.81%	93,730	4.81%	98,221	4.94%	98,304	4.85%	98,389	4.76%	98,476	4.67%
TOTAL OPERATING EXPENSES	148,129	7.75%	170,013	8.72%	172,844	8.69%	175,731	8.67%	178,675	8.64%	181,679	8.61%
OPERATING PROFIT	$270,008	14.13%	$281,635	14.45%	$298,770	15.03%	$305,831	15.08%	$318,600	15.40%	$331,622	15.72%
OTHER EXPENSES												
Permanent Capital Expenditures	$20,000	1.05%	$20,000	1.03%	$20,000	1.01%	$20,000	0.99%	$20,000	0.97%	$20,000	0.95%
Legal & Accounting	15,000	0.78%	15,000	0.77%	$15,000	0.75%	$15,000	0.74%	$15,000	0.73%	$15,000	0.71%
Depreciation	11,319	0.59%	14,176	0.73%	17,033	0.86%	19,890	0.98%	22,747	1.10%	25,604	1.21%
Amortization	60,800	3.18%	60,800	3.12%	60,800	3.06%	60,800	3.00%	60,800	2.94%	0	0.00%
TOTAL OTHER EXPENSES	$107,119	5.61%	$109,976	5.64%	$112,833	5.68%	$115,690	5.70%	$118,547	5.73%	$60,604	2.87%
PRE-TAX INCOME	$162,889	8.52%	$171,659	8.81%	$185,937	9.35%	$190,140	9.38%	$200,053	9.67%	$271,018	12.85%
ADD:												
Depreciation	$11,319		$14,176		$17,033		$19,890		$22,747		$25,604	
Amortization	60,800		60,800		60,800		60,800		60,800		0	
NET PRE-TAX CASH FLOW	$235,008		$246,635		$263,770		$270,831		$283,600		$296,622	

PROJECTED BALANCE SHEET
FOR THE FISCAL YEAR ENDING DECEMBER 31

ASSETS	Pro Forma	1996	1997	1998	1999	2000	2001
CURRENT ASSETS							
Cash	$60,000	$60,000	$60,000	$60,000	$60,000	$60,000	$60,000
Inventory	30,000	36,649	37,382	38,130	38,893	39,670	40,464
Prepaid Insurance	5,000	5,000	5,000	5,000	5,000	5,000	5,000
TOTAL CURRENT ASSETS	$95,000	$101,649	$102,382	$103,130	$103,893	$104,670	$105,464
FIXED ASSETS							
Decor	$20,000	$20,000	$20,000	$20,000	$20,000	$20,000	$20,000
Equipment	100,000	100,000	100,000	100,000	100,000	100,000	100,000
Leasehold Improvements	140,000	140,000	140,000	140,000	140,000	140,000	140,000
Liquor License	25,000	25,000	25,000	25,000	25,000	25,000	25,000
Permanent Capital Expenditures	0	20,000	40,000	60,000	80,000	100,000	120,000
P.O.S. System	20,000	20,000	20,000	20,000	20,000	20,000	20,000
Smallwares	25,000	25,000	25,000	25,000	25,000	25,000	25,000
NET FIXED ASSETS	$330,000	$350,000	$370,000	$390,000	$410,000	$430,000	$450,000
Accounting Svcs.	$5,000	$5,000	$5,000	$5,000	$5,000	$5,000	$5,000
Architect Fees	25,000	25,000	25,000	25,000	25,000	25,000	25,000
Key Money	100,000	100,000	100,000	100,000	100,000	100,000	100,000
Legal Fees	15,000	15,000	15,000	15,000	15,000	15,000	15,000
Miscellaneous	6,000	6,000	6,000	6,000	6,000	6,000	6,000
Permits	3,000	3,000	3,000	3,000	3,000	3,000	3,000
Promotional Fees	35,000	35,000	35,000	35,000	35,000	35,000	35,000
Staff for Opening	75,000	75,000	75,000	75,000	75,000	75,000	75,000
Uniforms	10,000	10,000	10,000	10,000	10,000	10,000	10,000
Deposits	1,000	1,000	1,000	1,000	1,000	1,000	1,000
TOTAL OTHER NONCURRENT ASSETS	$275,000	$275,000	$275,000	$275,000	$275,000	$275,000	$275,000
Accumulated Amortization	$0	($60,800)	($121,600)	($182,400)	($243,200)	($304,000)	($304,000)
Accumulated Depreciation	0	(11,319)	(25,495)	(42,527)	(62,418)	(85,165)	(110,769)
TOTAL DEPRECIATION & AMORTIZATION	$0	($72,119)	($147,095)	($224,927)	($305,618)	($389,165)	($414,769)
TOTAL ASSETS	$700,000	$654,531	$600,288	$543,202	$483,275	$420,506	$415,695
LIABILITIES							
CURRENT LIABILITIES							
Accounts Payable	$0	$48,534	$48,864	$49,514	$50,171	$51,175	$52,198
Current Portion of Note	0	0	0	0	0	0	0
TOTAL CURRENT LIABILITIES	$0	$48,534	$48,864	$49,514	$50,171	$51,175	$52,198
LONG TERM LIABILITIES							
Note Payable	$0	$0	$0	$0	$0	$0	$0
TOTAL LIABILITIES	$0	$48,534	$48,864	$49,514	$50,171	$51,175	$52,198
OWNER'S EQUITY							
Accumulated Surplus (Deficit)	$700,000	$700,000	$605,996	$551,424	$493,688	$433,104	$369,331
Current Period Surplus (Deficit)	0	(94,004)	(54,573)	(57,736)	(60,584)	(63,773)	(5,834)
TOTAL OWNER'S EQUITY	700,000	$605,996	$551,424	$493,688	$433,104	$369,331	$363,496
TOTAL LIABILITIES AND EQUITY	$700,000	$654,531	$600,288	$543,202	$483,275	$420,506	$415,695

PROJECTED STAFFING NEEDS - TABLE #2
FOR THE FIRST YEAR OF OPERATION

FUNCTION	Percent Of Cost	Number Of Employees	Hours Per Employee	Total Hours Worked	Hourly Wage	Wages Per Week	Weeks Per Year	Wages Per Year
MANAGER	8.00%	4	NA	NA	NA	$2,940	52	$152,880
KITCHEN	9.00%	24	19	456	$7.25	$3,308	52	$171,990
SERVICE	5.05%	40	20	793	$2.34	$1,856	52	$96,506
BUSING	1.00%	6	20	123	$3.00	$368	52	$19,110
HOST	1.60%	8	12	94	$6.25	$588	52	$30,576
BAR	1.35%	8	21	165	$3.00	$496	52	$25,799
MAINTENANCE	1.10%	2	32	65	$6.25	$404	52	$21,021
TOTALS	27.10%	92		1,696		$9,959		$517,881
		Total Number Of Employees		Total Non-Salaried Hours Worked Per Week		Total Wages Per Week		Total Wages Per Year
BENEFITS & TAXES								
FICA		7.50%				$747	52	$38,841
Health Insurance		2.00%				199	52	10,358
State Unemployment Tax		3.00%				299	52	15,536
Federal Unemployment Tax		1.50%				149	52	7,768
TOTAL BENEFITS & TAXES		14%				$1,394		$72,503
TOTAL SALARY COSTS						$11,354		$590,384
						Total Wages Per Week With Taxes		Total Wages Per Year With Taxes

PROJECTED FOOD & BEVERAGE SALES - TABLE #1
FOR THE FISCAL YEAR ENDING DECEMBER 31

	Growth	1996	1997	1998	1999	2000	2001
LUNCH ASSUMPTIONS:							
Seats		175	175	175	175	175	175
Daily Covers		175	175	175	175	175	175
Weekly Covers		1,225	1,225	1,225	1,225	1,225	1,225
# of Weeks		52	52	52	52	52	52
Avg. Check	2.00%	$8.00	$8.16	$8.32	$8.49	$8.66	$8.83
TOTAL SALES		$509,600	$519,792	$530,188	$540,792	$551,607	$562,640
DINNER ASSUMPTIONS:							
Seats		175	175	175	175	175	175
Daily Covers		350	350	350	350	350	350
Weekly Covers		2,450	2,450	2,450	2,450	2,450	2,450
# of Weeks		52	52	52	52	52	52
Avg. Check	2.00%	$11.00	$11.22	$11.44	$11.67	$11.91	$12.14
TOTAL SALES		$1,401,400	$1,429,428	$1,458,017	$1,487,177	$1,516,920	$1,547,259
TOTAL FOOD & BEVERAGE SALES		$1,911,000	$1,949,220	$1,988,204	$2,027,968	$2,068,528	$2,109,898

PROJECTED RENT AND OCCUPANCY EXPENSE - TABLE #3
FOR THE FISCAL YEAR ENDING DECEMBER 31

SQUARE FEET 5,700	Growth	1996	1997	1998	1999	2000	2001
Rental Rate per Sq./Ft.		15.00	15.00	15.00	17.25	17.25	17.25
Dollar Value		$85,500	$85,500	$85,500	$98,325	$98,325	$98,325
Common Area Maint. per Sq./Ft.		2.50	2.50	2.50	2.90	2.90	2.90
Dollar Value		$14,250	$14,250	$14,250	$16,530	$16,530	$16,530
Property Taxes per Sq./Ft.	3%	1.75	1.80	1.86	1.91	1.97	2.03
Dollar Value		$9,975	$10,274	$10,582	$10,900	$11,227	$11,564

PROJECTED BOOK DEPRECIATION SCHEDULE - TABLE #4
FOR THE FISCAL YEAR ENDING DECEMBER 31

	Pro Forma	1996	1997	1998	1999	2000	2001
Furniture, Fixtures & Equipment							
Existing Net Asset Balance (Table #5)	$330,000	-------	-------	-------	-------	-------	-------
Estimated Capital Additions	-------	20,000	20,000	20,000	20,000	20,000	20,000
Estimated Asset Sales	-------	$0	$0	$0	$0	$0	$0
Existing Net Asset Balance							
Remaining Average Life (Yrs.)	39						
Annual Depreciation		$8,462	$8,462	$8,462	$8,462	$8,462	$8,462
TOTAL		$8,462	$8,462	$8,462	$8,462	$8,462	$8,462
Estimated Capital Additions							
Depreciable Life (Yrs.)	7						
Annual Depreciation		$2,857	$2,857	$2,857	$2,857	$2,857	$2,857
			2,857	2,857	2,857	2,857	2,857
				2,857	2,857	2,857	2,857
					2,857	2,857	2,857
						2,857	2,857
							2,857
TOTAL		$2,857	$5,714	$8,571	$11,429	$14,286	$17,143
TOTAL BOOK DEPRECIATION		$11,319	$14,176	$17,033	$19,890	$22,747	$25,604

PROJECTED AMORTIZATION SCHEDULE
FOR THE FISCAL YEAR ENDING DECEMBER 31

	Pro Forma	1996	1997	1998	1999	2000	2001
Startup Costs (Table #5)							
Gross Balance	$304,000	-------	-------	-------	-------	-------	-------
Periods Amortized (Yrs.)	5						
TOTAL AMORTIZATION		$60,800	$60,800	$60,800	$60,800	$60,800	$0

SOURCES & APPLICATIONS OF FUNDING - TABLE #5
FOR THE FISCAL YEAR ENDING DECEMBER 31

SOURCES	AMOUNT
Capital Investment	$700,000
Note	0
TOTAL SOURCES	$700,000

APPLICATIONS	AMOUNT
Decor	20,000
Equipment	100,000
Leasehold Improvements	140,000
Liquor License	20,000
P.O.S. System	25,000
Smallwares	25,000
TOTAL FURNITURE, FIXTURES & EQUIPMENT	$330,000
Accounting	$5,000
Architect Fees	25,000
Food/Inventory	30,000
Key Money	100,000
Legal Fees	15,000
Miscellaneous	6,000
Permits	3,000
Promotional Fees	35,000
Staff for Opening	75,000
Uniforms	10,000
TOTAL STARTUP COSTS	$304,000
Deposits	$1,000
Prepaid Insurance	5,000
Working Capital	60,000
TOTAL OTHER COSTS	$66,000
TOTAL APPLICATIONS	$700,000

Banners	$1,000
Creative/P.R.	10,000
Food	2,500
Menus: Take Out, Insert	5,000
Newspaper	5,000
Photo Shoot	3,500
Radio	4,000
V.I.P. Invitations	500
Viewmasters	3,500
	$35,000

Healthcare Automation, Inc.

Location: Providence, R.I.
Founder: Kenneth J. Pereira
Year Founded: 1988
Starting Capital: $0
Sales 1995: $5.2 million
Owner's Equity: $0
Employees: 55

Before attempting to strike out on his own, Ken Pereira gained significant knowledge of his potential market while working within the industry. As an MIS director for companies that provided health care infusion, Pereira spotted an unfilled niche in the market: a need for software to support health care services. He then joined a start-up company, where he designed such a software system. After several years with this start-up, he broke out on his own. As soon as he signed on his first client, his company, Healthcare Automation, Inc., was born.

Pereira was as deliberate in writing his business plan as he was in selecting a business opportunity for his company. In 1989 he wrote the plan in six weeks, but took six to nine months to get feedback on and fine-tune it, since it was written for the purpose of obtaining financing. Pereira received $500,000 from a private investor (a quasi-venture group) for his company. He has since revised the plan three times, to obtain additional financing.

Pereira attributes the success of Healthcare Automation to the fact that he had so much experience in the industry before starting his own business.

EXPERT EVALUATION
Healthcare Automation

SECTION

Executive Summary: Sections I & II should be combined to provide for a more comprehensive Executive Summary. Most pertinent issues are well covered. However, items such as capital requirements and scope of operations are not addressed.

Description of Business: Section III is well written, straightforward, but too concise. Description of services to be provided should contain more examples. Should also be presented in laymen's terms. Needs more explanation for reader who is not familiar with the industry.

Market: Good, thorough analysis. Good segmentation. Adequate documentation.

Market Share: Not adequately addressed in the plan. Table on page 8 does a good job of laying out market size and share projections. However, this is an area where there needs to be more explanation, such as source(s) of market-size data and assumptions regarding market share. Additional narrative in this area would strengthen it significantly.

Competition: This section appears to have most relevant information about the competitors identified (pricing comparisons are incomplete). It would be helpful to include a table or grid here that would compare and contrast all service attributes and competitive advantages for all companies.

Location: The lack of location information is a serious omission in this plan. Reader needs to know where and why the business plans to operate and the costs associated with that location.

Pricing: Although pricing and royalty fees are discussed and one can compare this structure to some of the competition, pricing per se in this plan needs to be evaluated separately. Currently, one has to go to several sections of the plan to get information, and its intended strategy is still unclear (i.e., is this a premium price service?)

Promotional Strategy: It appears that the owners plan on marketing their products via direct sales, evidently by one person identified in a note to their Income Statement. Although they have indicated this effort will be supplemented by trade shows, it lacks detail. Promotional strategy and plans for the future must be explained in more detail.

Insurance: Insurance expenses are included in the income statement and a brief explanation in a note, which is probably adequate. A bit more detail would be useful, however, such as the amount of key-person insurance.

Forms of Ownership: Although it appears from the finance section that the proposed company is a form of corporation, that is not explained or rationalized.

Management/ Personnel: This section only includes an abbreviated resume of the CEO and the identification of other management and administrative positions. There are no job descriptions for these positions or for the salesperson, identification of outside professional advisers, or mention of any type of advisory board.

Financial Information: Good narrative and notes to statements. Contingency, private, and legal placement costs appear to be high. No break-even analysis included.

Overall Comments: A well written, well thought-out plan with substantial market opportunity. The plan could be improved by the addition of information mentioned in this evaluation, which would make it more engaging for someone not familiar with the industry.

HEALTHCARE AUTOMATION, INC. BUSINESS PLAN

OCTOBER 14, 1991

18352 Dallas Parkway • Suite 136 • Dallas, TX 75287
Tel: (214) 931-7097 • Fax: (214) 931-7098

TABLE OF CONTENTS

I. EXECUTIVE SUMMARY

Healthcare Automation, Inc. (HAI) was founded in December, 1988 and is engaged in the development and marketing of software solutions for the Home Infusion Therapy industry, a fast-growing segment of the healthcare service delivery market. HAI has realized sales and profits in its three-year history as follows:

	Net Sales	Growth	Net Profit
1989	$197,744		$ 34,300 (17%)
1990	$438,157	122%	$180,973 (41%)
1991	$596,880	36%	$ 67,101 (11%)

HAI has completed the development of a software application that facilitates the management of a Home I.V. Center's patients, pricing, billing, accounts receivable, pharmacy, and inventory activities. In its three-year existence, the major activity has been the development of a marketable product, working with its major account, a subsidiary company of Hoffman LaRoche of Basil, Switzerland (Roche). By retaining the proprietary rights to the software product, HAI proposes to capitalize on the industry's 30% growth, which is projected to grow from $1.6 billion in 1989 to $15 billion by the year 2000,[1] and market the product nationwide.

With this software product completed, and having had it installed and operating in 12 sites throughout the U.S.A., HAI is in a position to enter the marketplace and sell these high-demand software systems, which we believe will constitute a $24 million market in 1992 and grow to be a $200-to $250-million market by the year 2000. By specializing in Home I.V., HAI's established team led by Ken Pereira (the CEO and founder) can focus on the needs of this dynamic industry. As we address this market, we expect to capture at least 8% of the market by the end of 1994. We expect our sales and profits to be as follows:

	Net Sales	Growth	Net Profit (Loss)
1992	$ 803,484	19%	($ 275,487)
1993	$1,512,300	88%	$ 144,297 (10%)
1994	$2,323,650	54%	$ 452,507 (19%)
1995	$3,379,725	45%	$ 860,120 (25%)
1996	$4,488,300	33%	$1,180,669 (26%)

Healthcare Automation, Inc. is interested in raising $500,000 in equity capital through the sale of its stock to private investors.

We view this fundraising as ensuring our success by providing us with the capital resources to effectively market this product and to continue to retain an experienced and dedicated support staff. The industry is strong and growing rapidly and our product has the strong potential to quickly become the dominant product in the Home Therapy industry. In 1992, we have financial commitments of $275,000 from Roche and $160,000 from Chartwell, a Boston-based Home I.V. Provider, and are in the process of negotiating significant sales with other companies in the industry. We have a trained staff of 10 people and have a successful history of profitability.

Looking forward, we expect to be positioned in other outpatient areas beyond infusion therapy. We expect to harvest the firm to one of the many growing software giants, whose strategy is to build an array of vertical software products. We believe our financial projections are fair and very attainable and intend to build Healthcare Automation, Inc. into a well respected provider of quality healthcare software.

---

[1] *Prudential-Bache Securities Report on New England Critical Care and the Infusion Therapy Market, January 1990, page 6.*

II. THE OPPORTUNITY

A. THE HOME INFUSION THERAPY INDUSTRY

The healthcare service delivery market, traditionally dominated by hospitals, is undergoing radical changes. Insurers are embarking upon serious efforts to contain costs by moving patients from hospitals to alternative settings, most notably the patients' homes. This movement, along with significant developments in technology, has spawned a new industry experiencing rapid growth.

A typical Home I.V. center is an outpatient pharmacy that mixes and delivers intravenous drugs to a patient's home, delivers all of the required supplies, provides the nursing care and training to patients and caretakers, and coordinates all of the medical services (i.e. labs, wheelchairs, etc.) needed by the patient at home.

In 1983, the home infusion therapy industry generated approximately $265 million in revenues[2] and in 1989 an estimated $1.6 billion in revenues.[3] According to a February 1990 industry report issued by Prudential-Bache, this growth (35% compounded) is expected to continue throughout the 1990s. They also note that this $1.6 billion of revenues represents less than .7% (7/1000) of total hospital costs,[4] presenting a clear opportunity for significant savings in health care costs by sending more patients home or to alternative (less expensive) settings.

Prudential-Bache also estimates that home infusion therapy may account for 1.5% to 2.5% of hospital costs in ten years, generating $10 to $15 billion a year in revenues.[5] Yet, experts agree that home infusion is only the start of an ever-expanding trend to decentralize health care from the hospital setting into the home or into specialized centers.[6] This industry has the beginnings of a major shift away from institutionalized care to more decentralized and specialized care, with the intention of reducing health care costs while providing for the needs of an aging population.

---

[2]The Home Drug Delivery Industry: An Outlook, Bama B. Rucker and Susan T. Whitters, Hambrecht & Quest, January 1987, page 2.

[3]Prudential-Bache Securities Report on New England Critical Care and the Infusion Therapy Market, January 1990, page 6.

[4]Prudential-Bache Securities Report on New England Critical Care and the Infusion Therapy Market, January 1990, page 13.

[5]Prudential-Bache Securities Report on New England Critical Care and the Infusion Therapy Market, January 1990, Page 13.

[6]Prudential-Bache Securities Report on New England Critical Care and the Infusion Therapy Market, January 1990, page 13.

B. THE NEED TO AUTOMATE

This new and growing industry is highly regulated and is faced by the challenges of a new industry. Many of these challenges can be met with the introduction of efficiency in the operations. In its 1988 industry report, Prudential-Bache said that information systems are the key to successful management. The report continues, "Because health care delivery is executed at the local level, conveying what was delivered, at what price, and at what cost– to headquarters–is a systems problem that few companies (in Home I.V.) have sufficiently developed."[7]

The Home I.V. center is in need of an integrated information system for the following reasons:

Billing
To reimburse providers for the patient's care at home, insurers require that the provider submit to their set of rules in billing. Preparation of bills is a time-consuming and error-prone activity. Misspelling or omission can result in rejected claims, with poor cash flow as a consequence. The need to have consistent recording, pricing, and presentation of bills is a requirement that is poorly met by personnel without the use of a system.

Managed Care
Increasingly, HMOs, large employers, and managed care firms are demanding reduced prices for their patients. Very often, negotiated prices involve complex formulas or accumulated tracking of billings. A computer system can simplify this process and allow a Home I.V. firm to enter into complex contracts without burdening its limited personnel resources.

State and Local Pharmacy Regulations
Since a Home I.V. center delivers drugs to the patient, it must adhere to the strict and locally driven regulations with regards to labeling, prescription records, and patient instructions. Using a pharmacist to type labels directly reduces the center's ability to be profitable. In addition, the pharmacy must adhere to quality guidelines (JCAHO) and legal requirements, all of which require paperwork and tracking systems.

Management Information
As the industry consolidates, information about the local Home I.V. provider becomes essential to allow local, regional, and national headquarters management to make informed decisions. Information concerning referral sources, payer mix, profitability of contract arrangements, and patient mix is of great concern to managers of Home I.V. operations.

Financial Controls
Two major financial factors influence a Home I.V. Center's success: (1) control over accounts receivable (usually 100 days outstanding), and (2) control over inventory costs (usually 25% to 30% of sales).

Recognition of Medicare
Medicare does not currently reimburse most Home I.V. therapies. Its implementation was to occur when the Catastrophic Insurance Coverage Bill was passed by Congress, though it has since been repealed. In the next few years, Medicare will reimburse for Home I.V. because it saves money. The regulatory burden of such a program will only increase the need for a system.

---

[7]Prudential-Bache Securities Report on New England Critical Care and the Infusion Therapy Market, January 1990, page 26.

III. THE PRODUCTS

Healthcare Automation has developed and intends to market a main product, initially targeted for the Home Infusion Therapy market. This system will be marketed in two versions, one for those only interested in the reimbursement aspects of the system and those interested in the Pharmacy/Inventory functionality as an addition to the Reimbursement System.

A. THE I.V. REIMBURSEMENT SOLUTION — PATIENT MANAGEMENT AND REIMBURSEMENT

Completed and installed in 12 Home I.V. sites (11 Roche and Deaconess), this system, called "The I.V. Reimbursement Solution," allows the management of patient information and produces all of the paperwork needed to process a patient being cared for at home. This system accommodates the pricing mechanisms, prints bills, and tracks accounts receivable activity. This system is sold from $12,000 (single user license) and up ($36,000 for a 12-user license). Monthly rental cost is 4% of the product purchase price. From our sales efforts to date, it is clear that this product is seen as top shelf and geared directly at the Home I.V. market.

Since December 1990, this product has operated successfully at our 12 sites. We have invested a great deal of time and effort in improving this product and in ironing out any initial problems. Our customers are very satisfied with the product's functionality, and many new referrals come from existing customers and a large network of industry contacts.

B. FULL HOME I.V. SYSTEM — ADDITION OF THE PHARMACY/INVENTORY SYSTEM

This system will be the full Reimbursement system along with a fully functional Pharmacy and Inventory application called "The I.V. Solution". This system will automate almost all of the Home I.V. center, and will be priced from $17,000 (single-user license) to $41,000 (12-user license). Monthly rentals are charged at the rate of 4% per month of the purchase price.

This system was put into a Beta Test in Roche's Livingston, N. J. facility on July 8, 1991. We are in the process of running this system in parallel with their manual system of processing prescriptions to compare the results. Results of the initial test have been very favorable. We expect that this pilot will continue through November, at which point we will install it in the remaining installed sites. We expect this system to be able to be installed for new customers in January 1992.

IV. THE MARKET

Pressures on hospital length-of-stays, advances in technology, reforms in insurance reimbursements, and the patient's desire to be treated in the comfort of his or her own home have all contributed to growth in the Infusion Therapy market. Since its inception, the home infusion therapy market has experienced explosive growth. The potential size of the market for our product consists of the expenditures health care companies allocate for their management information systems.

A. INDUSTRY SEGMENTS

An analysis of the home infusion therapy industry and each segment's market potential is as follows:

Independent Providers
These providers have been entering the market in increasing numbers because of the relatively low barriers to entry and high profit potential. Typically, these operations average around $1.5 million in annual revenues. The 1990 Prudential-Bache industry report put the total annual revenue for independent providers at $707 million.[8] At $1.5 million annual average revenue, this equates to approximately 500 independent providers in the United States. We feel that these companies constitute a potential market for our product of approximately $11 million.

Durable Medical Equipment (DME) Providers
DME companies are beginning to offer home infusion services to improve their profit margins, finding home infusion services to be a natural extension of their business. Of the 1,412 DME facilities operating in the U.S., roughly 15% are involved with home infusion,[9] generating an average of $100,000 in annual revenues. DME's home infusion total revenues for 1989 came to $21 million. A 3.5% annual MIS budget, usually spent for this size firm, would mean a $742,000 potential market.

Retail Pharmacies
Some pharmacies have seen the home infusion market as not only highly profitable but also an opportunity to integrate forward with their product and services. There are approximately 21,000 retail pharmacies in the United States. A recent *Homecare Magazine* article stated that 7% of retail pharmacies currently offer home infusion services.[10] We feel this is high and 2% is a more conservative and accurate figure. Thus, approximately 430 retail pharmacies are involved in home infusion therapy services. At $100,000 average annual revenue, that comes to just over $43 million total revenue, with a 3.5% potential annual market for our product of $1.5 million.

---

[8]Prudential-Bache Securities Report on New England Critical Care and the Infusion Therapy Market, January 1990, page 4.

[9]Based on a count of facilities using Industry source books.

[10]"Pharmacists Forge Into Home Care," *Homecare Magazine*, February 1990.

Home Infusion Chains
These are the major players in the home infusion market. The Prudential-Bache report places their annual revenues at just over $900 million. Companies this size would allocate .5% of their annual revenues toward the purchase of such systems. Thus, their information systems' budget provides a potential market of $4.5 million.

Hospitals
Apparently very few hospitals have entered the home infusion market. Only the largest hospitals can justify a home infusion program. There are approximately 240 hospitals with 800- to 1,000-bed capacity that would generate average revenues of $360 million. Allocating 1.5% of their annual revenues for such systems, this translates into a potential market of $5.4 million.

Nursing Agencies
Currently 20 percent of the agencies providing home-care nursing have started offering home infusion services.[11] Annual revenues from their home infusion services average $500,000. In 1989, roughly 120 facilities offered home infusion,[12] equating to total revenues of $60 million. Thus, at a 1.5% allocation, the potential market is roughly $900,000.

While DME Providers, Retail Pharmacies, and Nursing Agencies are entering the business as a secondary opportunity, *Independents, Chains,* and *Hospital Programs* will tend to focus directly on infusion therapy. Our target market will focus on these three segments.

B. TOTAL MARKET SIZE

The potential annual market for this software comes out to roughly $24 million. Current reports and industry authorities and providers that we have interviewed say that hone infusion is just over a $2-billion market. Assuming an average 1.2% expenditure as a percentage of sales on MIS, a reasonable assumption based on interviews and experience would put our potential market at $24 million. The projected market size and penetration is as follows:

	1992	1993	1994	1995	1996
Market Size (Sites)	1,512	1,663	1,830	2,012	2,214
Market Size ($)	$24M	$32M	$43M	$59M	$78M
New Install Proj.	24	36	52	66	72
Install Base	26	62	114	180	252
Market Share (Sites)	1.7%	3.7%	6.2%	8.9%	11.4%
Projected Revenues	$803K	$1,512K	$2,324K	$3,380K	$4,488K
Market Sharre ($)	3.3%	4.7%	5.4%	6.3%	5.8%

The previous chart shows the number of home infusion therapy providers which constitute our market. With an average annual price for our product and services of $16,000, the 1,512 Home I.V. providers in 1992 would constitute a $24-mllion market. We have assumed 35% market growth in revenues and a 10% growth in the number of centers.

Future growth looks impressive as well. The Prudential-Bache study declared that 1989 revenues of $1.64 billion equalled less than 0.7 percent of total hospital costs. "Even if home infusion accounts for only 1.5% to 2.5% of hospital costs in ten years, it still could be a $10- to $15-billion-a-year business if hospital revenues grow 10% per year."[13] That would mean a potential future market for our product of $200- to $300 million.

[11]Based on a count of facilities using Industry source books.

[12]Based on a count of facilities using Industry source books.

[13]Prudential-Bache Securities Report on New Englad Critical Care and the Infusion Therapy Market, January 1990, page. 13.

C. EXISTING COMPETITION

There are five competitive computer systems available today for the Home Infusion Therapy Industry, none of which have satisfied the industry's needs. They are:

(1) Home Healthcare Systems, San Diego, CA
This software was sold along with a supplies contract by Kendall McGaw, a supplier of medical disposables, but is no longer done, so due to lack of support by the firm. Our system is price-competitive with the software for a four-station system and above. A one-station license for our software is $1,033 per month and a four-station license is $1,447 per month. We plan to compete with this firm by first offering a more comprehensive product. Their software only accommodates limited pharmacy labeling and billing. It does not accommodate functions to manage the patient referrals and pharmacy inventory, and does not offer complex pricing capabilities, a must for dealing with HMOs. Our second competitive edge is to provide strong system support. This firm does not offer telephone modem support and has one key employee who manages the operation. Existing customers have reported poor system support, and McGaw dropped this system for this reason.

(2) Specialized Clinical Services, Santa Ana, CA
This system was designed and is sold by pharmacists and is intended to produce TPN pharmacy labels and to perform clinical functions, primarily. This system has little pricing, billing, or inventory capabilities and has a poor accounting concept. The firm's intention is to address a part of the market interested in technical pharmacy software and not the business of operating a Home I.V. center. Most of this company's revenue is further derived from the implementation of pharmacy cleanroom procedures to allow compliance with JCAHO guidelines. Software is only a portion of their revenues.

(3) Kiyo Systems, Inc., Newport Beach, CA
This competitor offers a system that operates on AT&T equipment under the UNIX operating system. Its application is pharmacy-based and offers little in the way of accounting and reimbursement. We expect to compete with this firm successfully with our PC platform, a more flexible and desirable feature, and with our superior financial system. We are in the process of negotiating with a customer to replace this system at their chain.

(4) ICARE of Arkansas System, Little Rock, AK
Based on a custom system built for a Home I.V. operation in Arkansas, this system has begun to be marketed as part of a total program to facilitate new operations in entering the I.V. business. To date, there are few installations, and they apparently have faced some difficulties in implementation. One of the main obstacles a system such as this encounters is that it is too specific to the company that built it. Another key problem is that it is not supported by a staff to handle problems, incorporate enhancements, and improve the product. Chains will keep away from this product for these reasons and after a few installations into independent sites, the firm may decide it is not worth entering the marketplace. We do not feel that this firm will be a strong contender in the serious market for this type of systems.

(5) Central Coast Billing, Monterey, CA
Created by a successful Home I.V. firm, this product is also a home-grown system that has little support staff and low pricing, at under $10,000. It will make some headway with independents interested in price, but will not be a serious competitor for those firms that will rely on full automation.

D. COMPETITIVE ADVANTAGES

In competing with these Home I.V. software firms, we feel we can be competitive by:

1. Specializing in Home Infusion Therapy. We offer software services and advice for this industry with proven expertise.

2. Offering a comprehensive solution. Most of the competitive systems are partial solutions, very focused on pharmacy. Our base starts with a strong Reimbursement System, but encompasses all of the main areas to be automated.

3. Utilizing our extensive network of people in the industry for references and word-of-mouth leads, including several JCAHO Surveyors, who have had extensive participation in the design of the Pharmacy System. We will be seen as the JCAHO-friendly system.

4. Having a country-wide installed base, we have some established credibility in the Home I.V. Industry. Roche, Deaconess, and Chartwell are three well known names.

5. Reputation for excellent support, proven by a call to any existing customer.

6. Having a solid, well-designed, and easy-to-use product. The design of how our system is used has won praises by the twelve sites installed already. The remainder of the system will take advantage of this proven design to expand the functionality of the product.

7. Selling the product by visiting the Home I.V. Center, where the customer can have all of his/her personnel see our system and test our expertise, following proper qualification by our salespeople.

8. Using technology to sell the product. Demonstrations to prospective customers do not have to wait until on-site visits. Telephone/modem demonstrations are possible with no lead time, using existing technology.

9. Positioning on the two popular platforms, PC-Novell networks and Digital VAX.

V. MARKETING AND SALES PLAN

Healthcare Automation, Inc. will market its software product to companies in the home infusion industry. The product will be a high-quality, technically superior product answering the specific needs of the home infusion therapy market, and moving into other "alternative site care" markets as the primary market becomes saturated. Healthcare Automation has established a reputation for supplying high-quality products, dependable support service and the ability to fulfill a customer's software needs. The company's marketing plan will focus primarily on home infusion companies, chains, and hospitals.

During our existence, we have built a reliable database of Home I.V. players, some who have seen our product and others who are awaiting the January 1992 introduction of our Pharmacy module. The major obstacles to sales, to date, have been the upcoming Pharmacy System and a professional sales force. The Pharmacy System is currently in Beta Test and about to be installed in all of the Roche centers.

We intend to hire a Sales Manager on the East Coast to follow up on the sizable number of leads that we already have and to launch a professional sales program. In addition, as opportunities present themselves, we will consider hiring a salesperson on the West Coast or using independent representatives in the Home I.V. industry. Trade shows, three per year, will be used to generate leads and direct mail campaigns will be used extensively. We plan to attend "ASPEN," the industry's main trade show, in January 1992 to launch our Pharmacy product.

The product is priced to reflect the quality and service that will be offered. Purchase plans are attractive, compared to monthly lease plans, but monthly rental plans are offered to capture the customers not willing to purchase. Our pricing is competitive with other software firms, but our intent is not to be the least expensive. Our sales approach will emphasize our experience and knowledge of the Home I.V. industry, and our product's ability to address the needs of the Home I.V. center. Our pricing includes three components:

1. Software license purchase or rental
The I.V. Reimbursement Solution is priced at $12,000 for a single-user license and $16,000 for a multi-user license, with an additional $2,000 per user increment. Rental costs are 3.5% of the purchase cost per month. The I.V. Solution (Pharmacy) is priced at $20,000 for a single-user system and $24,000 for a multi-user system, with $2,000 increments for additional users. Rental costs are also 3.5% of the purchase cost per month.

2. Software Support and Maintenance
Annual fees are charged to allow the client the right to call our support lines to obtain help in operating the software. Also included will be an automatic right to obtain all of the related upgrades that are added to the product. The cost of this service will be set at 20% of the purchase cost of the product, billed on a monthly basis.

3. Consulting and Custom Programming
Custom reports and inquiries are to be positioned as a major opportunity to take advantage of the customer's dependence on our systems. Many customers want to produce output their way and we will position ourselves to not resist this, capitalizing on the need while keeping the integrity of the system intact.

VI. OPERATIONS AND STAFFING

A. SYSTEMS DEVELOPMENT

Throughout 1990 and 1991, Healthcare Automation's focus was to complete the development of The I.V. Solution. Beyond 1991, a Systems Development staff is needed to enhance the products already delivered and to produce new products where new opportunities in the industry arise. Our staffing needs over the next five years in Systems Development is projected as follows:

	1992	1993	1994	1995
Manager—System Developer	1	1	1	1
Sr. System Developer	2	2	2	2
System Developer	1	1	1	1
Maintenance Programmer	2	2	2	2
Technical Analyst	1	1	1	2
TOTAL DEVELOPMENT:	7	7	7	8

B. SYSTEM SUPPORT

System support is an essential activity with the installation of new sites. There are two functions that this portion of the operation is involved with:

Training and Installation

Usually a billable activity, this involves preparation of data and actual training of staff on the new computer system.

Support

Involves the day-to-day support of the customer personnel using the computer system. This includes answering questions, solving problems, and providing tools to assist the customers in the use of their system. This activity is usually self-sustaining with revenues paid by the customer for continuing support.

As the user base grows, it is essential to have personnel available to handle support activities. It is our philosophy and experience that we provide the very best support, utilizing experienced and customer-oriented personnel and the most advanced technology. We offer telephone and modem support, enabling us to dial into each customer site to diagnose problems. The staffing needs that we project are commensurate with the number of new installations and sites on service. They are:

	1992	1993	1994	1995	1996
New Sites	24	36	52	66	72
Install Base*	38	74	126	192	264
Mgr. Supp./Install.	1	1	1	1	1
Support Analysts	3	4	7	11	16
Q/C Analysts	1	1	2	2	2
TOTAL SUPPORT	5	6	10	14	19
Ratios:					
Support Personnel New Sites	1:4.8	1:6.0	1:5.2	1:4.7	1:3.8
Support Personnel Existing Sites	1:7.6	1:12.3	1:12.6	1:13.7	1:13.9

*Includes existing base of 12 sites

VII. MANAGEMENT

Kenneth J. Pereira is the founder and chief executive officer of the firm. He brings to this venture the following experience:

- 10 years in health care and M.I.S.
- In the Home Infusion Therapy industry for five years
- Successfully operated Healthcare Automation, Inc., 1988 to present
- M.I.S. Director for Protocare, Inc., Waltham, MA, 1986 to 1988
- Manager of Systems Development for National Medical Care, Inc., Waltham, MA, 1982 to 1986
- Project Leader for Acushnet Co., New Bedford, MA, 1981 to 1982
- Internal M.I.S. Auditor for Gulf and Western, New York, NY, 1979 to 1981

Ken currently has four people reporting directly to him, with an additional person for sales management to be added. They are:

Manager of System Development

- Two full-time employees

Manager of Maintenance and Technical Support

- One full-time employee

Manager of Support and Installation

- One full-time employee

Administrative Coordinator

- One part-time employee

Total: Principal plus nine employees

VIII. FINANCING THE COMPANY

A. PROPOSED PRIVATE PLACEMENT

The company is presently owned 100% by Kenneth Pereira, president and CEO, and Dianna Pereira. It is our intention to raise $500,000 in financing by March 1992 through the sale of its common stock. We intend to raise these funds through private investors or related industry firms.

Our projected net profits in 1996 are $1,180,669, providing a strong 24% after-tax profit as a percentage of sales. We feel that this firm can be harvested at a ratio of at least twelve times earnings. This would result in an acquisition value of $14 million for the company. A resulting payout could provide investors with very attractive returns. We feel the return on investment will be very favorable for this type of investment where an ongoing business is operating and where the development of the product is completed and a marketing program is about to escalate in a high-demand industry.

The use of these proceeds will be used to offset the projected cash deficit in working capital before the firm starts generating cash. The reason for the deficit is to fund the establishment of a full marketing program and to continue to maintain a high level of system support, while ramping up the client base.

The success of this venture will be influenced by the quality and motivation of the people on the team. We believe that the employees and board, whose wisdom will guide the direction of the company, should benefit from the success of the company to which they contribute. Up to 10% of the company's stock is reserved for employee and board stock options under the following provisions:

- Options vest 25% each year over a four-year period.
- Purchase price of options are set at the book value of the company when granted.
- Healthcare Automation retains a call option on all stock, if the employee leaves the company, set at the book value of the shares as set upon the previous year's accounting statements prior to termination.

B. USE OF PROCEEDS

The Use of Proceeds for the equity financing is as follows:

Sales and Marketing Costs	$115,000
Legal Costs for Private Placement	35,000
Costs for Private Placement	50,000
Development & Support Personnel	120,000
Capital Expenditures	50,000
Contingency	130,000
Total Use of Proceeds	$500,000

C. HARVEST STRATEGY

Our strategy to harvest this venture is to build a strong, dominant firm in this exploding industry and to make this venture attractive to large software companies seeking to build vertical market gains.

American Express, Baxter Travenol, and Computer Associates are three such firms currently building vertical market software segments. In the 1990s, we believe that a firm with strong product position in the correct computer operating environments will be an attractive target for acquisitions.

We intend to become a very visible company in the marketing of our product and to market our high-visibility customers, such as Hoffman-LaRoche.

IX. RISK FACTORS

As with any venture, there are inherent risks. We have itemized the risks in this venture and have planned for the reduction of these risks as follows:

1. Hoffman-LaRoche Dependency
In 1991, 90% of our revenues were from Roche. In 1992, we project that this percentage will be reduced to 40%. Our relationship with Roche has been very strong since it started in 1989. It has been so strong that the firm has opted to utilize HAI for all of its M.I.S. activities instead of building its own internal resources. This situation has benefited us and cannot be reversed quickly. We have operated under firm contracts with stated dollar commitments to date, and there have been no disputes with regard to billings or deliverables. The probability that this relationship will continue to be strong is very high. A new contract for 1992 has been completed and we expect the 40% revenue projection to hold steady. With all its benefits, this situation continues to present risks since it is dependent on Roche's continued need and desire for our services. We feel that this risk is low with our established history and relationship and firm contractual arrangements in place.

2. Technical Expertise
Building and maintaining a software product requires technical expertise. Evaluating, hiring, and keeping good, technically-oriented individuals is always a challenge. In the early years, it is a risk because there aren't the financial resources to maintain a large duplicating staff. This risk is reduced with time, as you build in duplication. We have come through the major part of this risk in building the software product and have reduced this risk by staffing four programmers in 1992, building in some duplication. Providing stock and cash bonus incentives into the compensation scheme provides for incentive for these individuals to stay with the company. We have also developed a network of contract programmers to utilize during peak development periods. This becomes an extra source of expertise to draw upon.

3. Acceptance by Other Home I.V. Companies
Because our customer base has been limited to two customers, the question of acceptance to other customers is a risk. We believe that the application has been built to appeal to general audiences. This can be demonstrated by Deaconess Home Healthcare's purchase and can be confirmed by industry sources who have reviewed the product. Additional sales have recently confirmed the abolition of this risk. Chartwell Home Therapies will deliver in excess of $150,000 of revenues to our venture in 1992 and two local Home I.V. providers have also agreed to our system, effective this year.

4. Acceptance of Pharmacy System
The Reimbursement System has been well accepted since it has been operational, since late 1990. The Pharmacy System is being implemented now and has not been operational long. The risk of acceptance by the market exists, but the system has received favorable reviews from customers, specifically Chartwell Home Therapies.

X. FINANCIAL PROJECTIONS

A. PRO-FORMA INCOME STATEMENT

Healthcare Automation, Inc. Profit and Loss Pro-Forma		1992	%	1993	%	1994	%	1995	%	1996	%
Revenues :											
Software Development		$180,000	22%	$300,000	20%	$336,000	14%	$360,000	11%	$408,000	9%
Software System Sales		$90,000	11%	$192,000	13%	$280,000	12%	$420,000	12%	$420,000	9%
Software System Rentals		$123,000	15%	$435,600	29%	$876,300	38%	$1,458,000	43%	$2,131,200	47%
Support & Training – Contracts		$174,000	22%	$120,000	8%	$72,000	3%	$48,000	1%	$48,000	1%
Training – New Customers		$72,000	9%	$118,800	8%	$182,000	8%	$231,000	7%	$252,000	6%
Support & Maintenance Fees		$49,284	6%	$191,100	13%	$399,750	17%	$667,125	20%	$965,500	22%
Consulting		$36,000	4%	$60,000	4%	$66,000	3%	$72,000	2%	$96,000	2%
Hardware Sales & Commissions		$7,200	1%	$4,800	0%	$3,600	0%	$3,600	0%	$3,600	0%
Expense Reimbursement		$72,000	9%	$90,000	6%	$108,000	5%	$120,000	4%	$144,000	3%
Total Revenues		$803,484		$1,512,300	88%	$2,323,650	54%	$3,379,725	45%	$4,488,300	33%
Cost of Sales :											
Salaries/Benefits For Operations		$495,833		$580,475		$757,304		$1,055,834		$1,453,891	
Amortization of Software		$70,465		$70,465		$70,465		$40,001		$0	
Billable Travel Expenses		$72,000		$90,000		$108,000		$120,000		$144,000	
Total Cost of Sales		$638,299	79%	$740,940	49%	$935,769	40%	$1,215,835	36%	$1,597,891	36%
Gross Profit		$165,185	21%	$771,360	51%	$1,387,881	60%	$2,163,890	64%	$2,890,409	64%
Expenses :											
Personnel Costs (Non Oper/Sales)		$110,000	14%	$123,300	8%	$133,056	6%	$143,630	4%	$186,706	4%
Sales Salaries/Benefits		$50,000	6%	$70,219	5%	$100,179	4%	$107,191	3%	$114,695	3%
Sales Commissions		$29,700	4%	$55,560	4%	$94,830	4%	$150,600	4%	$217,920	5%
Selling Expenses		$48,000	6%	$72,000	5%	$84,000	4%	$90,000	3%	$108,000	2%
Insurance		$4,200	1%	$7,200	0%	$7,920	0%	$10,200	0%	$14,400	0%
Insurance – Officer's Life		$4,800	1%	$4,800	0%	$4,800	0%	$4,800	0%	$4,800	0%
Professional Fees		$44,000	5%	$17,100	1%	$18,000	1%	$24,000	1%	$30,000	1%
Office Rental		$36,000	4%	$45,604	3%	$54,000	2%	$64,125	2%	$91,500	2%
Office Supplies		$4,200	1%	$5,400	0%	$6,600	0%	$7,800	0%	$9,600	0%
Telephone Service		$14,400	2%	$20,400	1%	$25,200	1%	$31,200	1%	$38,400	1%
Travel & Entertainment		$12,000	1%	$13,200	1%	$15,600	1%	$20,400	1%	$26,400	1%
Computer and Office Services		$3,600	0%	$5,400	0%	$6,600	0%	$7,800	0%	$9,600	0%
Software & Hardware Acces.		$3,600	0%	$7,200	0%	$10,800	0%	$14,400	0%	$18,000	0%
Automobile Expenses		$5,100	1%	$6,000	0%	$6,600	0%	$7,200	0%	$7,200	0%
Education & Seminars		$12,183	2%	$13,529	1%	$16,646	1%	$20,825	1%	$26,917	1%
Periodicals		$804	0%	$900	0%	$960	0%	$1,080	0%	$1,080	0%
Postal Expenses		$6,000	1%	$9,600	1%	$10,800	0%	$14,400	0%	$18,000	0%
Lease Expenses		$20,400	3%	$20,400	1%	$20,400	1%	$20,400	1%	$20,400	0%
Depreciation		$13,450	2%	$25,030	2%	$36,050	2%	$52,360	2%	$67,975	2%
Bad Debt Expenses		$6,235	1%	$12,123	1%	$19,877	1%	$30,197	1%	$40,803	1%
Misc Expenses		$12,000	1%	$14,400	1%	$16,800	1%	$18,000	1%	$21,600	0%
Total Expenses		$440,672	55%	$549,365	36%	$691,717	30%	$840,628	25%	$1,073,995	24%
Net Profit Before Taxes		($275,487)	-34%	$221,995	15%	$696,164	30%	$1,323,262	39%	$1,816,413	40%
Income Taxes	35.00%	$0	0%	$77,698	5%	$243,657	10%	$463,142	14%	$635,745	14%
Net Profit After Taxes		($275,487)	-34%	$144,297	10%	$452,507	19%	$860,120	25%	$1,180,669	26%

X. FINANCIAL PROJECTIONS

A. PRO-FORMA INCOME STATEMENT: Schedule of New Installations

Healthcare Automation, Inc. Home I.V. System Sales	1992	1993	1994	1995	1996
New Rental Sites	18	24	36	42	48
New Purchase Sites	6	12	16	24	24
Total New Sites	24	36	52	66	72
Install Base -- Rentals	20	44	80	122	170
Install Base	26	62	114	180	252
Average Monthly Rental	$1,000	$1,100	$1,150	$1,200	$1,200
Average Purchase Price	$15,000	$16,000	$17,500	$17,500	$17,500
Average Training Revenue Per Site	$3,000	$3,300	$3,500	$3,500	$3,500
Average Support & Maint/Month	$333	$350	$375	$375	$375

A. PRO-FORMA INCOME STATEMENT: Staffing Schedule

Healthcare Automation, Inc. Personnel & Salary Schedule		1992	1993	1994	1995	1996
President		$72,000	$80,640	$86,285	$92,325	$98,787
Seceratary		$16,000	$18,000	$20,160	$22,579	$50,577
Manager of Sys. Dev.		$46,000	$49,220	$52,665	$56,352	$60,297
Sr. System Developer		$74,000	$79,180	$84,723	$90,653	$96,999
Maintenance Programmer		$70,000	$74,900	$80,143	$85,753	$137,634
System Developer		$32,000	$34,240	$36,637	$55,535	$83,891
Technical Analyst		$35,000	$37,450	$40,072	$85,753	$91,756
Manager of Train. & Support		$39,000	$41,730	$44,651	$47,777	$51,121
Applic. Support Analyst		$74,667	$119,840	$219,821	$372,413	$573,255
Quality Control Analyst		$26,000	$27,820	$47,132	$50,431	$68,161
Manager of Sales (base)		$40,000	$42,800	$45,796	$49,002	$52,432
Salesperson		$0	$13,375	$34,347	$36,751	$39,324
				$0		
Total Monthly Salary		$524,667	$619,195	$792,431	$1,045,324	$1,404,234
Add : FICA by Employer	10.00%	$52,467	$61,920	$79,243	$104,532	$140,423
Fringe Benefits	15.00%	$78,700	$92,879	$118,865	$156,799	$210,635
	25.00%					
Total Salary, FICA & Fringe		$655,833	$773,994	$990,538	$1,306,655	$1,755,292
Less : Alloc. For Operations		($495,833)	($580,475)	($757,304)	($1,055,834)	($1,453,891)
Sales Salaries		($50,000)	($70,219)	($100,179)	($107,191)	($114,695)
Personnel Costs (non–operating)		$110,000	$123,300	$133,056	$143,630	$186,706
Average Salary/Ben – Overhead						
Average Salary/Ben – Sales						

Headcount (FTE) :	1992	1993	1994	1995	1996
President	1.0	1.0	1.0	1.0	1.0
Seceratary	1.0	1.0	1.0	1.0	2.0
Manager of Sys. Dev.	1.0	1.0	1.0	1.0	1.0
Sr. System Developer	2.0	2.0	2.0	2.0	2.0
Maintenance Programmer	2.0	2.0	2.0	2.0	2.0
System Developer	1.0	1.0	1.0	2.0	3.0
Technical Analyst	1.0	1.0	1.0	2.0	2.0
Manager of Train. & Support	1.0	1.0	1.0	2.0	2.0
Applic. Support Analyst	3.0	4.0	1.0	1.0	1.0
Quality Control Analyst	1.0	1.0	7.0	11.0	16.0
Manager of Sales (base)	1.0	1.0	2.0	2.0	2.0
Salesperson	0.0	0.0	1.0	1.0	1.0
			1.0	1.0	1.0
Total Headcount (FTE's)	15.0	16.0	21.0	27.0	34.0
FTE's : Overhead	2.0	2.0	2.0	2.0	3.0
FTE's : Development	0.0	0.0	0.0	0.0	0.0
FTE's : Operations	12.0	13.0	17.0	23.0	29.0
FTE's : Sales	1.0	1.0	2.0	2.0	2.0

A. PRO-FORMA INCOME STATEMENT: Explanations

In preparing this statement, the following projections, assumptions, and sub-schedules were used:

Revenues

The following revenues have been estimated based on experience in the industry, commitments made by existing customers, and the known potential from our initial marketing efforts. The following section details the assumptions that have been made and commitments that exist:

1. Software Development
This represents the income projected as a result of defined system-development products desired by customers. In 1990 and 1991, $400,000 of the $1,015,100 or 39% of our revenues were for this purpose. While retaining the proprietary rights to the software developed, we agree to deliver an additional $100,000 of software to Roche and $80,000 to new customers. The Roche development revenues should represent only 12% of our revenues, showing our reliance on development revenues drastically reduced.

2. Software System Sales
This represents the projected revenues to be derived from the sale of new Home I.V. sites, where the customer purchases the product (rather than rents on a monthly basis). Each sale assumes an average sale of $15,000 in 1992, $16,000 in 1993, $17,500 in 1994, 1995, and 1996. Our additional sale to Deaconess Home Healthcare resulted in a $32,000 sales for a site license (10 users), validating our assumptions as realistic. Our recent agreement with Chartwell is for $160,000 for a site license, operating on a DEC VAX.

3. Software System Rentals
This represents the projected revenues to be derived from the rental of new customer sites, assuming most customers will choose the rental plan for risk reduction reasons. The rental of the software is set at about 3.5% of the purchase price per month with no firm commitment of time by the customer. However, there are up-front training costs of about $3,000 per site, which will demonstrate commitment to the automation program. Average rental revenue is assumed to be $1,000 in 1991 and 1992, $1,100 in 1993, $1,150 in 1994, and $1,200 in 1995 and 1996. This results in the largest area of growth for the firm.

4. Support and Training — Contracts
This represents the projected revenues to be derived from providing support and update services to existing sites, namely the Roche facilities. In 1991, our contractual agreement called for fees of $120,000, but our actual billings will exceed $200,000. In July of 1991, we negotiated 1992 revenues to be set at $174,000 to cover support, updates, and training.

5. Training — New Customers
With each new customer, it is important that the personnel are trained in the use of the system. We have developed an extensive training program that can be covered in five working days, for which we currently charge $600 per day. For each new purchase and rental customer, we have projected revenue for training, assuming average revenue of $3,000 per new customer in 1992, $3,300 in 1993, and $3,500 in 1994, 1995, and 1996.

6. Support and Maintenance Fees
In addition to the purchase price of the system or the monthly rental, a charge is levied for the customer to access Customer Support personnel to resolve problems with the use of the software and to receive enhancements to the software. In our projections, we assumed that 20% of the purchase cost of the software will be charged for support and maintenance. This is justified by maintaining a strong support staff and continuing enhancements.

A. PRO-FORMA INCOME STATEMENT (continued)

Revenues

7. Consulting
This represents the revenues to be derived from consulting services associated with the implementation of our system or in assisting Home I.V. companies with their automation needs. As specialists in this niche industry, there is significant opportunity to assist companies in the implementation of policies and procedures and in assessing their automation needs. In 1991, the revenues for this activity will be in excess of $20,000, all with Home I.V. companies that currently do not use our system. We are in a terrific position to take advantage of our expertise in automating this industry.

8. Hardware Sales and Commissions
We are a Value Added Reseller for Dell Computer Corporation and will generate over $20,000 in commissions in 1991. We have estimated modest commissions for the ensuing years, taking advantage of direct account setups that we are credited with for Roche and for several other customers that we have initiated.

9. Expense Reimbursement
Revenues are derived from the receipt of reimbursed travel expenses when travel occurs at the customer's request. This is not a profitable activity. A corresponding entry into Cost of Goods Sold balances this out.

Cost of Goods Sold

The following costs are itemized in this section because they directly relate to the sale of new customers and support of existing customers, for which we derive revenue. The following section details the assumptions and logic used in computing the Cost of Sales or direct costs associated with providing software and services to our customers:

1. Salaries/Benefits for Operations
This figure is an allocation of the total personnel costs that are due to directly installing new customer sites or in maintaining a level of customer support that is required to keep the customers satisfied and the systems up and running.

2. Salaries/Benefits for Sales
This figure is an allocation of the total personnel costs attributable to the sales activity. This reflects the salary of the salesperson hired at the end of 1991 and of the second person hired in 1993.

3. Sales Commissions
This amount represents the commissions paid to the salespeople for the successful sales of new customers, assuming a commission rate of 10% for new customer purchases and rentals. Revenues received from Roche and from customers previously signed are exempt from the commissions due.

4. Selling Expenses
This figure represents the cost of selling, including travel, automobile expenses, trade shows, advertising, mailings, and the like. It is estimated based on the expected level of activity for each.

5. Billable Travel Expenses
Expense due as a result of reimbursed travel expenses when travel occurs at the customer's request. A corresponding entry into the Revenue section balances this amount.

A. PRO-FORMA INCOME STATEMENT (continued)

Expenses

The following expenses are estimated on the basis of experience, considering the expected projections of new customers. Annual increases have been included for inflation and growth and were done so with an eye toward conservatism. The following section details some of the assumptions used in the calculation of these expenses:

1. Personnel Cost (non-operating)
This figure reflects the costs of personnel, exclusive of those broken out for operations in the previous section. A separate headcount, salary, and allocation schedule has been provided to estimate these figures. All salaries for 1992 through 1996 reflect 7% annual increases for existing employees and reflect market competitive rates for new employees.

2. Insurance
Reflects insurance coverage for liability, automobile coverage, and the life of the officer.

3. Professional Fees
An estimate of the cost of legal, accounting, and recruiting fees, based on past experience and expected future activity.

4. Office Rental
We presently lease 2,500 square feet of office space at $5.52 per square foot per year ($1,150/month), including utilities. Although this is a very favorable arrangement, we will exceed our capacity by the end of 1991, will be seeking additional space and expect a less favorable arrangement, because of new landlords. I have assumed that we will lease 3,000 square feet at $12 per square foot, the market rate for office space in our area in 1992. In 1993 — 3,500 square feet at $13.00, 1994 — 3,822 square feet at $13.50, 1995 — 4,210 square feet at $14.25.

5. Office Supplies
Office paper and other supplies for the office administration, budgeted based on past experience.

6. Telephone Service
An estimate of local and long distance phone services, which is not billable to consulting clients. The 1992 amount reflects a 50% increase from the average in 1991, growing each year to accommodate the traffic due to an increased number of clients. This does not assume any 800 incoming service, which is not standard in such a niche industry.

7. Travel and Entertainment
Reflects the cost of travel and entertainment not related to sales or consulting.

8. Computer and Office Services
The costs of payroll processing, coffee service, cleaning service, answering services, and other miscellaneous service required to maintain the office.

9. Software and Hardware Accessories
The cost of software tools to facilitate the development and maintenance of programs, taking advantage of the latest technology to improve productivity.

10. Automobile Expenses
The cost of the officer's company transportation, a reimbursed lease.

A. PRO-FORMA INCOME STATEMENT (continued)

Expenses

11. Education and Seminars
The cost of educating employees in new and useful technologies, assuming $850 per employee per year.

12. Periodicals
The cost of technical journals and industry magazines, based on past experience.

13. Postal Expenses
The cost of mailings and express mail based on past experience and future activity.

14. Lease Expenses
The cost of lease payments, based on previous commitments to lease computer equipment. A constant rate of lease payments has been assumed for all years in the projection because no significant additional leases are intended to be added beyond the current load. Company financing is expected to accommodate our capital needs.

15. Depreciation
Assumed at a constant $500 starting amount, plus the addition of new fixed assets, depreciated over a four-year period. This is not a significant expense to the company, due to the minimum amount of fixed assets.

16. Amortization of Software
Includes the $30,465 aged over the remaining four years, as carried from the 1991 balance sheet, plus a portion of the capitalized software expenditures in the projected years, amortized over the same four-year period.

17. Bad Debt Expenses
An estimate of bad debt, assuming 1% bad debt for all revenues except System Development.

18. Miscellaneous Expense
An estimate of other expenses that may be incurred.

B. CASH FLOW PROJECTIONS

Healthcare Automation, Inc. Cash Flow Projections	1992	1993	1994	1995	1996
Cash Inflows:					
Net Profit After Taxes	($275,487)	$144,297	$452,507	$860,120	$1,180,669
Depreciation	$13,450	$25,030	$38,050	$52,380	$67,975
Amortization of Software	$70,465	$70,465	$70,465	$40,001	$0
Accounts Payable Float @30 Days	$0	$0	$0	$0	$0
Total Cash Inflows	($191,572)	$239,792	$561,022	$952,501	$1,248,644
Cash Outflows:					
Capital Expenditures	$104,000	$61,200	$68,400	$74,400	$81,000
Accounts Receivable @ 30 Days	$74,758	$47,142	$92,150	$84,150	$92,600
Total Outflows	$178,758	$108,342	$160,550	$158,550	$173,600
Net Cash Flow	($370,330)	$131,450	$400,472	$793,951	$1,075,044
Accum Cash Flow – Before Financing	($370,330)	($238,880)	$161,592	$955,543	$2,030,587
Debt Financing	$0	$0	$0	$0	$0
Equity Financing	$500,000	$0	$0	$0	$0
Accum Cash Flow – After Financing	$129,670	$261,120	$661,592	$1,455,543	$2,530,587
Debenture Interest Payment @ 15% Accumulated Interest Payout	$0	$0	$0	$0	$0
Cash Flow After Interest/Payout	$129,670	$261,120	$661,592	$1,455,543	$2,530,587

B. CASH FLOW PROJECTIONS: Capital Expenditure Schedule

Healthcare Automation, Inc. Capital Expenditure Schedule	1992	%	1993	%	1994	%	1995	%	1996	%
Office Furniture	$12,000	12%	$14,400	24%	$16,800	25%	$18,000	24%	$19,800	24%
Computer Equipment	$24,000	23%	$26,400	43%	$28,800	42%	$31,200	42%	$33,600	41%
Office Equipment	$18,000	17%	$20,400	33%	$22,800	33%	$25,200	34%	$27,600	34%
Organization Costs	$50,000	48%								
Totals	$104,000	100%	$61,200	100%	$68,400	100%	$74,400	100%	$81,000	100%

B. CASH FLOW PROJECTIONS: Explanations

An annual cash flow is shown for the five-year period through 1996. A graph of continuous accumulated cash flows is also shown throughout the five-year plan, assuming a starting balance of $0 at the start of 1992.

CASH INFLOWS

1. Net Profit After Taxes
Shown as a positive cash flow from the after-tax profit of the firm, as calculated in the Projected Profit and Loss Statement.

2. Depreciation
Shown as an inflow of cash because it was incorporated into the above Net Profit figure as an expense, being a noncash expense shown in the Profit and Loss Statement.

3. Amortization of Software
Shown as an inflow of cash because it was incorporated into the above Net Profit figure as an expense, being a noncash expense shown in the Profit and Loss Statement.

4. Accounts Payable Float
Assumed no inflow, due to Accounts Payable terms of 30 days, because no significant payables exist in the firm now and no significant payables are projected to exist, since our main expense is payroll.

5. Total Cash Inflows
The sum total of positive cash impact using the Profit and Loss projections as a base.

CASH OUTFLOWS

1. Capital Expenditures
Considering the attached schedule of capital expenditures, this is shown as a cash outflow because it is assumed that all capital items are purchased with cash from financing. Lease commitments beyond the current load are not anticipated.

2. Accounts Receivable
It is assumed that all revenues will be paid in a 30-day time frame, although our company terms are a combination of payable in advance and payable within 15 days. This is a conservative projection.

3. Total Outflows
The sum total of all the negative cash impacts, projected using the Profit and Loss projections and Capital Acquisition Schedule as a base.

B. CASH FLOW PROJECTIONS (continued)

CASH FLOW COMPUTATIONS

1. Net Cash Flow
The net effect of cash inflows/outflows for the period shown. This amount will show positive if more cash is received in the period than dispensed and will show negative for the opposite.

2. Accumulated Cash Flow — Before Financing
Without financing, this is the accumulated effect of the period-to-period net cash flows. This amount was used to gauge the extent of needed financing throughout the planning period.

3. Debt Financing
The amount shown here is the projected debt to be carried. We have assumed this to be zero.

4. Equity Financing
The amount of equity financing to be acquired to overcome negative accumulated cash flows. We have calculated the need for financing at $500,000 in 1992.

5. Accumulated Cash Flow — After Financing
After financing, the accumulated cash flow is shown. This amount remains positive throughout the duration of the plan.

6. Debenture Interest
No estimate is shown here since no debt is being assumed.

7. Accumulated Interest Payout
The accumulated amount of interest on any debenture, assumed at zero since there is no debt.

8. Cash Flow After Interest/Payout
No different than the accumulated cash flow after financing, since there is no debt.

C. BALANCE SHEET : Assets

Healthcare Automation, Inc.
Balance Sheet

ASSETS : Current Assets :	1991 Balance	1992	%	1993	%	1994	%	1995	%	1996	%
Cash	$0	$129,670		$261,120		$661,592		$1,455,543		$2,530,587	
Accounts Receivable	$22,000	$96,758		$143,900		$236,050		$320,200		$412,800	
Total Current Assets	$22,000	$226,428	44%	$405,020	62%	$897,642	81%	$1,775,743	90%	$2,943,387	93%
Fixed Assets											
Office Equipment	$15,000	$45,000		$79,800		$119,400		$162,600		$210,000	
Computers and Software	$23,000	$47,000		$73,400		$102,200		$133,400		$167,000	
Less: Accum Deprec.	($25,000)	($38,450)		($63,480)		($101,530)		($153,910)		($221,885)	
Net Fixed Assets	$13,000	$53,550	10%	$89,720	14%	$120,070	11%	$142,090	7%	$155,115	5%
Other Assets											
Software Development Costs	$352,326	$352,326		$352,326		$352,326		$352,326		$352,326	
Less : Accumulated Amort.	($100,930)	($171,395)		($241,860)		($312,326)		($352,326)		($352,326)	
Net Software Dev. Costs	$251,396	$180,931	35%	$110,466	17%	$40,000	4%	($0)	-0%	($0)	-0%
Organizational Costs	$70	$50,070		$50,070		$50,070		$50,070		$50,070	
Deposits	$1,878	$1,878		$1,878		$1,878		$1,878		$1,878	
Due From Officer	$194	$194		$194		$194		$194		$194	
Total Other Assets	$253,538	$233,073	45%	$162,608	25%	$92,142	8%	$52,142	3%	$52,142	2%
Total Assets	$288,538	$513,051	100%	$657,348	100%	$1,109,855	100%	$1,969,975	100%	$3,150,644	100%

C. BALANCE SHEET : Liabilities and Owners Equity

LIAB & EQUITY : Current Liab :	1991 Balance	1992	%	1993	%	1994	%	1995	%	1996	%
Accounts Payable	$0	$0		$0		$0		$0		$0	
Accrued Payroll Taxes	$4,000	$4,000		$4,000		$4,000		$4,000		$4,000	
Accrued Income Taxes	$100	$100		$100		$100		$100		$100	
Total Current Liabilities	$4,100	$4,100	1%	$4,100	1%	$4,100	0%	$4,100	0%	$4,100	0%
Long-Term Liabilities											
Due To Officer	$0	$0		$0		$0		$0		$0	
Long-Term Debt	$0	$0		$0		$0		$0		$0	
Total Long-Term Liabilities	$0	$0	0%	$0	0%	$0	0%	$0	0%	$0	0%
Stockholders Equity											
Common Stock	$100	$500,100	98%	$500,100	77%	$500,100	45%	$500,100	25%	$500,100	16%
Retained Earnings	$284,338	$8,851	2%	$153,148	23%	$605,655	55%	$1,465,775	75%	$2,646,444	84%
Total Stockholders Equity	$284,438	$508,951	99%	$653,248	99%	$1,105,755	100%	$1,965,875	100%	$3,146,544	
Total Liabilities & Equity	$288,538	$513,051	100%	$657,348	100%	$1,109,855	100%	$1,969,975	100%	$3,150,644	

C. BALANCE SHEET: Explanations

The Balance Sheet shows a baseline 1991 statement with $288,538 in assets, a $62,204 (27%) increase projected over the 1990 statements published. The baseline statement also projects $284,438 in Stockholders Equity, a $69,828 (33%) projected increase over the 1990 statements. Internal accounting statements of the firm show this projection to be a reasonable starting point for 1992.

D. GRAPHICAL REPRESENTATIONS OF FINANCIAL PROJECTIONS:

Revenue and Profit Projections

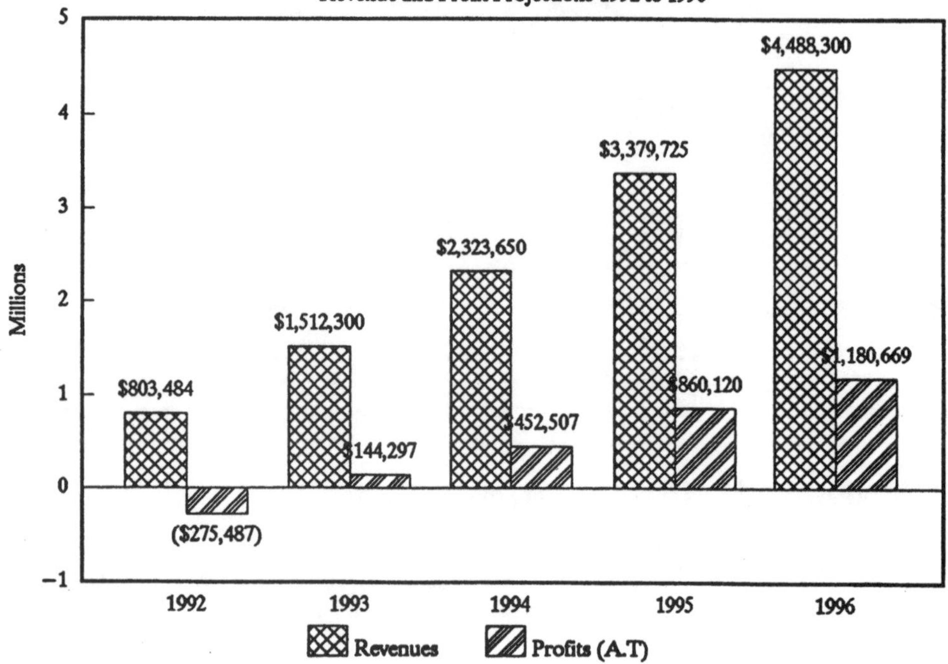

Cash Flow

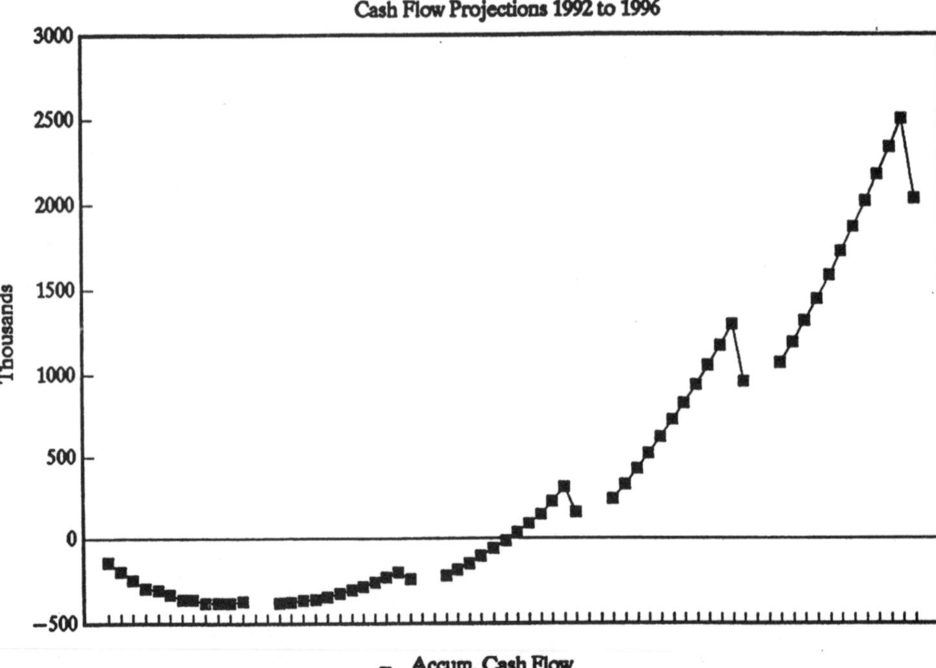

D. GRAPHICAL REPRESENTATIONS OF FINANCIAL PROJECTIONS:

Stockholder's Equity

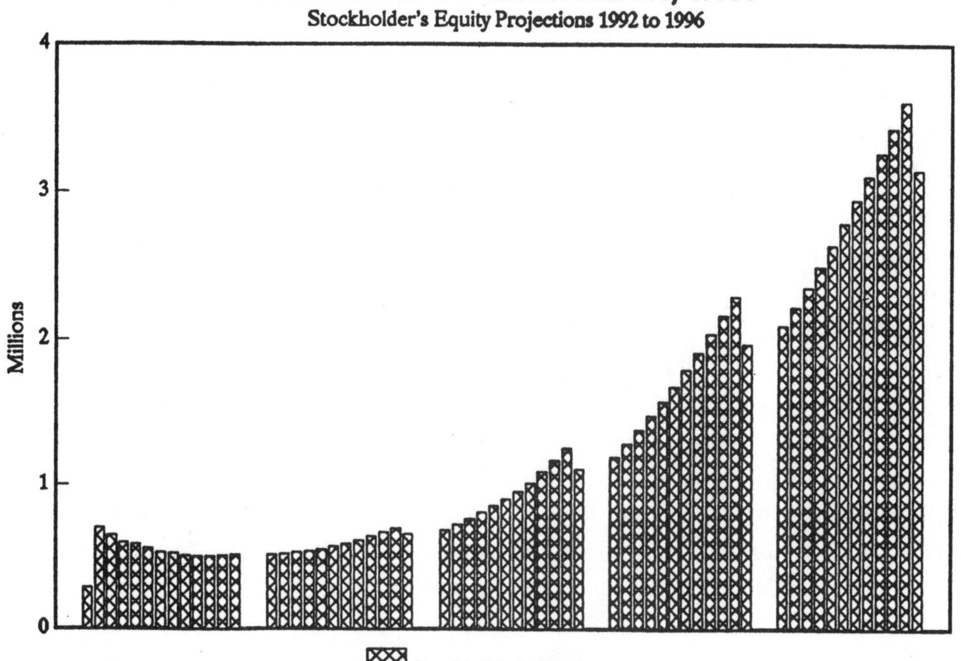

Revenue Breakdown

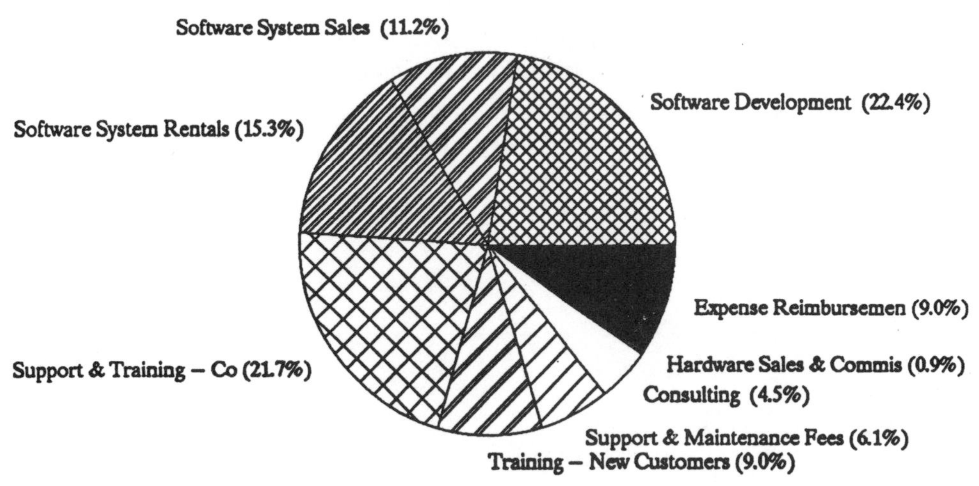

ASAPS Xpress—Car Wash and Lube

Location:	Woodstock, Ga.
Business Description:	Car wash and quick lube
Founders:	Shoqut and Pamela Hussien
Year Founded:	December 1995
Starting Capital:	$650,000
Sales 1st quarter 1996:	$65,000
Owners' Equity:	$80,000
Employees:	8 full-time, 2 part-time
Educational Background:	High school diploma

While patiently waiting for her daughters to finish gymnastics class in a suburb of Atlanta, Ga., Pam Hussien noticed a combination car wash/convenience store across the street doing a booming business. She counted dozens of cars per hour utilizing wash services as well as several young employees doing "auto detailing" work (engine cleaning, interior shampoo, leather treatments, etc.). Pam approached the manager, and began asking questions about the business.

After this short discussion, Pam knew this was a golden opportunity. She consulted her husband, Shoqut, who had been working for Volkswagen Services of America for over 30 years. Together, they felt that combining a car wash with a quick lube franchise seemed like a logical fit. The lube business could offset the weather-dependent car-wash business. As they began to collect data on the industry and talk to suppliers of cleaning supplies, they learned about auto detailing. Shoqut and Pam attended auto-detailing classes sponsored by manufacturers of the cleaners and solvents.

At this same time, the Hussiens were refinancing their home through a local bank. Aware of their business plans, their personal mortgage banker suggested that Pam and Shoqut attend a local SBDC-sponsored three-day course held at Kennesaw Community College. Upon completion of the course, the Hussiens had the tools necessary to begin writing their plan.

The plan took over one year to create. Pam considered it a full-time job to prepare a quality business plan. When it was nearing completion, Pam submitted the plan to the SBDC for review by one of their business-planning classes. The students returned the plan to the Hussiens with rave reviews. The Hussiens applied for bank financing and after SBA approval, were granted a $650,000 loan for the start of the business.

In the end, the Hussiens were very thankful for the entire business-plan process. "You have to start with something in order to go forward. Even though things have changed, we know where we should be. For example, it amazed me as to what numbers we didn't include (in the original plan): utility deposits, advertising costs, signage, and so on."

EXPERT EVALUATION
ASAPS Xpress-Car Wash and Lube

SECTION

Executive Summary: Well written, good overall summary. Relationship with Quaker State should be explained in this section. Detail on financing options would be better placed in a separate section. Also, it is unclear whether their loan request would qualify under SBA section 504 loan program. In addition, there are computational errors under project and loan recap.

Description of Business: Information contained in parts 2,3, and 4 should be combined into a Description of Business section. Although these parts are well written and contain most of the necessary information, one must read the whole plan to get a good understanding of the proposed business operation.

Market: Very good, well documented market data are provided and linked to a proposed location, the most critical factor for this type of business. Market assumptions, however, do not appear to consider the impact weather conditions may have on sales volume.

Market Share: Market share has to be inferred from the Competitive Analysis, Market Analysis, and Market Strategy sections. The plan would be stronger if this information were isolated and evaluated in a separate section.

Competition: The plan provides a very good analysis of the strengths and weaknesess of the competition, including services offered and competitive advantages. A side-by-side comparison might be useful here to provide more detail, such as specific operating hours and prices, and to offer information in a more user-friendly format.

Location: A specific location is identified, with good supporting documentation in the Appendices.

Pricing The competitive pricing model (coupled with superior service) makes sense, and pricing data on their closest competitor are provided. More narrative in this section would be helpful to garner support for this strategy.

Promotional Strategy: Although the strategy of offering a free exterior car wash with each lube job differentiates ASAPS from their competitors, the advertising plan needs to be more fully developed and provide more detail. The promotion section should probably be separate and include excerpts from appendices C and D, which, in turn, should be tied into the budget.

Insurance: There is no mention of insurance in the plan. There should, at least, be a brief explanation of types of insurance carried, as a note to the financial statements.

Forms of Ownership: Legal form of ownership is adequately covered.

Management/ Personnel: Very good, includes proper documentation in appendix A. Identifies critical professional advisers, with the exception of insurance, and gives significant detail in terms of staffing and training. Outside professional/technical support is also provided. Although owners have no direct experience in this type of business, they will receive substantial training which should be more than adequate.

Financial Information: All critical data are included, such as projections, income statement, cash flow, ratio analysis, and break-even analysis. However the information is scattered, forcing the reader to hunt for it. Financial information should be consolidated into a more readable format.

Overall Comments: A very good plan that includes all the necessary information. Organizationally, the plan could be strengthened by reordering the data/information into a section-by-section breakdown by topic.

TABLE OF CONTENTS

Section

**Not included in this guide due to space limitation and limited applicability of data.*

MARCH 1995

This document contains confidential and proprietary information belonging exclusively to:

ASAPS X*press* — Car Wash and Lube
Highway 92 & Londonderry Road
Woodstock, Georgia 30188

Shoqut Hussien
President

Pamela Hussien
Vice President

4650 Waters Road
Woodstock, Georgia 30188
404-928-9216

SECTION ONE

EXECUTIVE SUMMARY

"We've mythologized the typical start-up as one brave roll of the dice. But, real-life entrepreneurship is a long, hard pull." —David L. Birsch, President of Cognetics Inc.

In 1995, **ASAPS X*press* – Car Wash and Lube** was formed to build, own, and operate a full-service car wash and quick lube oil change business. **ASAPS X*press* – Car Wash and Lube** has plans to incorporate in the State of Georgia and notify the IRS of its election as a Subchapter "S" Corporation.

ASAPS X*press* – Car Wash and Lube will take advantage of Cherokee County's market niche for a quality, full-service car wash and the growing demand for quick-lube oil changes. By operating these two services at one location, **ASAPS X*press* – Car Wash and Lube** will provide today's convenience-oriented consumer with one-stop shopping at a single, easily accessible location.

Background

Car Wash— For several years people in this market have either used the area's only full service retail car wash (located in Cobb County) or have used various do-it-yourself or personal service options. Many people, particularly those who have moved from larger metropolitan areas, have been frustrated at the lack of a quality, modern, conveniently located full-service car wash facility.

Quick Lube– Freestanding quick lube/oil change operations have only begun serving this area in recent years. Market research and area demographics indicate that consumers will patronize an additional quick lube that features highly respected major-branded lubricants, is competitively priced, and is conveniently located.

By combining these services at a single location, **ASAPS X*press* – Car Wash and Lube** will capitalize on the customer's desire and need for our full-service car wash and quick lube services.

Technology and Technical Expertise

The "state of the art" of the car wash and quick lube industries today is such that customers are demanding the latest in car-care technologies. Car-wash customers want a wash that protects and enhances their car's finish. Quick-lube customers want well known, branded products that are proven to extend the wear of their car's engines with regular oil changes. Customers will not need to leave their cars at **ASAPS X*press* – Car Wash and Lube** because of the *express* services we will provide.

ASAPS X*press* – Car Wash and Lube will utilize the latest technology from both the ful-service car wash and quick lube industries—from brushless/touchless car wash, rinsing, and drying equipment from **PECO Corporation** to the latest in **Quaker State** synthetic and nonsynthetic motor lubricants from **Specialty Oil Company, Inc.**

Section 1 — Executive Summary *continued*

Concept

Uniquely for this market, **ASAPS X*press* – Car Wash and Lube** will offer a full-service car wash and quick lube at a single location, a concept that is growing in popularity throughout our industry and is growing in demand from customers.

Under normal circumstances, a customer can expect to receive a full-service car wash in 10 to 15 minutes and quick lube in 10 to 15 minutes; combined, both services will typically be complete in 30 minutes or less. This market targets busy consumers and fulfills their needs for quality car-care services delivered in a very short time.

By offering a free car wash to all quick lube customers, **ASAPS X*press* – Car Wash and Lube** expects to capture a sizable market share away from the two (2) existing freestanding quick lube operations. Compared to the competition, customers will perceive our pricing structure and service level as an excellent value and will give **ASAPS X*press* – Car Wash and Lube** a distinct market advantage over the competition.

Simply stated, our strategy for meeting and dominating the competition is convenience, quality, and greater value for the dollar by offering full-service car wash and quick lube service at a single location.

Board of Directors

Shoqut Hussien, President

Pamela Hussien, Vice President, Secretary, and Treasurer

Management

Our management team consists of Shoqut Hussien and Pamela Hussien, whose backgrounds and skills consist of a combined total of 30 years of management, marketing, and sales with prominent companies such as Volkswagen Services of America, Manuel's Auto Service, Afro Link Transport Company, Cox Enterprises, Tarkenton Group, Inc., DeKalb Community College, Kilpatrick Cody Law Firm, and Insurance Systems of America.

Additionally, our outside Management and Technical advisers will provide tremendous support for management decisions and creativity, and will serve as a valuable technical and industry resource.

Marketing

The fundamental thrust for our marketing strategy consists of utilizing:

- local and area newspaper advertising
- billboards
- direct mail and customer tracking
- local market radio/TV
- Quaker State's co-op advertising program
- word of mouth referrals
- "special days" such as Ladies Day, Senior Citizen Day, Rainy Day Special, etc.
- point-of-sale coupons, i.e., return in 10 days for $1.00 off on next car wash
- frequent buyer/customer promotions, discounts, and recognition

ASAPS Xpress–Car Wash and Lube

Section 1–Executive Summary *continued*

Loan Layout Summary

Type of Loan:	SBA Section 504 with 50/40/10 participation
Amount:	Total Project—$409,044 Borrowed Funds—$354,044 (plus $201,000 equipment lease)
Borrower's Equity:	$55,000 (down payment, working capital, reserve)
Use of Proceeds:	Fixed asset acquisition (land, building, and equipment)
Term:	20 years
Closing Date:	At earliest possible date
Closing Takedown:	As needed
Collateral:	Fixed assets
Guarantees:	Corporate Officers
Rate:	Prime + 2%
Repayment Schedule:	Monthly payments of principal and interest
Debt Services:	$102,653 per year (principal & interest on loan plus lease payment)
Source of Funds for Repayment:	Cash flow in excess of cash required for operations
Alternate Source of Funds for Repayment:	Land, building, equipment, and other assets

Finance

Our operation is forecast to produce first full-year annual gross revenues of $707,111 with $169,037 of net income. Gross revenue projected for the second fiscal year of operation, without external funding, is expected to be $810,192 with $198,017 of net income.

Annual growth is projected to be 10–15% per year through 1997 and will grow in subsequent years as the population, number of registered automobiles, and traffic counts grow.

Please refer to Section 9—Financial Data for further information on financial data and ratios.

Conclusion

ASAPS X*press* – Car Wash and Lube will be quickly established as an excellent service and value for our customers in this community. By achieving our goals of superior customer service, excellent quality, and competitive pricing, and with dedication and commitment to the "long, hard pull," **ASAPS X*press* – Car Wash and Lube** will quickly become a dominant force in this market.

Overall, our company will be characterized as focused on customer and market needs, a high-profile retail merchant, actively involved in community activities such as the Chamber of Commerce, United Way, Habitat for Humanity, and other similar organizations.

PROJECT AND LOAN RECAP
March 1995

Borrower: **ASAPS X*press* – Car Wash and Lube**
650 Waters Road, Woodstock, GA 30188

Guarantors: Shoqut Hussien, President
Pamela Hussien, Vice President

Loan Purpose: The proposed loan is for a full-service car wash and quick lube located at the corner of Highway 92 and Londonderry Drive, Woodstock, Georgia. **ASAPS X*press* – Car Wash and Lube** will take advantage of Cherokee County's market niche for a quality, full-service car wash and detail shop and the growing demand for quick lube oil changes. By operating these two services at one location, **ASAPS X*press* – Car Wash and Lube** will provide today's convenience-oriented consumer with one-stop shopping at a single, easily accessible location.

Description of Property:
Located at the corner of highway 92 and Londonderry Drive, Woodstock, Georgia. The property is .64 acres and is located at a busy intersection. Due to its ideal location, the property has high visibility and easy accessibility. The facility will utilize the latest technology from both the full-service car wash and quick lube industries—from Soft'N'Foamy® brushless/touchless car wash, rinsing, and drying equipment from PECO Corporation to the latest in Quaker State synthetic and non-synthetic motor lubricants from Specialty Oil Company.

Project Costs:

Land	$150,000
Building	$200,000
Equipment	$300,000
Working Capital	$ 7,831
Soft Costs	$ 7,831
Total Costs	**$409,044**

Borrower's Equity: $55,000

ASAPS Xpress–Car Wash and Lube

ASAPS *Xpress* - Car Wash and Lube
**** SBA 504 Loan (Bank Name) with Car Wash Equipment Lease ****
FINANCIAL ANALYSIS SUMMARY
March, 1995

FINANCIAL ANALYSIS

Loan Terms

Principal	354,044
Rate	11.00%
Term	20 Year

	As of 12/31/96	As of 12/31/97	As of 12/31/98	As of 12/31/99	As of 12/31/00
Current Assets	187,351	452,133	810,066	1,249,862	1,783,600
Current Liabilities	5,761	6,427	7,171	8,001	8,927
Total Assets	557,733	799,515	1,134,448	1,551,244	2,061,982
Total Liabilites	348,881	343,120	336,693	329,522	321,521
Net Worth	208,852	456,394	797,755	1,221,723	1,740,461
Gross Income	710,818	818,627	926,933	1,024,403	1,134,415
Expenses	556,966	571,085	585,572	600,435	615,677
Net Income	153,852	247,542	341,360	423,968	518,738
Depreciation	23,000	23,000	23,000	23,000	23,000
Interest	38,690	38,092	37,426	36,682	35,852
Rent	-	-	-	-	-
Cash Flow	187,351	452,133	810,066	1,249,862	1,783,600
Annual Debt Service (inc. lease payment)	102,653	102,653	102,653	102,653	102,653

Ratios:

Current Ratio	(Current Assets/Current Liabilites)	32.52	70.35	112.96	156.22	199.81
Debt to Worth	(Total Liabilites/Net Worth)	1.67	0.75	0.42	0.27	0.18
Debt Service Ratio	(Cash Flow/Annual Debt Service)	1.83	4.40	7.89	12.18	17.38

PROJECT SUMMARY
Sales Projections and Net Income
SBA 504 Loan with Car Wash Equipment Lease

Car Wash	Break Even	1st Year	2nd Year	3rd Year
Daily Volume (Cars)	94	127	152	178
Monthly Volume (Cars)	2,115	2,858	3,420	4,005
Net Income	$14,661	43,880	$108,922	$170,801
Quick Lube				
Daily Volume (Cars)	24	46	50	52
Monthly Volume (Cars)	621	1,162	1,268	1,320
Net Income	$43,131	$109,972	$138,620	$170,559
TOTAL NET INCOME	$57,792	$153,852	$247,542	$341,360

NOTE:

Car Wash "monthly volume" is calculated by multiplying daily volume by 6 days per week times 45 weeks divided by 12 months.

Quick Lube "monthly volume" is calculated by multiplying daily volume by 6 days per week times 51 weeks divided by 12 months.

SECTION TWO

"Customerize: to make a company more responsive to its customer and better able to attract new ones. When you customerize, you put the customer at the heart of your world, rather than at the periphery." —Unisys Corporation

MISSION STATEMENT

To Our Customers:

We know that you, as a convenience-oriented consumer, want important car-care services that are high-quality, convenient and accessible, competitively priced, and quickly delivered.

ASAPS X*press* – Car Wash and Lube will work hard to serve your needs, while becoming a market leader, by providing you with superior service, outstanding quality, and an excellent value for the price, delivered by smiling, well-trained staff who will make every effort to please you, our customer.

We want you to keep coming back!

It will be our goal to treat customers the way they want to be treated; give customers what they want, when they want it, and how they want it; develop good communication and human relations skills—the backbone of good customer service; and to "customerize" every aspect of our business.

SECTION THREE

OBJECTIVES

The primary objectives of **ASAPS X*press* – Car Wash and Lube** are to:

A. Build, own, and operate a superior quality full-service car wash and quick lube center
B. Establish a market presence that assures short-term and long-term profitability, growth, and success
C. Provide a satisfactory return on investment to investors and owners

The dominant driving forces behind our success will be:

A. Quality services offered
B. Satisfying an existing market need
C. Profit and income capabilities
D. Building a solid customer base

Business Goals

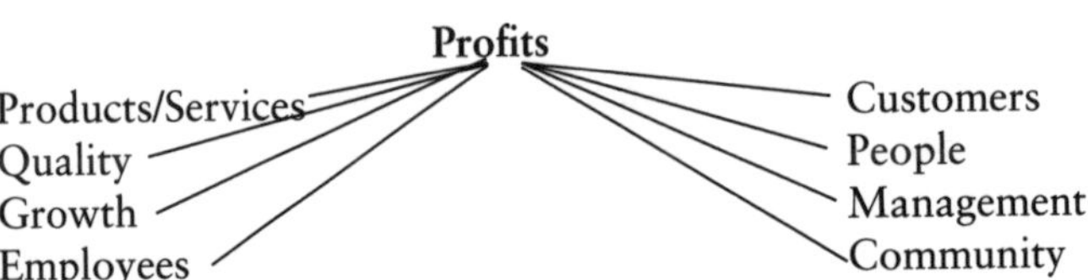

Compared to past performances and industry averages from the full-service car wash and quick lube industries, we are forecasting extremely conservative first-year gross revenues.

Car Wash — Industry averages for the full-service car wash industry suggest that **ASAPS X*press* – Car Wash and Lube** could reasonably expect to capture .7% to .9% of the existing "annual average daily traffic" (DOT - AADT). In our projections, we are forecasting to capture only .5% of this traffic.

Quick Lube — Similarly, first-year projections for new locations in the quick lube industry, in a market of our size, who offer free or heavily discounted car washes with each lube, as compared to the competition who does not, suggest that **ASAPS X*press* – Car Wash and Lube** would capture 60% to 65% of the market. In our projection, we are forecasting to capture only 44% of the available market.

Rationale

Based on the competition in this market, DOT traffic studies, market demographics, and the business potential, we feel our conservative projections will be easily achieved and most likely be surpassed.

Please refer to Section 6 — Market Analysis for information that substantiates business goals.

Position for Growth

1. Understand customer needs, competition, and industry
2. Respond to service needs and demands in the market
3. Balance management/business/people goals
4. Operate at minimal/optimal staffing
5. Develop values and culture — live them in our work and the way we treat our customers and employees
6. Hire the best people

SECTION FOUR

PRODUCT/SERVICE DESCRIPTION

ASAPS X*press* – Car Wash and Lube will offer customers a wide selection of services and products. Upon entering the premises, the customer proceeds either to the full-service car wash staging area or to the quick lube bays. At this point, the customer is presented with a menu of available services:

- CAR WASH — basic car wash and choice of optional additional services
- LUBE — basic oil change with a choice of oil brands, grades, and optional additional services
- Combination CAR WASH and LUBE — choice of the various options from CAR WASH and LUBE menus

Each customer's vehicle will be vacuumed, regardless of whether the customer selects a full-service car wash or quick lube.

FULL-SERVICE CAR WASH:

The full-service car wash will provide every customer with complete interior vacuuming, exterior car wash, rinse, and detailing (wipe down). These services are considered "basic services."

There will be additional services that the customer may select from a menu of available services:

- exterior car wash only
- polyseal wax
- foaming polish wax
- undercarriage/rust inhibitor
- full detailing (premium service)

QUICK LUBE:

The quick lube will provide every customer with a free exterior car wash in addition to the complete "14 point oil change service" which includes:

- oil change
- replacement oil filter
- check and refill of fluids
- check of other miscellaneous service items such as air filters, tire pressure, etc.

Although **ASAPS X*press* – Car Wash and Lube** will feature Quaker State lubricants from the Specialty Oil Company, the customer will have the option of selecting from other various popular brands and grades of oil.

Useful Purpose and Benefits

ASAPS X*press* – Car Wash and Lube will provide customers with important services that they need in order to maintain their cars, at prices that are competitive and attractive, in a comfortable, convenient location.

We believe, given all of the benefits offered by **ASAPS X*press* – Car Wash and Lube** that customers in this market will choose **ASAPS X*press* – Car Wash and Lube** for their full-service car wash and quick lube service needs.

SECTION FIVE

COMPETITION

According to our review and analysis of the competition, supported by the analysis of professionals from the full service car wash and quick lube industries, **ASAPS X*press* – Car Wash and Lube** will offer more services, better location, and a better product than any of the car wash or quick lube competitors currently operating in this market.

Please refer to the chart at the end of this section for a listing of area car wash and quick lube competitors.

Car Washes

According to industry experts, "coin operated," "backdoor" operations, personal service operations, "mobile" car washes, and car washes that are "secondary operations" to a company's primary business are not considered strong competition to a quality, full-service car wash. These car wash options address a different segment of the market.

Realistically, a segment of the market currently uses and will continue to use these non-full service car wash alternatives.

ASAPS X*press* – Car Wash and Lube Market Strengths:

- only business of its kind to service the Woodstock and surrounding areas in Cherokee County
- convenient, easily accessible location
- new, modern facility
- technologically advanced equipment
- extensive professional marketing and advertising support through Quaker State's marketing and advertising programs

Our competitive assessment of the only full-service car wash operating in this market is as follows:

Competition Market Strengths

- located in Cobb County, only game available to the Woodstock community and surrounding areas
- well known by virtue of having operated at the same location for many years
- longtime business investors

Competition Market Weaknesses:

- extremely poor location
- short operating hours
- closes whenever there is a hint of rain
- building is old
- equipment has not been updated in many years
- high volume of employee turnover
- waiting room is not customer-oriented
- pricing is high
- rarely advertises or markets services
- inadequate staging and detail areas—size of the lot gives drive-by appearance of long lines when only 2–3 cars are in line

Quick Lubes

In this market there are two (2) freestanding quick lubes which will be in direct competition to **ASAPS X*press* – Car Wash and Lube**. The other quick lube operations, which are "secondary operations" to the company's primary business, such as car dealerships and other auto repair or discount retailers, are not considered strong competition to convenient, freestanding quick lube operations.

Realistically, a segment of the market currently uses and will continue to use these secondary quick lube alternatives.

There are distinct competitive advantages that **ASAPS X*press* – Car Wash and Lube** will have over all of the area's quick lubes, in particular the freestanding quick lube operations:

- free exterior car wash with every oil change
- products and affiliation with Quaker State, a highly respected major oil company
- 250,000-mile new car engine warranty provided by Quaker State
- extensive professional marketing and advertising support from Quaker State
- credit cards

Our competitive assessment of the freestanding quick lubes operating in this market is as follows:

Competition Market Strengths

- Econo Lube: well known by virtue of having operated at the same locations for many years
- Brady's Street: no discernible market strengths other than the business offers customers an alternative to Econo Lube
- pricing for both is competitive for the market

Competition Market Weaknesses

- less than ideal locations
- waiting rooms are not customer-oriented
- advertising and marketing efforts are weak
- owners are not highly visible within the community

Competitive Roundup

The chart at the end of this section lists the area car wash and quick lube competitors and their locations.

Observations and Conclusions

It appears from the above information that **ASAPS X*press* – Car Wash and Lube** will have major competitive and market advantages over all types of competitors in the area.

Section 5 — Competition *continued*

Summary of Car Wash Competitors

Name	Type of Operation	Address
(Cobb County)	Full-service	3028 Canton Rd. Marietta
Wash n Go Car Wash	Coin-operated	Highway 92 Woodstock
Val's Auto Clean-Up	Secondary operation	S. Main St. Woodstock
The Bubble & Brush	Coin operated	Main St. Woodstock
1-575 Amoco Food Store	Drive-through tunnel	1601 Highway 92 Woodstock
BP Oil	Drive-through tunnel	195 W. Church St. Woodstock
Chevron	Drive-through tunnel	Hwy. 92 & Canton Rd. Woodstock

Summary of Quick Lube Competitors

Name	Type of Operation	Address
Econo Lube	Freestanding	S. Main St. Woodstock
Brady's Street	Freestanding	Highway 92 Woodstock
DP Care Car Center	Secondary operation	Londonderry Dr. Woodstock
Goodyear	Secondary operation	Highway 92 Woodstock
Firestone	Secondary operation	Highway 92 Woodstock
Hennessy Honda	Secondary operation	Highway 92 Woodstock
Cherokee Ford	Secondary operation	Town Lake Parkway Woodstock
Wal-Mart Express Oil Change	Secondary operation	Highway 92 Woodstock

SECTION SIX

MARKET ANALYSIS: THE CUSTOMER, THE LOCATION, AND DEMOGRAPHICS

The Customer

According to car wash and quick lube industry data, the typical customer who will utilize the services of **ASAPS X*press* – Car Wash and Lube** is:

- between the ages of 24 and 50
- owns or leases a car
- is in a white collar job
- is in the middle to upper income brackets
- lives or works within five miles of the business location
- is likely to be female (65% of car wash customers are typically female)

Proposed Location

Address: Highway 92 & Londonderry Rd.
Woodstock, GA 30188

The property is located in Cherokee Country and is zoned highway commercial, the zoning required to operate a full service car wash and quick lube operation (zoning verified by Ken Patton, Cherokee County Zoning Administrator).

The property is .64 acres in size, has approximately a 199-foot frontage on Highway 92, is approximately 140 feet deep, and sits at the corner of the intersection of Highway 92 and Londonderry Drive. Due to its ideal location, the property has high visibility and easy accessibility.

All utility services are either in use on the property or are available at the property line.

A real estate contract has been negotiated and signed with the current property owners *(copy in Appendix 10-K— Legal Documents).*

Please refer to Appendix 10-E for a copy of the Site Survey Plat for the proposed location.

Market Area

Market Area (the actual market area may be larger):

Five-mile radius, originating at the intersection of Highway 92 and Londonderry Drive

All data shown in the Demographic Data section below are for this Market Area.

Demographic Data

The following is a summary of demographic data that is pertinent to evaluating the demographic success of a full-service car wash and quick lube operating at the proposed location and within our Market Area. **The "Market Area" is defined in the box above.**

Section 6 — Market Analysis *continued*

Demographic Data Source: Except for the DOT traffic counts *(Appendix 10-F)*, all specific demographic data were obtained from two sources, Urban Decision Systems *(Appendix 10-G)* and Georgia Power Company *(Appendix 10-H)*, dated February 1995.

Average Daily Traffic Count (passing by the location):

25,390 vehicles every 24 hours, 365 days per year.

NOTE: This GA DOT traffic count was compiled as of February 1995 in interest of the widening of Highway 92 to a four-lane road with median breaks. According to Glen Scarborough, Director of Projects & Traffic Counts, the DOT estimates an increase of traffic flow to 29,500 in February 1997 after completing road construction.

Number of Registered Automobiles (market area):

64,999

Population (market area):

91,338 — 1990 census
107,535 — 1994 estimate
118,735 — 1999 estimate

Households by Number of Vehicles (market area):

98.39% of households have 1, 2, 3, or more vehicles

Population by Transportation to Work (market area):

84.22% drive alone
10.85% car pool

Estimated Population by Age (market area):

60.33% between age 21 and 59

Median Age/Average Age (market area):

30 - 32 years of age

Section 6 — Market Analysis *continued*

TARGET MARKET CUSTOMER PROFILE

Full Service Car Wash

Industry Data Source: The following data were collected and reported in the 1993 survey by *Professional Car Washing and Detailing Magazine (Appendix 10-I)* of 450 full service car wash owners, who operate approximately 1,000 automatic car wash locations nationwide; where available, data shown are for the Southeast.

Traffic Count Washed

0.9% of traffic passing the location every 24 hours

Average Daily Traffic Count (passing by the location):

32,000 every 24 hours, 365 days per year

Average Per-Car Gross Revenue:

$8.61 per car

Average Number of Days Open:

312 days of operation

Average Number of Competing Full-Service Locations:

3 full-service car wash locations

Quick Lubes

Industry Data Source: Quaker State Oil Company's "Qlube Fast Lube" Division *(Appendix 10-J).*

Average Number of Registered Automobiles (utilizing quick lubes):

39% of registered automobiles are serviced at quick lubes

Average Daily Traffic Count (passing by the location):

28,000 every 24 hours, 365 days per year

Average Number of Competing Free-Standing Quick Lubes:

2.4 quick lube locations

Average Per-Car Gross Revenue:

$21.22 per car for basic service

Average Age of Quick Lube Customer:

24–59 years of age (upper age limit is growing)

Section 6 - Market Analysis *continued*

Analysis and Conclusion
The demographic data for the proposed market/location, when compared against industry averages and trends, strongly supports the conclusion that **ASAPS X*press* – Car Wash and Lube** will be extremely successful.

Strengths

Clearly **ASAPS X*press* – Car Wash and Lube**'s location, traffic counts, and positive demographic data coupled with the advantages of operating a combination full-service car wash and quick lube at the same location (convenience, value, and time savings) gives **ASAPS X*press* – Car Wash and Lube** a distinct advantage over the competition.

In marketing **ASAPS X*press* – Car Wash and Lube**, our most powerful assets are:

- Only game in town serving Cherokee County
- Location, location, location
- Demographics
- Convenience
- New, modern facility
- Positive word of mouth
- Latest technology in equipment and products

Weaknesses

New business needing to establish customer base and market presence

Opportunities

There is tremendous upside potential for **ASAPS X*press* – Car Wash and Lube** to capture and maintain a large share of the market's full-service car wash and quick lube business and, therefore, to exceed all expectations and projections.

The keys to our success are that we must consistently deliver excellent customer service and quality products.

Threats

1. Existing competition wages price war
   Response Tactic : stand firm and continue to deliver quality services and products
2. Death or disability of owner
   Response Tactic: prepare with life insurance to cover debt and operating costs until business is continued or sold
3. Natural disaster
   *Response Tactic : i*nsurance and preparedness
4. Additional competition
   Response Tactic: rely heavily on existing loyal customer base, additional promotion, and strength of location; target marketing
5. Weather
   Response Tactic: be known to customers and community as a business that rarely, if ever, closes due to weather

SECTION SEVEN

MARKETING STRATEGY

"He who excels at resolving difficulties does so before they arise. He who excels in conquering his enemies triumphs before threats materialize." —Sun Tzu, The Art of War

ASAPS X*press* – Car Wash and Lube's marketing strategy is to enhance, promote, and support the fact that our products and services:

- are far superior to any other in the area
- are competitively priced (equal to the area's quick lubes and below the area's full-service car washes)
- offer value-added services the competition does not offer for the same or lower price
- offer products and services using the latest technology
- provide greater convenience and accessibility
- feature high-quality, major-branded products supported by an outstanding name brand reputation

Target Market/Area

ASAPS X*press* – Car Wash and Lube is targeting the market who live, work, shop, or travel in the five (5)-mile radius centering at the intersection of Highway 92 and Londonderry Drive and who drive any size vehicle.

Please refer to Section 6 — Market Analysis for a recap of the "target market" customer profile.

Pricing

Full-Service Car Wash

ASAPS X*press* – Car Wash and Lube's full-service car wash will be priced at a figure that is competitive for the Southeast and is below prices currently charged by the area's only full-service car wash, located in Cobb County:

Service	ASAPS X*press*	Calibur
Full-Service Car Wash	$7.50	$7.99
Exterior Wash only	$5.50	$5.99
Small Truck/Station Wagon	$9.00	$9.99
Passenger Vans	$9.00	$9.99
Sport Utility Vehicles	$9.00	$9.99
Poly Seal	$2.50	$2.50
Polish Wax	$3.50	$4.00
Air Freshener	$1.00	$1.00
Full Detailing	$75.00	not offered

Section 7 - Marketing Strategy *continued*

Quick Lube

The quick lube will be priced equal to the "going price" in the market — typically $21.95 to $22.95. However, for that price, the customer will also receive a free exterior car wash.

Advertising and Promotion

Company Positioning: to be the market leader on service, quality, and value for the price

Advertising

Within established budgets, **ASAPS X*press* – Car Wash and Lube** will advertise in all of the area newspapers and on local radio/TV, and will use billboard advertising (particularly in the first year of operation).

In addition, by being an independent operator for Specialty Oil Company's program, **ASAPS X*press* – Car Wash and Lube** will have access to the marketing and advertising resources of Quaker State including:

- Quaker State's signage — provided free to **ASAPS X*press* – Car Wash and Lube**
- use of Quaker State's local credit card mailing list for direct mail
- participation in Quaker State's extensive co-op advertising programs
- Quaker State's name and trademark logo identity and recognition
- Quaker State's trademark logo will appear in all advertising material

> NOTE: Quaker State's "Q" trademark is one of the most highly recognized trademark symbols behind McDonald's golden arches.

Please refer to Appendix 10-C and 10-D for further information on Quaker State's Xpress Lube and Advertising Allowance Programs.

Public Relations

The owner/operators of **ASAPS X*press* – Car Wash and Lube** will continue to be active in a number of civic, community, and church activities. We will also focus on activities within the company such as service projects, our employees and their families, and bringing new technologies to the business.

SECTION EIGHT

MANAGEMENT

"Generally, management of many is the same as management of few. It is a matter of organization." —Sun Tzu, The Art of War

How We Started

ASAPS X*press* – Car Wash and Lube was created in 1995 by Shoqut Hussien and Pamela Hussien, who saw a need in this market for a combined full-service car wash and quick lube business.

The legal form of **ASAPS X*press* – Car Wash and Lube** will be a Subchapter "S" Corporation. **ASAPS X*press* – Car Wash and Lube** has plans to incorporate in the State of Georgia and notify the IRS of its election as a Subchapter "S" Corporation.

This legal form was chosen to provide the owners with the most advantageous tax treatment that is presently available.

Management Team

The two people who make up the management team and who are also the founders of **ASAPS X*press* – Car Wash and Lube** hold the following positions:

Shoqut Hussien, Corporate President and Chief Executive Officer
Pamela Hussien, Vice President of Finance and Operations
Shoqut Hussien, Vice President of Marketing and Sales

Please refer to Appendix 10-A for management team résumés.

The founders and key managers of **ASAPS X*press* – Car Wash and Lube** have combined experience and skills exceeding 30 years in service, automotive repair, management consulting, and computer industries.

We believe that the skill, leadership, and characteristics of the management team will result in strong and flexible goal setting and goal achievement to meet the demands of the marketplace requiring our services. We anticipate that this expertise will produce outstanding results.

Responsibilities

Pamela Hussien, Vice President - Finance and Operations

Manage the day-to-day activities and staffing

Manage working capital, including inventory, cash, and marketable securities

Perform financial forecasting, including capital budgeting, cash budgeting, monthly financial statements, and external financing. Perform daily and routine physical maintenance, inventory management, and cost allocation functions.

Section 8 — Management *continued*

Shoqut Hussien, Vice President - Marketing and Sales

Manage market planning, advertising, public relations, sales promotion, merchandising, and facilitating staff services

Identify new markets and conduct market research

Manage sales activities, including customer service and quality

Outside Management and Technical Support

Outside support for **ASAPS X*press* – Car Wash and Lube** includes highly qualified business and industry professionals/experts who will assist our management team to make appropriate decisions and take the most effective actions. However, our outside support professionals will not be responsible for management decisions.

Outside Management Support (hourly basis)

Kevin Houston: Accountant/CPA
Ralph Walker: Attorney
Carlotta Roberts: Consultant, Georgia Small Business Development Center

Outside Technical Support (no fee)

Tommy LeMonis: Account Manager, Specialty Oil Company
Leon Hartman: President, Action Car Wash Systems, Inc.

Quick Lube Technical Support and Expertise

The quick lube portion of the business is being developed with the assistance of and in cooperation with Tommy LeMonis, Account Manager with Specialty Oil Company. **ASAPS X*press* – Car Wash and Lube** will be considered an "independent operator" of Quaker State's Xpress Lube Division.

Specialty Oil Company will be the principal supplier for all of the quick lube equipment, supplies, and products.

Specialty Oil Company, Express Lube Division, provides independent oil change owner/operators with a broad range of support services to assist the owner/operator with the set-up and ongoing operation of the quick lube business.

The services provided by Specialty Oil Company to **ASAPS X*press* – Car Wash and Lube** include or will include:

- complete demographic analysis
- competitive market survey and analysis
- complete set of oil change facility plans
- initial and ongoing training for the owner/operators
- training/certification programs for the oil change technicians
- marketing and advertising co-op programs and support
- oil reclamation service that *fully indemnifies* **ASAPS X*press* – Car Wash and Lube** from all liabilities regarding disposal of used oil and oil filters

Mr. LeMonis and the Specialty Oil Team will be available for continuing service and support on an ongoing basis.

Section 8 - Management *continued*

Training

As part of preparing to set up and operate **ASAPS X*press* – Car Wash and Lube**, Shoqut and Pamela Hussien will receive intensive, specialized operations and business management training.

Shoqut and Pamela will be provided in-house/on-site consulting and training classes with a Specialty Oil Company team of professionals. The consulting and training provides quick lube owner/operators with technical and business management skills training necessary to successfully set up, operate, and manage a quick lube center. Shoqut and Pamela will also receive two to four weeks of training at one or more established, successful quick lube operations in Georgia. During the training Shoqut and Pamela will receive hands-on experience in operating a quick lube on a day-to-day basis.

Shoqut and Pamela will also spend two to four weeks in training at one or more established, successful full-service car wash operations in Georgia. During the training Shoqut and Pamela will receive hands-on experience in operating a full-service car wash on a day-to-day basis.

These specialized training programs, when combined with the extensive business experience and skills of Shoqut Hussien and Pamela Hussien, will aid tremendously in ensuring the success and profitability of **ASAPS X*press* – Car Wash and Lube.**

People/Talent We Require

The development team recognizes that additional staff is required to properly support the **ASAPS X*press* – Car Wash and Lube** operation. We plan to employ a combination of eleven (11) full-time and part-time employees to cover the 60 hours per week of operating hours.

Title	Number of Employees
Manager (Pamela Hussien)	1
Cashier/Office	2
Car Wash Attendants	5
Lube Technicians	3
TOTAL	**11**

Government Regulations

The business operated by **ASAPS X*press* – Car Wash and Lube** is not considered to be a "regulated business" and is therefore subject only to normal business and governmental regulatory agencies, i.e. ,OSHA, EEOC, EPA (federal, state, and local), and the Cherokee County Business License Office.

The only license required to open and operate **ASAPS X*press* – Car Wash and Lube** is a Cherokee County Business License.

Discussions with the Directors of the Cherokee County Water Authority revealed no unusual wastewater treatment or water run-off concerns. Similarly, discussions with the State Environmental Protection Agency also revealed no particular concerns about the operation of the business.

Section 8 - Management *continued*

Environmental Issues and Concerns

The founders of **ASAPS X*press* – Car Wash and Lube** are very concerned about the environment.

It will be our goal and objective to ensure that **ASAPS X*press* – Car Wash and Lube** operates in such a way as to be in full compliance with all local, state, and federal environmental laws and regulations. We will strive to be good environmental citizens by using recycled products and by recycling waste by-products as much as is practical in operating the business.

- All of the car wash products are biodegradable, phosphate free, and oil free.
- 70%-80% of the water used in the car wash is recycled.
- Used oil removed from vehicles will be collected and disposed of by a licensed, certified oil reclamation service company.

Note Regarding Used Oil Collection

Specialty Oil Company will be providing **ASAPS X*press* – Car Wash and Lube** with used oil collection services through their "Used Oil Collection Program." By participating in this program, **ASAPS X*press* – Car Wash and Lube** will be fully indemnified regarding the disposal of the used oil.

SECTION NINE

FINANCIAL DATA

ASAPS Xpress - Car Wash and Lube
ProForma

Equipment and Start Up Costs
Detail of Miscellaneous Expenses

Computer System (Hardware/Software)	$10,362
Office Equipment	$3,020
(blank)	$0
(blank)	$0
(blank)	$0
(blank)	$0
	$13,382

OFFICE EQUIPMENT:	
Desks or Tables	300
Office Chairs	300
Filing Cabinets	180
Customer Lounge Furniture	300
Letterhead Stationery	500
Letterhead/Souvenir Memo Pads	60
"Service Writer" forms	125
Phone Call Record Books	40
Imprinted Pens & Pencils	125
Cash register	600
Calculator with tape	90
Employee time clock	200
Miscellaneous	200
TOTAL	3,020

ASAPS Xpress - Car Wash and Lube
ProForma

INSURANCE

Property/Casualty/Liability $4,500 Estimated

TAXES

PAYROLL

FICA/FUTA/SUTA	% of Payroll	11.15%
Workers Compensation	% of Payroll	6.90%
	temporarily set as 6.9% of payroll	

PROPERTY		Car Wash	Lube
	Millage	0.01675	0.01675
	Assessed Value	40%	40%
	Land & Equipment	$185,000	$195,000
	NOTE: property tax excludes lease equipment		
	Tax	$1,240	$1,307

ASAPS *Xpress* - Car Wash and Lube
CONSOLIDATED FINANCIALS

*** BUDGET (Year 1 by month) ***

	Jan	Feb	Mar	Apr	May	Jun	Jul	Aug	Sep	Oct	Nov	Dec	Year 1
Sales													
Full Service Wash	$19,237	$19,621	$19,818	$19,818	$19,619	$19,227	$18,650	$18,277	$18,094	$18,275	$18,458	$18,827	$227,923
% of Total Sales	32%	32%	32%	32%	32%	32%	32%	32%	32%	32%	32%	32%	32%
Exterior Wash	$1,924	$1,962	$1,982	$1,982	$1,962	$1,923	$1,865	$1,828	$1,809	$1,828	$1,846	$1,883	$22,792
% of Total Sales	3%	3%	3%	3%	3%	3%	3%	3%	3%	3%	3%	3%	3%
Poly Seal	$1,822	$1,858	$1,877	$1,877	$1,858	$1,821	$1,766	$1,731	$1,713	$1,731	$1,748	$1,783	$21,584
% of Total Sales	3%	3%	3%	3%	3%	3%	3%	3%	3%	3%	3%	3%	3%
Foaming Polish Wax	$2,550	$2,601	$2,627	$2,627	$2,601	$2,549	$2,473	$2,423	$2,399	$2,423	$2,447	$2,496	$30,217
% of Total Sales	4%	4%	4%	4%	4%	4%	4%	4%	4%	4%	4%	4%	4%
Under Carriage/Rust Inhibitor	$1,093	$1,115	$1,126	$1,126	$1,115	$1,092	$1,060	$1,038	$1,028	$1,038	$1,049	$1,070	$12,950
% of Total Sales	2%	2%	2%	2%	2%	2%	2%	2%	2%	2%	2%	2%	2%
Full Detailing	$4,372	$4,459	$4,504	$4,504	$4,459	$4,370	$4,239	$4,154	$4,112	$4,154	$4,195	$4,279	$51,801
% of Total Sales	7%	7%	7%	7%	7%	7%	7%	7%	7%	7%	7%	7%	7%
Basic Oil Change	$27,198	$27,742	$28,020	$28,020	$27,740	$27,185	$26,369	$25,842	$25,583	$25,839	$26,098	$26,620	$322,255
% of Total Sales	45%	45%	45%	45%	45%	45%	45%	45%	45%	45%	45%	45%	45%
Add-on Services (Oil Change)	$1,778	$1,813	$1,795	$1,778	$1,760	$1,742	$1,724	$1,742	$1,760	$1,795	$1,795	$1,813	$21,296
% of Total Sales	3%	3%	3%	3%	3%	3%	3%	3%	3%	3%	3%	3%	3%
Total Sales	$59,973	$61,173	$61,749	$61,731	$61,114	$59,909	$58,146	$57,035	$56,500	$57,083	$57,636	$58,770	$710,818
Cost of Goods Sold													
Supplies	$9,679	$9,873	$9,961	$9,955	$9,856	$9,664	$9,385	$9,213	$9,131	$9,228	$9,315	$9,496	$114,756
% of Total Sales	16%	16%	16%	16%	16%	16%	16%	16%	16%	16%	16%	16%	16%
Labor (including P/R taxes)	$13,445	$13,714	$13,844	$13,841	$13,703	$13,432	$13,036	$12,785	$12,664	$12,794	$12,918	$13,173	$159,348
% of Total Sales	22%	22%	22%	22%	22%	22%	22%	22%	22%	22%	22%	22%	22%
Overhead	$0	$0	$0	$0	$0	$0	$0	$0	$0	$0	$0	$0	$0
% of Total Sales	0%	0%	0%	0%	0%	0%	0%	0%	0%	0%	0%	0%	0%
Total Cost of Goods Sold	$23,125	$23,587	$23,805	$23,796	$23,558	$23,096	$22,420	$21,998	$21,795	$22,022	$22,233	$22,669	$274,104
Gross Profit	$36,849	$37,586	$37,944	$37,935	$37,555	$36,813	$35,726	$35,038	$34,705	$35,061	$35,403	$36,102	$436,714
Gross Margin	61%	61%	61%	61%	61%	61%	61%	61%	61%	61%	61%	61%	61%
Operating Expenses													
Sales & Marketing													
Advertising	$1,202	$1,226	$1,238	$1,238	$1,226	$1,201	$1,165	$1,142	$1,131	$1,142	$1,153	$1,177	$14,243
Commissions	$0	$0	$0	$0	$0	$0	$0	$0	$0	$0	$0	$0	$0
Entertainment	$0	$0	$0	$0	$0	$0	$0	$0	$0	$0	$0	$0	$0
Literature	$0	$0	$0	$0	$0	$0	$0	$0	$0	$0	$0	$0	$0
Promotions	$0	$0	$0	$0	$0	$0	$0	$0	$0	$0	$0	$0	$0
Salaries	$0	$0	$0	$0	$0	$0	$0	$0	$0	$0	$0	$0	$0
Trade Shows	$0	$0	$0	$0	$0	$0	$0	$0	$0	$0	$0	$0	$0
Travel	$0	$0	$0	$0	$0	$0	$0	$0	$0	$0	$0	$0	$0
Total Sales & Marketing Costs	$1,202	$1,226	$1,238	$1,238	$1,226	$1,201	$1,165	$1,142	$1,131	$1,142	$1,153	$1,177	$14,243
% of Total Sales	2%	2%	2%	2%	2%	2%	2%	2%	2%	2%	2%	2%	2%
Research & Development													
Consulting	$0	$0	$0	$0	$0	$0	$0	$0	$0	$0	$0	$0	$0
Equipment (Expensed Purchases)	$0	$0	$0	$0	$0	$0	$0	$0	$0	$0	$0	$0	$0
R & D Materials	$0	$0	$0	$0	$0	$0	$0	$0	$0	$0	$0	$0	$0
R & D Salaries	$0	$0	$0	$0	$0	$0	$0	$0	$0	$0	$0	$0	$0
Total R & D Costs	$0	$0	$0	$0	$0	$0	$0	$0	$0	$0	$0	$0	$0

Prepared by Shoqut and Pamela Husslen 3/11/95

Page 1 of 2

ASAPS *Xpress* - Car Wash and Lube
CONSOLIDATED FINANCIALS

% of Total Sales	Jan 0%	Feb 0%	Mar 0%	Apr 0%	May 0%	Jun 0%	Jul 0%	Aug 0%	Sep 0%	Oct 0%	Nov 0%	Dec 0%	Year 1 0%
General & Administrative													
Accounting (CPA)	$395	$395	$395	$395	$395	$395	$395	$395	$395	$395	$395	$395	$4,738
Admin Salaries	$5,780	$5,794	$5,752	$5,709	$5,666	$5,622	$5,579	$5,650	$5,722	$5,852	$5,866	$5,939	$68,929
Customer Claims ()	$601	$601	$595	$589	$583	$577	$572	$577	$583	$595	$595	$601	$7,071
Depreciation (10 yr/straight line)	$1,917	$1,917	$1,917	$1,917	$1,917	$1,917	$1,917	$1,917	$1,917	$1,917	$1,917	$1,917	$23,000
Repairs & Maintenance ()	$1,202	$1,202	$1,190	$1,179	$1,167	$1,155	$1,143	$1,155	$1,167	$1,190	$1,190	$1,202	$14,142
Insurance	$375	$375	$375	$375	$375	$375	$375	$375	$375	$375	$375	$375	$4,500
Legal Fees	$101	$101	$101	$101	$101	$101	$101	$101	$101	$101	$101	$101	$1,209
Licenses and Permits	$10	$10	$10	$10	$10	$10	$10	$10	$10	$10	$10	$10	$120
Office Expenses (miscellaneous)	$481	$481	$476	$471	$467	$462	$457	$462	$467	$476	$476	$481	$5,657
Lease Equipment	$4,900	.$4,900	$4,900	$4,900	$4,900	$4,900	$4,900	$4,900	$4,900	$4,900	$4,900	$4,900	$58,800
Taxes (non-income, ie. FICA/FUTA/SUT	$1,235	$1,235	$1,235	$1,235	$1,235	$1,235	$1,235	$1,235	$1,235	$1,235	$1,235	$1,235	$14,820
Telephone	$240	$240	$238	$236	$233	$231	$229	$231	$233	$238	$238	$240	$2,828
Utilities (water/sewer/electric)	$2,050	$2,050	$2,030	$2,010	$1,990	$1,969	$1,949	$1,969	$1,990	$2,030	$2,030	$2,050	$24,116
Total G & A Costs	$19,286	$19,301	$19,213	$19,125	$19,037	$18,949	$18,861	$18,977	$19,094	$19,313	$19,328	$19,445	$229,930
% of Total Sales	32%	32%	31%	31%	31%	32%	32%	33%	34%	34%	34%	33%	32%
Total Operating Expenses	$20,489	$20,527	$20,452	$20,364	$20,263	$20,151	$20,026	$20,119	$20,224	$20,455	$20,481	$20,622	$244,173
% of Total Sales	34%	34%	33%	33%	33%	34%	34%	35%	36%	36%	36%	35%	34%
Income From Operations	$16,360	$17,059	$17,492	$17,571	$17,292	$16,662	$15,700	$14,919	$14,481	$14,606	$14,922	$15,480	$192,542
% of Total Sales	27%	28%	28%	28%	28%	28%	27%	26%	26%	26%	26%	26%	27%
Interest Income	$0	$0	$0	$0	$0	$0	$0	$0	$0	$0	$0	$0	$0
Interest Expense	$3,245	$3,242	$3,238	$3,234	$3,230	$3,226	$3,222	$3,218	$3,214	$3,210	$3,206	$3,202	$38,690
Income before Taxes	$13,115	$13,817	$14,254	$14,337	$14,062	$13,436	$12,477	$11,700	$11,266	$11,395	$11,715	$12,278	$153,852
Taxes on Income	$0	$0	$0	$0	$0	$0	$0	$0	$0	$0	$0	$0	$0
Net Income After Taxes	$13,115	$13,817	$14,254	$14,337	$14,062	$13,436	$12,477	$11,700	$11,266	$11,395	$11,715	$12,278	$153,852
% of Total Sales	22%	23%	23%	23%	23%	22%	21%	21%	20%	20%	20%	21%	22%

Prepared by Shoqut and Pamela Husslen 3/11/95 **Page 2 of 2**

ASAPS *Xpress* - Car Wash and Lube
CONSOLIDATED FINANCIALS

*** INCOME STATEMENT (Years 1 - 5) ***

Sales	Year 1	Year 2	Year 3	Year 4	Year 5
Full Service Wash	$227,923	$273,507	$317,269	$364,859	$419,588
% of Total Sales	32%	33%	34%	36%	37%
Exterior Wash	$22,792	$27,351	$31,727	$36,486	$41,959
% of Total Sales	3%	3%	3%	4%	4%
Poly Seal	$21,584	$25,900	$30,044	$34,551	$39,734
% of Total Sales	3%	3%	3%	3%	4%
Foaming Polish Wax	$30,217	$36,260	$42,062	$48,371	$55,627
% of Total Sales	4%	4%	5%	5%	5%
Under Carriage/Rust Inhibitor	$12,950	$15,540	$18,027	$20,731	$23,840
% of Total Sales	2%	2%	2%	2%	2%
Full Detailing	$51,801	$62,161	$72,107	$82,922	$95,361
% of Total Sales	7%	8%	8%	8%	8%
Basic Oil Change	$322,255	$354,481	$389,929	$409,425	$429,896
% of Total Sales	45%	43%	42%	40%	38%
Add-on Services (Oil Change)	$21,296	$23,426	$25,769	$27,057	$28,410
% of Total Sales	3%	3%	3%	3%	3%
Total Sales	$710,818	$818,627	$926,933	$1,024,403	$1,134,415
Cost of Goods Sold					
Supplies	$114,756	$118,198	$121,744	$125,396	$129,158
% of Total Sales	16%	14%	13%	12%	11%
Labor (including P/R taxes)	$159,348	$164,129	$169,053	$174,124	$179,348
% of Total Sales	22%	20%	18%	17%	16%
Overhead	$0	$0	$0	$0	$0
% of Total Sales	0%	0%	0%	0%	0%
Total Cost of Goods Sold	$274,104	$282,327	$290,797	$299,521	$308,506
Gross Profit	$436,714	$536,300	$636,136	$724,882	$825,909
Gross Margin	61%	66%	69%	71%	73%
Operating Expenses					
Sales & Marketing	$14,243	$14,528	$14,818	$15,115	$15,417
% of Total Sales	2%	2%	2%	1%	1%
Research & Development	$0	$0	$0	$0	$0
% of Total Sales	0%	0%	0%	0%	0%
G & A (without Depreciation)	$206,930	$213,138	$219,532	$226,118	$232,901
% of Total Sales	29%	26%	24%	22%	21%
Depreciation	$23,000	$23,000	$23,000	$23,000	$23,000
% of Total Sales	3%	3%	2%	2%	2%
Total Operating Expenses	$244,173	$250,665	$257,350	$264,232	$271,318
% of Total Sales	34%	31%	28%	26%	24%
Income From Operations	$192,542	$285,634	$378,786	$460,650	$554,590
% of Total Sales	27%	35%	41%	45%	49%
Interest Income	$0	$0	$0	$0	$0
Interest Expense	$38,690	$38,092	$37,426	$36,682	$35,852
Income before Taxes	$153,852	$247,542	$341,360	$423,968	$518,738
Taxes on Income	$0	$0	$0	$0	$0
Net Income After Taxes	$153,852	$247,542	$341,360	$423,968	$518,738
% of Total Sales	22%	30%	37%	41%	46%

Prepared by Shoqut and Pamela Hussien 3/11/95 **Page 1 of 1**

ASAPS *Xpress* - ~ar Wash and Lube
CONSOLIDATED FINANCIALS

***** CASH FLOW STATEMENT (Year 1 by month) *****

	Jan	Feb	Mar	Apr	May	Jun	Jul	Aug	Sep	Oct	Nov	Dec	Year 1
Beginning Cash Balance	$15,662	$30,284	$45,606	$61,360	$77,193	$92,747	$107,671	$121,633	$134,814	$147,557	$160,425	$173,609	$15,662
Cash Receipts													
Total Sales	$59,973	$61,173	$61,749	$61,731	$61,114	$59,909	$58,146	$57,035	$56,500	$57,083	$57,636	$58,770	$710,818
Interest Income	$0	$0	$0	$0	$0	$0	$0	$0	$0	$0	$0	$0	$0
Total Cash Receipts	$59,973	$61,173	$61,749	$61,731	$61,114	$59,909	$58,146	$57,035	$56,500	$57,083	$57,636	$58,770	$710,818
Cash Disbursements													
Salaries & Labor	$19,225	$19,508	$19,596	$19,550	$19,368	$19,054	$18,614	$18,435	$18,385	$18,645	$18,784	$19,112	$228,277
Advertising	$1,202	$1,226	$1,238	$1,238	$1,226	$1,201	$1,165	$1,142	$1,131	$1,142	$1,153	$1,177	$14,243
Commissions	$0	$0	$0	$0	$0	$0	$0	$0	$0	$0	$0	$0	$0
Cost of Goods Sold (non-labor)	$9,679	$9,873	$9,961	$9,955	$9,856	$9,664	$9,385	$9,213	$9,131	$9,228	$9,315	$9,496	$114,756
Lease Equipment	$4,900	$4,900	$4,900	$4,900	$4,900	$4,900	$4,900	$4,900	$4,900	$4,900	$4,900	$4,900	$58,800
Other Disbursements	$5,455	$5,455	$5,410	$5,365	$5,320	$5,275	$5,231	$5,275	$5,320	$5,410	$5,410	$5,455	$64,381
Interest Expense	$3,245	$3,242	$3,238	$3,234	$3,230	$3,226	$3,222	$3,218	$3,214	$3,210	$3,206	$3,202	$38,690
Tax Payments	$1,235	$1,235	$1,235	$1,235	$1,235	$1,235	$1,235	$1,235	$1,235	$1,235	$1,235	$1,235	$14,820
Total Cash Disbursements	$44,942	$45,439	$45,578	$45,477	$45,135	$44,556	$43,752	$43,418	$43,317	$43,771	$44,004	$44,576	$533,966
Net Cash from Operations	$15,031	$15,734	$16,171	$16,253	$15,978	$15,353	$14,394	$13,617	$13,183	$13,312	$13,632	$14,194	$176,852
Non-Operational Expenditures													
Investments	$0	$0	$0	$0	$0	$0	$0	$0	$0	$0	$0	$0	$0
Building (& land)	$350,000	$0	$0	$0	$0	$0	$0	$0	$0	$0	$0	$0	$350,000
Equipment (Capitalized Purchases)	$43,382	$0	$0	$0	$0	$0	$0	$0	$0	$0	$0	$0	$43,382
Leasehold Improvements	$0	$0	$0	$0	$0	$0	$0	$0	$0	$0	$0	$0	$0
Current Maturity - Long Term Debt	$409	$413	$417	$420	$424	$428	$432	$436	$440	$444	$448	$452	$5,163
Long Term Loan Repayment	$0	$0	$0	$0	$0	$0	$0	$0	$0	$0	$0	$0	$0
Payment of Cash Dividends	$0	$0	$0	$0	$0	$0	$0	$0	$0	$0	$0	$0	$0
Owner Equity	$39,338	$0	$0	$0	$0	$0	$0	$0	$0	$0	$0	$0	$39,338
Proceeds from Short Term Loan	$0	$0	$0	$0	$0	$0	$0	$0	$0	$0	$0	$0	$0
Proceeds from Long Term Loan	$354,044	$0	$0	$0	$0	$0	$0	$0	$0	$0	$0	$0	$354,044
Net Cash Balance	$30,284	$45,606	$61,360	$77,193	$92,747	$107,671	$121,633	$134,814	$147,557	$160,425	$173,609	$187,351	$187,351

Prepared by Shoqut and Pamela Hussien 3/11/95 **Page 1 of 1**

ASAPS *Xpress* - Car Wash and Lube
CONSOLIDATED FINANCIALS

*** SOURCE & USE OF FUNDS ***

Source of Funds	**Year 1**	**Year 2**	**Year 3**	**Year 4**	**Year 5**
Net Income After Taxes	$153,852	$247,542	$341,360	$423,968	$518,738
Depreciation	$23,000	$23,000	$23,000	$23,000	$23,000
Funds From Operations	$176,852	$270,542	$364,360	$446,968	$541,738
Owner Equity	$39,338	$0	$0	$0	$0
Proceeds from Long Term Loan	$354,044	$0	$0	$0	$0
Total Source of Funds	$570,234	$270,542	$364,360	$446,968	$541,738
Use of Funds					
Building (& land)	$350,000	$0	$0	$0	$0
Equipment (Capitalized Purchases)	$43,382	$0	$0	$0	$0
Leasehold Improvements	$0	$0	$0	$0	$0
Long Term Loan Repayment	$0	$0	$0	$0	$0
Cash Dividends	$0	$0	$0	$0	$0
Increased Working Capital*	$171,091	$264,115	$357,189	$438,967	$532,812
Total Use of Funds	$564,473	$264,115	$357,189	$438,967	$532,812
Summary of Changes in Working Capital:					
Cash	$171,689	$264,782	$357,933	$439,797	$533,738
Investments	$0	$0	$0	$0	$0
Accounts Receivable	$0	$0	$0	$0	$0
Notes Receivable	$0	$0	$0	$0	$0
Other Current Assets	$0	$0	$0	$0	$0
Current Maturity - Long Term Debt	($597)	($667)	($744)	($830)	($926)
Accounts Payable	$0	$0	$0	$0	$0
Other Payables	$0	$0	$0	$0	$0
Accrued Liabilities	$0	$0	$0	$0	$0
Increased Working Capital*	$171,091	$264,115	$357,189	$438,967	$532,812

Prepared by Shoqut and Pamela Hussien 3/11/95 **Page 1 of 1**

ASAPS *Xpress* - Car Wash and Lube
CONSOLIDATED FINANCIALS

***** BALANCE SHEET *****

Assets	**Year 1**	**Year 2**	**Year 3**	**Year 4**	**Year 5**
Current Assets					
Cash	$187,351	$452,133	$810,066	$1,249,862	$1,783,600
Investments	$0	$0	$0	$0	$0
Accounts Receivable	$0	$0	$0	$0	$0
Notes Receivable	$0	$0	$0	$0	$0
Other Current Assets	$0	$0	$0	$0	$0
Total Current Assets	$187,351	$452,133	$810,066	$1,249,862	$1,783,600
Plant and Equipment					
Building	$350,000	$350,000	$350,000	$350,000	$350,000
Equipment (Capitalized Purchases)	$43,382	$43,382	$43,382	$43,382	$43,382
Leasehold Improvements	$0	$0	$0	$0	$0
Less Accumulated Depreciation	$23,000	$46,000	$69,000	$92,000	$115,000
Total Net Property & Equip	$370,382	$347,382	$324,382	$301,382	$278,382
Other Assets	$0	$0	$0	$0	$0
Total Assets	$557,733	$799,515	$1,134,448	$1,551,244	$2,061,982
Liabilities & Owner Equity					
Current Liabilities					
Short Term Debt	$5,761	$6,427	$7,171	$8,001	$8,927
Accounts Payable	$0	$0	$0	$0	$0
Other Payables	$0	$0	$0	$0	$0
Accrued Liabilities	$0	$0	$0	$0	$0
Total Current Liabilities	$5,761	$6,427	$7,171	$8,001	$8,927
Long Term Debt	$343,120	$336,693	$329,522	$321,521	$312,594
Total Liabilities	$348,881	$343,120	$336,693	$329,522	$321,521
Owner Equity					
Owner Equity	$39,338	$39,338	$39,338	$39,338	$39,338
Retained Earnings	$153,852	$401,394	$742,754	$1,166,722	$1,685,461
Paid In Capital	$15,662	$15,662	$15,662	$15,662	$15,662
Total Owners' Equity	$208,852	$456,394	$797,755	$1,221,723	$1,740,461
Total Liabilities & Equity	$557,733	$799,515	$1,134,448	$1,551,244	$2,061,982

Prepared by Shoqut and Pamela Hussien 3/11/95 **Page 1 of 1**

ASAPS *Xpress* - Car Wash and Lube
CONSOLIDATED FINANCIALS

***** RATIO ANALYSIS *****

Ratios	Year 1	Year 2	Year 3	Year 4	Year 5	
Current Ratio	32.52	70.35	112.96	156.22	199.81	Current Assets / Current Liabilities
Quick Ratio (Acid Test)	32.52	70.35	112.96	156.22	199.81	Quick Assets (Cash + Receivables) / Current Liabili
Return on Total Assets	34.52%	35.73%	33.39%	29.70%	26.90%	Net Income After Taxes / Total Assets (at year end)
Total Assets Turnover	1.27	1.02	0.82	0.66	0.55	Total Sales / Total Assets (at year end)
Total Debt to Total Assets	0.63	0.43	0.30	0.21	0.16	Total Liabilities / Total Assets
Gross Profit Margin	61.44%	65.51%	68.63%	70.76%	72.80%	Gross Profit (Net Sales) / Total Sales
Operating Profit Margin	27.09%	34.89%	40.86%	44.97%	48.89%	Income From Operations (Before Interest & Taxes) .
Net Profit Margin	21.64%	30.24%	36.83%	41.39%	45.73%	Net Income After Taxes / Total Sales
Return on Sales	35.23%	46.16%	53.66%	58.49%	62.81%	Net Income After Taxes / Gross Profit (Net Sales)
Return on Owners' Equity	73.67%	54.24%	42.79%	34.70%	29.80%	Net Income After Taxes / Total Owners' Equity (at y
Total Debt to Owners' Equity	1.67	0.75	0.42	0.27	0.18	Total Liabilities / Total Owners' Equity

Prepared by Shoqut and Pamela Hussien 3/11/95 **Page 1 of 1**

Adventure Media, Inc.

Location:	Cambridge, Mass.
Founder:	Andrew McKee
Education:	M.B.A., Harvard University
Year Founded:	1994
Starting Capital:	$150,000
Sales, 1995:	new venture
Owner's Equity:	$0
Employees:	5

After receiving his M.B.A., Andrew McKee worked for the Direct Mail Division of Time Warner. Using skills developed there as well as at Goldman, Sachs & Company, McKee eventually started his own music cataloguing company called HEAR Music. After successful growth, McKee sold the company to a conglomerate in 1992. Following the sale, McKee put together a group of investors to purchase Overseas Adventure Travel, a company which specialized in adventure vacations (e.g., safaris). Again, after successful growth, he was able to sell the business to a large database marketer of travel services.

While working at Overseas Adventure Travel, McKee found it difficult to market the company's services in an affordable way. Catalog printings and mailings were expensive, as were other forms of media. With experience in online services, McKee felt there would be an appropriate marketing application for his company via the Internet. Not only did the technology lower the advertising rates significantly, but the company was able to specifically target the audience with the appropriate demographic profile.

In order to launch a new online business (Adventure Media, Inc.), McKee wrote a business plan in 1994 to obtain financing from venture capitalists. Over the course of two months, McKee utilized business school case material, experienced faculty members, and classmates in the venture capital business to help develop his plan. To date, McKee has a contract with the Microsoft Network and a draft contract with Prodigy, as well as relationships with some of the larger Web sites including Pathfinder, Time Warner's Web site. Each of these Web sites will eventually incorporate Adventure Media, Inc.'s services.

"The plan was very important. It helped us to market our business and concept to the financial community. Without a business plan, we couldn't get our foot in the door. If you don't have it ready in a terse, concise readable format with a good Executive Summary, you'll never get beyond the word go."

Note*: Since this is a preliminary — or* venture *— plan, it was not submitted to our panel of experts for evaluation as were the business plans for Picaro's, Healthcare Automation, and ASAPS Xpress.*

Preliminary Business Plan for

Adventure Media, Inc.

This document contains proprietary and confidential information related to the business plan of Adventure Media, Inc. and has been provided for analysis by the person to whom it has been transmitted by the Company. This document may not be reproduced, distributed, nor its contents divulged or otherwise used, in whole or in part, without the prior written consent of Adventure Media, Inc.

This is not an offer to sell, nor the solicitation of an offer to buy, any securities. Such an offer, if made, will be made only through a prospectus or private placement memorandum issued in accordance with the United States Securities Act and other applicable laws, rules, and regulations.

Prepared By:

Andrew McKee, Chief Executive Officer
Adventure Media, Inc.

Adventure Media, Inc.

THE COMPANY

Adventure Media, Inc. is a vacation marketing company that delivers leisure travel offerings to customers and users of the Internet and commercial online services. Adventure Media Inc.'s proprietary database, *Travelon,* is a comprehensive visual database of worldwide travel products including the largest selection of adventure, special interest travel, and expedition cruises, as well as traditional travel offerings. *Travelon* allows users to browse these extensive travel offerings in real time while the user is online. Or, based upon a profile supplied by the user that is maintained in the *Travelon* database, the system will notify the consumer that a desired product is available, based upon the user's specified budget, activity preference, and/or destination interest. The Company's Internet address is: http://www.travelon.com.

Acceptance of the Company's service by commercial online services has been outstanding. Agreements have either been signed or are in negotiation with the following commercial providers:

America Online

Prodigy

The Microsoft Network

Pathfinder (Time Warner's site on the World Wide Web)

The company has also had joint venture discussions with other service providers who are soon to enter the online arena, including:

AT&T WorldNet (a new consumer online service)

Travelocity (joint venture between Sabre and Worldview)

Travel Connect (a joint venture between the *New York Times* and Advanced Publications, which includes Random House and Condé Nast)

Success with travel providers has also been outstanding. The Company has established relationships with 30 specialty tour operators, providing over 350 trips annually and has established a strategic relationship with National Leisure Group, a subsidiary of the Ideon Group (formerly Safecard Services).

NLG is the largest provider of private label endorsement travel programs in the country. NLG will provide a private label program for *Travelon*, traditional travel offerings, and last-minute bargains.

Adventure Media, Inc.

SERVICE

Travelon is a comprehensive visual database that will be incorporated into the Travel Sections of various commercial online services such as Prodigy, America Online, and The Microsoft Network, as well as the World Wide Web. The Company's easy-to-use software guides the consumer through all the travel offerings in the database and helps consumers narrow their choices and eventually select a trip based on their predefined vacation criteria.

This analysis is performed based on a user profile, set up by the consumer, which includes preferences such as budget, activities, destination, and time of travel. This guide is the most unique aspect of the service. A consumer will be able to search the system online based on his or her preferences, identify matches currently available, and then view comprehensive information regarding the package, including color photography.

Once consumers have found the vacation they want on the system, they will call an 800 number visible on the computer screen that will connect the consumers directly to the travel provider to book their vacation. Adventure Media will track the number of calls to each tour operator, using software developed by AT&T, which will provide the company with valuable marketing information as well as data for billing purposes.

PROPRIETARY DATABASE

Users of the *Travelon* service will have the option to identify themselves when they log on to use the system. Most users will complete an online questionnaire that provides demographic information as well as travel and destination preferences.

This valuable consumer data will be the property of *Travelon* and could be marketed to a variety of product and service providers. Such activity would provide a secondary source of revenue for the Company and will comprise a valuable asset for the Company.

REVENUE ACTIVITIES

The Company will generate revenues from the following activities:

1) Commissions from certain products sold through sales generated on the *Travelon* system;
2) Fees earned by charging specialty and adventure travel companies based on leads or inquiries generated;
3) Shared usage fees from certain commercial online services;
4) Advertising sales from companies who pay to have their ads appear on the *Travelon* home pages;
5) List rental income.

Adventure Media's strategy has three aspects: consumers, commercial service providers, and travel providers. *Travelon* offers unique benefits to all of these customers, which positions it to be the premier travel provider in cyberspace.

Consumers

Consumers are the ultimate customers and will determine the success of *Travelon.* To ensure their use, the system is flexible, simple to use, easily accessible, and loaded with information to facilitate their vacation planning. Benefits consumers will receive are as follows:

- Largest culmination of specialty tour operators and adventure travel outfitters
- Access to travel products offered by National Leisure Group, the largest provider of "private label" endorsement travel programs in the country (see discussion below)
- Online research of travel destinations and activities
- Online forum for posting questions and "chatting" with other vacationers
- Access to last-minute travel bargains

OnLine Providers

OnLine service providers are continuously searching for content that will attract and retain subscribers. As discussed in the competition section, online travel has not been presented in a manner similar to *Travelon* by any source.

The Company is designing proprietary aspects of its service that will be unique to each online service provider, to help ensure they attract and retain subscribers, such as:

- Service to purchase vacation packages, not just flight information
- Create online community in which adventure and special interest travel is the focus
- Online "events" involving industry experts

Travel Providers

Travelon is being developed as a comprehensive resource of travel products. The system can be thought of as an online travel agency, except that the information is communicated electronically and bookings and inquiries are handled by the tour operators directly. The benefits to the travel providers are most obvious:

- Advertising without up-front cost; commission payments or finders fees are only due if a trip is booked or a qualified lead contacts the specialty travel provider.

THE MARKET

As the interest in online communication grows, there has been increased demand for innovative services that cater to specific audiences. As the information superhighway penetrates a growing number of households, whether by computer, telephone, or television, consumers will be clamoring for more information. Adventure Media's competitive advantage will come from the quality of the information and service provided, regardless of the platform.

Of all the uncertainty surrounding this emerging media, one fact is certain: interactive communication is here to stay; the only question is how large the market will become.

The Direct Marketing Association predicts that electronic home shopping will evolve into $150 billion industry, up from $3 billion today. However large the market ultimately becomes, the Company strongly believes that travel will be an important component of this revolutionary marketplace.

The following chart displays the variety of mechanisms through which Americans plan their vacations. It is important to note that traditional methods of information gathering are rapidly changing. As the online population increases, industry analysts predict consumers will use online services as a resource to obtain information as well as to purchase products. With respect to travel, the traditional methods of researching information (guidebooks, magazines, TV), purchasing products (travel agents, direct contact with supplier), and even travel clubs will all be located online.

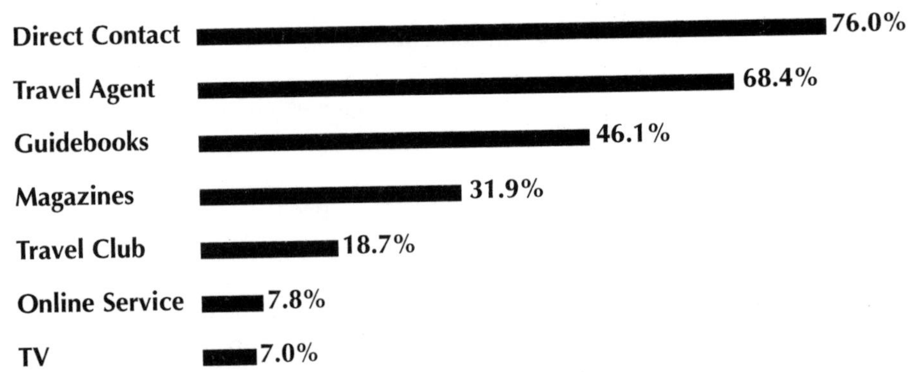

Source: U. S. Travel Data Center (TIAA)

Adventure Media, Inc.

STRATEGIC ALLIANCES

Commercial Online Service Providers

Prodigy
Prodigy Services Corporation has committed to incorporate the *Travelon* system into Prodigy's online travel section, one of the most popular areas on its service.

Adventure Media will create two separate services on Prodigy:

1) Prodigy Vacations, which will incorporate vacation products offered by National Leisure Group and fulfilled by NLG's Boston call center. Adventure Media will remit to Prodigy a portion of all Gross Profit earned by Adventure Media (prior to deduction of any Adventure Media expenses) on all Prodigy vacation bookings.

2) Adventure Media will also incorporate *Travelon* into Prodigy and will retain 100% of the lead generation revenues earned by *Travelon* on Prodigy.

America Online
Adventure Media has been selected by America Online to develop new programming for AOL that builds on the company's *Travelon* database.

The new service, called ***"Outtahere!"*** will combine expertise and personality to the vacation planning process by commingling rich content, expert guidance, stimulating graphics, and a robust database of travel products from which to choose. Unlike other travel resources, *Outtahere!* will be interactive and will speak with a voice designed to appeal to the adventure traveler. *Outtahere!* will build on the *Travelon* product database of Adventure Media by surrounding it with a variety of editorial content and functionality that will make the vacation-planning process both entertaining and satisfying.

The Microsoft Network
Adventure Media was selected by Microsoft to be one of approximately 160 ICPs on the service this year. Although the size and scope of the opportunity is uncertain, it is clear that MSN will have a substantial impact on the online world, given the simple fact that access to MSN will be universal to customers worldwide who upgrade to Windows 95.

Adventure Media will develop a Forum on MSN, an environment in which we will be able to feature all of the products of our clients, as well as to create an online community in which adventure and travel is our expertise.

MSN allows ICPs to set fees which members pay for goods and services in each forum. MSN splits the revenues with the ICPs, and allows the ICP to keep the majority of this revenue.

Travel Providers

National Leisure Group

NLG will be providing Adventure Media with an extensive selection of vacation products and will create a separate private-label travel program.

Specialty Tour Operators

These are smaller travel companies who operate specialty tours, adventure vacations and other unique travel products. They all share one thing in common: their products are not widely marketed and they are operated by small companies. Their products include safaris, treks, hiking tours, bicycle trips, scuba-diving excursions, etc.

REVENUE SOURCES

Lead Generation Revenues

Adventure Media will bill the tour operator for each call received, charging them a fee of $4.75 per call, far less than the inquiry costs from other media. Market research suggests that tour operators are accustomed to the notion of costs associated with leads generated, and that fees of $10–$20 per qualified lead are customary. As such, we believe that a low, $4.75 cost per lead will be highly attractive to a large number of operators.

Profit Sharing with NLG

National Leisure Group will supply cruises and resort vacation packages on *Travelon* and will be the supplier for Prodigy Vacations. Once consumers have found the vacation they want on the system, they will call a dedicated 800 number terminating at National Leisure Group to book the package. Adventure Media will be paid 30% of NLG's gross profit for each booking or about 4% of the gross package price. By sharing profits, our interests will be aligned as we are both motivated to promote the highest-margin products. The Company will receive reports from NLG of sales activity to ensure that bookings generated as a result of exposure to *Travelon* are captured. The relationship with NLG will allow Adventure Media to operate with a small head-office staff, avoiding the staffing, hardware, and other costs associated with having a dedicated inbound call center.

Online Usage Fees
America Online will pay Adventure Media a percentage of the hourly usage when consumers spend time in the *Travelon* area on AOL. Currently, the hourly fees charged to the consumer are $2.95, but they are expected to decrease over time.

USE OF FUNDS

Adventure Media is seeking investors in order to finance the development and execution of the business plan. As of August 1995, the founder has invested over $50,000 in the Company and has secured additional bank financing of $100,000. The Company is seeking commitments for a total of $1,000,000 of equity capital, allocated as follows:

Business Segment	Investment Required
Travelon Software	$350,000
Capital Costs	$150,000
Working Capital	$500,000
Total	**$1,000,000**

Uses of Proceeds
A substantial portion of the use of proceeds will be used to enhance and develop the functionality of the Web site, especially the consumer database. Funds will be used to develop the notification option, in which the consumers will build a profile of their preferences and the system will alert them when a product that matches their profile becomes available. We will also use a portion of the proceeds to develop editorial content. The Company's working capital base will be used to acquire new clients, as well as to promote the service to consumers using traditional means (advertising and PR) as well as nontraditional methods (electronic promotions). Working capital will be also invested in sales to the travel trade.

The long-term cash requirements for Adventure Media are relatively modest. Most of the development expenses are incurred during the initial site development phase. Once the service is built and deployed in the various online distribution channels (AOL, Prodigy, Microsoft, etc.) the Company will "lock in" an audience, from which our revenue base will be derived.

Adventure Media, Inc.

COMPETITION

There are several travel-related web sites that offer services to travel companies and the travel industry generally. Overall, what distinguishes them all from Adventure Media is that none have established significant relationships with the consumer-oriented, high-traffic commercial online services. Of the larger Web service providers, TEN-IO (http://www.ten-io.com) offers Internet services to the travel, tourism, and entertainment industries. Specifically in travel, TEN-IO created the Internet Web presence for CLIA (Cruise Line Industry Association), as well as a service for Travel Agents to have a listing on the TEN-IO web site. The TEN-IO Web site is designed for the travel industry by building "pocket presences" for their clients. By comparison, *Travelon* is designed for the *end user* in its functionality.

Another travel-oriented Web site is Axeta Travel 2000 (http://www.travel2000.com). The Travel 2000 Web site allows the user to research destination information. Their strategy includes serving three audiences: the meeting planner, the business traveler, and the leisure traveler. Travel 2000 provides information about accommodations, transportation, meeting planner services, business traveler service, and vacation packages (mostly of the cruise and resort variety).

Another source of competition is travel companies building their own Web sites. One of the early users of the Internet was Mountain Travel Sobek (http://www.mtsobek.com), one of the leading adventure tour operators and the biggest competitor to Andrew McKee's previous company, Overseas Adventure Travel. Mountain Travel reports that they are very happy with their experience because the Internet has provided them with a source of new leads. Mountain Travel has committed to working with *Travelon.*

Andrew McKee — CEO

Mr. McKee started his publishing career at Hamilton College, where he was the editor of the weekly newspaper, *The Spectator*. Under his leadership, the paper won the Columbia University Scholastic Press Association "Medalist" award, the highest citation given for a publication. After Hamilton, Mr. McKee spent two years as an investment banker at Goldman, Sachs & Co. From there he went to Harvard Business School where he became Publisher of *The Harbus News,* the weekly student paper. During his business school summer, he worked at Time Inc. in magazine circulation, where he specialized in direct mail marketing. Mr. McKee is the co-founder of HEAR Music, a company he started after sharing a Harvard Business School award with his co-founder as Entrepreneur of the Year. HEAR Music markets music to adults through the company's 12 specialty retail stores. After two years, he attracted the interest of CML Group, the parent of the Nature Company and Nordic Track, which acquired the company in 1992. In 1992, Mr. McKee put together a group of private investors to acquire Overseas Adventure Travel, a leading direct marketer of adventure and nature travel programs. In September 1993, Mr. McKee sold the company to Grand Circle Corporation, a leading database marketer of travel and related financial services. Mr. McKee was a White House Fellow Finalist in 1994 and is now CEO of Adventure Media, Inc.

Lisa Ikle Gieger— Marketing Director

Ms. Gieger has over 10 years' experience in the travel industry, most recently as Northeast Region Sales manager for Maupintour, one of the largest tour operators in the country, specializing in luxury tours worldwide. Prior to working at Maupintour, Ms. Gieger spent five years at Overseas Adventure Travel, where she was a specialist in Africa and South America. Ms. Gieger will handle all responsibilities with respect to business development to the travel industry. Ms. Gieger holds a B.A. from Amherst College.

Kathy Martin — Editorial Director

Ms. Martin spent five years with *Outside* Magazine, most recently as Managing Editor, where she was responsible for editorial direction and staff management for the magazine. Prior to Managing Editor, Ms. Martin was the Associate Editor responsible for the Travel section. Before *Outside* magazine, Ms. Martin was a media planner and buyer for Leo Burnett USA Advertising. Ms. Martin has an M.S. from the Medill School of Journalism, Northwestern University, and a B.A. from the University of Notre Dame.

David Fish — Application Developer/Consultant

From 1990 to 1993, Mr. Fish was the Engineering Director for Lotus Development Corporation's One Source Division (the world's leading provider of business information delivered by CD-ROM). In this capacity he set overall technical direction for the division, developed high-performance technology to support delivery of CD-ROM-based information over large corporate networks (released as the Lotus CD/Networker product), and managed the production and distribution of over 200 electronic publication editions annually, spanning 20 subscription product lines delivered via CD-ROM and data communications.

Prior to Lotus, Mr. Fish served as Vice President of Marketing at Articulate Systems, Inc., a startup company in the area of Macintosh-based voice recognition. From 1980 to 1989, Mr. Fish was with Epsilon Data Management, most recently as Vice President of Systems, with responsibility for all technical operations and product development at this $50 million marketing information services firm. Mr. Fish holds an M.B.A. from Harvard Business School, an M.S. in Information Sciences from Harvard University, and a B.S. in Computer Sciences from MIT.

Philip Wolf — Director
Mr. Wolf is President of PhoCus Wright, a consulting firm to the cable, telecommunications, travel, and online services industries. Mr. Wolf is Chairman of the Independent Travel Technology Association. ITTA is an international education and advocacy trade group, co-founded by Mr. Wolf in 1992, which now claims over 80 member companies. Mr. Wolf is also the Chairman of the Interactive Travel Marketing Conference, an annual symposium on interactive technology and its applications to the travel industry.

Mr. Wolf is former President and CEO of Travelmation Corporation, a software developer and information provider. Mr. Wolf joined the firm in 1989 as Vice President of Operations and became CEO in 1991. Travelmation was sold to Rosenbluth International in late 1992. Mr. Wolf is a magna cum laude graduate of Duke University and holds an M.B.A. from Vanderbilt University.

SUMMARY OF FINANCIAL PROJECTIONS

	1996	**1997**	**1998**	**1999**
Revenue	$660,796	$3,116,005	$4,768,590	$6,925,614
Expenses	-865,315	1,216,557	1,378,238	1,666,713
Pretax profit	(204,519)	1,899,447	3,390,352	5,258,901
Income Taxes	-(77,717)	721,790	1,288,334	1,998,382
Net income	($126,802)	$1,177,657	$2,102,018	$3,260,519

EXIT STRATEGY

We believe that, within five years of development, several natural exit strategies will be available for investors in Adventure Media. Although a public offering may be a viable alternative, a more likely scenario would involve an acquisition by a company interested in buying the cash flow stream and business assets (tight supplier relationships, network access, database content, and consumer mailing lists) of Adventure Media.

The exit scenario would be to be acquired by one of four types of entities:
1) a diversified travel industry player (Carlson Travel, American Express, Rosenbluth International, etc.) seeking new channels of distribution,
2) a communications company (online service, telco, cable operator) seeking to purchase content,
3) a diversified media company with existing travel related assets (New York Times Company, Condé Nast, Times Mirror, Time Warner) seeking to leverage its existing assets, or
4) a communications-related investment fund seeking to acquire a portfolio for businesses offering content solutions through emerging distribution channels.

Adventure Media, Inc.

STATUS

Incorporation

Commonwealth of Massachusetts, S Corporation

Management

Andrew McKee	CEO
Lisa Ikle Gieger	Marketing Director
David Fish	Application Developer

Advisory Board

Philip Wolf	PhoCusWright Consulting
James Cash	Chairman, M.B.A. Program, Harvard Business School
Jack Shields	Consultant; former CEO, Prime Computer
Don Steiner	CEO, The Cornerstone Group
R. Ronald Guerriero	Director, Emerging Business Consulting, Arthur Andersen

Legal Counsel

Bingham, Dana & Gould (General Counsel)

Accountant

The Company has had preliminary discussions with and plans to retain Arthur Andersen.

Adventure Media, Inc.

CONTACT:

Mr. Andrew McKee
Adventure Media, Inc.
71 Martin St.
Cambridge, MA 02138
Phone: 617- 437-6017
Fax: 617-437-6194

Summary Financials

SUMMARY FINANCIALS - ANNUAL							
INCOME STATEMENT PERIOD							
REVENUE		1/1/95	12/31/96	12/31/97	12/31/98	12/31/99	12/31/00
Underlying Discount Travel Bookings			*6,840,000*	*55,870,500*	*86,292,675*	*131,400,219*	*166,154,557*
-Commissions Earned			273,600	2,234,820	3,451,707	5,256,009	6,646,182
Underlying Specialty Travel Bookings			*2,539,200*	*5,274,955*	*7,545,044*	*10,402,750*	*13,957,473*
-Lead Generated Revenues			160,816	350,785	526,833	762,691	1,074,475
-Online Time-Related			166,380	290,400	490,050	618,915	695,448
-Display Advertising			60,000	240,000	300,000	288,000	336,000
TOTAL REVENUE			660,796	3,116,005	4,768,590	6,925,614	8,752,105
TOTAL EXPENSES			865,315	1,216,557	1,378,238	1,666,713	2,089,172
PRETAX PROFIT			(204,519)	1,899,447	3,390,352	5,258,901	6,662,933
PROVISION FOR INCOME TAXES			(77,717)	721,790	1,288,334	1,998,382	2,531,915
NET INCOME			(126,802)	1,177,657	2,102,018	3,260,519	4,131,018
BALANCE SHEET							
Cash surplus / needs		0	(379,469)	884,322	3,037,527	5,796,388	9,822,143
Accounts receivable		0	65,080	307,600	471,859	577,135	729,342
Total current assets		0	(314,389)	1,191,922	3,509,386	6,373,522	10,551,485
Capital equipment		0	167,000	205,000	219,000	245,000	271,000
accumulated depreciation		0	22,850	60,333	103,133	152,133	206,333
Net fixed assets		0	144,150	144,667	115,867	92,867	64,667
TOTAL ASSETS		0	(170,239)	1,336,589	3,625,252	6,466,389	10,616,152
Accounts payable		0	34,280	39,900	53,533	52,996	71,741
Tax payable		0	(77,717)	245,833	418,846	2,417,228	2,531,915
Tax installments paid this period		0	0	0	0	2,417,228	2,531,915
Net tax payable		0	(77,717)	245,833	418,846	0	0
TOTAL LIABILITIES		0	(43,437)	285,733	472,379	52,996	71,741
Retained earnings		0	(126,802)	1,050,856	3,152,874	6,413,392	10,544,411
TOTAL OWNER'S EQUITY		0	(126,802)	1,050,856	3,152,874	6,413,392	10,544,411
CASH FLOW							
Net income			(126,802)	1,177,657	2,102,018	3,260,519	4,131,018
Depreciation			22,850	37,483	42,800	49,000	54,200
Changes in working capital			(108,517)	86,650	22,387	(524,658)	(133,463)
Capital expenditures			(140,000)	(38,000)	(14,000)	(26,000)	(26,000)
Annual cash flow			(352,469)	1,263,790	2,153,205	2,758,861	4,025,756
Terminal value @ PE of 15	15						61,965,277
Tax on gain on sale @ 28%							(17,350,278)
Total cash flow, after-tax			(352,469)	1,263,790	2,153,205	2,758,861	48,640,755
*							

Adventure Media Inc.

Notes to Financials –

Underlying Discount Travel

The imputed value of gross discount travel booking derived from *Travelon* marketing activities based on an assumption of an average booking of $1,000 per transaction, 4% commission

Bookings
Commission Earned

Commissions paid to Adventure Media by the booking service that handles reservations

Underlying Specialty Travel Bookings

The imputed value of gross specialty travel bookings derived from *Travelon* marketing activities based on an assumption of an average booking of $1,000 per transaction, 4% commission

Lead-Generated Revenues

Fees paid to Adventure Media based on leads generated by phone or E-mail request

Online Time-Related

Fees paid to Adventure Media from the commercial online services based on usage

Display Advertising

Ads purchased on the *Travelon* Pages by display advertisers

Section IV

Inc.Sheets

Inc.Sheets are hands-on worksheets you can use to build your business. They were developed to facilitate the gathering and analysis of data that should be included in your business plan. *Inc.Sheets* are a combination of checklists, templates, and forms that closely parallel each section of the planning guide. Make copies as tools for drafting your plan. Use them as you complete the corresponding sections of your business plan, and then file them by topic as suggested in Section I.

Executive Summary Checklist/Worksheet

As a statement of your vision for your business, the Executive Summary should be well thought-out and drafted prior to developing your plan. It can be revised or corrected once your plan has been completed. It must give concise answers to the following questions:

What services will be offered?

❑ Now—

❑ Future—

What is the projected demand for these services?

❑ Now—

❑ Future—

Who constitutes the primary market?

❑ Now—

❑ Future—

How large is the primary market?

❑ Now—

❑ Future—

When will the business begin operations?

Where will the business be located?

Who will make up your management team?

What organizational structure will your business have?

What are your business's major short-term and long-term goals?

How will financing be obtained?

Inc.
SHEETS
Worksheets To Build Your Business

The Market

Information Needs

Information Needs Assessment

Identifying information needs before actually looking for data will help maximize your research efforts. Refer to the Resource Directory for possible sources or ask your library's reference librarian for additional help. Use one Inc.Sheet for each level.

❑ National Level ❑ Regional Level ❑ Local Level

Data/Information Needed	Potential Sources

Trend Information

This worksheet (use one for each question) helps you examine the trends in your market to assist you in your planning effort. To get you started, a few generic questions are provided. You will also need to develop additional topics that are specific to your business's market environment. Refer to the Resource Directory for possible sources of trend information.

- ❑ How are other businesses similar to yours doing? Are they experiencing growth, maintaining at a plateau, or in decline? If the industry is in decline, how will your company avoid the trend?
- ❑ If the industry is growing, how will you compete with companies already in existence?
- ❑ Is the field becoming overcrowded with competitors?
- ❑ Is there (or will there be) a rapid change in technology in your industry? How will you stay on top of technological changes?
- ❑ Are trends in your local marketplace different from those on the national and regional levels? If so, how can they be used to your advantage?

Question:

❑ National ❑ Regional ❑ Local

Specific Data/Information:

Inc. SHEETS
Worksheets To Build Your Business

The Market

Segmentation Strategy (Consumer)

Segmentation Strategy: Consumer Market

There are several ways to define a *target market(s)* (i.e., those consumers toward whom you are *specifically* aiming your services). This worksheet helps identify the characteristics of those markets that are most important, serving as a guide for developing your target market profile(s). Fill out one worksheet for each of your proposed target market segments.

Age:	**Sex:**	**Marital-family status:**	**Family size:**

Education level:

Occupation:

Income:

Geographic location:

Housing (rent/own):

Interests:

Frequency of need for your service:

Other:

Segmentation Strategy: Business Market

There are several ways to define a *target market(s)*, (i.e., those businesses towards which you are *specifically* aiming your services). This worksheet helps identify the characteristics of those markets that are most important, serving as a guide for developing your target market profile(s). General categories have been provided; however, characteristics will vary with the types of business being targeted. Fill out one worksheet for each of your proposed target market segments.

Business type:

Size of business:

Geographic location:

Possible uses of your service:

Frequency of need for your service:

Other:

Competition

Competitive Data

Competitive Data

Fill out this sheet for each competitor identified. Some of the data may be impossible to obtain; therefore, estimates will be necessary. The information collected will be used in developing your competitive grid.

Company____

Street Address: ____________________________________

City: ____________________ State: _______ Zip: __________

Years in business: __________________________________

Telephone: (____) ____—_______ Fax: (____) ____—_______

E-mail address: ____________________________________

Services offered:

Service features (hours, pricing, customer service, etc.):

Estimated size:

- ❑ Annual Sales
- ❑ Market share
- ❑ Number of employees

Advertising methods used (give names of newspapers, radio stations, outdoor locations, Internet sites, and so on):

Greatest perceived strength:

Greatest perceived weakness:

How you will compete with this company (i.e., what are your competitive advantages)?

Inc.® SHEETS
Worksheets To Build Your Business

Competition

Competitive Grid

Competitive Grid

After completing a Competitor Data Sheet on each competitor in your market area, collect the most significant information on this table for inclusion in your business plan. Your actual worksheet will probably contain more detail than the completed grid.

Company	Market Share & Sales (estimated)	Services Offered
Name _____ Address: _____ City: _____ State: ___ Zip: _____ Years in business: _____ Telephone: (___) ___—____ E-mail address: _____	Market Share: Annual Sales: No. of Employees:	
Name _____ Address: _____ City: _____ State: ___ Zip: _____ Years in business: _____ Telephone: (___) ___—____ E-mail address: _____	Market Share: Annual Sales: No. of Employees:	
Name _____ Address: _____ City: _____ State: ___ Zip: _____ Years in business: _____ Telephone: (___) ___—____ E-mail address: _____	Market Share: Annual Sales: No. of Employees:	

Competition

Competitive Grid

	Strengths	Weaknesses	My Competitive Advantages

Inc. SHEETS
Worksheets To Build Your Business

Market Share

Sales & Customer Estimates

Estimated Competitor Sales & Customer Base

The following calculations will provide you with an estimate of the **average sales** *(in dollars)* and the **average number of people served** per existing competitor.

Average Competitor Sales

Sales: What are the total sales for competitors' services statewide?
[Note: This can also be calculated at the citywide, regional, or national levels.]

(Source: State Bureau of Taxation)

Number of Establishments: How many competitors are there in your state?

(Source: County Business Patterns)

$$\frac{\text{Total Sales}}{\text{Number of Establishments}} = \text{Average Sales per Establishment}$$

$$\frac{\qquad\qquad}{\qquad\qquad} = \$$$

Average Customer Base

Population: What is the total number of *people* in your state?

(Source: Statistical Abstract)

$$\frac{\text{Population}}{\text{Number of Establishments}} = \text{Average Number of People per Business}$$

$$\frac{\qquad\qquad}{\qquad\qquad} = \$$$

Projections Using National Data

If it has been difficult to access service demand data for your market area, you can gather it for regional or national markets then apply that information to your local market to obtain demand estimates. Use the Reference Guide to identify appropriate data sources.

Example:

You want to open a sports-themed bar/restaurant serving lunch and dinner in the greater Manchester, N.H. area. Since there is no local survey information on how many times a week your target market dines out in Manchester, you will have to use national data to help determine market size.

From *national* demographic data, you find out that:

- ❑ At least 44.3% of *all* Americans dine out for lunch or dinner *one or more* times per week. *(Source: National Restaurant Association)*
- ❑ 22.1% of the total population of the United States have watched the sports channel ESPN within the last seven days. *(Source: Simmons Media and Market Report)*

Combine the data: .443 x .221 = .0979

Result: 9.79% of the given population fit your customer profile (people who watch ESPN and eat out at least once a week).

Local Market Conditions: There are 32,557 people in the greater Manchester area. *(Source: Sourcebook of Zip Code Demographics)*

By applying the 9.79% to the local market population, you get:

32,557 x .0979 = 3,118

Conclusion: There are approximately 3,118 people per week who fit your customer profile in the Manchester area.

> Note: When combining data from different sources, bear in mind that the data sets may include different categories (e.g., income class or time periods). It may be necessary to interpolate the data to fit your needs. Remember that you are looking for approximations. The results of your calculations are just estimates that, combined with other data (such as breakeven), can be used to reduce uncertainty about market size and sales projections.

...continued

Projections Using National Data *(continued)*

Projection Worksheet

Target Profile:

Develop a target customer profile by using factors such as:

- ❑ Income
- ❑ Marital status
- ❑ Occupation
- ❑ Family size
- ❑ Geographic region
- ❑ Home ownership
- ❑ Cable subscribers
- ❑ Pet owners
- ❑ Frequent travelers

Be sure to note the source, category description, and time frame of each piece of data you collect.

My target customer's characteristics are:	____% of national/regional population	Source
A		
B		

Calculate the national/regional percentage:

_____% (A) x _____% (B) =

Result: _______________%

Local Market Conditions:

(Population in your trading area) ________________________________

Estimated size of my target market:

____________ (National/regional percent) x ____________ (Trading area population) = ____________ (No. of potential customers)

Note: There may be situations in which you use more than two characteristics to define your target population.

Location Needs Assessment

The first step in choosing your new location is determining the operating environment your business needs. Once you have identified your business location requirements, you can use this information to identify locations that best fulfill those needs. (Some of the categories given here may not be applicable to your business.)

Budget range (improvements/deposits/utilities/rent/or debt service if you plan on purchasing your business's premises): $______________ to $ ______________

Location Factors	Your Requirements
Site Requirements Square footage, improvements, utilities, zoning/future expansion, office sharing, other *Note: If you are considering a home office, include any improvements you will have to make to the space.*	
Proximity to Customers Customers' need to come to business Business's need to go to customers Retail space availability	
Proximity to Competition Optimum distance to competitors	
Traffic Patterns Customer volume required Foot traffic Vehicular traffic	
Parking Customer, Employee	
Permits & Licenses Federal/State, Local	
Other Considerations	

Location

Needs Assessment

Site Evaluation

Use this form to gather information on each potential business location. Cross-check with the information on the "Location Needs Assessment" to evaluate the site's advantages and disadvantages in order to determine an overall "grade" for the site.

Location Address____

Structure (configuration, square footage, age, materials, condition, architecture, heating/air):

Rent/Lease (duration, cost, terms, etc.):

Other Costs:

Proximity to Customers:

Proximity to Competition:

Traffic Patterns (foot and vehicular):

Parking:

Zoning:

Permits/Licenses Required:

Key Advantages:

Key Disadvantages:

Other:

Site Grade: (check one) ❏ **A** (Ideal) ❏ **B** (Desirable) ❏ **C** (Suitable) ❏ **D** (Last resort) ❏ **F** (Unsuitable)

Worksheets To Build Your Business

Pricing

Break-Even

Break-Even Quantity

Calculate the break-even quantity for your business.

$$BEQ = \frac{FC}{P-VC}$$

BEQ = Number of transactions necessary to break even (such as cars washed or hours worked)

FC = Fixed costs for one year

P = Price you plan to charge for a single service or transaction to break even

VC = Direct or variable costs related to each transaction

BEQ = ______________________
—

Break-Even Price

Calculate the break-even price for your business.

$$BEP = \frac{FC}{Q} + VC$$

BEP = Price you need to charge for a single service or transaction to break even

FC = Fixed costs for one year

VC = Direct or variable costs related to each transaction

Q = Number of transactions necessary to break even (such as cars washed or hours worked)

BEP = $\frac{\$\_\_\_\_\_\_}{}$ + $

Objectives

From the following list, prioritize your objectives to help form your promotional strategy. In the early stage of your business, you may have only one or two goals on which to focus.

✍ **Establish and/or expand customer base**

✍ **Differentiate service**

✍ **Influence people to become customers**

✍ **Build goodwill**

Objectives	Methods to Achieve Objectives

Inc. SHEETS
Worksheets To Build Your Business

Promotion

Evaluating Media

Evaluating Media Reach

Use this worksheet to evaluate potential media options for your business message. List the name and type of each media support (e.g., Radio: KSEA, WBWK; TV: Channel 6, ABC; Print: *Washington Journal, Rye Examiner*), its reach, its cost, and the message you plan to promote via that medium. This information, coupled with a calculation of CPM (cost per thousand) for each vehicle, will further assist you in determining which media mix will be most cost-effective.

Promotional Medium: ____________________

Reach: ____________ Cost: ____________ CPM: ____________

Market Targeted: ____________________

Message:

Promotional Medium: ____________________

Reach: ____________ Cost: ____________ CPM: ____________

Market Targeted: ____________________

Message:

Promotional Medium: ____________________

Reach: ____________ Cost: ____________ CPM: ____________

Market Targeted: ____________________

Message:

Information Needs Checklist

You will need to gather information on each of following items for the Management section of your business plan. As you complete each section, use this checklist to track your progress.

Biographical Sketch & Qualifications

- ❑ Yourself
- ❑ Partners
- ❑ Other Management
- ❑ Key Personnel (non-management)

Professional Advisers

- ❑ Attorney
- ❑ Accountant
- ❑ Insurance Agent
- ❑ Consultants (qualifications and descriptions of services)
- ❑ Other

Staff & Organization

- ❑ Description of Jobs
- ❑ Salary and Benefits
- ❑ Special Requirements/Qualifications

Other:

- ❑ Board of Directors/Advisers: Qualifications
- ❑ Organizational Chart
- ❑ Staffing Plan

Inc. SHEETS
Worksheets To Build Your Business

Financials

Capital Equipment

Capital Equipment List

List all the capital equipment you need to buy for your business. Be sure to note any major items with the vendors' names, addresses, and phone numbers. This form will help you to project how much fixed-asset financing you may need.

Capital Equipment List

Item	Description	Quantity	Unit Cost	Total Cost
			$	$
TOTAL COST				$

Notes

Start-Up Cost Estimate Statement

This statement helps you calculate the amount of funds required to open and maintain your business until your sales revenues can support operations. This first section identifies Pre-Start-Up expenses, including items such as equipment, legal and professional fees, and Grand Openings. The second section identifies other start-up costs and allows for estimating a "financial cushion" to get you through the first few months of business. Some common business expense items have been included. Be sure to expand your worksheet to include all of your specific business needs.

Management

Start-Up Costs

Start-Up Cost Estimate

Pre-Start-Up Items	Estimated Cost
	$
Subtotal	$

Other Start-Up Items	Est. Cost per Month	# Months Coverage	
Salary of Owner	$		$
Other Salaries/Wages/Fees			
Rent/Mortgage			
Advertising			
Delivery			
Supplies			
Telephone/Fax/Postage			
Utilities			
Insurance			
Taxes, Social Security			
Interest			
Maintenance			
Legal/Professional Assistance			
Other			
TOTAL START-UP COSTS	$		$

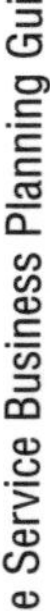

Inc. SHEETS
Worksheets To Build Your Business

Financials

Sources & Uses of Cash

Sources & Uses of Cash

On this worksheet, you must list all individual sources of funds used to start your business and the specific uses to which this money will be put. Sources must *always* equal uses.

Sources & Uses of Cash

Sources	Amount
	$
TOTAL SOURCES:	**$**

Uses	Amount
	$
TOTAL USES:	**$**

Balance Sheet

A balance sheet is calculated on an annual basis reflecting your business condition as of a particular date. Fill out this balance sheet projected for the day you open your business (*pro forma*). Your specific business may require additional categories, and some of those listed below may not apply to you. Adjust your Balance Sheet accordingly.

BALANCE SHEET

Date:

ASSETS		**LIABILITIES**	
CURRENT ASSETS		**CURRENT LIABILITIES**	
Cash	$ ________	Notes Payable	$ ________
Accounts Receivable	________	Accounts Payable	________
Supplies	________	Accrued Expenses	________
Prepaid Expenses	________		
Other Current Assets	________	TOTAL CURRENT LIABILITIES	$ ________
TOTAL CURRENT ASSETS	$ ________	LONG-TERM LIABILITIES	
		Installment Debt Payable	________
PROPERTY, PLANT & EQUIPMENT		TOTAL LONG-TERM LIABILITIES	________
Land	$ ________	TOTAL LIABILITIES	________
Buildings	________		
Equipment	________	OWNER'S EQUITY	
Vehicles and Boats	________	Paid-In Capital	$ ________
Depreciation	________		
		Retained Earnings	$ ________
TOTAL NET FIXED ASSETS	$ ________		
		TOTAL OWNER'S EQUITY	$ ________
TOTAL ASSETS	$ ________	**TOTAL LIABILITIES & OWNER'S EQUITY**	$ ________

Worksheets To Build Your Business

Financials

Income Statement

Income Statement

The Income Statement is a record of your business's financial activities over a period of time, and is generally calculated on a quarterly basis. Fill out this Income Statement on a (*pro forma*) basis before you open. You may also complete this statement at various times throughout the year to obtain an idea of your current finances. Your particular business may require additional categories, and some of those listed below may not apply to you. Adjust your Income Statement accordingly.

Company Name ______________________________ Date ______________

INCOME STATEMENT

NET SALES (Revenues) $ ______________

OPERATING EXPENSES

Salaries	$ ________	
Fees	$ ________	
Rent	$ ________	
Telephone & Utilities	$ ________	
Insurance	$ ________	
Advertising	$ ________	
Professional Fees	$ ________	
Office Administration	$ ________	
Depreciation	$ ________	
Travel & Entertainment	$ ________	
Food Supplies	$ ________	
Miscellaneous	$ ________	
Nonincome Taxes	$ ________	
Food Supplies	$ ________	
Miscellaneous	$ ________	
Nonincome Taxes	$ ________	
TOTAL OPERATING EXPENSES		$ ______________
OTHER REVENUE		$ ______________
(OTHER EXPENSES)		($______________)
INCOME BEFORE TAXES		$ ______________

Monthly Cash Flow Projection Statement

The cash flow statement documents all cash transactions (income and expenses) on a monthly basis. Use the forms on these pages as a guide to creating your Cash Flow Statement (extend to 12 months by copying the blank form on the following pages). Begin with figures form your Sources & Uses of Cash statements. As you receive funds and accrue expenses, be sure to fill in the "Actual" column for each month (including Pre-Start-Up). This statement can be modified to suit your specific needs. It can be more easily created and updated using spreadsheet software. *Note: it may be helpful to copy and tape this statement (10 pages) together.)*

Monthly Cash Flow Projection (Pre-Start-Up—Month 2)

YEAR MONTH:	Pre-Start-Up		Month 1		Month 2	
	Estimate	Actual	Estimate	Actual	Estimate	Actual
1. Cash on Hand (beginning of month)	$	$	$	$	$	$
2. Cash Receipts (a) Cash Sales						
(b) Collections from Credit Accts.						
(c) Loan or Other Cash (specify)						
3. Total Cash Receipts (2a+2b+2c)						
4. Total Cash Available (before cash out) (1 + 3)						
5. Cash Paid Out (a) Purchases (merchandise)						
(b) Gross Wages						
(c) Payroll Expenses						
(d) Outside Services						
(e) Supplies (office/operating)						
(f) Repairs and Maintenance						
(g) Advertising						
(h) Car, Delivery, & Travel						
(i) Accounting & Legal						
(j) Rent						

continued next page

Note: Copy and fill in the month by name or number.

Financials

Cash Flow Statement *continued*

Monthly Cash Flow Projection (Pre-Start-Up—Month 2)

YEAR MONTH:	Pre-Start-Up		Month 1		Month 2	
	Estimate	Actual	Estimate	Actual	Estimate	Actual
5. Cash Paid Out (*cont.)* (k) Telephone	$	$	$	$	$	$
(l) Utilities						
(m) Insurance						
(n) Taxes (real estate, other)						
(o) Interest						
(p) Other Expenses (specify) food for customers						
(q) Miscellaneous						
(r) Subtotal (5a through 5q)						
(s) Loan Principal Payment						
(t) Capital Purchases						
(u) Other Start-Up Costs						
(v) Reserve and/or Escrow						
(w) Owner's Withdrawal						
6. Total Cash Paid Out (Total 5r through 5w)						
7. Cash Position End of the Month (line 4 minus line 6)	$	$	$	$	$	$

Monthly Cash Flow Projection (Month 3—Month 5)

YEAR **MONTH:**	**Month 3**		**Month 4**		**Month 5**	
	Estimate	Actual	Estimate	Actual	Estimate	Actual
1. Cash on Hand (beginning of month)	$	$	$	$	$	$
2. Cash Receipts (a) Cash Sales						
(b) Collections from Credit Accts.						
(c) Loan or Other Cash (specify)						
3. Total Cash Receipts (2a+2b+2c)						
4. Total Cash Available (before cash out) (1 + 3)						
5. Cash Paid Out (a) Purchases (merchandise)						
(b) Gross Wages						
(c) Payroll Expenses						
(d) Outside Services						
(e) Supplies (office/operating)						
(f) Repairs and Maintenance						
(g) Advertising						
(h) Car, Delivery, & Travel						
(i) Accounting & Legal						
(j) Rent						

continued next page

Monthly Cash Flow Projection (Month 3—Month 5)

YEAR MONTH:	Month 3		Month 4		Month 5	
	Estimate	Actual	Estimate	Actual	Estimate	Actual
5. Cash Paid Out (*cont.*) (k) Telephone	$	$	$	$	$	$
(l) Utilities						
(m) Insurance						
(n) Taxes (real estate, other)						
(o) Interest						
(p) Other Expenses (specify) food for customers						
(q) Miscellaneous						
(r) Subtotal (5a through 5q)						
(s) Loan Principal Payment						
(t) Capital Purchases						
(u) Other Start-Up Costs						
(v) Reserve and/or Escrow						
(w) Owner's Withdrawal						
6. Total Cash Paid Out (Total 5r through 5w)						
7. Cash Position End of the Month (line 4 minus line 6)	$	$	$	$	$	$

Monthly Cash Flow Projection (Month 6—Month 8)

YEAR MONTH:	Month 6		Month 7		Month 8	
	Estimate	Actual	Estimate	Actual	Estimate	Actual
1. Cash on Hand (beginning of month)	$	$	$	$	$	$
2. Cash Receipts (a) Cash Sales						
(b) Collections from Credit Accts.						
(c) Loan or Other Cash (specify)						
3. Total Cash Receipts (2a+2b+2c)						
4. Total Cash Available (before cash out) (1 + 3)						
5. Cash Paid Out (a) Purchases (merchandise)						
(b) Gross Wages						
(c) Payroll Expenses						
(d) Outside Services						
(e) Supplies (office/operating)						
(f) Repairs and Maintenance						
(g) Advertising						
(h) Car, Delivery, & Travel						
(i) Accounting & Legal						
(j) Rent						

continued next page

Monthly Cash Flow Projection (Month 6—Month 8)

YEAR MONTH:	Month 6		Month 7		Month 8	
	Estimate	Actual	Estimate	Actual	Estimate	Actual
5. Cash Paid Out (*cont.)*	$	$	$	$	$	$
(k) Telephone						
(l) Utilities						
(m) Insurance						
(n) Taxes (real estate, other)						
(o) Interest						
(p) Other Expenses (specify) food for customers						
(q) Miscellaneous						
(r) Subtotal (5a through 5q)						
(s) Loan Principal Payment						
(t) Capital Purchases						
(u) Other Start-Up Costs						
(v) Reserve and/or Escrow						
(w) Owner's Withdrawal						
6. Total Cash Paid Out (Total 5r through 5w)						
7. Cash Position End of the Month (line 4 minus line 6)	$	$	$	$	$	$

Monthly Cash Flow Projection (Month 9—Month 11)

YEAR MONTH:	Month 9		Month 10		Month 11	
	Estimate	Actual	Estimate	Actual	Estimate	Actual
1. Cash on Hand (beginning of month)	$	$	$	$	$	$
2. Cash Receipts (a) Cash Sales						
(b) Collections from Credit Accts.						
(c) Loan or Other Cash (specify)						
3. Total Cash Receipts (2a+2b+2c)						
4. Total Cash Available (before cash out) (1 + 3)						
5. Cash Paid Out (a) Purchases (merchandise)						
(b) Gross Wages						
(c) Payroll Expenses						
(d) Outside Services						
(e) Supplies (office/operating)						
(f) Repairs and Maintenance						
(g) Advertising						
(h) Car, Delivery, & Travel						
(i) Accounting & Legal						
(j) Rent						

continued next page

Monthly Cash Flow Projection (Month 9—Month 11)

YEAR MONTH:	Month 9		Month 10		Month 11	
	Estimate	Actual	Estimate	Actual	Estimate	Actual
5. Cash Paid Out (*cont.*) (k) Telephone	$	$	$	$	$	$
(l) Utilities						
(m) Insurance						
(n) Taxes (real estate, other)						
(o) Interest						
(p) Other Expenses (specify) food for customers						
(q) Miscellaneous						
(r) Subtotal (5a through 5q)						
(s) Loan Principal Payment						
(t) Capital Purchases						
(u) Other Start-Up Costs						
(v) Reserve and/or Escrow						
(w) Owner's Withdrawal						
6. Total Cash Paid Out (Total 5r through 5w)						
7. Cash Position End of the Month (line 4 minus line 6)	$	$	$	$	$	$

Monthly Cash Flow Projection (Month 12)

YEAR MONTH:	Month 12		TOTAL	
	Estimate	Actual		
1. Cash on Hand (beginning of month)	$	$	$	
2. Cash Receipts (a) Cash Sales				
(b) Collections from Credit Accts.				
(c) Loan or Other Cash (specify)				
3. Total Cash Receipts (2a+2b+2c)				
4. Total Cash Available (before cash out) (1 + 3)				
5. Cash Paid Out (a) Purchases (merchandise)				
(b) Gross Wages				
(c) Payroll Expenses				
(d) Outside Services				
(e) Supplies (office/operating)				
(f) Repairs and Maintenance				
(g) Advertising				
(h) Car, Delivery, & Travel				
(i) Accounting & Legal				
(j) Rent				

continued next page

continued

Monthly Cash Flow Projection (Month 12)

YEAR MONTH:	Month 12		TOTAL
	Estimate	Actual	
5. Cash Paid Out (*cont.*)	$	$	$
(k) Telephone			
(l) Utilities			
(m) Insurance			
(n) Taxes (real estate, other)			
(o) Interest			
(p) Other Expenses (specify) food for customers			
(q) Miscellaneous			
(r) Subtotal (5a through 5q)			
(s) Loan Principal Payment			
(t) Capital Purchases			
(u) Other Start-Up Costs			
(v) Reserve and/or Escrow			
(w) Owner's Withdrawal			
6. Total Cash Paid Out (Total 5r through 5w)			
7. Cash Position End of the Month (line 4 minus line 6)	$	$	$

Insurance Needs List

There are various types of insurance your business will need. Before contacting an insurance agent, list each type you anticipate needing, including information such as coverage levels required, deductible limits, and maximum premium costs. You can usually find this information through trade associations, in industry publications, and by asking local counterparts. Examples include: fire, health, workers' compensation, title, and other risks specific to your business.

Type of insurance: ____________________

Coverage required: ____________________

Deductible limit: ____________________

Maximum premium: ____________________

Questions for agent: ____________________

____

Type of insurance: ____________________

Coverage required: ____________________

Deductible limit: ____________________

Maximum premium: ____________________

Questions for agent: ____________________

____

Type of insurance: ____________________

Coverage required: ____________________

Deductible limit: ____________________

Maximum premium: ____________________

Questions for agent: ____________________

____

Inc. SHEETS
Worksheets To Build Your Business

Insurance

Coverage

Insurance Quotes

Use this worksheet to identify vendors who can provide services to meet your insurance needs. Create grids for each potential insurance category required by your business, and use them to evaluate and select policies that best meet your needs.

Note: As you speak to insurance brokers, they may inform you of coverage/plans that you had not previously considered.

Broker	Premium/ Deductible	Coverage Provided
Name ____ Address: ____ City: ____ State: ____ Zip: ____ Telephone: (____) ____—____ Fax: (____) ____—____ E-mail address: ____ Policy Carrier: ____		
Name ____ Address: ____ City: ____ State: ____ Zip: ____ Telephone: (____) ____—____ Fax: (____) ____—____ E-mail address: ____ Policy Carrier: ____		
Name ____ Address: ____ City: ____ State: ____ Zip: ____ Telephone: (____) ____—____ Fax: (____) ____—____ E-mail address: ____ Policy Carrier: ____		

Business Description Checklist

A Description of Business section may be necessary for your plan in order to elaborate on certain aspects of your business which cannot be adequately covered in your Executive Summary. Following are three situations in which a Description of Business section may help clarify to the reader exactly what your business is trying to accomplish and how you plan to do it.

Buying an Existing Business

- ❑ The company history.
- ❑ How is it organized?
- ❑ Performance history.
- ❑ Reasons the owner(s) are selling.
- ❑ What is its existing customer base?
- ❑ What ownership transition strategies will you use?
- ❑ Business valuation.

A New Type of Service

- ❑ Why is your service really different?
- ❑ What existing service(s) represents your closest competition?
- ❑ Overview of new technology and/or methods you plan on using.
- ❑ Why do you feel there is a demand for this service?

Complex Service Offerings

- ❑ What is the rationale for your service offerings?
- ❑ Explain each service you will provide and how they interrelate.
- ❑ Identify all of your potential target markets.

Section V

Appendices

Sample Corporate Charter

Articles of Incorporation, or "corporate charter", are governed by each individual state. That is, each state will have its own laws, requirements, restrictions, and forms for the different types of corporation. What follows are Articles of Incorporation for the state of Maine. Contact your secretary of state for the forms required.

BUSINESS CORPORATION

STATE OF MAINE

ARTICLES OF INCORPORATION

(Check box only if applicable)
❑ This is a professional service corporation formed pursuant to 13 MRSA Chapter 22.

____
Deputy Secretary of State

True Copy When Attested By Signature

____
Deputy Secretary of State

Pursuant to 13-A MRSA 403, the undersigned, acting as incorporator(s) of a corporation, adopt(s) the following Articles of Incorporation:

FIRST: The name of the corporation is ______________________

and its principal place of business location in Maine is

____

____
(physical location - street (not P.O. Box), city, state, and zip code)

SECOND: The name of its Clerk, who must be a Maine resident, and the registered office shall be:

____
(name)

____
(physical location - street (not P.O. Box), city, state, and zip code)

____
(mailing address if different from above)

THIRD: ("X" one box only)

❑ A. 1. The number of directors constituting the initial board of directors of the corporation is _____ (See Section 703.1.A.)
2. If the initial directors have been selected, the names and addresses of the persons who are to serve as directors until the first annual meeting of the shareholders or until their successors are elected and shall qualify are:

NAME	ADDRESS
____________________	______________________________
____________________	______________________________
____________________	______________________________

3. The board of directors ❑ is ❑ is not authorized to increase or decrease the number of directors.

4. If the board is so authorized, the minimum number, if any, shall be _______ directors, (See Section 703.1.A.) and the maximum number, if any, shall be _______ directors.

❑ B. There shall be no directors initially; the shares of the corporation will not be sold to more than twenty (20) persons; the business of the corporation will be managed by the shareholders. (See Section 701.2.)

FOURTH: ("X" one box only)

❑ There will only be one class of shares (title of class) ______________________________

Par value of each share (if none, so state) _________ Number of shares authorized: ___________

❑ There will be two or more classes of shares. The information required by Section 403 concerning each such class is set out in Exhibit _______ attached hereto and made a part hereof.

SUMMARY

The aggregate par value of all authorized shares (of all classes) **having a par value** is $___________

The total number of authorized shares (of all classes) **without par value** is $_______________

FIFTH: ("X" one box only) Meetings of shareholders may may not be held outside of the State of Maine.

SIXTH: ("X" if applicable) There are no preemptive rights.

SEVENTH: Other provisions of these articles, if any, including provisions for the regulation of the internal affairs of the corporation, are set out in Exhibit _______ attached hereto and made a part hereof.

INCORPORATORS DATED ______________________

______________________________ (signature) ______________________________ (residence address)

______________________________ (type or print name) ______________________________ (city, state, and zip code) (signature) (residence address)

(type or print name) (city, state, and zip code)

(signature) (residence address)

(type or print name) (city, state, and zip code)

For Corporate Incorporators*

Name of Corporate Incorporator ______________________________

By ______________________________

(signature of officer) (principal business location)

(type or print name and capacity) (city, state, and zip code)

*** Articles are to be executed as follows:**

If a corporation is an incorporator (Section 402), the name of the corporation should be typed and signed on its behalf by an officer of the corporation. The articles of incorporation must be accompanied by a certificate of an appropriate officer of the corporation certifying that the person executing the articles on behalf of the corporation was duly authorized to do so.

Partnership Agreement

1. Introduction. Agreement to form a partnership (Partnership) made on [date], between [name], residing at [address], and [name], residing at [address].

2. Partnership Purpose and Name. The parties agree to form Partnership on the terms set out below to engage in the business of [nature of business]. Partnership's name shall be [name], and its principal office shall be at [address].

3. Duration of Partnership. Partnership will begin on [date] and will continue until it terminates in accordance with the provisions of this Agreement.

[Alternative Paragraph]

3. Duration of Partnership. Partnership will begin on [date] and end on [date].

4. Partners' Capital Contributions. The Partnership capital shall be contributed by the Partners, partly in cash and partly in personal property. The cash contributions shall be:

   [schedule of Partners' names and cash amounts]

   The contributions of personal property and the values to be placed upon them shall be:

   [schedule of Partners' names, descriptions of property, and values of property]

5. Partners' Capital Accounts. Partnership shall maintain a separate capital account for each Partner. Neither Partner may withdraw any part of the Partner's contributed capital without the other's consent. If a Partner's capital account falls below the amount of the Partner's contributed capital because of losses or permitted withdrawals, the Partner's share of profits will be credited to the Partner's capital account until the capital contribution has been restored, and before any profits can be credited to the Partner's income account.

6. Division of Profits and Losses. The net profits and losses of Partnership will be equally divided between the Partners.

[Alternative Paragraph A]

6. Division of Profits and Losses. The net profits and losses of Partnership will be divided

in accordance with the proportion that the amount of each Partner's contributed capital bears to Partnership's total contributed capital.

[Alternative Paragraph B]

6. Division of Profits and Losses. The net profits and losses of Partnership will be divided or charged to the Partners in the following proportions:

[schedule of Partners' names and percentages of profit or loss allotted]

7. Partners' Income Accounts. Partnership shall maintain a separate income account for each Partner to which each Partner's share of Partnership's income or losses shall be credited or charged. If there is no credit balance in a Partner's income account, losses shall be charged to the Partner's capital account.

8. Partners' Right to Salary and Drawings. Neither Partner shall receive any salary for the Partner's services to Partnership. Each Partner may withdraw any credit balance in the Partner's income account at any time. Neither Partner shall be entitled to an additional share of profits solely because the Partner's capital account exceeds that of the other, except as otherwise provided in this Agreement.

[Alternative Paragraph]

8. Partner's Right to Salary and Drawings. Partner [name] shall draw a salary of __________ dollars ($__________) weekly, and Partner [name] shall draw a salary of __________ dollars ($__________) weekly. The Partners' salaries shall not be charged to their capital or income accounts but shall be charges for the purposes of determining Partnership's net income. Withdrawals of credit balances from the Partners' income accounts shall be made only at the times and in the amounts that the Partners agree upon from time to time.

9. No Interest on Capital. No interest will be paid on any balances in the Partners' capital accounts.

10. Management of the Partnership. Each Partner shall have an equal voice in the management of Partnership, and each shall be devoted full time to the conduct of its business. Without the other's written consent, no Partner shall, on Partnership's behalf:

a. Borrow or lend money;

b. Make, deliver, or accept commercial paper;

c. Execute any mortgage, security agreement, bond, or lease; or

d. Buy or execute a purchase agreement, or sell or execute a sales agreement for any property other than that bought or sold in the regular course of Partnership's business.

11. Sale of, Assignment of, or Granting Lien on Partnership Interest. Without the other's written consent, no Partner shall:

a. Assign, mortgage, give a security interest in, or sell the Partner's Partnership interest;

b. Agree with a party not privy to this Agreement that such party will have an interest in Partnership; or

c. Do anything that would be detrimental to Partnership's ability to conduct its business.

12. Partnership Bank Account. All Partnership funds shall be deposited in its name in an account with the [name of bank] located at [address], or such other bank or banks as the Partners may agree upon from time to time. All withdrawals from these accounts shall be by check signed by either Partner.

13. Partnership Books and Records. Partnership books of account will be kept in accordance with generally accepted accounting principles. The books and supporting records will be maintained at Partnership's principal office and will be examined by Partnership's certified public accountants at least [frequency]. Partnership's fiscal year shall start on [month and day] and close on [month and day]. Partnership's certified public accountants shall prepare an income statement and balance sheet for each fiscal year within [number] months after the end of the fiscal year. These financial statements shall be binding upon the Partners as to income or losses and the balances in the Partners' income and capital accounts.

14. Voluntary Dissolution of Partnership. The Partners may agree to dissolve Partnership at any time. Should the Partners so agree, they will liquidate Partnership in an orderly fashion. The proceeds derived from the sale of Partnership's property, including its name and goodwill, shall be applied in the following order:

a. Discharge all Partnership liabilities and pay the costs of liquidation;

b. Bring the Partners' income accounts into balance;

c. Pay the balance shown in each Partner's income account to that Partner;

d. Bring the Partners' capital accounts into balance; and

e. Pay the balance shown in each Partner's capital account to that Partner.

15. Effect of Partner's Retirement. A Partner may retire from Partnership at the end of any Partnership fiscal year by serving written notice of his or her intention to retire upon the other Partner no later than [number] months before the end of the fiscal year. The remaining Partner may elect either to purchase the retiring Partner's interest or to terminate and liquidate Partnership together with the retiring Partner. Written notice of the remaining Partner's election shall be served on the retiring Partner no later than [number] months after receipt of the notice of intention to retire.

If the remaining Partner elects to purchase the retiring Partner's interest, the purchase price and terms of payment shall be those set out in Paragraph 17.

If the remaining Partner elects to terminate and liquidate Partnership together with the retiring Partner, the termination and liquidation shall be carried out in the manner described in Paragraph 14.

16. Effect of Partner's Death. If one of the Partners dies, the survivor may either purchase the deceased Partner's interest or terminate and liquidate Partnership.

17. Election to Purchase the Deceased Partner's Interest in the Partnership.

a. Notice of Election. If the surviving Partner elects to purchase the deceased Partner's interest, the Partner shall serve written notice of this election within [number] months after the Partner's death upon the executor or administrator of the decedent if one has been appointed and qualified or, if none has qualified, upon the decedent's heirs at their last known addresses.

b. Purchase Price. The purchase price will be an amount equal to the balance in the decedent's capital account as of the date of the decedent's death, plus or minus the balance in the decedent's income account at the end of the fiscal year immediately preceding the Partner's death, increased or decreased by the decedent's share of Partnership profits or losses for the period beginning with the start of the fiscal year in which the Partner died and ending the last day of the month in which death occurred, reduced by any withdrawals from the deceased Partner's income account during the same period. The purchase price will not include any separate amounts for goodwill, trade name, patents, or other intangible assets. The surviving Partner will be entitled to use Partnership trade name. The purchase price will be paid without interest in [number] equal monthly payments commencing [number] months after the month in which the decedent died.

[Alternative Paragraph]

b. Purchase Price. The purchase price will be an amount equal to the balance in the deceased Partner's capital account together with a sum equal to [number] times the average net income earned by Partnership in the [number] fiscal years immediately prior to the deceased Partner's death. If the deceased Partner's death occurs in the last six months of any fiscal year, that fiscal year shall be one of the [number] fiscal years included for the computation of average net income. The determination by Partnership's certified public accountants of Partnership's average net income shall be conclusive upon all parties.

18. Election to Liquidate Partnership. If the surviving Partner elects to liquidate Partnership, the liquidation will proceed as quickly as possible, following the procedure described in Paragraph 14 of this Agreement. In addition to its share of the proceeds from the liquidation, the deceased Partner's estate shall be entitled to any profits that have not been withdrawn and that have been earned up to and including the date of the deceased Partner's death. If there have been losses up to and including the date of the deceased Partner's death that have not been charged to the Partner's income account, they shall be so charged before any distribution is made to the deceased Partner's estate.

19. Arbitration of Disputes. Any controversy concerning this Agreement will be settled by arbitration according to the rules of the American Arbitration Association, and judgment upon the award may be entered and enforced in any court.

[signatures]

Partners

Source: Basic Legal Forms
© Warren, Gorham, & Lamont

Articles of Organization for Limited Liability Company
Generalized Form

ARTICLES OF ORGANIZATION
OF
[name of limited liability company]

The undersigned hereby execute and acknowledge the following Articles of Organization for the purpose of forming a limited liability company under the [specify state statue].

1. The name of the limited liability company is ________________, LLC.

   NOTE: The name of each limited liability company must contain the words "limited liability company," "limited company," or an appropriate abbreviation such as LLC or LC.

2. The street address of the registered office in [state of organization] is [address].

3. a. The name of the registered agent for service of process in [state of organization] is ______________________.

   b. The address of the registered agent for service of process is [address]

   c. The registered agent is [mark appropriate box]:

      An individual resident of [state of organization]

      A domestic corporation

      A foreign corporation authorized to do business within [state of organization]

      A domestic limited liability company

      A foreign limited liability company authorized to do business within [state of organization].

4. The [appropriate state official] is hereby appointed the agent of [name of LLC] for service of process if the registered agent has resigned, the registered agent's authority has been revoked, or the agent cannot be found or served with the exercise of reasonable diligence. The address within [state of organization] to which the [appropriate state official] shall mail a copy of any process against [name of LLC] is ______________

5. The name and business address of each organizer is: [list name and address of each organizer].

6. The latest date on which the limited liability company is to be dissolved [and its affairs wound up] is [date].

   NOTE: Some states set a thirty-year ceiling on the life of an LLC. The trend, however, is to leave the precise period open, since the setting of a specific term will not necessarily negate the corporate attribute of "continuity of life." Ordinarily, state law or the operating agreement will specify events such as the bankruptcy, retirement, or death of a member that will interrupt the existence of the LLC, unless all (or a majority of) the remaining members vote to continue it.

[Alternative Clause]

6. The period of duration of [name of LLC] is from [date articles are filed] to [date of final dissolution].

7. The management of [name of LLC] shall be vested pursuant to the Operating Agreement in a manager/managers, who shall be appointed by the members and who shall have the exclusive right to control and manage [name of LLC]. The members shall not take part in the management and control of [name of LLC] and shall have no power to bind [name of LLC].

NOTE: Some states provide that management of the LLC will be vested in the members in proportion to their membership interests, unless the articles provide otherwise.

[Alternative Clause]

7. The management of [name of LLC] shall be vested pursuant to an operating agreement in the following managers, who shall be appointed by the members. The names and street addresses of the managers are: [names of addresses of managers].

[Alternative Clause]

7. The management of [name of LLC] shall be vested in the members. The names and street addresses of the members are: [names of addresses of members].

8. [name of LLC] has been formed for the following purposes: [specify purposes], and to conduct or promote any lawful business or purpose permitted by the laws of [state of organization].

9. In the event of the death, retirement, resignation, expulsion, bankruptcy, or dissolution of a member or the occurrence of any other event that terminates the continued membership of a member in [name of LLC], the remaining members have the right [under the operating agreement] to continue the business of [name of LLC].

10. [Name of LLC] is intended to be treated as a partnership [or corporation] for purposes of federal income taxation.

11. A member's interest in [name of LLC] may be evidenced by a certificate of membership interest signed by [person or persons with signing authority], which may be assigned or transferred. The right to assign or transfer a member's interest in [name of LLC] is limited by the provisions of Article ______, Paragraph ______ of the Operating Agreement.

Source: Basic Legal Forms
© Warren, Gorham, and Lamont

Income Statement from a Restaurant Business

Benjamin & Abigail's Italian Eatery
STATEMENT OF INCOME
Year Ended August 31, 1996

Sales	Amount	% of Sales
	$544,576	100%
Cost of sales:		
Cost of Food	161,194	29.6
Cost of Paper	18,516	3.4
Salaries and wages	115,450	21.2
Payroll taxes	19,060	3.5
	314,220	57.7
Gross profit	230,356	42.3
Operating expenses	208,573	38.3
Gross margin on operations	21,783	4
General administrative expenses	11,980	2.2
Operating income	9,803	1.8
Other income (expense)	8,168	
Income before income taxes	$17,971	

Source: Macdonald, Page & Co.

SAFEGUARDING YOUR BUSINESS

Trademark. . . *To protect your name*

A trademark, or service mark, in the service industry, is defined as a word, name, symbol, device, design, slogan, distinctive sound, or any combination thereof that distinguishes your service(s) from those of your competitors. Prior to choosing a name for your business you should check with your secretary of state's office to be sure that name is not already reserved and if not, complete the paperwork to register it. If you intend to provide services out-of-state (let's say you own a landscaping business in eastern Kentucky and plan to conduct business in West Virginia), you might want to register your name in both states. If, on the other hand, you plan to do business nationwide, as in the case of a newsletter, you would want to register your trademark through the U.S. Patent and Trademark Office, at the following address:

U.S. Patent and Trademark Office
2121 Crystal Dr.
Arlington, VA 22202
703-305-8341
800-786-9199

Copyright. . .T*o protect your writings*

A copyright as the term implies, protects an author against someone copying his or her works. To be copyrighted, a work must be original. The Copyright Act of 1976 gives several rights to copyright owners, including: the rights of reproduction, adaptation, distribution, performance, and display. These rights can be sold to others in the form of licenses. Copyrights are registered at the copyright office at the Library of Congress. Information can be obtained by calling 202-707-3000 or 202-707-9100 for applications. You can also write to the address below. Your original work is considered copyrighted as soon as it is created. You are not required to register it with the Register of Copyrights. However, once your work has been registered, the symbol ©, the year of first publication, and the name of the copyright owner should be displayed on your work. There is a $10 fee for registration of copyright which lasts for the life of the creator plus 50 years.

Register of Copyrights
Information and Publication Section, LM-455
Library of Congress
Washington, DC 20559

Online

Patents. . . *To protect your inventions*

A patent is the registered, exclusive right to make, use, and sell an invention. A patent is granted by the government through the Patent and Trademark Office. The process for obtaining a patent is complicated, time consuming, and expensive. A copy of the "General Information Concerning Patents" can be obtained from the U.S. Patent and Trademark Office, at the address listed above. If you are considering conducting a patent search or filing for a patent, a patent attorney or agent should be consulted.

The U.S. Patent and Trademark Office now offers a great deal of useful information about patents, trademarks, and copyrights via the Internet (http://www.uspto.gov/).

RATIO ANALYSIS

A **ratio analysis** is a simple mathematical comparison that examines the relationship between certain Income Statement and Balance Sheet items. Once a ratio analysis has been completed for your business, the results can then be compared to industry averages. Ratio analysis is important in ongoing financial analysis for a business that's up and running or in the analysis of a business you are considering purchasing. It can also be useful to test some of the assumptions you have made on *pro forma* statements for a start-up. In addition, bankers use comparative ratios as they analyze financial statements in response to loan requests.

Types of Ratios

There are various kinds of ratios grouped into four categories: Liquidity Ratios, Activity Ratios, Leverage Ratios, and Profitability Ratios. Following is an example of a commonly used ratio from each category. The numbers shown are for illustrative purposes only. More information about ratios and ratio analysis is readily available in most business finance texts or a publication such as *Financial Studies of the Small Business.*

Financial Studies of the Small Business p 102

Liquidity Ratio — *Current ratio*

Liquidity is an indication of the ability of a business to cover its current liabilities on a day-to-day basis. Liquidity analysis focuses on Balance Sheet asset and liability relationships that indicate how well a firm's assets cover its debts. In other words, the analyst (or user of this data) wants to know if the debts could actually be liquidated (paid off). The *current ratio* is one such measure. It is calculated by dividing Current Assets by Current Liabilities.

$$\frac{\text{Current assets}}{\text{Current liabilities}} = \text{Current ratio} \qquad \frac{\$125{,}000}{\$100{,}000} = 1.25$$

A current ratio of 1.25 means that there is $1.25 in current assets (including cash, receivables, and inventory) for every $1.00 in current liabilities (such as accounts payable, notes payable, and accrued expenses). In general, to assure liquidity the current ratio should be between 1 and 2. The actual figure depends on the type of firm, the volatility of economic conditions, and the quality of current assets.

Activity Ratios — *Average collection period*

Activity ratios focus on the speed with which receivables are collected, inventory is sold (turned over), or payables are being paid. This analysis allows you to determine whether common operating activities are being handled efficiently. The average number of days it takes to collect receivables is calculated in two steps:

$$\frac{\text{Net sales}}{\text{Average receivables}} = \text{Receivables turnover} \qquad \frac{\$290{,}000}{\$29{,}500} = 9.8$$

$$\frac{\text{Business days in a year}}{\text{Receivables turnover}} = \text{Average collection period} \qquad \frac{360}{9.8} = 36.7 \text{ days}$$

Ideally, only a monthly average of receivables and sales on credit is used in the sales figure. (For simplicity's sake, in this example all sales have been assumed to be on credit.)

Leverage Ratio — *Times interest earned*

Long-term investors and creditors of a firm want to know whether a firm's income is adequate to allow for promised returns to them, as well as to allow for reinvestment toward future growth. For example, the *times interest earned* ratio provides long-term creditors with a measure of how well the interest on their debt can be covered by income.

In another sense, *times interest earned* indicates the extent to which earnings can decline before the firm is unable to meet its annual interest costs. Banks use this measure to assess the firm's ability to meet interest obligations. It is calculated by dividing *net operating income* by total *interest expense.*

$$\frac{\text{Net operating income}}{\text{Interest expense}} = \text{Times interest earned} \qquad \frac{\$23,707}{\$2,800} = 8.5$$

This is considered to be an indication of general financial strength. The appropriate level varies from industry to industry. A ratio of 5.0 or better would be considered to be a strong position in many industries, but in the utilities industry, for example, a *times interest earned* ratio of 3.0 is considered adequate.

Financial Studies of the Small Business p 102

Profitablility Ratio — *Return on owner's equity*

Profitability is the assessment of a company's bottom line (profit) in relation to the size of its sales, assets, debts, or owner's equity. Profitability measures can show how effectively a business controls its expenses or utilizes its assets and investments. *Return on owner's equity* is calculated by dividing *net income* by *total owner's equity.*

$$\frac{\text{Net income}}{\text{Owner's equity}} = \text{Return on owner's equity} \qquad \frac{\$17,771}{\$209,900} = 8.5\%$$

The *return on owner's equity* ratio provides a measure of the earnings on the owner's investment in the business, which, at the very least, can be compared to the rate of return on current money market investments. In general, investors want to know whether the return on their investment is remaining stable over time, and whether or not it exceeds the rate of return on other Balance Sheet factors like *total assets* and *total debt.*

Once you have calculated your ratios, compare them to those of similar businesses. This information can be found in the publications of Robert Morris Associates, Dun & Bradstreet, Prentice Hall Publishing, and FRA's *Financial Studies of the Small Business.* Each of these publications lists ratios by industry types, and some of them break them down further by size of business. You can get copies of them from your banker, who uses them to compare your company to others, or try your local or state library.

Remember, the ratios presented in the publications cited above are industry averages. Some companies produce better, some worse. To remain viable, your target ratio should be above the average. Also, your business will probably be smaller than the industry average. *Financial Studies of the Small Business* includes smaller sales categories, making it a particularly good reference for start-ups.

Bibliography

Accounting, Bookkeeping, and Taxes

Accounting and Financial Fundamentals for Nonfinancial Executives, by Robert Rachlin and Allen Sweeney (AMACOM, 1996, 256 pages; $18.95; 800-262-9699).

Bottom Line Basics: Understand and Control Business Finances, by Robert J. Low (Oasis Press, 1995, 304 pages; $19.95; 800-228-2275).

Budgeting for a Small Business, by Terry Dickey (Crisp Publications, 1994, 200 pages; $15.95; 415-323-6100).

The Ernst & Young Tax Guide: 1996 (John Wiley & Sons, updated annually, 752 pages; $14.95; 800-225-5945).

The Ernst & Young Tax Saver's Guide: 1996 (John Wiley & Sons, updated annually, 280 pages; $10.95; 800-225-5945).

Financial Basics of Small Business, by James O. Gill (Crisp Publications, 1994, 250 pages; $15.95; 415-323-6100).

Banking, Financing, Cash and Capital Resources

Banking Smarter: How to Save Money in Your Business Banking Relationship, by Dennis M. Suchocki and Andrew M. Smith (BCS & Associates, 1995, 120 pages; $39.95; 602-423-8384).

Free Money for Small Businesses and Entrepreneurs, by Laurie Blum (John Wiley & Sons, 4th ed., 1995, 293 pages; $14.95; 800-225-5945).

How to Finance a Growing Business: An Insider's Guide to Negotiating the Capital Markets, by Royce Diener (Merritt Professional Publishing, 4th ed., 1995, 328 pages; $24.95; 800-638-7597).

Business Valuation, Buying a Business

Business Analysis & Valuation Using Financial Statements: Text and Cases, by Krishna G. Palepu, Victor L.Bernard, and Paul M. Healy (Southwestern College Publishing, 1996, 896 pages; $85.50; 800-865-5840).

Business Valuation: Theory and Practice, by Dr. Joesph Vinso (J & H Publishing, 1995, updated annually, 400 to 500 pages; $95; 406-542-1213).

Guide to Business Valuations, by Jay Fishman, Shannon Pratt, Cliff Griffith, and Keith Wilson (Practitioners Publishing, 6th ed., 1996, updated annually, 900 pages; $165; 800-323-8724).

Handbook of Small Business Valuation Formulas and Rules of Thumb, by Glenn Desmond (Valuation Press, 3rd ed., 1994, 371 pages; $74.95; 800-421-8042).

Valuation: Measuring and Managing the Value of Companies, by T. Copeland, T. Coller, and J. Murrin, McKinsey & Co. (New York Institute of Finance, 1994, 480 pages; $69.95; book and disk, $139.95; 212-859-5000).

Computers and Other Office Equipment

Business Consumer Guide (Beacon Research Group, monthly, 40 to 50 pages per issue, $119 per year; back issues, $25; 800-938-0088).

. . . For Dummies Series, by various authors (IDG Books Worldwide, many updated annually, 200 to 700 pages; $16.95 to $34.95; 800-762-2974).

The Office Equipment Adviser, by John Derrick (What to Buy for Business, 3rd ed., 1995, 634 pages; $24.95; 800-247-2185).

Direct Marketing

Direct Marketing Rules of Thumb, by Nat G. Bodian (McGraw-Hill, 1995, 448 pages; $59.95; 800-722-4726).

T*he New Direct Marketing: How to Implement a Profit-Driven Database Marketing Strategy*, by David Shepard Associates (Irwin Professional Publishing, 2nd ed., 1995 ,493 pages; $65; 800-634-3966).

Electronic Commerce, Internet/Web

101 Businesses You Can Start on the Internet, by Daniel S. Janal (International Thomson Publishing, 1996, 503 pages; $24.95; 800-842-3636).

Build a Web Site: The Programmer's Guide to Creating, Building, and Maintaining a Web Presence, by net.Genesis, Devra Hall (Prima Publishing, 1995, 656 pages; $34.95; 800-632-8676).

Business Development: Doing More Business on the Internet, by Mary Cronin (International Thomson Publishing, 2nd ed., 1995, 368 pages; $29.95; 800-842-3636).

World Wide Web Bible, by Bryan Pfaffenberger (MIS Press, 2nd ed., 1996, 688 pages; $29.95; 800 488-5233).

World Wide Web Marketing: Integrating the Internet into Your Marketing Strategy, by Jim Sterne (John Wiley & Sons, 1995, 352 pages; $24.95; 800-225-5945).

Forms of Ownership and Organization

Basic Legal Forms (1995 Cumulative Supplement No. 2, "Articles of Organization for a Limited Liability Company"), by Marvin Hyman and Clifford R. Ennico (Warren, Gorham & Lamont, 1995, published semiannually, 976 pages; $69; 800-950-1205)

The Essential Limited Liability Company Handbook, by Corporate Agents, Inc. (Oasis Press, 1995, 260 pages; $19.95; 800-228-2275).

The Essential Corporation Handbook, by Carl R.J. Sniffen (Oasis Press, 2nd ed., 1995, 244 pages; $19.95; 800-228-2275).

Human Resources, Managing People

CompControl: The Secrets of Reducing Workers' Compensation Costs, by Edward J. Priz (Oasis Press, 1995, 155 pages; $19.95; 800-228-2275).

How to Really Recruit, Motivate, & Lead Your Team: Managing People, edited by Ruth G. Newman and Bradford W. Ketchum, Jr. (*Inc.* magazine, 1994, 260 pages; $15.95; 800-468-0800).

Managing Human Resources in Small & Mid-Sized Companies, by Diane Arthur (AMACOM, 1995, 352 pages; $59.95; 800-262-9699)

Insurance

Dictionary of Insurance, by Lewis E. Davids (Littlefield, Adams Quality Paperbacks, 7th ed., 1990, 504 pages; $17.95; 800-462-6420).

Understanding Insurance Law, by Robert H. Jerry II (Matthew Bender, 3rd ed., 1996, 700 pages; $25; 212-967-7707).

Legal Issues, Agreements, and Contracts

A Legal Guide for Small Business, by Charles P. Lickson (Crisp Publications, 1994, 210 pages; $15.95; 415-323-6100).

Basic Legal Forms, by Marvin Hyman (Warren, Gorham & Lamont, 2nd. ed., 1995, updated annually, 864 pages; $140; 800-950-1205)

Law & Advertising, by Dean Keith Fueroghne (The Copy Workshop, 1995, 505 pages; $37.50; 800-651-3133, ext. 1179).

Location Analysis

Location, Location, Location, by Luigi Salvaneschi (Oasis Press, 1996, 250 pages; $19.95; 800-228-2275).

Management and Planning

301 Great Management Ideas, edited by Leslie Brokaw (*Inc.* magazine, 2nd ed., 1995, 360 pages; $14.95, 800-468-0800).

How to Really Start Your Own Business, by David E. Gumpert (*Inc.* magazine, 1994, 238 pages; $19.95; 800-468-0800).

Marketing and Market Research (Advertising, Customer Service, and Pricing)

Advertising Campaign Planning, by Jim Avery (The Copy Workshop, 2nd ed., 1993, 200 pages; $19.50; 800-651-3133, ext. 1179).

Customer Service for Dummies, by Karen Leland and Keith Bailey (IDG Books Worldwide, 1995, 346 pages; $19.99; 800-762-2974).

How to Really Create a Successful Marketing Plan, by David E. Gumpert (*Inc.* magazine, 1994, 280 pages; $19.95, 800-468-0800).

How to Really Deliver Superior Customer Service, edited by John R. Halbrooks (*Inc.* magazine, 1994, 268 pages; $15.95; 800-468-0800).

The Strategy and Tactics of Pricing, by Thomas Nagle (Prentice Hall, 2nd ed., 1995, 432 pages; $39; 800-223-1360).

Patents, Copyrights, and Trademarks

Patent It Yourself, by David Pressman (Nolo Press, 4th ed., 1995, 300 pages; $39.95; 800-992-6656).

Licensing Intellectual Property, by Diane E. Cornish (Carswell, 1995, 110 pages; $30.35; 800-387-5164).

GLOSSARY

Asset: Any item owned that has cash value, such as real estate, equipment, stocks, or licenses, that can be used to satisfy debts.

Browser A software program that allows the user to view the World Wide Web in its entirety.

Cooperative direct marketing
A group of businesses sharing a single mailing (usually via a direct marketing firm) to promote their products or services, thereby lowering their promotional costs.

Demographics Statistics for various socioeconomic variables such as age, race, income, etc. Often used to determine target market.

Depreciation For tax reporting and accounting purposes, the deduction in value of property (asset) over its useful life.

Discounts and allowances
Reduction in price of services or merchandise to customers based on classification of customer (i.e. commercial versus individual) and/or volume of sales activity. Allowances are typically offered to the retailer by the manufacturer, as in the case of retail display allowances.

Download/upload To use a computer to retrieve or send electronic files to another computer or disk.

Electronic commerce
Methods for ordering and selling goods over the Internet, which can involve various payment methods, including credit cards and automatic bank transfers.

Equity Ownership interest in a business in the form of stock, paid-in capital, and/or retained earnings.

File transfer protocol (FTP)
A method for retrieving files from the Internet.

Firewall A security measure used to protect computers on a local area network from outside access.

Footprint The layout of a business location to scale.

Goodwill Intangible but valuable asset (e.g., reputation) of a business that is developed from the sale and/or distribution of quality services or merchandise. Also, community involvement by the business to promote the public good.

Home page An electronic "billboard" on the World Wide Web used for advertising a business. A home page can include a listing of services offered, pictures of products, E-mail addresses, hours of operation, and other helpful information.

Hypertext A system that directly links documents scattered across many sites.

Hypertext markup language (HTML) The standard format for documents on the World Wide Web.

Internet (the Net) A global information network created by the interconnection of millions of computers worldwide. The Net makes it possible to obtain information from resources ranging from the New York Public Library and U.S. Congress, to your local school board and hundreds of colleges and universities. It can also be used to send electronic mail (E-mail) messages to anyone across the globe who has a computer and telephone.

Java A programming language for the World Wide Web that allows developers to create mini-programs or "applets" that can be easily transferred over the Internet.

Links (hyperlinks) A connection between two locations on the Web. A link can be used to direct a person from a particular home page to a resource containing more in-depth information on a particular subject, or to an E-mail address.

Mission statement Outline of business purpose that includes long-term organizational objectives, management philosophy, and community outreach goals.

Net worth The amount by which a business's assets exceed its liabilities.

Niche A particular segment of the market in which a business specializes. By focusing efforts on a discrete sector, a company can help ensure efficient use of its marketing efforts.

Operating expenses Amounts paid to maintain and/or operate property, such as the cost of utilities, supplies, taxes, depreciation, and insurance.

Organizational chart A tree chart diagramming the structure of responsibility and authority within an organization.

Owner equity The amount of capital investment by the owner(s) after retained earnings, dividends, and other financial obligations.

Revenue The gross amount of money received for services rendered or merchandise sold.

Search engine Applications on the World Wide Web that allow the user to enter key words and search for documents on the Internet.

Service provider A company that provides connections to the Internet.

Small Business Development Center (SBDC)
A small-business assistance center that provides counseling, training, and other services — in most cases at no charge. Partially funded by the U.S. Small Business Administration, SBDCs are located in all 50 states, plus the District of Columbia, Puerto Rico, and the U.S. Virgin Islands (see directory on page 127).

SOHO Acronym for Small Office/Home Office.

Telecommunications
Transmission of information by telephone, wire, or computer.

Uniform resource locator (URL)
A type of address that points to a specific document on the World Wide Web (e.g., *Inc.* magazine's http://www.inc.com).

U. S. Small Business Administration (SBA)
A division of the federal government dedicated to promoting small business by providing management and technical assistance and loan guaranties through various programs such as the Service Corps of Retired Executives (SCORE), Small Business Development Centers (SBDCs), and Business Information Centers (BICs).

Venture capital Source of financing for start-up or emerging businesses that present greater than average investment risk for the short term, but will potentially produce greater returns in the long run. Typically used by high-tech or emerging-technology companies.

Web site See Home page.

World Wide Web A service of the Internet, the Web is a connection of millions of computers forming a super-network of electronic information. It allows users to retrieve hyertext and graphics from various Internet sites.

Index

K

L

M

NOTES